Course   Classic Edition Sources:
          American Government, 4e

http://create.mheducation.com

Copyright 2016 by McGraw-Hill Education. All rights
reserved. Printed in the United States of America. Except as
permitted under the United States Copyright Act of 1976, no part
of this publication may be reproduced or distributed in any form
or by any means, or stored in a database or retrieval system,
without prior written permission of the publisher.

This McGraw-Hill Create text may include materials submitted to
McGraw-Hill for publication by the instructor of this course.
The instructor is solely responsible for the editorial content of such
materials. Instructors retain copyright of these additional materials.

ISBN-10: 130800883X   ISBN-13: 9781308008837

Contents

Credits

Preface

*P*olitics is dynamic! The study of American government entails a critical analysis of human political behavior within the context of diverse institutions and processes. The fundamental objective of political scientists who study American government is to acquire a broad understanding of American politics through descriptions, explanations, and evaluations of often complex political phenomena. Political scientists systematically attempt to make intelligible those governmental activities that often seem remote, obscure, inaccessible, complicated, and unintelligible to most citizens. Observations, explanations, and analyses of American politics also offer ample opportunities for evaluative critiques of how the government ought to function.

American government has been explored through a rich diversity of perspectives, approaches, and interpretations. Political scientists who focus on the American government do not conform to one particular mode of inquiry; they follow different paths of investigation and use distinct tools, techniques, and methods of analysis. *Classic Edition Sources: American Government* brings together selections from classic primary sources that have dramatically impacted upon the ways in which people think about American government and politics. Many of these selections have not only influenced contemporary understanding of complex institutions, processes, and behavior, but they have directly shaped and altered the critical political decisions and acts of a multitude of policymakers and political practitioners (e.g., voters, lobbyists, legislators, judges, presidents, bureaucrats, and political party leaders). The literature included here reflects the efforts of numerous American government scholars to intertwine insights and interpretations of the political system with invaluable predictions and suggestions for reform.

The selections chosen for this book cover a wide range of substantive topics and incorporate an extensive variation of the most notable perspectives found within the study of American government. For example, the selections in the opening unit provide exposure to the distinct world views and interpretative analyses of the classical liberal theoretical tradition, the democratic-egalitarian tradition, and the communitarian school of American political thought in reference to the cultural, ideological, and intellectual context of the American political system.

This format is consistent throughout this book, as alternative scholarly views and explanatory models are offered to the critically active reader for her or his interpretation and assessment.

This volume of readings is designed to inspire the reader to become enthusiastic in their discovery of topics that have been of profound significance to the evolution of the American government and to seriously think about key issues, topics, themes, theories, concepts, problems, and solutions pertinent to the literature on American government. A good number of selections provide examples of how concrete political behavior or policies are linked to abstract political concepts and political theories. Sources rich in their depth and scope of coverage of the American political system include a source that was written in the seventeenth century to many sources from the twentieth century; from English and French theorists to many American analysts; and from sources that are highly laudatory of the American government to sources that suggest major political, social, and economic reforms. Although most of the sources were written by traditional political scientists who primarily study American government, several of the selections were authored by nonpolitical scientists (e.g., sociologists, historians, and mass media communication experts). The selections to articulate as lucidly as possible the multiple tensions endemic to the American political system and the continuous struggle of ethnic and racial minorities and women to fully achieve their democratic rights. Finally, and perhaps most important, a fundamental objective of this book is to enable students to develop some proficiency in their critical thinking, critical reading, reasoning, and analysis skills, in addition to acquiring general information on the American government.

ORGANIZATION OF THE BOOK: The selections are organized into units that correspond to most introductory American government textbooks and therefore offer ample opportunities for students to read and analyze the original sources of topics as they are presented throughout the course. Selections can be assigned as independent entities or in sets of readings, depending upon the preference of the instructor. Each selection is introduced by a brief headnote that establishes the selection's significance to the literature and offers pertinent biographical information on the author.

SUGGESTIONS FOR READING THE SELECTIONS: It is strongly recommended that students first read the introductory headnotes before reading the selections, as they provide substantial commentary on significant issues in American government and elaborate on the general context from which the text is derived. The reader should be sensitive to the direct impact and influence of context (e.g., conventional and scholarly language usage of the period and the cultural, intellectual, social, economic, demographic, and political forces) upon the content of each particular selection. In this regard, the reader should remember the evolutionary nature of language. Each selection is culturally and socially derived and consequently reflects the language used in the period. For example, many of the older selections use the masculine pronouns *he* and *him* to refer to all humans regardless of gender. Contemporary authors are much more sensitive to such gender-biased language.

The reader should be aggressive in the reading, analysis, and interpretation of each selection and should not hesitate to raise both explanatory and evaluative questions.

For example, when reading a selection on interest groups or political parties, the reader should consider what factors might help to explain their behavior and whether or not such behavior is legitimate.

A WORD TO THE INSTRUCTOR: An *Instructor's Resource Guide with test questions* (multiple-choice and essay) is available through the publisher for instructors using *Classic Edition Sources: American Government* in the classroom. Visit www.mhhe.com/createcentral.

Academic Advisory Board

Members of the Academic Advisory Board are instrumental in the final selection of articles for the *Classic Edition Sources* series. Their review of the articles for content, level, and appropriateness provides critical direction to the editor(s) and staff. We think that you will find their careful consideration reflected in this book.

JEAN-GABRIEL JOLIVET, ASHFORD UNIVERSITY
JAMES NEWMAN, UNIVERSITY OF MARYLAND UNIVERSITY COLLEGE

Correlation Guide

*E*ach volume in the *Classic Edition Sources* series brings together selections of enduring intellectual value—classic articles, book excerpts, and research studies—that have shaped a discipline of study. Edited for length and level, the selections are organized topically around the major areas of study within the discipline. For more information on *Classic Edition Sources* and other *McGraw-Hill Create*™ titles and collections, visit www.mcgrawhillcreate.com.

This convenient guide matches the chapters in **Classic Edition Sources: American Government, 4/e** with the corresponding chapters in two of our best-selling McGraw-Hill Education Political Science textbooks by **Patterson**.

Classic Edition Sources: American Government, 4/e	We the People, 10/e by Patterson	The American Democracy, 11/e by Patterson
Chapter 1: American Political Culture and Ideology	**Chapter 1:** Political Thinking and Political Culture: Becoming a Responsible Citizen	**Chapter 1:** Political Thinking and Political Culture: Becoming a Responsible Citizen
Chapter 2: The Constitutional Foundation of American Government	**Chapter 2:** Constitutional Democracy: Promoting Liberty and Self-Government	**Chapter 2:** Constitutional Democracy: Promoting Liberty and Self-Government
Chapter 3: The Evolution of American Federalism	**Chapter 3:** Federalism: Forging a Nation	**Chapter 3:** Federalism: Forging a Nation
Chapter 4: Civil Liberties	**Chapter 4:** Civil Liberties: Protecting Individual Rights	**Chapter 4:** Civil Liberties: Protecting Individual Rights
Chapter 5: Civil Rights	**Chapter 5:** Equal Rights: Struggling Toward Fairness	**Chapter 5:** Equal Rights: Struggling Toward Fairness
Chapter 6: Interest Groups	**Chapter 9:** Interest Groups: Organizing for Influence	**Chapter 9:** Interest Groups: Organizing Influence
Chapter 7: Political Parties	**Chapter 8:** Political Parties, Candidates, and Campaigns: Defining the Voter's Choice	**Chapter 8:** Political Parties, Candidates, and Campaigns: Defining the Voter's Choice
Chapter 8: Electoral Politics	**Chapter 7:** Political Participation and Voting: Activating the Popular Will	**Chapter 7:** Political Participation: Activating the Popular Will
Chapter 9: The Media and Public Opinion	**Chapter 6:** Public Opinion and Political Socialization: Shaping the People's Voice **Chapter 10:** The News Media: Communicating Political Images	**Chapter 6:** Public Opinion and Political Socialization: Shaping the People's Voice **Chapter 10:** The News Media: Communicating Political Images
Chapter 10: Congress	**Chapter 11:** Congress: Balancing National Goals and Local Interests	**Chapter 11:** Congress: Balancing National Goals and Local Interests

Classic Edition Sources: American Government, 4/e	We the People, 10/e by Patterson	The American Democracy, 11/e by Patterson
Chapter 11: The Presidency	**Chapter 12:** The Presidency: Leading the Nation	**Chapter 12:** The Presidency: Leading the Nation
Chapter 12: The Bureaucracy	**Chapter 13:** The Federal Bureaucracy: Administering the Government	**Chapter 13:** The Federal Bureaucracy: Administering the Government
Chapter 13: The Judiciary	**Chapter 14:** The Judiciary: Applying the Law	**Chapter 14:** The Federal Judicial System: Applying the Law
Chapter 14: Domestic Public Policy Making	**Chapter 15:** Economic and Environmental Policy: Contributing to Prosperity **Chapter 16:** Welfare and Education Policy: Providing for Personal Security and Need	**Chapter 15:** Economic and Environmental Policy: Contributing to Prosperity **Chapter 16:** Welfare and Education Policy: Providing for Personal Security and Need **Chapter 18:** State and Local Politics: Maintaining Our Differences
Chapter 15: American Foreign Policy	**Chapter 17:** Foreign and Defense Policy: Protecting the American Way	**Chapter 17:** Foreign Policy: Protecting the American Way

Topic Guide

Unit 1: American Political Culture and Ideology

The Second Treatise

John Locke

Learning Outcomes

After reading this selection, you should be able to:

1. Define the "law of nature," as understood by Locke.
2. Recognize the connection between classical liberalism and the creation of the U.S. government.
3. Discuss the difference between a "state of liberty" and a "state of license."

John Locke (1632–1704), the English political philosopher and the founder of classical liberalism, articulated a political theory of natural rights, individualism, private property ownership, constitutionalism, and limited government that greatly influenced the framers' design of the U.S. Constitution. Classical liberalism emphasizes human rationality, the legitimacy of a constitutional limited government, the central significance of natural rights (particularly property rights), the freedom of the individual, and the critical need of privacy. In particular, the idea of legitimate government based upon a social contract and the consent of individuals inspired James Madison and the other framers.

In the following selection, excerpted from his classic work *Two Treatises of Government* (1690), Locke expounds on his political theory, which was derived from his interpretation of human nature in the context of a state of nature. He depicts the state of nature as a primitive society without government, in which individuals are relatively equal, free, independent, rational agents primarily motivated by the pursuit to acquire private property. The law of nature is defined as an objective moral principle obliging individuals to preserve their own lives and property and not to harm the lives and property of others. The universal applicability of this normative principle of natural rights directly influenced Thomas Jefferson's writing of the Declaration of Independence.

Locke's classical republican justification of citizen rebellion against a tyrannical government also influenced the development of the American political system. Locke's radical political theory has remained a dominant element of American political ideology.

Key Concept: the political ideology of classical liberalism

Of the State of Nature

To understand Political Power right, and derive it from its Original, we must consider what State all Men are naturally in, and that is, a *State of the perfect Freedom* to order their Actions, and dispose of their Possessions, and Persons as they think fit, within the bounds of the Law of Nature, without asking leave, or depending upon the Will of any other Man.

A *State* also *of Equality*, wherein all the Power and Jurisdiction is reciprocal, no one having more than another: there being nothing more evident, than that Creatures of the same species and rank promiscuously born to all the same advantages of Nature, and the use of the same faculties, should also be equal one amongst another with Subordination or Subjection, unless the Lord and Master of them all, should by any manifest Declaration of his Will set one above another, and confer on him by an

evident and clear appointment an undoubted Right to Dominion and Sovereignty. . . .

But though this be a *State of Liberty*, yet it is *not a State of Licence*, though Man in that State have an uncontroleable Liberty, to dispose of his Person or Possessions, yet he has not Liberty to destroy himself, or so much as any Creature in his Possession, but where some nobler use, than its bare Preservation calls for it. The *State of Nature* has a Law of Nature to govern it, which obliges every one: And Reason, which is that Law, teaches all Mankind, who will but consult it, that being all equal and independent, no one ought to harm another in his Life, Health, Liberty, or Possessions. . . . And being furnished with like Faculties, sharing all in one Community of Nature, there cannot be supposed any such *Subordination* among us, that may Authorize us to destroy one another, as if we were made for one another's uses, as the inferior ranks of Creatures are for ours. Every one as he is *bound to preserve himself*, and not to quit his Station wilfully; so by the like reason when his own Preservation comes not in competition, ought he, as much as he can, *to preserve the rest of Mankind*, and may not unless it be to do Justice on an Offender, take away, or impair the life, or what tends to the Preservation of the Life, the Liberty, Health, Limb or Goods of another.

And that all Men may be restrained from invading others Rights, and from doing hurt to one another, and the Law of Nature be observed, which willeth the Peace and *Preservation of all Mankind*, the *Execution* of the Law of Nature is in that State, put into every Mans hands, whereby every one has a right to punish the transgressors of that Law to such a Degree, as may hinder its Violation. For the *Law of Nature* would, as all other Laws that concern Men in this World, be in vain, if there were no body that in the State of Nature, had a *Power to Execute* that Law, and thereby preserve the innocent and restrain offenders, and if any one in the State of Nature may punish another, for any evil he has done, every one may do so. For in that *State of perfect Equality*, where naturally there is no superiority or jurisdiction of one, over another, what any may do in Prosecution of that Law, every one must needs have a Right to do.

And thus in the State of Nature, *one Man comes by a Power over another*; but yet no Absolute or Arbitrary Power, to use a Criminal when he has got him in his hands, according to the passionate heats, or boundless extravagancy of his own Will, but only to retribute to him, so far as calm reason and conscience dictates, what is proportionate to his Transgression, which is so much as may serve for *Reparation* and *Restraint*. . . .

Every Offence that can be committed in the State of Nature, may in the State of Nature be also punished, equally, and as far forth as it may, in a Common-wealth; for though it would be besides my present purpose, to enter here into the particulars of the Law of Nature, or its *measures of punishment*; yet, it is certain there is such a Law, and that too, as intelligible and plain to a rational Creature, and a Studier of that Law, as the positive Laws of Common-wealths, nay possibly plainer. . . .

Of the Ends of Political Society and Government

If Man in the State of Nature be so free, as has been said; If he be absolute Lord of his own Person and Possessions, equal to the greatest, and subject to no Body, why will he part with his Freedom? Why will he give up this Empire, and subject himself to the Dominion and Controul of any other Power? To which 'tis obvious to Answer, that though in the state of Nature he hath such a right, yet the Enjoyment of it is very uncertain, and constantly exposed to the Invasion of others. For all being Kings as much as he, every Man his Equal, and the greater part no strict Observers of Equity and Justice, the enjoyment of the property he has in this state is very unsafe, very unsecure. This makes

him willing to quit this Condition, which however free, is full of fears and continual dangers: And 'tis not without reason, that he seeks out, and is willing to joyn in Society with others who are already united, or have a mind to unite for the mutual *Preservation* of their Lives, Liberties and Estates, which I call by the general Name, *Property*.

The great and *chief end* therefore, of Mens uniting into Common-wealths, and putting themselves under Government, *is the Preservation of their Property*. To which in the state of Nature there are many things wanting.

First, There wants an *establish'd*, settled, known *Law*, received and allowed by common consent to be the Standard of Right and Wrong, and the common measure to decide all Controversies between them. For though the Law of Nature be plain and intelligible to all rational Creatures; yet Men being biassed by their Interest, as well as ignorant for want of study of it, are not apt to allow of it as a Law binding to them in the application of it to their particular Cases.

Secondly, In the State of Nature there wants *a known and indifferent Judge*, with Authority to determine all differences according to the established Law. For every one in that state being both Judge and Executioner of the Law of Nature, Men being partial to themselves, Passion and Revenge is very apt to carry them too far, and with too much heat, in their own Cases; as well as negligence, and unconcernedness, to make them too remiss, in other Mens.

Thirdly, In the State of Nature there often wants *Power* to back and support the Sentence when right, and to *give* it due *Execution*. They who by any Injustice offended, will seldom fail, where they are able, by force to make good their Injustice: such resistance many times makes the punishment dangerous, and frequently destructive, to those who attempt it.

Thus Mankind, notwithstanding all the Priviledges of the State of Nature, being but in an ill condition, while they remain in it, are quickly driven into Society. Hence it comes to pass, that we seldom find any number of Men live any time together in this State. The inconveniencies, that they are therein exposed to, by the irregular and uncertain exercise of the Power every Man has of punishing the transgressions of others, make them take Sanctuary under the establish'd Laws of Government, and therein seek *the preservation of their Property*. 'Tis this makes them so willingly give up every one his single power of punishing to be exercised by such alone as shall be appointed to it amongst them; and by such Rules as the Community, or those authorised by them to that purpose, shall agree on. And in this we have the original *right and rise* of both *the Legislative and Executive Power*, as well as of the Governments and Societies themselves.

For in the State of Nature, to omit the liberty he has of innocent Delights, a Man has two Powers.

The first is to do whatsoever he thinks fit for the preservation of himself and others within the permission of the *Law of Nature*: by which Law common to them all, he and all the rest of *Mankind are one Community,* make up one Society distinct from all other Creatures. And were it not for the corruption, and vitiousness of degenerate Men, there would be no need of any other; no necessity that Men should separate from this great and natural Community, and by positive agreements combine into smaller and divided associations.

The other power a Man has in the State of Nature, is the *power to punish the Crimes* committed against that Law. Both these he gives up, when he joyns in a private, if I may so call it, or particular Political Society, and incorporates into any Common-wealth, separate from the rest of Mankind.

The first *Power, viz. of doing whatsoever he thought fit for the Preservation of himself,* and the rest of Mankind, *he gives up* to be regulated by Laws made by the Society, so far forth as the preservation of himself, and the rest of that Society shall require; which Laws of the Society in many things confine the liberty he had by the Law of Nature.

Secondly, the *Power of punishing* he wholly *gives up,* and engages his natural force, (which he might before imploy in the Execution of the Law of Nature, by his own single Authority, as he thought fit) to assist the Executive Power of the Society, as the Law thereof shall require. For being now in a new State, wherein he is to enjoy many Conveniencies, from the labour, assistance, and society of others in the same Community, as well as protection from its whole strength; he is to part also with as much of his natural liberty in providing for himself, as the good, prosperity, and safety of the Society shall require: which is not only necessary, but just; since the other Members of the Society do the like.

But though Men when they enter into Society, give up the Equality, Liberty, and Executive Power they had in the State of Nature, into the hands of the Society, to be so far disposed of by the Legislative, as the good of the Society shall require; yet it being only with an intention in every one the better to preserve himself his Liberty and Property; (For no rational Creature can be supposed to change his condition with an intention to be worse) the power of the Society, or *Legislative* constituted by them, *can never be suppos'd to extend farther than the common good;* but is obliged to secure every ones Property by providing against those three defects above-mentioned, that made the State of Nature so unsafe and uneasie. And so whoever has the Legislative or Supream Power of any Common-wealth, is bound to govern by establish'd *standing Laws,* promulgated and known to the People, and not by Extemporary Decrees; by *indifferent* and upright *Judges,* who are to decide Controversies by those Laws; And to imploy the force of the Community at home, *only in the Execution of such Laws,* or abroad to prevent or redress Foreign Injuries, and secure the Community from Inroads and Invasion. And all this to be directed to no other *end,* but the *Peace, Safety,* and *publick good* of the People. . . .

Of the Extent of the Legislative Power

The great end of Mens entering into Society, being the enjoyment of their Properties in Peace and Safety, and the great instrument and means of that being the Laws establish'd in that Society; the *first and fundamental positive Law* of all Common-wealths, *is the establishing of the Legislative* Power; as the *first and fundamental natural Law,* which is to govern even the Legislative it self, is *the preservation of the Society,* and (as far as will consist with the publick good) of every person in it. This *Legislative* is not only *the supream power* of the Commonwealth, but sacred and unalterable in the hands where the Community have once placed it; nor can any Edict of any Body else, in what Form soever conceived, or by what Power soever backed, have the force and obligation of a *Law,* which has not its *Sanction from* that *Legislative,* which the publick has chosen and appointed. For without this the Law could not have that, which is absolutely necessary to its being a *Law, the consent of the Society,* over whom no Body can have a power to make Laws, but by their own consent, and by Authority received from them. . . .

These are the *Bounds* which the trust that is put in them by the Society, and the Law of God and Nature, have *set to the Legislative* Power of every Commonwealth, in all Forms of Government.

First, they are to govern by *promulgated establish'd Laws,* not to be varied in particular Cases, but to have one Rule for Rich and Poor, for the Favourite at Court, and the Country Man at Plough.

Secondly, these *Laws* also ought to be designed *for no* other end ultimately but *the good of the People.*

Thirdly, they must *not raise Taxes* on the Property of the People, *without the Consent of the People,* given by themselves, or their Deputies. And this properly concerns only such Governments where the *Legislative* is always in being, or at least where the People have not reserv'd any part of the Legislative to Deputies, to be from time to time chosen by themselves.

Fourthly, the *Legislative* neither must *nor can transfer the Power of making Laws* to any Body else, or place it any where but where the People have. . . .

Whosoever uses *force without Right,* as every one does in Society, who does it without Law, puts himself into a *state of War* with those, against whom he so uses it, and in that state all former Ties are cancelled, all other Rights cease, and every one has a *Right* to defend himself, and *to resist the Aggressor.* . . .

[T]he common Question will be made, *Who shall be Judge* whether the Prince or Legislative act contrary to their Trust? This, perhaps, ill affected and factious Men may spread amongst the People, when the Prince only makes use of his due Prerogative. To this I reply, *The People shall be Judge;* for who shall be *Judge* whether his Trustee or Deputy acts well, and according to the Trust reposed in him, but he who deputes him, and must, by having deputed him have still a Power to discard him, when he fails in his Trust? If this be reasonable in particular Cases of private Men, why should it be otherwise in that of the greatest moment; where the Welfare of Millions is concerned, and also where the evil, if not prevented, is greater, and the Redress very difficult, dear, and dangerous? . . .

To conclude, The *Power that every individual gave the Society,* when he entered into it, can never revert to the Individuals again, as long as the Society lasts, but will always remain in the Community; because without this, there can be no Community, no Common-wealth, which is contrary to the original Agreement: So also when the Society hath placed the Legislative in any Assembly of Men, to continue in them and their Successors, with Direction and Authority for providing such Successors, *the Legislative can never revert to the People* whilst that Government lasts: Because having provided a Legislative with Power to continue for ever, they have given up their Political Power to the Legislative, and cannot resume it. But if they have set Limits to the Duration of their Legislative, and made this Supreme Power in any Person, or Assembly, only temporary: Or else when by the Miscarriages of those in Authority, it is forfeited; upon the Forfeiture of their Rulers, or at the Determination of the Time set, *it reverts to the Society,* and the People have a Right to act as Supreme, and continue the Legislative in themselves, or erect a new Form, or under the old form place it in new hands, as they think good.

Critical Thinking

1. How much of the content of Jefferson's "Declaration of Independence" is an apparent parallel to the content of Locke's "Second Treatise"?
2. Why does the preservation of one's property more rationally rely on one's submission to a government than on the unilateral actions of oneself?
3. Would it be possible to establish and maintain a democracy that does not adhere to the basic tenets of classical liberalism?

Create Central

www.mhhe.com/createcentral

Internet References

The American Political Science Association
www.apsanet.org/index.cfm

The Communitarian Network
www.gwu.edu/~ccps/index.html

Stanford Encyclopedia of Philosophy
http://plato.stanford.edu

From *Two Treaties of Government* by John Locke (1690).

Democracy in America

Alexis de Tocqueville

Learning Outcomes

After reading this selection, you should be able to:

1. Recognize the unparalleled results of America's experiment with democracy.
2. Discuss the "eminently democratic" social condition of Anglo-Americans in the 1830s.

The first comprehensive social and political analysis of the early American republic was written by Alexis de Tocqueville (1805–1859), a young French aristocrat. His observations of American society and political culture were documented during his nine-month visit to the United States in 1831 and led to the publication of the two-volume classic *Democracy in America* (1835), from which the following selection has been taken. *Democracy in America* was a scholarly political philosophical and sociological work intended to provide an objective understanding of the unique American experiment in democracy.

American social scientists have focused on issues of political behavior and governmental institutions emphasized in the first volume of *Democracy in America*. The general theme of democracy and the particular issues of social, political, and economic equality and freedom examined in Tocqueville's treatise have been continuously debated and reexamined by American political scientists. Both American and European commentators have studied Tocqueville's argumentation on the political and sociological implications of popular democratic institutions.

In the following selection, Tocqueville articulates a causal linkage between the great number of diverse voluntary associations and autonomous local communities and the rapid development of political equality, opportunity, and freedom in the American context. However, Tocqueville expresses serious concerns about the potential tyranny of the majority, in which individuals and minorities are open to the coercion of mass conformity and dominant public opinion.

Key Concept: American democratic beliefs and practices

Social Condition of the Anglo-Americans

Social condition is commonly the result of circumstances, sometimes of laws, oftener still of these two causes united; but when once established, it may justly be considered as itself the source of almost all the laws, the usages, and the ideas which regulate the conduct of nations: whatever it does not produce, it modifies.

If we would become acquainted with the legislation and the manners of a nation, therefore, we must begin by the study of its social condition. . . .

*M*any important observations suggest themselves upon the social condition of the Anglo-Americans; but there is one that takes precedence of all the rest. The social condition of the Americans is eminently democratic; this was its character at the foundation of the colonies, and it is still more strongly marked at the present day.

I have stated . . . that great equality existed among the immigrants who settled on the shores of New England. Even the germs of aristocracy were never planted in that part of the Union. The only influence which obtained there was that of intellect; the people became accustomed to revere certain names as representatives of knowledge and virtue. Some of their fellow citizens acquired a power over the others that might truly have been called aristocratic if it had been capable of transmission from father to son. . . .

At this period society was shaken to its center. The people, in whose name the struggle had taken place, conceived the desire of exercising the authority that it had acquired; its democratic tendencies were awakened; and having thrown off the yoke of the mother country, it aspired to independence of every kind. The influence of individuals gradually ceased to be felt, and custom and law united to produce the same result.

But the law of inheritance was the last step to equality. I am surprised that ancient and modern jurists have not attributed to this law a greater influence on human affairs. . . .

In the United States it has nearly completed its work of destruction, and there we can best study its results. The English laws concerning the transmission of property were abolished in almost all the states at the time of the Revolution. The law of entail was so modified as not materially to interrupt the free circulation of property. The first generation having passed away, estates began to be parceled out; and the change became more and more rapid with the progress of time. And now, after a lapse of a little more than sixty years, the aspect of society is totally altered; the families of the great landed proprietors are almost all commingled with the general mass. In the state of New York, which formerly contained many of these, there are but two who still keep their heads above the stream; and they must shortly disappear. The sons of these opulent citizens have become merchants, lawyers, or physicians. Most of them have lapsed into obscurity. The last trace of hereditary ranks and distinctions is destroyed; the law of partition has reduced all to one level.

I do not mean that there is any lack of wealthy individuals in the United States; I know of no country, indeed, where the love of money has taken stronger hold on the affections of men and where a profounder contempt is expressed for the theory of the permanent equality of property. But wealth circulates with inconceivable rapidity, and experience shows that it is rare to find two succeeding generations in the full enjoyment of it.

This picture, which may, perhaps, be thought to be overcharged, still gives a very imperfect idea of what is taking place in the new states of the West and Southwest. At the end of the last century a few bold adventurers began to penetrate into the valley of the Mississippi, and the mass of the population very soon began to move in that direction: communities unheard of till then suddenly appeared in the desert. States whose names were not in existence a few years before, claimed their place in the American Union; and in the Western settlements we may behold democracy arrived at its utmost limits. In these states, founded offhand and as it were by chance, the inhabitants are but of yesterday. Scarcely known to one another, the nearest neighbors are ignorant of each other's history. In this part of the American continent, therefore, the population has escaped the influence not only of great names and great wealth, but even of the natural aristocracy of knowledge and virtue. None is there able to wield that respectable power which men willingly grant to the remembrance of a life spent in doing good before their eyes. The new states of the West are already inhabited, but society has no existence among them.

It is not only the fortunes of men that are equal in America; even their acquirements partake in some degree of the same uniformity. I do not believe that there is a country in the world where, in proportion to the population, there are so few ignorant and at the same time so few learned individuals. Primary instruction is within the reach of everybody; superior instruction is scarcely to be obtained by any. This is not surprising; it is, in fact, the necessary consequence of what I have advanced above. Almost all the Americans are in easy circumstances and can therefore obtain the first elements of human knowledge.

In America there are but few wealthy persons; nearly all Americans have to take a profession. Now, every profession requires an apprenticeship. The Americans can devote to general education only the early years of life. At fifteen they enter upon their calling, and thus their education generally ends at the age when ours begins. If it is continued beyond that point, it aims only towards a particular specialized and profitable purpose; one studies science as one takes up a business; and one takes up only those applications whose immediate practicality is recognized.

In America most of the rich men were formerly poor; most of those who now enjoy leisure were absorbed in business during their youth; the consequence of this is that when they might have had a taste for study, they had no time for it, and when the time is at their disposal, they have no longer the inclination.

There is no class, then, in America, in which the taste for intellectual pleasures is transmitted with hereditary fortune and leisure and by which the labors of the intellect are held in honor. Accordingly, there is an equal want of the desire and the power of application to these objects.

A middling standard is fixed in America for human knowledge. All approach as near to it as they can; some as they rise, others as they descend. Of course, a multitude of persons are to be found who entertain the same number of ideas on religion, history, science, political economy, legislation, and government. The gifts of intellect proceed directly from God, and man cannot prevent their unequal distribution. But it is at least a consequence of what I have just said that although the capacities of men are different, as the Creator intended they should be, the means that Americans find for putting them to use are equal.

In America the aristocratic element has always been feeble from its birth; and if at the present day it is not actually destroyed, it is at any rate so completely disabled that we can scarcely assign to it any degree of influence on the course of affairs.

The democratic principle, on the contrary, has gained so much strength by time, by events, and by legislation, as to have become not only predominant, but all-powerful. No family or corporate authority can be perceived; very often one cannot even discover in it any very lasting individual influence.

America, then, exhibits in her social state an extraordinary phenomenon. Men are there seen on a greater equality in point of fortune and intellect, or, in other words, more equal in their strength, than in any other country of the world, or in any age of which history has preserved the remembrance.

Political Consequences of the Social Condition of the Anglo-Americans

The political consequences of such a social condition as this are easily deducible.

It is impossible to believe that equality will not eventually find its way into the political world, as it does everywhere else. To conceive of men remaining forever unequal upon a single point, yet equal on all others, is impossible; they must come in the end to be equal upon all.

Now, I know of only two methods of establishing equality in the political world; rights must be given to every citizen, or none at all to anyone. For nations which are arrived at the same stage of social existence as the Anglo-Americans, it is, therefore, very difficult to discover a medium between the sovereignty of all and the absolute power of one man: and it would be vain to deny that the social condition which I have been describing is just as liable to one of these consequences as to the other.

There is, in fact, a manly and lawful passion for equality that incites men to wish all to be powerful and honored. This passion tends to elevate the humble to the rank of the great; but there exists also in the human heart a depraved taste for equality, which impels the weak to attempt to lower the powerful to their own level and reduces men to prefer equality in slavery to inequality with freedom. Not that those nations whose social condition is democratic naturally despise liberty; on the contrary, they have an instinctive love of it. But liberty is not the chief and constant object of their desires; equality is their idol: they make rapid and sudden efforts to obtain liberty and, if they miss their aim, resign themselves to their disappointment; but nothing can satisfy them without equality, and they would rather perish than lose it.

On the other hand, in a state where the citizens are all practically equal, it becomes difficult for them to preserve their independence against the aggressions of power. No one among them being strong enough to engage in the struggle alone with advantage, nothing but a general combination can protect their liberty. Now, such a union is not always possible.

From the same social position, then, nations may derive one or the other of two great political results; these results are extremely different from each other, but they both proceed from the same cause.

The Anglo-Americans are the first nation who, having been exposed to this formidable alternative, have been happy enough to escape the dominion of absolute power. They have been allowed by their circumstances, their origin, their intelligence, and especially by their morals to establish and maintain the sovereignty of the people.

The Principle of the Sovereignty of the People of America

Whenever the political laws of the United States are to be discussed, it is with the doctrine of the sovereignty of the people that we must begin.

The principle of the sovereignty of the people, which is always to be found, more or less, at the bottom of almost all human institutions, generally remains there concealed from view. It is obeyed without being recognized, or if for a moment it is brought to light, it is hastily cast back into the gloom of the sanctuary.

"The will of the nation" is one of those phrases that have been most largely abused by the wily and the despotic of every age. Some have seen the expression of it in the purchased suffrages of a few of the satellites of power; others, in the votes of a timid or an interested minority; and some have even discovered it in the silence of a people, on the supposition that the fact of submission established the right to command.

In America the principle of the sovereignty of the people is neither barren nor concealed, as it is with some other nations; it is recognized by the customs and proclaimed by the laws; it spreads freely, and arrives without impediment at its most remote consequences. If there is a country in the world where the doctrine of the sovereignty of the people can be fairly appreciated, where it can be studied in its application to the affairs of society, and where its dangers and its advantages may be judged, that country is assuredly America.

I have already observed that, from their origin, the sovereignty of the people was the fundamental principle of most of the British colonies in America. It was far, however, from then exercising as much influence on the government of society as it now does. Two obstacles, the one external, the other internal, checked its invasive progress.

It could not ostensibly disclose itself in the laws of colonies which were still forced to obey the mother country; it was therefore obliged to rule secretly in the provincial assemblies, and especially in the townships.

American society at that time was not yet prepared to adopt it with all its consequences. Intelligence in New England and wealth in the country to the south of the Hudson . . . long exercised a sort of aristocratic influence, which tended to keep the exercise of social power in the hands of a few. Not all the public functionaries were chosen by popular vote, nor were all the citizens voters. The electoral franchise was everywhere somewhat restricted and made dependent on a certain qualification, which was very low in the North and more considerable in the South.

The American Revolution broke out, and the doctrine of the sovereignty of the people came out of the townships and took possession of the state. Every class was enlisted in its cause; battles were fought and victories obtained for it; it became the law of laws.

A change almost as rapid was effected in the interior of society, where the law of inheritance completed the abolition of local influences.

As soon as this effect of the laws and of the Revolution became apparent to every eye, victory was irrevocably pronounced in favor of the democratic cause. All power was, in fact, in its hands, and resistance was no longer possible. The higher orders submitted without a murmur and without a struggle to an evil that was thenceforth inevitable. The ordinary fate of falling powers awaited them: each of their members followed his own interest; and as it was impossible to wring the power from the hands of a people whom they did not detest sufficiently to brave, their only aim was to secure its goodwill at any price. The most democratic laws were consequently voted by the very men whose interests they impaired: and thus, although the higher classes did not excite the passions of the people against their order, they themselves accelerated the triumph of the new state of things; so that, by a singular change, the democratic impulse was found to be most irresistible in the very states where the aristocracy had the firmest hold. The state of Maryland, which had been founded by men of rank, was the first to proclaim universal suffrage and to introduce the most democratic forms into the whole of its government.

When a nation begins to modify the elective qualification, it may easily be foreseen that, sooner or later, that qualification will be entirely abolished. There is no more invariable rule in the history of society: the further electoral rights are extended, the greater is the need of extending them; for after each concession the strength of the democracy increases, and its demands increase with its strength. The ambition of those who are below the appointed rate is irritated in exact proportion to the great number of those who are above it. The exception at last becomes the rule, concession follows concession, and no stop can be made short of universal suffrage.

At the present day the principle of the sovereignty of the people has acquired in the United States all the practical development that the imagination can conceive. It is unencumbered by those fictions that are thrown over it in other countries, and it appears in every possible form, according to the exigency of the occasion. Sometimes the laws are made by the people in a body, as at Athens; and sometimes its representatives, chosen by universal suffrage, transact business in its name and under its immediate supervision.

In some countries a power exists which, though it is in a degree foreign to the social body, directs it, and forces it to pursue a certain track. In others the ruling force is divided, being partly within and partly without the ranks of the people. But nothing of the kind is to be seen in the United States; there society governs itself for itself. All power centers in its bosom, and scarcely an individual is to be met with who would venture to conceive or, still less, to express the idea of seeking it elsewhere. The nation participates in the making of its laws by the choice of its legislators, and in the execution of them by the choice of the agents of the executive government; it may almost be said to govern itself, so feeble and so restricted is the share left to the administration, so little do the authorities forget their popular origin and the power from which they emanate. The people reign in the American political world as the Deity does in the universe. They are the cause and the aim of all things; everything comes from them, and everything is absorbed in them.

Critical Thinking

1. Why is that, even before the American Revolution, the tradition of aristocracy could not be preserved on American soil?
2. What would give de Tocqueville the impression that the new states of the West, although already inhabited, were bereft of society?
3. If de Tocqueville were here today, what encouragement and/or admonition might he give to emerging democracies that want to pattern themselves on the principles of American democracy?

Create Central

www.mhhe.com/createcentral

Internet References

The Alexis de Tocqueville Tour
www.tocqueville.org

From *Democracy in America* by Alexis de Tocqueville (1835).

Individualism

Robert N. Bellah et al.

Learning Outcomes

After reading this selection, you should be able to:

1. Recognize the distinctions and commonalities among biblical, civic, and utilitarian individualism.
2. Discuss how the mythical heroism of the cowboy and the hard-boiled detective tells us something important about American individualism.
3. Explain what Alasdair MacIntyre means by the term "bureaucratic individualism."

Habits of the Heart: Individualism and Commitment in American Life (University of California Press, 1985), from which the following selection has been taken, established authors Robert N. Bellah (b. 1927), Richard Madsen (b. 1941), William M. Sullivan (b. 1945), Ann Swidler (b. 1944), and Steven M. Tipton as scholars of the communitarian school of American political thought. This school of thought links political theory to practical proposals for social and political reform of the American political system. In order to reestablish the connection between rights and duties, it emphasizes civic responsibilities and obligations, social commitments in the private and public sector, and the concept of a shared community or public interest. The communitarian philosophy insists that as social beings, citizens fulfill their lives by engaging in meaningful group activities and relations in their respective communities (e.g., religious, recreational, family, educational, and cultural activities).

Habits of the Heart was written in the context of the Ronald Reagan administration during a period of extreme individualism, egoism, and rejection of the welfare state. The book has been considered an influential analysis and critique of contemporary American political ideology. In the following selection, the authors contend that the forces of personal material gratification and self-fulfillment operating in contemporary American political culture result in shallow social relations, unfulfilled lives, and alienation. The prescribed remedy to a false conception of individualism is linked to a comprehensive strengthening of communal social bonds and associations.

Bellah is the Elliott Professor of Sociology Emeritus at the University of California at Berkeley, and a scholar of religious studies. Madsen is a professor of sociology and chairman of the Department of Sociology at the University of California, San Diego. Sullivan is a Senior Scholar at the Carnegie Foundation for the Advancement of Teaching and an associate faculty at La Salle University in Philadelphia, Pennsylvania. Swidler is a professor of sociology at the University of California, Berkeley. Tipton is professor of the sociology of religion and Director of the Graduate Division of Religion at Emory University in Atlanta, Georgia.

Key Concept: individualism as the core of American political culture

The Ambiguities of Individualism

Individualism lies at the very core of American culture. Every one of the four traditions we have singled out is in a profound sense individualistic. There is a biblical individualism and a civic individualism as well as a utilitarian and an expressive individualism. Whatever the differences among the traditions and the consequent differences in their understandings of individualism, there are some things they all share, things that are basic to American identity. We believe in the dignity, indeed the sacredness, of the individual. Anything that would violate our right to think for ourselves, judge for ourselves, make our own decisions, live our lives as we see fit, is not only morally wrong, it is sacrilegious. Our highest and noblest aspirations, not only for ourselves, but for those we care about, for our society and for the world, are closely linked to our individualism. Yet, . . . some of our deepest problems both as individuals and as a society are also closely linked to our individualism. We do not argue that Americans should abandon individualism—that would mean for us to abandon our deepest identity. But individualism has come to mean so many things and to contain such contradictions and paradoxes that even to defend it requires that we analyze it critically, that we consider especially those tendencies that would destroy it from within.

Modern individualism emerged out of the struggle against monarchical and aristocratic authority that seemed arbitrary and oppressive to citizens prepared to assert the right to govern themselves. In that struggle, classical political philosophy and biblical religion were important cultural resources. Classical republicanism evoked an image of the active citizen contributing to the public good and Reformation Christianity, in both Puritan and sectarian forms, inspired a notion of government based on the voluntary participation of individuals. Yet both these traditions placed individual autonomy in a context of moral and religious obligation that in some contexts justified obedience as well as freedom.

In seventeenth-century England, a radical philosophical defense of individual rights emerged that owed little to either classical or biblical sources. Rather, it consciously started with the biological individual in a "state of nature" and derived a social order from the actions of such individuals, first in relation to nature and then in relation to one another. John Locke is the key figure and one enormously influential in America. The essence of the Lockean position is an almost ontological individualism. The individual is prior to society, which comes into existence only through the voluntary contract of individuals trying to maximize their own self-interest. It is from this position that we have derived the tradition of utilitarian individualism. But because one can only know what is useful to one by consulting one's desires and sentiments, this is also ultimately the source of the expressive individualist tradition as well.

Modern individualism has long coexisted with classical republicanism and biblical religion. The conflict in their basic assumptions was initially muted because they all, in the forms commonest in America, stressed the dignity and autonomy of the individual. But as modern individualism became more dominant in the United States and classical republicanism and biblical religion less effective, some of the difficulties in modern individualism began to become apparent. The therapeutic ethos to which we have devoted so much attention is suggestive of these because it is the way in which contemporary Americans live out the tenets of modern individualism. For psychology, as Robert Coles has written, the self is "the only or main form of reality."

The question is whether an individualism in which the self has become the main form of reality can really be sustained. What is at issue is not simply whether self-contained individuals might withdraw from the public sphere to pursue purely private ends, but whether such individuals are capable of sustaining either a public *or* a private life. If this is the danger, perhaps only the civic and biblical forms of individualism—forms that see the individual in relation to a larger whole, a community and a tradition—are capable of sustaining genuine individuality and nurturing both public and private life.

There are both ideological and sociological reasons for the growing strength of modern individualism at the expense of the civic and biblical traditions. Modern individualism has pursued individual rights and individual autonomy in ever new realms. In so doing, it has come into confrontation with those aspects of biblical and republican thought that accepted, even enshrined, unequal rights and obligations—between husbands and wives, masters and servants, leaders and followers, rich and poor. As the absolute commitment to individual dignity has condemned those inequalities, it has also seemed to invalidate the biblical and republican traditions. And in undermining these traditions, as Tocqueville warned, individualism also weakens the very meanings that give content and substance to the ideal of individual dignity.

We thus face a profound impasse. Modern individualism seems to be producing a way of life that is neither individually nor socially viable, yet a return to traditional forms would be to return to intolerable discrimination and oppression. The question, then, is whether the older civic and biblical traditions have the capacity to reformulate themselves while simultaneously remaining faithful to their own deepest insights.

Many Americans would prefer not to see the impasse as starkly as we have put it. Philosophical defenders of modern individualism have frequently presumed a social and cultural context for the individual that their theories cannot justify, or they have added ad hoc arguments that mitigate the harshness of their theoretical model. . . . Parents advocate "values" for their children even when they do not know what those "values" are. What this suggests is that there is a profound ambivalence about individualism in America among its most articulate defenders. This ambivalence shows up particularly clearly at the level of myth in our literature and our popular culture. There we find the fear that society may overwhelm the individual and destroy any chance of autonomy unless he stands against it, but also recognition that it is only in relation to society that the individual can fulfill himself and that if the break with society is too radical, life has no meaning at all.

Mythic Individualism

A deep and continuing theme in American literature is the hero who must leave society, alone or with one or a few others, in order to realize the moral good in the wilderness, at sea, or on the margins of settled society. Sometimes the withdrawal involves a contribution to society, as in James Fenimore Cooper's *The Deerslayer*. Sometimes the new marginal community realizes ethical ends impossible in the larger society, as in the interracial harmony between Huckleberry Finn and Jim. Sometimes the flight from society is simply mad and ends in general disaster, as in *Moby Dick*. When it is not in and through society but in flight from it that the good is to be realized, as in the case of Melville's Ahab, the line between ethical heroism and madness vanishes, and the destructive potentiality of a completely asocial individualism is revealed.

America is also the inventor of that most mythic individual hero, the cowboy, who again and again saves a society he can never completely fit into. The cowboy has a special talent—he can shoot straighter and faster than other men—and a special sense of justice. But these characteristics make him so unique that he can never fully belong to society. His destiny is to defend society without ever really joining it. He rides off alone into the sunset like Shane, or like the Lone Ranger moves on accompanied only by his Indian companion. But the cowboy's importance is not that he is isolated or antisocial. Rather, his significance lies in his unique, individual virtue and special skill and it is because of those qualities that society needs and welcomes him. Shane, after all, starts as a real outsider, but ends up with the gratitude of the community and the love of a woman and a boy. And while the Lone Ranger never settles down and marries the local schoolteacher, he always leaves with the affection and gratitude of the people he has helped. It is as if the myth says you can be a truly good person, worthy of admiration and love, only if you resist fully joining the group. But sometimes the tension leads to an irreparable break. Will Kane, the hero of *High Noon*, abandoned by the cowardly townspeople, saves them from an unrestrained killer, but then throws his sheriff's badge in the dust and goes off into the desert with his bride. One is left wondering where they will go, for there is no longer any link with any town.

The connection of moral courage and lonely individualism is even tighter for that other, more modern American hero, the hard-boiled detective. From Sam Spade to Serpico, the detective is a loner. He is often unsuccessful in conventional terms, working out of a shabby office where the phone never rings. Wily, tough, smart, he is nonetheless unappreciated. But his marginality is also his strength. When a bit of business finally comes their way, Philip Marlowe, Lew Archer, and Travis McGee are tenacious. They pursue justice and help the unprotected even when it threatens to unravel the fabric of society itself. . . .

Both the cowboy and the hard-boiled detective tell us something important about American individualism. The cowboy, like the detective, can be valuable to society only because he is a completely autonomous individual who stands outside it. To serve society, one must be able to stand alone, not needing others, not depending on their judgment, and not submitting to their wishes. Yet this individualism is not selfishness. Indeed, it is a kind of heroic selflessness. One accepts the necessity of remaining alone in order to serve the values of the group. And this obligation to aloneness is an important key to the American moral imagination. Yet it is part of the profound ambiguity of the mythology of American individualism that its moral heroism is always just a step away from despair. For an Ahab, and occasionally for a cowboy or a detective, there is no return to society, no moral

redemption. The hero's lonely quest for moral excellence ends in absolute nihilism.

If we may turn from the mythical heroes of fiction to a mythic, but historically real, hero, Abraham Lincoln, we may begin to see what is necessary if the nihilistic alternative is to be avoided. In many respects, Lincoln conforms perfectly to the archetype of the lonely, individualistic hero. He was a self-made man, never comfortable with the eastern upper classes. His dual moral commitment to the preservation of the Union and the belief that "all men are created equal" roused the hostility of abolitionists and Southern sympathizers alike. In the war years, he was more and more isolated, misunderstood by Congress and cabinet, and unhappy at home. In the face of almost universal mistrust, he nonetheless completed his self-appointed task of bringing the nation through its most devastating war, preaching reconciliation as he did so, only to be brought down by an assassin's bullet. What saved Lincoln from nihilism was the larger whole for which he felt it was important to live and worthwhile to die. No one understood better the meaning of the Republic and of the freedom and equality that it only very imperfectly embodies. But it was not only civic republicanism that gave his life value. Reinhold Niebuhr has said that Lincoln's biblical understanding of the Civil War was deeper than that of any contemporary theologian. The great symbols of death and rebirth that Lincoln invoked to give meaning to the sacrifice of those who died at Gettysburg, in a war he knew to be senseless and evil, came to redeem his own senseless death at the hand of an assassin. It is through his identification with a community and a tradition that Lincoln became the deeply and typically American individual that he was.

The Social Sources of Ambivalence

. . . [I]ndividualism is deeply rooted in America's social history. Here the bondservant became free, the tenant became a small landowner, and what Benjamin Franklin called the self-respecting "middling" condition of men became the norm. Yet the incipient "independent citizen" of colonial times found himself in a cohesive community, the "peaceable kingdoms" that were colonial towns, where ties to family and church and respect for the "natural leaders" of the community were still strong. Individualism was so embedded in the civic and religious structures of colonial life that it had not yet found a name, even though John Locke's ideas about individual autonomy were well known. It took the geographical and economic expansion of the new nation, especially in the years after 1800, to produce the restless quest for material betterment that led Tocqueville to use the word "individualism" to describe what he saw. The new social and economic conditions did not create the ideology of modern individualism, most of whose elements are considerably older than the nineteenth century, but those conditions did make it possible for what we have called utilitarian and, later, expressive individualism to develop their own inherent tendencies in relative independence from civic and religious forms of life, important though those still were.

Tocqueville was quick to point out one of the central ambiguities in the new individualism—that it was strangely compatible with conformism. He described the American insistence that one always rely on one's own judgment, rather than on received authority, in forming one's opinions and that one stand by one's own opinions. We have already heard many examples of this attitude . . . in the assertion, for example, that compromise with others is desirable, but not if you sacrifice your own "values." But, as Tocqueville observed, when one can no longer rely on tradition or authority, one inevitably looks to others for confirmation of one's judgments. Refusal to accept established opinion and anxious conformity to the opinions of one's peers turn out to be two sides of the same coin. . . .

The ambiguity and ambivalence of American individualism derive from both cultural and social contradictions. We insist, perhaps more than ever before, on finding our true selves independent of any cultural or social influence, being responsible to that self alone, and making its fulfillment the very meaning of our lives. Yet we spend much of our time navigating through immense bureaucratic structures—multiversities, corporations, government agencies—manipulating and being manipulated by others. In describing this situation, Alasdair MacIntyre has spoken of "bureaucratic individualism," the form of life exemplified by the manager and the therapist. In bureaucratic individualism, the ambiguities and contradictions of individualism are frighteningly revealed, as freedom to make private decisions is bought at the cost of turning over most public decisions to bureaucratic managers and experts. A bureaucratic individualism in which the consent of the governed, the first demand of modern enlightened individualism, has been abandoned in all but form, illustrates the tendency of individualism to destroy its own conditions.

But in our interviews, though we saw tendencies toward bureaucratic individualism, we cannot say that it has yet become dominant. Rather we found all the classic polarities of American individualism still operating: the deep desire for autonomy and self-reliance combined with an equally deep conviction that life has no meaning unless shared with others in the context of community; a commitment to the equal right to dignity of every individual combined with an effort to justify inequality of reward, which, when extreme, may deprive people of dignity; an insistence that life requires practical effectiveness and "realism" combined with the feeling that compromise is ethically fatal. The inner tensions of American individualism add up to a classic case of ambivalence. We strongly assert the value of our self-reliance and autonomy. We deeply feel the emptiness of a life without sustaining social commitments. Yet we are hesitant to articulate our sense that we need one another as much

as we need to stand alone, for fear that if we did we would lose our independence altogether. The tensions of our lives would be even greater if we did not, in fact, engage in practices that constantly limit the effects of an isolating individualism, even though we cannot articulate those practices nearly as well as we can the quest for autonomy.

The Limits of Individualism

We have pointed out the peculiar resonance between middle-class life and individualism in America. We have also stressed the special nature of the middle class, the fact that it is not simply a "layer" in a "system of stratification" but rather a group that seeks to embody in its own continuous progress and advancement the very meaning of the American project. To a large extent, it has succeeded in this aspiration. It so dominates our culture that, as Schneider and Smith put it, "middle-class values can be said to encompass both lower- and upper-class values." This is true for the lower class in that not only are middle-class values understood and respected but "lower-class people explain their inferior position in terms of circumstances that have prevented them from behaving in a middle-class fashion." The upper class sometimes takes comfort in its special sense of family and tradition, but it does not try to substitute its values for the dominant ones. On the contrary, its members praise middle-class rationality and achievement as the values on which our society is based, even when they do not choose to follow them.

The nature of middle-class individualism becomes even clearer when we contrast it to lower-class and upper-class culture. Schneider and Smith describe the contrast very suggestively when they say that the middle class sees "individual and social behavior as predominantly determined by the application of technical rules to any situation that arises," whereas the lower class (and, interestingly enough, the upper class) have a more "dramaturgical view of social action." By "dramaturgical" they mean action that takes on meaning because of a particular history of relationships. Abstract rules are less important than the examples set by individuals. Schneider and Smith argue, for example, that it is in the lower class that ethnicity, as a specific pattern of cultural life, survives in America, and that as individuals enter the middle class, ethnicity loses distinctive social content even when it is symbolically emphasized. The point is not that lower- and upper-class Americans are not individualistic, but rather that their individualism is embedded in specific patterns of relationship and solidarity that mitigate the tendency toward an empty self and empty relationships in middle-class life. The contrast is expressed by middle-class Americans themselves when they entertain envious fantasies about more "meaningful community" among lower-class racial and ethnic groups or among (usually European) aristocracies.

Important though the distinctions we have been drawing are, we should not overemphasize the degree to which rationality and technical rules govern middle-class life. Children do not grow up through abstract injunctions. They identify with their parents, they learn through role modeling, and they are influenced by the historic specificity of their family, church, and local community. It is the middle-class orientation toward technical education, bureaucratic occupational hierarchies, and the market economy that encourages the greater emphasis on universal rules and technical rationality. The upper and lower classes can maintain greater cultural specificity (though in the United States that specificity is only relative) because they are less oriented to these rationalizing institutions.

Since middle-class people, too, are embedded in families, churches, and local communities, they also experience conflict between the more rational and the more dramaturgic spheres of life. The tensions that divide middle-class Americans from other Americans also exist within the middle class itself. Much is said about the cultural diversity and pluralism of American life. But perhaps what divides us most is not that diversity, but the conflict between the monoculture of technical and bureaucratic rationality and the specificity of our concrete commitments.

Critical Thinking

1. To what extent has the American middle class succeeded in its aspiration to "embody in its own continuous progress and advancement the very meaning of the American project"?
2. How might a strengthening of communal social bonds and associations work to counter a false conception of individualism?
3. In what way was Lincoln's commitment to the preservation of the Union and to the belief that "all men are created equal" a moral duality?

Create Central

www.mhhe.com/createcentral

Internet References

The American Political Science Association
www.apsanet.org/index.cfm

The Communitarian Network
www.gwu.edu/~ccps/index.html

Stanford Encyclopedia of Philosophy
http://plato.stanford.edu

From *Habits of the Heart: Individualism and Commitment in American Life* (University of California Press, 1985), pp. 142–148, 150–152. Copyright © 1985 by Regents of the University of California. Reprinted by permission of University of California Press via Rightslink.

Prepared by: James Newman, *University of Maryland University College*

Give Me Liberty, or Give Me Death!

Patrick Henry

Learning Outcomes

After reading this selection, you should be able to:

1. Understand why Henry placed such a high value on freedom.
2. Develop a sense of what freedoms Henry views as sacrosanct.

Patrick Henry (1736–1799) served in the Virginia House of Burgesses, the Continental Congress, and as Governor of Virginia. He was a champion of states' rights and a supporter of limited authority for the federal government.

Key concept: freedom

No man thinks more highly than I do of the patriotism, as well as abilities, of the very worthy gentlemen who have just addressed the House. But different men often see the same subject in different lights; and, therefore, I hope that it will not be thought disrespectful to those gentlemen, if, entertaining as I do opinions of a character very opposite to theirs, I shall speak forth my sentiments freely and without reserve.

This is no time for ceremony. The question before the House is one of awful moment to this country. For my own part I consider it as nothing less than a question of freedom or slavery; and in proportion to the magnitude of the subject ought to be the freedom of the debate. It is only in this way that we can hope to arrive at truth, and fulfill the great responsibility which we hold to God and our country. Should I keep back my opinions at such a time, through fear of giving offense, I should consider myself as guilty of treason towards my country, and of an act of disloyalty towards the majesty of heaven, which I revere above all earthly kings.

Mr. President, it is natural to man to indulge in the illusions of hope. We are apt to shut our eyes against a painful truth, and listen to the song of that siren, till she transforms us into beasts. Is this the part of wise men, engaged in a great and arduous struggle for liberty? Are we disposed to be of the number of those who, having eyes, see not, and having ears, hear not, the things which so nearly concern their temporal salvation?

For my part, whatever anguish of spirit it may cost, I am willing to know the whole truth—to know the worst and to provide for it. I have but one lamp by which my feet are guided; and that is the lamp of experience. I know of no way of judging of the future but by the past. And judging by the past, I wish to know what there has been in the conduct of the British ministry for the last ten years, to justify those hopes with which gentlemen have been pleased to solace themselves and the House?

Is it that insidious smile with which our petition has been lately received? Trust it not, sir; it will prove a snare to your feet. Suffer not yourselves to be betrayed with a kiss. Ask yourselves how this gracious reception of our petition comports with these warlike preparations which cover our waters and darken our land. Are fleets and armies necessary to a work of love and reconciliation? Have we shown ourselves so unwilling to be reconciled that force must be called in to win back our love? Let us not deceive ourselves, sir. These are the implements of war and subjugation—the last arguments to which kings resort. I ask gentlemen, sir, what means this martial array, if its purpose be not to force us to submission? Can gentlemen assign any other possible motives for it? Has Great Britain any enemy, in this quarter of the world, to call for all this accumulation of navies and armies?

No, sir, she has none. They are meant for us; they can be meant for no other. They are sent over to bind and rivet upon us those chains which the British ministry have been so long forging. And what have we to oppose to them? Shall we try argument? Sir, we have been trying that for the last ten years. Have we anything new to offer on the subject? Nothing.

We have held the subject up in every light of which it is capable; but it has been all in vain. Shall we resort to entreaty and humble supplication? What terms shall we find which have not been already exhausted? Let us not, I beseech you, sir, deceive ourselves longer.

Sir, we have done everything that could be done to avert the storm which is now coming on. We have petitioned; we have remonstrated; we have supplicated; we have prostrated ourselves before the throne, and have implored its interposition to arrest the tyrannical hands of the ministry and Parliament.

Our petitions have been slighted; our remonstrances have produced additional violence and insult; our supplications have been disregarded; and we have been spurned, with contempt, from the foot of the throne. In vain, after these things, may we indulge the fond hope of peace and reconciliation. There is no longer any room for hope.

If we wish to be free—if we mean to preserve inviolate those inestimable privileges for which we have been so long contending—if we mean not basely to abandon the noble struggle in which we have been so long engaged, and which we have pledged ourselves never to abandon until the glorious object of our contest shall be obtained, we must fight! I repeat it, sir, we must fight! An appeal to arms and to the God of Hosts is all that is left us!

They tell us, sir, that we are weak—unable to cope with so formidable an adversary. But when shall we be stronger? Will it be the next week, or the next year? Will it be when we are totally disarmed, and when a British guard shall be stationed in every house? Shall we gather strength by irresolution and inaction? Shall we acquire the means of effectual resistance, by lying supinely on our backs, and hugging the delusive phantom of hope, until our enemies shall have bound us hand and foot?

Sir, we are not weak, if we make a proper use of the means which the God of nature hath placed in our power. Three millions of people, armed in the holy cause of liberty, and in such a country as that which we possess, are invincible by any force which our enemy can send against us. Besides, sir, we shall not fight our battles alone. There is a just God who presides over the destinies of nations, and who will raise up friends to fight our battles for us.

The battle, sir, is not to the strong alone; it is to the vigilant, the active, the brave. Besides, sir, we have no election. If we were base enough to desire it, it is now too late to retire from the contest. There is no retreat but in submission and slavery! Our chains are forged! Their clanking may be heard on the plains of Boston! The war is inevitable—and let it come! I repeat it, sir, let it come!

It is in vain, sir, to extenuate the matter. Gentlemen may cry, "Peace! Peace!"—but there is no peace. The war is actually begun! The next gale that sweeps from the north will bring to our ears the clash of resounding arms! Our brethren are already in the field! Why stand we here idle? What is it that gentlemen wish? What would they have? Is life so dear, or peace so sweet, as to be purchased at the price of chains and slavery? Forbid it, Almighty God! I know not what course others may take; but as for me, give me liberty, or give me death!

Critical Thinking

1. Why does the king wish to suppress these freedoms?
2. What freedoms are worth sacrificing?

Create Central

www.mhhe.com/createcentral

Internet References

Patrick Henry Center for Individual Liberty
www.patrickhenrycenter.com/Speeches.aspx

From *Lit2Go*, March 23, 1775. Copyright © 1775 by Florida Center for Instruction Technology. http://etc.usf.edu/lit2go/133/historic-american-documents/4956/patrick-henrys-speech-to-the-virginia-house-of-burgess-richmond-virginia-march-23-1775/.

Unit 2: The Constitutional Foundation of American Government

Federalist, *Nos. 47, 48, and 51*

James Madison

Learning Outcomes

After reading this selection, you should be able to:

1. Discuss Madison's defense of the Constitution as a tyranny-proof instrument.
2. Identify the direct influence of Montesquieu on the U.S. Constitution, as well as the state constitutions that preceded it.
3. Cite Madison's contention that in republican government, the legislative authority necessarily predominates.

The framers of the U.S. Constitution, James Madison (1751–1836), Alexander Hamilton (1757–1804), and John Jay (1745–1829), wrote the *Federalist Papers* (1788) under the pseudonym "Publius" (identifying with Publius Valerius, a Roman emperor and defender of the Republic). This collection of 85 persuasive, political, theoretical articles and letters was published in New York City newspapers from October 1787 to March 1788 during New York's debates on the ratification of the U.S. Constitution. Although a pseudonym was used to conceal the identity of the authors during the publication of the essays, subsequent scholarly research has confirmed that Hamilton wrote 51 of them, Madison 26, Jay 5, and Hamilton and Madison collaborated on 3. The authors thought that it was necessary to publish the articles in this context due to New York's strong Anti-Federalist resistance to the ratification of the U.S. Constitution. The papers had a powerful impact upon the ratification debates in New York and were immediately reprinted in several other critical states. The objective of this collection of essays was to critique the many significant defects of the Articles of Confederation and to forcefully argue for the proposed federal legal framework.

In the following selection from the *Federalist Papers* (1788), Madison dispassionately defends the U.S. Constitution. In *Federalist*, Nos. 47 and 48, Madison prescribes a national government with a configuration of three distinct, independent, and equal branches of public authority. He refers to the historical cases of state governments and the British Constitution to document the problems and limitations of the principle of separation of powers. These papers defend those constitutional principles that promote a strong unified national government and protect against the potential of any one branch usurping the powers and functions of the others, in addition to avoiding excessive consolidation or concentration of power in any one particular branch of the national government. In *Federalist*, No. 51, Madison focuses on the problems of the principle of separation of powers and the objective of avoiding governmental tyranny.

The *Federalist Papers* have had an enduring impact as the most comprehensive and substantive interpretation of the U.S. Constitution. They are considered by many scholars to be the most significant and creative work in American political philosophy.

Key Concept: proposed constitutional principles to avoid governmental tyranny

No. 47

Having reviewed the general form of the proposed government, and the general mass of power allotted to it, I proceed to examine the particular structure of this government, and the distribution of this mass of power among its constituent parts.

One of the principal objections inculcated by the more respectable adversaries to the Constitution is its supposed violation of the political maxim that the legislative, executive, and judiciary departments ought to be separate and distinct. In the structure of the federal government no regard, it is said, seems to have been paid to this essential precaution in favor of liberty. The several departments of power are distributed and blended in such a manner as at once to destroy all symmetry and beauty of form, and to expose some of the essential parts of the edifice to the danger of being crushed by the disproportionate weight of other parts.

No political truth is certainly of greater intrinsic value, or is stamped with the authority of more enlightened patrons of liberty than that on which the objection is founded. The accumulation of all powers, legislative, executive, and judiciary, in the same hands, whether or one, a few, or many, and whether hereditary, self-appointed, or elective, may justly be pronounced the very definition of tyranny. Were the federal Constitution, therefore, really chargeable with this accumulation of power, or with a mixture of powers, having a dangerous tendency to such an accumulation, no further arguments would be necessary to inspire a universal reprobation of the system. I persuade myself, however, that it will be made apparent to everyone that the charge cannot be supported, and that the maxim on which it relies has been totally misconceived and misapplied. In order to form correct ideas on this important subject it will be proper to investigate the sense in which the preservation of liberty requires that the three great departments of power should be separate and distinct.

The oracle who is always consulted and cited on this subject is the celebrated Montesquieu. If he be not the author of this invaluable precept in the science of politics, he has the merit at least of displaying and recommending it most effectually to the attention of mankind. . . .

From . . . facts, by which Montesquieu was guided, it may clearly be inferred that in saying "There can be no liberty where the legislative and executive powers are united in the same person, or body of magistrates," or, "if the power of judging be not separated from the legislative and executive powers," he did not mean that these departments ought to have no *partial agency* in, or no *control* over, the acts of each other. His meaning, as his own words import, and still more conclusively as illustrated by the example in his eye, can amount to no more than this, that where the *whole* power of one department is exercised by the same hands which possess the *whole* power of another department, the fundamental principles of a free constitution are subverted. . . .

If we look into the constitutions of the several States we find that, notwithstanding the emphatical and, in some instances, the unqualified terms in which this axiom has been laid down, there is not a single instance in which the several departments of power have been kept absolutely separate and distinct. . . .

The constitution of Massachusetts has observed a sufficient though less pointed caution in expressing this fundamental article of liberty. It declares "that the legislative department shall never exercise the executive and judicial powers, or either of them; the executive shall never exercise the legislative and judicial powers, or either of them; the judicial shall never exercise the legislative and executive powers, or either of them." This declaration corresponds precisely with the doctrine of Montesquieu . . . and is not in a single point violated by the plan of the convention. It goes no farther than to prohibit any one of the entire departments from exercising the powers of another department. In the very Constitution to which it is prefixed, a partial mixture of powers has been admitted. The executive magistrate has a qualified negative on the legislative body, and the Senate, which is a part of the legislature, is a court of impeachment for members both of the executive and judiciary departments. The members of the judiciary department, again, are appointable by the executive department, and removable by the same authority on the address of the two legislative branches. . . .

No. 48

It was shown in the last paper that the political apothegm there examined does not require that the legislative, executive, and judiciary departments should be wholly unconnected with each other. I shall undertake, in the next place, to show that unless these departments be so far connected and blended as to give to each a constitutional control over the others, the degree of separation which the maxim requires, as essential to a free government, can never in practice be duly maintained.

It is agreed on all sides that the powers properly belonging to one of the departments ought not to be directly and completely administered by either of the other departments. It is equally evident that none of them ought to possess, directly or indirectly, an overruling influence over the others in the administration of their respective powers. It will not be denied that power is of an encroaching nature and that it ought to be effectually restrained from passing the limits assigned to it. After discriminating, therefore, in theory, the several classes of power, as they may in their nature be legislative, executive, or judiciary, the next and most difficult task is to provide some practical security for each, against the invasion of the others. What this security ought to be is the great problem to be solved.

Will it be sufficient to mark, with precision, the boundaries of these departments in the constitution of the government, and to trust to these parchment barriers against the encroaching spirit of power? This is the security which appears to have been principally relied on by the compliers of most of the American constitutions. But experience assures us that the efficacy of the provision has been greatly overrated; and that some more adequate defense is indispensably necessary for the more feeble against the more powerful members of the government. The legislative department is everywhere extending the sphere of its activity and drawing all power into its impetuous vortex. . . .

In a government where numerous and extensive prerogatives are placed in the hands of an hereditary monarch, the executive department is very justly regarded as the source of danger, and watched with all the jealousy which a zeal for liberty ought to inspire. In a democracy, where a multitude of people exercise in person the legislative functions and are continually exposed, by their incapacity for regular deliberation and concerted measures, to the ambitious intrigues of their executive magistrates, tyranny may well be apprehended, on some favorable emergency, to start up in the same quarter. But in a representative republic where the executive magistracy is carefully limited, both in the extent and the duration of its power; and where the legislative power is exercised by an assembly, which is inspired by a supposed influence over the people with an intrepid confidence in its own strength; which is sufficiently numerous to feel all the passions which actuate a multitude, yet not so numerous as to be incapable of pursuing the objects of its passions by means which reason prescribes; it is against the enterprising ambition of this department that the people ought to indulge all their jealousy and exhaust all their precautions.

The legislative department derives a superiority in our governments from other circumstances. Its constitutional powers being at once more extensive, and less susceptible of precise limits, it can, with the greater facility, mask, under complicated and indirect measures, the encroachments which it makes on the co-ordinate departments. It is not unfrequently a question of real nicety in legislative bodies whether the operation of a particular measure will, or will not, extend beyond the legislative sphere. On the other side, the executive power being restrained within a narrower compass and being more simple in its nature, and the judiciary being described by landmarks still less uncertain, projects of usurpation by either of these departments would immediately betray and defeat themselves. Nor is this all: as the legislative department alone has access to the pockets of the people, and has in some constitutions full discretion, and in all a prevailing influence, over the pecuniary rewards of those who fill the other departments, a dependence is thus created in the latter, which gives still greater facility to encroachments of the former. . . .

No. 51

To what expedient, then, shall we finally resort, for maintaining in practice the necessary partition of power among the several departments as laid down in the Constitution? The only answer that can be given is that as all these exterior provisions are found to be inadequate the defect must be supplied, by so contriving the interior structure of the government as that its several constituent parts may, by their mutual relations, be the means of keeping each other in their proper places. . . .

In order to lay a due foundation for that separate and distinct exercise of the different powers of government, which to a certain extent is admitted on all hands to be essential to the preservation of liberty, it is evident that each department should have a will of its own; and consequently should be so constituted that the members of each should have as little agency as possible in the appointment of the members of the others. . . .

It is equally evident that the members of each department should be as little dependent as possible on those of the others for the emoluments annexed to their offices. Were the executive magistrate, or the judges, not independent of the legislature in this particular, their independence in every other would be merely nominal.

But the great security against a gradual concentration of the several powers in the same department consists in giving to those who administer each department the necessary constitutional means and personal motives to

resist encroachments of the others. The provision for defense must in this, as in all other cases, be made commensurate to the danger of attack. Ambition must be made to counteract ambition. The interest of the man must be connected with the constitutional rights of the place. It may be a reflection on human nature that such devices should be necessary to control the abuses of government. But what is government itself but the greatest of all reflections on human nature? If men were angels, no government would be necessary. If angels were to govern men, neither external nor internal controls on government would be necessary. In framing a government which is to be administered by men over men, the great difficulty lies in this: you must first enable the government to control the governed; and in the next place oblige it to control itself. A dependence on the people is, no doubt, the primary control on the government; but experience has taught mankind the necessity of auxiliary precautions.

This policy of supplying, by opposite and rival interests, the defect of better motives, might be traced through the whole system of human affairs, private as well as public. We see it particularly displayed in all the subordinate distributions of power, where the constant aim is to divide and arrange the several offices in such a manner as that each may be a check on the other—that the private interest of every individual may be a sentinel over the public rights. These inventions of prudence cannot be less requisite in the distribution of the supreme powers of the State.

But it is not possible to give to each department an equal power of self-defense. In republican government, the legislative authority necessarily predominates. The remedy for this inconveniency is to divide the legislature into different branches; and to render them, by different modes of election and different principles of action, as little connected with each other as the nature of their common functions and their common dependence on the society will admit. It may even be necessary to guard against dangerous encroachments by still further precautions. As the weight of the legislative authority requires that it should be thus divided, the weakness of the executive may require, on the other hand, that it should be fortified. An absolute negative on the legislature appears, at first view, to be the natural defense with which the executive magistrate should be armed. But perhaps it would be neither altogether safe nor alone sufficient. On ordinary occasions it might not be exerted with the requisite firmness, and on extraordinary occasions it might be perfidiously abused. May not this defect of an absolute negative be supplied by some qualified connection between this weaker department and the weaker branch of the stronger department, by which the latter may be led to support the constitutional rights of the former, without being too much detached from the rights of its own department?

Critical Thinking

1. How would you assess Madison's ability to argue convincingly to those in passionate opposition, yet remain respectful of those in opposition?
2. Which of the three branches of authority—executive, legislative, judicial—was probably of the greatest concern to those most reluctant to ratify the Constitution, and why?

Create Central

www.mhhe.com/createcentral

Internet References

Emory University School of Law
http://library.law.emory.edu/for-law-students/emory-law
-subject-guides/constitutional-and-statutory-research/
us-constitution

The National Archives and Records Administration
www.archives.gov

The National Governors Association
www.nga.org/portal/site/nga

From *The Federalist* by James Madison (1788).

An Economic Interpretation of the Constitution of the United States

Charles A. Beard

Learning Outcomes

After reading this selection, you should be able to:

1. Provide a general socioeconomic profile of the majority of members of the Constitutional Convention.
2. Discuss the Constitution's provisions for indirect taxation.
3. Identify the core great powers conferred on the federal government by the Constitution.

Charles A. Beard's *An Economic Interpretation of the Constitution of the United States* (Macmillan, 1935), from which the following selection is excerpted, offers a historical revisionist interpretation of the U.S. Constitution. This political study was controversial because it strongly rejected the conventional democratic interpretation of the nature of the Constitution and the public-spirited, virtuous motivation of the framers of the U.S. Constitution. In sharp contrast to alternative studies that focus on the pragmatic character of the framers and on the Constitution as a flexible and stable blueprint based upon negotiated compromises, Beard contended that the document is a reflection exclusively of the private economic self-interests of an elite, or minority, of the American population. Beard claimed that the delegate membership of the Constitutional Convention consisted in a social economic elite of wealthy and powerful individuals.

In the following selection, Beard contends that the fundamental objective of the framers was to consolidate and expand their property holdings. The delegates strongly desired to limit the power of the masses, or majority rule, and consequently to protect their private property from potential tyranny of the majority and mob rule. The Constitution was designed with provisions consisting of specific political procedures and governmental institutions with the purposes of limiting majority rule, reducing popular accessibility and influence on public policy, and preserving elite dominance.

Various political scientists and historians have offered a rebuttal to Beard's thesis due to theoretical and historical deficiencies of evidence. However, several contemporary political theorists have adopted Beard's thesis and antidemocratic interpretation of the political ideas of the framers.

Beard (1874–1948) was the author of numerous books on American political history, and his scholarly reputation was recognized by both political scientists and historians. He was elected president of the American Political Science Association in 1926 and president of the American Historical Association in 1933. He was also awarded the prestigious Gold Medal for distinguished achievement by the National Institute of Arts and Letters in 1948.

Key Concept: the economic intention of the framers of the U.S. Constitution

A Survey of Economic Interests in 1787

The whole theory of the economic interpretation of history rests upon the concept that social progress in general is the result of contending interests in society—some favorable, others opposed, to change. On this hypothesis, we are required to discover at the very outset of the present study what classes and social groups existed in the United States just previous to the adoption of the Constitution and which of them, from the nature of their property, might have expected to benefit immediately and definitely by the overthrow of the old system and the establishment of the new. On the other hand, it must be discovered which of them might have expected more beneficial immediate results, on the whole, from maintenance of the existing legal arrangements.

The importance of a survey of the distribution of property in 1787 for economic as well as political history is so evident that it is strange that no attempt has been made to undertake it on a large scale. Not even a beginning has been made. It is, therefore, necessary for us to rely for the present upon the general statements of historians who have written more or less at length about the period under consideration; but in the meanwhile it can do no harm to suggest, by way of a preface, the outlines of such a survey and some of the chief sources of information. . . .

A survey of the economic interests of the members of the Convention presents certain conclusions:

A majority of the members were lawyers by profession.

Most of the members came from towns, on or near the coast, that is, from the regions in which personalty was largely concentrated.

Not one member represented in his immediate personal economic interests the small farming or mechanic classes.

The overwhelming majority of members, at least five-sixths, were immediately, directly, and personally interested in the outcome of their labors at Philadelphia, and were to a greater or less extent economic beneficiaries from the adoption of the Constitution. . . .

It cannot be said. . . that the members of the Convention were "disinterested." On the contrary, we are forced to accept the profoundly significant conclusion that they knew through their personal experiences in economic affairs the precise results which the new government that they were setting up was designed to attain. As a group of doctrinaires, like the Frankfort assembly of 1848, they would have failed miserably; but as practical men they were able to build the new government upon the only foundations which could be stable: fundamental economic interests.[1]

The Constitution As an Economic Document

It is difficult for the superficial student of the Constitution, who has read only the commentaries of the legists, to conceive of that instrument as an economic document. It places no property qualifications on voters or officers; it gives no outward recognition of any economic groups in society; it mentions no special privileges to be conferred upon any class. It betrays no feeling, such as vibrates through the French constitution of 1791; its language is cold, formal, and severe.

The true inwardness of the Constitution is not revealed by an examination of its provisions as simple propositions of law; but by a long and careful study of the voluminous correspondence of the period, contemporary newspapers and pamphlets, the records of the debates in the Convention at Philadelphia and in the several state conventions, and particularly, *The Federalist*, which was widely circulated during the struggle over ratification. The correspondence shows the exact character of the evils which the Constitution was intended to remedy; the records of the proceedings in the Philadelphia Convention reveal the successive steps in the building of the framework of the government under the pressure of economic interests; the pamphlets and newspapers disclose the ideas of the contestants over the ratification; and *The Federalist* presents the political science of the new system as conceived by three of the profoundest thinkers of the period, Hamilton, Madison, and Jay.

Doubtless, the most illuminating of these sources on the economic character of the Constitution are the records of the debates in the Convention, which have come down to us in fragmentary form; and a thorough treatment of material forces reflected in the several clauses of the instrument of government created by the grave assembly at Philadelphia would require a rewriting of the history of the proceedings in the light of the great interests represented there. But an entire volume would scarcely suffice to present the results of such a survey, and an undertaking of this character is accordingly impossible here.

The Federalist, on the other hand, presents in a relatively brief and systematic form an economic interpretation of the Constitution by the men best fitted, through an intimate knowledge of the ideals of the framers, to expound the political science of the new government. This wonderful piece of argumentation by Hamilton, Madison, and Jay is in fact the finest study in the economic interpretation of politics which exists in any language; and whoever would understand the Constitution as an economic document need hardly go beyond it. It is true that the tone of the writers is somewhat modified on account of the fact that they are appealing to the voters to ratify the Constitution, but at the same time they are, by the force of circumstances, compelled to convince large economic groups that safety and strength lie in the adoption of the new system.

Indeed, every fundamental appeal in it is to some material and substantial interest. Sometimes it is to the people at large in the name of protection against invading armies and European coalitions. Sometimes it is to the commercial classes whose business is represented as prostrate before the follies of the Confederation. Now it is to creditors seeking relief against paper money and the assaults of the agrarians in general; now it is to the holders of federal securities which are depreciating toward the vanishing point. But above all, it is to the owners of personalty anxious to find a foil against the attacks of levelling democracy, that the authors of *The Federalist* address their most cogent arguments in favor of ratification. It is true there is much discussion of the details of the new frame-work of government, to which even some friends of reform took exceptions; but Madison and Hamilton both knew that these were incidental matters when compared with the sound basis upon which the superstructure rested.

In reading the pages of this remarkable work as a study in political economy, it is important to bear in mind that the system, which the authors are describing, consisted of two fundamental parts—one positive, the other negative:

I. A government endowed to certain positive powers, but so constructed as to break the force of majority rule and prevent invasions of the property rights of minorities.

II. Restrictions on the state legislatures which had been so vigorous in their attacks on capital. . . .

The Powers Conferred Upon the Federal Government

1. The powers for positive action conferred upon the new government were few, but they were adequate to the purposes of the framers. They included, first, the power to lay and collect taxes; but here the rural interests were conciliated by the provision that direct taxes must be apportioned among the states according to population, counting three-fifths of the slaves. This, in the opinion of contemporaries eminently qualified to speak, was designed to prevent the populations of the manufacturing states from shifting the burdens of taxation to the sparsely settled agricultural regions. . . .

The taxing power was the basis of all other positive powers, and it afforded the revenues that were to discharge the public debt in full. Provision was made for this discharge in Article VI to the effect that "All debts contracted and engagements entered into before the adoption of this Constitution shall be valid against the United States under this Constitution as under the Confederation."

But the cautious student of public economy, remembering the difficulties which Congress encountered under the Articles of Confederation in its attempts to raise the money to meet the interest on the debt, may ask how the framers of the Constitution could expect to overcome the hostile economic forces which had hitherto blocked the payment of the requisitions. The answer is short. Under the Articles, Congress had no power to lay and collect taxes immediately; it could only make requisitions on the state legislatures. Inasmuch as most of the states relied largely on direct taxes for their revenues, the demands of Congress were keenly felt and stoutly resisted. Under the new system, however, Congress is authorized to lay taxes on its own account, but it is evident that the framers contemplated placing practically all of the national burden on the consumer. The provision requiring the apportionment of direct taxes on a basis of population obviously implied that such taxes were to be viewed as a last resort when indirect taxes failed to provide the required revenue.

With his usual acumen, Hamilton conciliates the freeholders and property owners in general by pointing out that they will not be called upon to support the national government by payments proportioned to their wealth.[2] Experience has demonstrated that it is impracticable to raise any considerable sums by direct taxation. Even where the government is strong, as in Great Britain, resort must be had chiefly to indirect taxation. The pockets of the farmers "will reluctantly yield but scanty supplies,

in the unwelcome shape of impositions on their houses and lands; and personal property is too precarious and invisible a fund to be laid hold of in any other way than by the imperceptible agency of taxes on consumption." Real and personal property are thus assured a generous immunity from such burdens as Congress had attempted to impose under the Articles; taxes under the new system will, therefore, be less troublesome than under the old.

2. Congress was given, in the second place, plenary power to raise and support military and naval forces, for the defence of the country against foreign and domestic foes. These forces were to be at the disposal of the President in the execution of national laws; and to guard the states against renewed attempts of "desperate debtors" like Shays, the United States guaranteed to every commonwealth a republican form of government and promised to aid in quelling internal disorder on call of the proper authorities.

The army and navy are considered by the authors of *The Federalist* as genuine economic instrumentalities. As will be pointed out below, they regarded trade and commerce as the fundamental cause of wars between nations; and the source of domestic insurrection they traced to class conflicts within society. "Nations in general," says Jay, "will make war whenever they have a prospect of getting anything by it";[3] and it is obvious that the United States dissevered and discordant will be the easy prey to the commercial ambitions of their neighbors and rivals.

The material gains to be made by other nations at the expense of the United States are so apparent that the former cannot restrain themselves from aggression. France and Great Britain feel the pressure of our rivalry in the fisheries; they and other European nations are our competitors in navigation and the carrying trade; our independent voyages to China interfere with the monopolies enjoyed by other countries there; Spain would like to shut the Mississippi against us on one side and Great Britain fain would close the St. Lawrence on the other. The cheapness and excellence of our productions will excite their jealousy, and the enterprise and address of our merchants will not be consistent with the wishes or policy of the sovereigns of Europe. But, adds the commentator, by way of clinching the argument, "if they see that our national government is efficient and well administered, our trade prudently regulated, our militia properly organized and disciplined, our resources and finances discreetly managed, our credit re-established, our people free, contented, and united, they will be much more disposed to cultivate our friendship than provoke our resentment."[4]

All the powers of Europe could not prevail against us. "Under a vigorous national government the natural strength and resources of the country, directed to a common interest, would baffle all the combinations of European jealousy to restrain our growth. . . . An active commerce, an extensive navigation, and a flourishing marine would then be the offspring of moral and physical necessity. We might defy the little arts of the little politicians to control or vary the irresistible and unchangeable course of nature."[5] In the present state of disunion the profits of trade are snatched from us; our commerce languishes; and poverty threatens to overspread a country which might outrival the world in riches.

The army and navy are to be not only instruments of defence in protecting the United States against the commercial and territorial ambitions of other countries; but they may be used also in forcing open foreign markets. What discriminatory tariffs and navigation laws may not accomplish the sword may achieve. The authors of *The Federalist* do not contemplate that policy of mild and innocuous isolation which was later made famous by Washington's farewell address. On the contrary—they do not expect the United States to change human nature and make our commercial classes less ambitious than those of other countries to extend their spheres of trade. A strong navy will command the respect of European states. . . .

3. In addition to the power to lay and collect taxes and raise and maintain armed forces on land and sea, the Constitution vests in Congress plenary control over foreign and interstate commerce, and thus authorizes it to institute protective and discriminatory laws in favor of American interests, and to create a wide sweep for free trade throughout the whole American empire. A single clause thus reflects the strong impulse of economic forces in the towns and young manufacturing centres. In a few simple words the mercantile and manufacturing interests wrote their *Zweck im Recht*; and they paid for their victory by large concessions to the slave-owning planters of the south.

While dealing with commerce in *The Federalist*[6] Hamilton does not neglect the subject of interstate traffic and intercourse. He shows how free trade over a wide range will be to reciprocal advantage, will give great diversity to commercial enterprise, and will render stagnation less liable by offering more distant markets when local demands fall off. "The speculative trader," he concludes, "will at once perceive the force of these observations and will acknowledge that the aggregate balance of the commerce of the United States would bid fair to be much more favorable than that of the thirteen states without union or with partial unions.". . .

*T*hese are the great powers conferred on the new government: taxation, war, commercial control, and disposition of western lands. Through them public creditors may be paid in full, domestic peace maintained, advantages obtained in dealing with foreign nations, manufactures protected, and the development of the territories go forward with full swing. The remaining powers are minor and need not be examined here. What implied powers lay in the minds of the framers likewise need not be inquired into; they have long been the subject of juridical speculation.

None of the powers conferred by the Constitution on Congress permits a direct attack on property. The federal government is given no general authority to define property. It may tax, but indirect taxes must be uniform, and these are to fall upon consumers. Direct taxes may be laid, but resort to this form of taxation is rendered practically impossible, save on extraordinary occasions, by the provision that they must be apportioned according to population—so that numbers cannot transfer the burden to accumulated wealth. The slave trade may be destroyed, it is true, after the lapse of a few years; but slavery as a domestic institution is better safeguarded than before.

Notes

1. The fact that a few members of the Convention, who had considerable economic interests at stake, refused to support the Constitution does not invalidate the general conclusions here presented.
2. *The Federalist*, No. 12.
3. *The Federalist*, No. 4.
4. *Ibid.*
5. *The Federalist*, No. 11.
6. No. 11.

Critical Thinking

1. In what ways could the framers, by their own design, have financially benefited from the provisions of the Constitution?
2. Is it a valid argument to claim that the only stable foundations on which the new American government could have been built were "fundamental economic interests"?
3. Why is an examination of the Constitution as an economic document an atypical approach?

Create Central

www.mhhe.com/createcentral

Internet References

Emory University School of Law
http://library.law.emory.edu/for-law-students/emory-law-subject-guides/constitutional-and-statutory-research/us-constitution

The National Archives and Records Administration
www.archives.gov

The National Governors Association
www.nga.org/portal/site/nga

From *An Economic Interpretation of the Constitution of the United States* by Charles Beard (Macmillan, 1935).

The Intellectual Origins of the American Constitution

Gordon S. Wood

Learning Outcomes

After reading this selection, you should be able to:

1. Discuss the concept of separation of powers.
2. Define the characteristics of monarchy, aristocracy, and democracy, as categorized since the time of Aristotle.
3. Recognize classical republicanism as the basic premise of American thinking in 1787.

Gordon S. Wood (b. 1933) has taught with great distinction as a professor of history at numerous institutions, including the College of William and Mary, Harvard University, and the University of Michigan, and he was the Pitt Professor at Cambridge University in 1982–1983. From 1969 to the present he has taught at Brown University, where he is currently University Professor and a professor of history. He has received several awards and honors, including the John H. Dunning Prize from the American Historical Association and the Bancroft Award in 1970 for his book *The Creation of the American Republic, 1776–1787* (University of North Carolina Press, 1969). His book *The Radicalism of the American Revolution* (Random House, 1991) won a Pulitzer Prize. Wood has also published many scholarly articles in various American historical journals.

In the following selection from "The Intellectual Origins of the American Constitution," *National Forum: The Phi Kappa Phi Journal* (Fall 1984), Wood emphasizes the central ideological and intellectual role and dominant historical significance of classical republican political thought during the American Revolution and the designing of the Constitution. Classical republicanism refers to a political theory or ideology that is articulated through such values as civic virtue, governmental accountability, civic education, citizen obligations, and the public good as the ultimate criterion evaluating the worth of public policy. Wood develops the claim that the republican value of civic virtue performed a central role in the political culture of the American Revolution and in the period of the drafting of the U.S. Constitution. However, Wood also identifies other intellectual sources that influenced the Founders, such as a political theory of balanced or mixed government, a political theory of separation of powers, and a commitment to a particular interpretation of liberty.

Key Concept: the political culture of the U.S. Constitution

The Constitution was created at a stroke in the summer of 1787, but its intellectual origins and sources, like those of all great events, reached back deep into the past. The Constitution has been described as the climax of the Enlightenment—that great eighteenth-century attempt to apply the results of Western science and learning to human affairs. As the product of Western "enlightened" thinking, the Constitution could scarcely have sprung simply from a summer's meeting. Its sources have often seemed to be the whole of previous history. No thinker, no idea, has been too remote, too obscure, to have been involved somehow in the making of the Constitution. Thus historians and political theorists have rummaged through the past looking for the particular philosopher or book that might have especially influenced the Framers of the Constitution. Some have seized on the Englishman John Locke; others, the Frenchman Montesquieu; still others, the Scot David Hume or the Swiss Burlamaqui; and some have even made a case for the ancient Greek Polybius. . . .

Although isolating the influence of any one thinker on the Founding Fathers may be impossible, describing the currents of the political culture in which they were immersed in 1787 is not. The Founders were experienced, pragmatic political leaders, but they were not such practical, down-to-earth men that they could not be bothered by questions of political philosophy and theory. On the contrary, they were men intensely interested in ideas and especially concerned with making theoretical sense of what they were doing. They were participants in a rich, dynamic political culture that helped determine the nature of the Constitution they created. Understanding the Constitution requires an understanding of that political culture.

Republicanism

The most pervasive characteristic of that political culture was republicanism, a body of ideas and values so deeply rooted that it formed the presuppositions of American thinking. This body of thought not only determined the elective political system the Founders believed in; it also determined their moral and social goals. To become republican was what the American Revolution had been about.

. . . Republicanism was the ideology of the democratic revolutions of the late eighteenth century; it was the ideology of the people against monarchs and hereditary aristocracies. Even the English who held on to their king and their House of Lords through the upheavals of this period nevertheless felt compelled to claim that, because of the power of the House of Commons, their constitution was already greatly republicanized. By the last quarter of the eighteenth century, being enlightened in the Western world, it seemed, was nearly equivalent to believing in republican values.

The deepest origins of these civic and moral values went all the way back to ancient Rome and the great era of the Roman Republic. . . .

This great body of classical literature was revived and updated by the Renaissance, especially in the writings of the Italian philosopher Machiavelli. All was blended into a tradition of what has been called "civic humanism.". . .

What precisely did this body of ideas mean? It meant most obviously the elimination of a king and the institution of an electoral system of government. But these were just incidental means to a larger end. Republicanism really meant creating a political system concerned with the *res publica*, public things, the welfare of the people. Liberal critics of eighteenth-century monarchism believed that kings had become too wrapped up in their own selfish dynastic purposes and were ignoring the good of their people. By eliminating hereditary kings and instituting governments in which the people themselves would elect their political leaders, liberal reformers hoped that governments at last would promote only the public's welfare.

This civic culture, however, had more than political significance; it had social and moral significance as well. Republics required a particular sort of egalitarian and virtuous people: independent, property-holding citizens without artificial hereditary distinctions who were willing to sacrifice many of their private, selfish interests for the good of the whole community. This dependence on a relatively equal and virtuous populace was what made republics such fragile and often short-lived polities. Monarchies were long-lasting; they could maintain order from the top down over large, diverse, and stratified populations through their use of hereditary privilege, executive power, standing armies, and religious establishments. But republics had to be held together from below, from the consent and sacrifice of the people themselves; and therefore, as Montesquieu and other theorists had warned, republics necessarily had to be small in territory and homogeneous and moral in character. . . .

Americans of 1787 were not the republican enthusiasts they had been in 1776. In a decade's time many of them had had their earlier dreams and illusions about republicanism considerably dampened. Experience with popular government, especially in the state legislatures, had cast doubt on the American people's capacity for virtue and disinterestedness. By 1787 many leaders, therefore, were ready for what James Madison called a "systematic change" of government, a change that resulted in the creation of the federal Constitution. But dissatisfied as many American leaders were with the Confederation and with the state legislatures, none of them—not even Alexander Hamilton who was the most monarchically minded among them— was prepared to give up on republican government. They knew, as Madison said, that "no other form would be reconcileable with the genius of the people of America; with the fundamental principles of the revolution; or with that honorable determination, which animates every votary of freedom, to rest all our political experiments on the capacity of mankind for self-government." Hence in the new Constitution, the Framers provided for periodically elected officers of the executive and legislative branches, and they made the federal government guarantee a republican form of government for each state (Article IV, Section 4), and forbade the United States from granting any titles of nobility (Article I, Section 9).

Still, the new federal government was sufficiently different from the Confederation and the governments of the states to arouse fears among many people that it was not "strictly republican." Did it not have a strong king-like executive and a powerful Senate with an aristocratic bearing? Unlike the Confederation, did it not operate directly on diverse peoples over half a continent despite the warnings of theorists and experience that such a large republic could not last? Fears and questions like these are what led Hamilton, Madison, and John Jay to spend so much time in *The Federalist* trying to prove that the Constitution was really "conformable to the true principles of republican government." In the process they helped to develop and shape further American ideas of republicanism.

Balanced Government

In 1787, classical republicanism was the basic premise of American thinking—the central presupposition behind all other ideas. However, it alone was not responsible for the peculiar structure of the revolutionary governments, including that of the federal government created by the Constitution. There was another set of ideas encapsulated in the theory of balanced or mixed government. It came likewise out of antiquity and was closely if not inextricably entwined with the tradition of classical republicanism. The classical theory of balanced government provided much more than the foundational ideas for the structures of the several state governments. The classical theory also included the notion of an independent president, the aristocratic Senate, and the popular House of Representatives.

Since at least the time of Aristotle, theorists had categorized forms of government into three ideal types—monarchy, aristocracy, and democracy. These types were derived from the number of rulers in each: for monarchy, one person; for aristocracy, a few nobles; for democracy, all the people. Aristotle and others believed that each of these rulers when alone entrusted with political power tended to run amok and to become perverted. By itself monarchy became tyranny; aristocracy became oligarchy; and democracy became anarchy. Only by mixing each of these types together in the same constitution, only by balancing the tendencies of each of them, could order be maintained and the perfections of each type of simple government be achieved. The result would be a governmental system in equilibrium—the very kind of static model that the eighteenth-century Enlightenment admired.

For most enlightened thinkers of the eighteenth century, including those of the American colonies, there already existed at least in theory such a perfectly balanced government—the English constitution. . . .

When Americans in 1776 revolted from this perfect English constitution, most of them had no intention of repudiating the classical ideal behind it. Nor did they believe that this ideal of balanced government was incompatible with republicanism. . . . They and other English critics, speaking out of the civic humanist tradition of republicanism, thought that in the course of the eighteenth century the ideal English constitution had degenerated and become corrupted. The king was using his power to appoint men to crown offices in order to bribe and influence members of the House of Lords and House of Commons. . . .

Most of America's revolutionary state governments created in 1776–77 were meant to be miniature republican copies of the ideal English constitution. Although elected, the governors, senates, and houses of representatives of the several states were intended to resemble the king, House of Lords, and House of Commons of the English constitution; indeed, they still do. But in order

to prevent their balanced governments from degenerating in the way the English constitution had, most of the states in 1776 severely limited the appointing powers of the governors or chief executives; and, more important for American constitutional development, all of them forbade members of both houses of the legislature and the judiciary from simultaneously holding office in the executive branch. In justifying this prohibition, some of the states in 1776 invoked a doctrine made famous by Montesquieu of separating the executive, legislative, and judicial powers from each other. This triad of functioning powers was really not the same as the classical triad of ruling elements—governors, senates, and houses of representatives—but the goal of the two triads—the prevention of corruption—was the same.

There is no exaggerating the importance of this American exclusion of the legislators from simultaneous executive or ministerial office. This fundamentally divided America's constitutional tradition from that of the former mother country. By this prohibition alone, Americans prevented the development of an English or European-style parliamentary cabinet form of government. Members of America's executive branch, unlike those of most of the democracies in the world, cannot at the same time hold seats in the legislatures. The separation of the legislature from what was thought to be the perverse, corrupting influence of the executive was written into the revolutionary state constitutions of 1776–77. This division was instituted for the sake of maintaining the independence of the ruling parts and the balance that an ideal government ought to have. Since separation of powers was often used to justify the maintenance of this independence and balance, there was the likelihood that separating powers and balancing parts of the government would blend in people's minds.

Separation of Powers

By the time Americans came to form the federal Constitution in 1787–88, the two sets of ideas had become thoroughly confused. Undoubtedly most of the Framers at Philadelphia thought they were creating a balanced government much in the form of the several state governments—only with a stronger chief executive and Senate than in most of the states. Although the ultimate source of this structure was the ideal English constitution, by 1787 few American political leaders felt comfortable any longer saying so in public. (John Adams was a conspicuous exception.) Referring to the chief executive as the monarchical element and the Senate as the aristocracy in a balanced government was politically impossible in the popular atmosphere of the 1780s. Thus the Framers had to find justifications for their two-house legislature and their strong, independent president in some place other than the English constitution and the classical ideal of mixed government.

What they did was blend the notion of separating the functional powers of government—executive, legislative, and judicial—with the older theory of balanced government; and they used both indiscriminately to describe the now incredibly fragmented and countervailing character of America's political system. "The constant aim," wrote Madison in *The Federalist* No. 51, which summed up the Founders' thinking on their parcelling of power, "is to divide and arrange the several offices in such a manner as that each may be a check on the other." Bicameralism, the presidential veto power, the independent judiciary, even federalism itself—the apportioning of authority between the national and state governments—all became various means of dividing, checking, and balancing a mistrusted political power.

Liberty

... Although the classical traditions of republicanism and mixed government formed the presuppositions of American thinking, they were presuppositions shared by the whole Western world. Other nations, such as eighteenth-century France, were influenced by republicanism; indeed, most countries in the world now have republican governments. Other states also have attempted balanced governments, two-house legislatures, independent executives, and separated powers. But few of them have our particular concern for personal and political liberty: for the rule of law, for private personal and property rights, for constitutional and judicial limitations on the use of governmental power. If the origins of these concerns are to be found in sources other than America's own experience, then they must be found neither in the ideas of classical antiquity nor in those of Renaissance civic humanism but in the peculiarities of the English legal tradition.

Nothing was more important for the development of American constitutionalism in 1787 and in the years following than the fact that most of the Founders had been reared as Englishmen and had thus shared in the English preoccupation with liberty and in the unique protections of the English common law. England was, as Montesquieu said in 1731, "the freest country that exists in the world," and eighteenth-century Englishmen on both sides of the Atlantic prided themselves on that reputation. The colonists began the Revolution in defense of their English liberties. Liberty was an English obsession before it was an American one.

... Whatever Americans did to extend liberty and protect individual rights from the encroachments of governmental power, the English had done it first: trial by jury, writs of *habeas corpus*, concern for property rights, fear of standing armies, bills of rights—all were English before they were American. Without the influence of the English constitutional and legal tradition, it is inconceivable that Americans in 1787 or later would have believed and acted as they did.

Yet ultimately, of course, the American political and legal system is not the English system, and this difference should make us aware that looking for intellectual origins and tracing intellectual influences are only part of the explanation of how we have come to be what we are. More important perhaps is what Americans have done with these inherited ideas, how they have used, expanded, and reshaped their intellectual legacies to fit the dynamics of their changing experience.

Critical Thinking

1. Why is it that the English constitution, from which Americans revolted in 1776, was clearly an influential model for the U.S. Constitution in 1787?
2. How might the ratification of the Constitution have been affected if it provided for members of America's executive branch to simultaneously hold seats in the legislatures (which is common in most of the world's democracies)?
3. If classical republicanism is still the basic premise of American thinking, explain why it has survived since the birth of the nation; if not, then what premise of thinking has replaced it?

Create Central

www.mhhe.com/createcentral

Internet References

Emory University School of Law
http://library.law.emory.edu/for-law-students/emory-law
-subject-guides/constitutional-and-statutory-research/
us-constitution

The National Archives and Records Administration
www.archives.gov

The National Governors Association
www.nga.org/portal/site/nga

Reprinted from *National Forum* (now called *Phi Kappa Phi Forum*), vol. LXIV, no. 4 (fall 1984). Copyright (©) by Gordon S. Wood. By permission of the publishers.

Unit 3: The Evolution of American Federalism

McCulloch v. Maryland

John Marshall

Learning Outcomes

After reading this selection, you should be able to:

1. Discuss the unanimous Supreme Court decision in this landmark case.

2. Explain how the "elastic" or "necessary and proper" clause of the Constitution assures the implied powers of the federal government.

The 1819 landmark decision *McCulloch v. Maryland* (4 Wheaton 316), from which the following selection is taken, had major constitutional and political consequences, including the dramatic growth of the federal government. The opinion of the U.S. Supreme Court reflected a fundamental attempt to identify the legitimate relationship between the federal and state governments. In 1791, after an intense national partisan debate, Congress chartered the First National Bank of the United States. As a leader of the Federalist political party and a strong advocate for the construction of the bank, Alexander Hamilton defended the bank, interpreting its legitimate existence to be based upon an implied power. As a leader of the Anti-Federalist political party and a strong opponent of the bank, Thomas Jefferson contended that any congressional power must be explicitly expressed. However, the First National Bank's constitutionality was not challenged in the courts, and its charter expired in 1811. In 1816 Congress created the Second National Bank of the United States, and it met immediate intense political opposition by various state legislatures. In 1818 the state of Maryland passed legislation designed to tax a branch of the National Bank in Baltimore. The cashier of the bank, James McCulloch, refused to pay the tax, so Maryland sued. A Maryland state court upheld the tax legislation; McCulloch subsequently appealed the decision to the U.S. Supreme Court.

Chief Justice John Marshall articulated that in addition to the expressed or enumerated powers listed in the Constitution, the federal government, and Congress in particular, have implied powers due to the "elastic" or "necessary and proper clause" of the Constitution. Thus, Marshall established the constitutionality of Congress's establishment of the bank and the illegitimacy of Maryland's legislation to tax the bank. The Court's decision had a highly significant impact upon the general expansion of the federal government's power. In particular, *McCulloch v. Maryland* established a legal foundation and a precedent for the expanded commercial powers of the national government.

Key Concept: implied powers of the national government under the "necessary and proper clause"

*M*r. Chief Justice Marshall delivered the opinion of the Court, saying in part:

In the case now to be determined, the defendant, a sovereign State, denies the obligation of a law enacted by the legislature of the Union; and the plaintiff, on his part, contests the validity of an Act which has been passed by the legislature of that State. The Constitution of our country, in its most interesting and vital parts, is to be considered; the conflicting powers of the government of the Union and of its members, as marked in that Constitution, are to be discussed; and an opinion given, which may essentially influence the great operations of the government. . . .

The first question made in the cause is, has Congress power to incorporate a bank? . . .

In discussing this question, the counsel for the State of Maryland have deemed it of some importance, in the construction of the Constitution, to consider that instrument not as emanating from the people, but as the act of sovereign and independent states. The powers of the general government, it has been said, are delegated by the states, who alone are truly sovereign; and must be exercised in subordination to the states, who alone possess supreme dominion. . . .

If any one proposition could command the universal assent of mankind, we might expect it would be this: that the government of the Union, though limited in its powers, is supreme within its sphere of action. This would seem to result necessarily from its nature. It is the government of all; its powers are delegated by all;

it represents all, and acts for all. Though any one State may be willing to control its operations, no State is willing to allow others to control them. The nation, on those subjects on which it can act, must necessarily bind its component parts. But this question is not left to mere reason: the people have, in express terms, decided it, by saying, "this Constitution, and the laws of the United States, which shall be made in pursuance thereof," "shall be the supreme law of the land," and by requiring that the members of the State legislatures, and the officers of the executive and judicial departments of the States, shall take the oath of fidelity to it.

The government of the United States, then, though limited in its powers, is supreme; and its laws, when made in pursuance of the Constitution, form the supreme law of the land, "anything in the Constitution or laws of any State to the contrary notwithstanding."

Among the enumerated powers, we do not find that of establishing a bank or creating a corporation. But there is no phrase in the instrument which, like the Articles of Confederation, excludes incidental or implied powers; and which requires that everything granted shall be expressly and minutely described. Even the Tenth Amendment, which was framed for the purpose of quieting the excessive jealousies which had been excited, omits the word "expressly," and declares only that the powers "not delegated to the United States, nor prohibited to the States, are reserved to the States or to the people"; thus leaving the question, whether the particular power which may become the subject of contest, has been delegated to the one government, or prohibited to the other, to depend on a fair construction of the whole instrument. The men who drew and adopted this amendment, had experienced the embarrassments resulting from the insertion of this word in the Articles of Confederation, and probably omitted it to avoid those embarrassments. A constitution, to contain an accurate detail of all the subdivisions of which its great powers will admit, and of all the means by which they may be carried into execution, would partake of the prolixity of a legal code, and could scarcely be embraced by the human mind. It would probably never be understood by the public. Its nature, therefore, requires, that only its great outlines should be marked, its important objects designated, and the minor ingredients which compose those objects be deduced from the nature of the objects themselves. That this idea was entertained by the framers of the American Constitution, is not only to be inferred from the nature of the instrument, but from the language. . . .

Although, among the enumerated powers of government, we do not find the word "bank," or "incorporation," we find the great powers to lay and collect taxes; to borrow money; to regulate commerce; to declare and conduct a war; and to raise and support armies and navies. The sword and the purse, all the external relations, and no inconsiderable portion of the industry of the nation, are entrusted to its government. It can never

be pretended that these vast powers draw after them others of inferior importance, merely because they are inferior. Such an idea can never be advanced. But it may, with great reason, be contended, that a government, entrusted with such ample powers, on the due execution of which the happiness and prosperity of the nation so vitally depends, must also be entrusted with ample means for their execution. The power being given, it is the interest of the nation to facilitate its execution. It can never be their interest, and cannot be presumed to have been their intention, to clog and embarrass its execution by withholding the most appropriate means. Throughout this vast republic, from the St. Croix to the Gulf of Mexico, from the Atlantic to the Pacific, revenue is to be collected and expended, armies are to be marched and supported. The exigencies of the nation may require, that the treasure raised in the North should be transported to the South, that raised in the East conveyed to the West, or that this order should be reversed. Is that construction of the Constitution to be preferred which would render these operations difficult, hazardous, and expensive? Can we adopt that construction (unless the words imperiously require it) which would impute to the framers of that instrument, when granting these powers for the public good, the intention of impeding their exercise by withholding a choice of means? If, indeed, such be the mandate of the Constitution, we have only to obey; but that instrument does not profess to enumerate the means by which the powers it confers may be executed; nor does it prohibit the creation of a corporation, if the existence of such a being be essential to the beneficial exercise of those powers. It is, then, the subject of fair inquiry, how far such means may be employed. . . .

But the Constitution of the United States has not left the right of Congress to employ the necessary means, for the execution of the powers conferred on the government, to general reasoning. To its enumeration of powers is added that of making "all laws which shall be necessary and proper, for carrying into execution the foregoing powers, and all other powers vested by this Constitution, in the government of the United States, or in any department thereof." . . .

But the argument on which most reliance is placed, is drawn from the peculiar language of this clause. Congress is not empowered by it to make all laws, which may have relation to the powers conferred on the government, but such only as may be "necessary and proper" for carrying them into execution. The word "necessary" is considered as controlling the whole sentence, and as limiting the right to pass laws for the execution of the granted powers, to such as are indispensable, and without which the power would be nugatory. That it excludes the choice of means, and leaves to Congress, in each case, that only which is most direct and simple.

Is it true, that this is the sense in which the word "necessary" is always used? Does it always import an absolute physical necessity, so strong, that one thing, to which another may be termed necessary, cannot exist without that other? We think it does not. If reference be had to its use, in the common affairs of the world, or in approved authors, we find that it frequently imports no more than that one thing is convenient, or useful, or essential to another. To employ the means necessary to an end, is generally understood as employing any means calculated to produce the end, and not as being confined to those single means, without which the end would be entirely unattainable. . . .

This provision is made in a constitution intended to endure for ages to come, and, consequently, to be adapted to the various crises of human affairs. To have prescribed the means by which government should, in all future time, execute its powers, would have been to change, entirely, the character of the instrument, and give it the properties of a legal code. It would have been an unwise attempt to provide, by immutable rules, for exigencies which, if foreseen at all, must have been seen dimly, and which can be best provided for as they occur. To have declared that the best means shall not be used, but those alone without which the power given would be nugatory, would have been to deprive the legislature of the capacity to avail itself of experience, to exercise its reason, and to accommodate its legislation to circumstances. . . .

But the argument which most conclusively demonstrates the error of the construction contended for by the counsel for the State of Maryland, is founded on the intention of the convention, as manifested in the whole clause. To waste time and argument in proving that, without it, Congress might carry its powers into execution, would be not much less idle than to hold a lighted taper to the sun. As little can it be required to prove, that in the absence of this clause, Congress would have some choice of means. That it might employ those which, in its judgment, would most advantageously effect the object to be accomplished. That any means adapted to the end, any means which tended directly to the execution of the constitutional powers of the government, were in themselves constitutional. This clause, as construed by the State of Maryland, would abridge and almost annihilate this useful and necessary right of the legislature to select its means. That this could not be intended, is, we should think, had it not been already controverted, too apparent for controversy. We think so for the following reasons:

1st. The clause is placed among the powers of Congress, not among the limitations on those powers.

2d. Its terms purport to enlarge, not to diminish the powers vested in the government. It purports to be an additional power, not a restriction on those already granted. No reason has been or can be assigned, for thus concealing an intention to narrow the discretion of the national legislature, under words which purport to enlarge it. The framers of the Constitution wished its adoption, and well knew that it would be endangered by its strength, not by its weakness. Had they been capable of using language which would convey to the eye one idea, and after deep reflection, impress on the mind another, they would rather have disguised the grant of power, than its limitation. If then, their intention had been, by this clause, to restrain the free use of means which might otherwise have been implied, that intention would have been inserted in another place, and would have been expressed in terms resembling these: "In carrying into execution the foregoing powers, and all others," etc., "no laws shall be passed but such as are necessary and proper." Had the intention been to make this clause restrictive, it would unquestionably have been so in form as well as in effect.

The result of the most careful and attentive consideration bestowed upon this clause is, that if it does not enlarge, it cannot be construed to restrain the powers of Congress, or to impair the right of the legislature to exercise its best judgment in the selection of measures, to carry into execution the constitutional powers of the government. If no other motive for its insertion can be suggested, a sufficient one is found in the desire to remove all doubts respecting the right to legislate on that vast mass of incidental powers which must be involved in the Constitution, if that instrument be not a splendid bauble.

We admit, as all must admit, that the powers of the government are limited, and that its limits are not to be transcended. But we think the sound construction of the Constitution must allow to the national legislature that discretion, with respect to the means by which the powers it confers are to be carried into execution, which will enable that body to perform the high duties assigned to it, in the manner most beneficial to the people. Let the end be legitimate, let it be within the scope of the Constitution, and all means which are appropriate, which are plainly adapted to that end, which are not prohibited, but consist with the letter and spirit of the Constitution, are constitutional. . . .

It being the opinion of the court that the act incorporating the bank is constitutional; and that the power of establishing a branch in the State of Maryland might be properly exercised by the bank itself, we proceed to inquire:

2. Whether the State of Maryland may, without violating the Constitution, tax that branch?

That the power of taxation is one of vital importance; that it is retained by the States; that it is not abridged by the grant of a similar power to the government of the Union; that it is to be concurrently exercised by the two governments: are truths which have never been denied. But, such is the paramount character of the Constitution, that its capacity to withdraw any subject from the action of even this power, is admitted. The States are expressly forbidden to lay any duties on imports or exports, except what may be absolutely necessary for executing their inspection laws. If the obligation of this prohibition must be conceded—if it may restrain a State from the exercise of its taxing power on imports and exports; the same paramount character would seem to restrain, as it certainly may restrain, a State from such other exercise of this power, as is in its nature incompatible with, and repugnant to, the constitutional laws of the Union. A law, absolutely repugnant to another, as entirely repeals that other as if express terms of repeal were used.

On this ground the counsel for the bank place its claim to be exempted from the power of a State to tax its operations. There is no express provision for the case, but the claim has been sustained on a principle which so entirely pervades the Constitution, is so intermixed with the materials which compose it, so interwoven with its web, so blended with its texture, as to be incapable of being separated from it, without rending it into shreds.

This great principle is, that the Constitution and the laws made in pursuance thereof are supreme; that they control the Constitution and laws of the respective States, and cannot be controlled by them. From this, which may be almost termed an axiom, other propositions are deduced as corollaries, on the truth or error of which, and on their application to this case, the cause has been supposed to depend. These are, 1st. That a power to create implies a power to preserve. 2d. That a power to destroy, if wielded by a different hand, is hostile to, and incompatible with, these powers to create and preserve. 3d. That where this repugnancy exists, that authority which is supreme must control, not yield to that over which it is supreme. . . .

If we apply the principle for which the State of Maryland contends, to the Constitution generally, we shall find it capable of changing totally the character of that instrument. We shall find it capable of arresting all the measures of the government and of prostrating it at the foot of the States. The American people have declared their Constitution, and the laws made in pursuance thereof, to be supreme; but this principle would transfer the supremacy, in fact, to the States. . . .

The court has bestowed on this subject its most deliberate consideration. The result is a conviction that the States have no power, by taxation or otherwise, to retard, impede, burden or in any manner control, the operations of the constitutional laws enacted by Congress to carry into execution the powers vested in the general government. This is, we think, the unavoidable consequence of that supremacy which the Constitution has declared.

We are unanimously of opinion, that the law passed by the legislature of Maryland, imposing a tax on the Bank of the United States, is unconstitutional and void.

Critical Thinking

1. In terms of historical implications, how significant is it that the Supreme Court's opinion in *McCulloch v. Maryland* was unanimous?
2. Assuming that a definitive case involving the implied powers of the federal government would eventually appear in the Supreme Court, what circumstances (unrelated to the national bank) may have brought this about had not the Maryland bank-tax issue occurred?
3. Try to frame an argument that may have persuaded the Court to uphold Maryland's bank-tax legislation.

Create Central

www.mhhe.com/createcentral

Internet References

Emory University School of Law
http://library.law.emory.edu/for-law-students/emory-law-subject-guides/caselaw-and-citators/supreme-court

The National Archives and Records Administration
www.archives.gov

The National Governors Association
www.nga.org/portal/site/nga

Supreme Court of the United States, 1819.

Federalism, Nationalism, and Democracy in America

Samuel H. Beer

Learning Outcomes

After reading this selection, you should be able to:

1. Discuss how the framers of the U.S. Constitution borrowed from two incompatible ideologies to craft a unique federal design.
2. Explain the meaning of "representational federalism."
3. Analyze the role of compact theory in justifying extensive states' rights.

Samuel H. Beer (b. 1911) received his Ph.D. from Harvard University, where he served as professor of government since 1938 and where he is the Eaton Professor of Science of Government Emeritus. He has received several awards and honors, including a Rhodes Scholarship from 1932 to 1935, Fulbright and Guggenheim Fellowships from 1953 to 1954, and a Woodrow Wilson Foundation Award in 1966 for his work *British Politics in the Collectivist Age* (Alfred A. Knopf, 1965). Beer is a prolific author who has published numerous books on American government, comparative politics, and British politics, such as *The City of Reason* (Harvard University Press, 1968) and *Treasury Control: The Coordination of Financial and Economic Policy in Great Britain* (Clarendon Press, 1956). He has published numerous scholarly articles in various political science and public policy journals. Beer has also served as associate editor of the journal *American Political Science Review*.

In the following selection, which is excerpted from "Federalism, Nationalism, and Democracy in America," *American Political Science Review* (March 1978), Beer analyzes the apparently contradictory developments of centralization and decentralization, which have occurred simultaneously with the dramatic expansion of American governmental institutions in recent decades. He argues that the most dramatic development of American federalism has been the emergence of multiple contexts of cooperative interaction and interdependence among distinct layers of government. This, he feels, represents the most significant transformation of American federalism, more so than any of particular transference of public authority or governmental roles and responsibilities among levels of government. The recently accelerated blurring of distinction between national and state powers and functions is referred to as *cooperative federalism*. Beer contends that these new developments closely conform to the framers' original model of representational federalism. The original design of representation was based upon a theory of territorial diffusion of powers as a preventative measure against a highly centralized tyrannical government and as a means to promote expanded political representation.

Beer's analysis, a critical addition and necessary contribution to the literature on federalism, helped shift the focus of debate and analysis on this topic.

Key Concept: the impact of intergovernmental relations upon representation

$\mathcal{D}$uring the 1960s in the United States, as in most advanced countries, there was a large and sudden surge upward in the growth of the public sector, largely under the impetus of the central government. Supporters of this new phase of centralization sometimes see it as one more, and perhaps the final, stage in the transformation of the American polity into virtually a unitary system. Critics, on the other hand, seek to revive federalism, frequently proposing a reallocation of functions between levels of government. Some find evidence of such a revival in the decentralization accomplished by recent less restrictive schemes of federal aid.

I should like to present a third position. My thesis is that more important than any shifts of power or function between levels of government has been the emergence of new arenas of mutual influence among levels of government. Within the field of intergovernmental relations a new and powerful system of representation has arisen, as the federal government has made a vast new use of state and local governments and these governments in turn have asserted a new direct influence on the federal government. What is interesting about American federalism today is not its particular allocation of functions or powers between levels of government, but rather what it is adding to our national system of representation.

Moreover, I should say that these developments, while new, are in harmony with the original design of the federal system. Federalism as the mutually exclusive allocation of powers between the general and the state governments—dual federalism it may be called—belongs to the past. Dual federalism was indeed a feature of the original design and, broadly speaking, characterized our system of multilevel government until the New Deal. Federalism in this sense does not apply, and given the realities of our times, could not be made to apply, to that system today.

But dual federalism was only one and a secondary feature of the original design. The theory governing that design made its territorial allocation of powers an instrument of a far more important purpose. That purpose was so to divide and organize power as to avert the evils and realize the benefits of free government. Within this general scheme, the federal division of powers served a representative function by creating a structure of mutual balance and influence between the two main levels of government. In this manner, dual federalism was a means to representational federalism.

In the first part of this article I shall, therefore, be talking about the original federal design, in order, in the second part, to direct attention to the way that representational federalism has been reconstituted by recent developments in intergovernmental relations. Since these developments have parallels in other countries, I shall conclude with a few questions for comparative study suggested by American experience.

The Original Federal Design

The Democratic Purpose. To see the original federal design as the solution to a problem of representation links it directly and intimately to the great cause that led to the American Revolution. That cause was liberty. To the colonial dissidents liberty meant certain personal rights, such as freedom of conscience, but above all political liberty, the right to government by "the consent of the governed." And by "consent" they meant not some presumed agreement to a form of government delivered by social contract in the distant past, but rather a consent that closely and actively joined voter and representative. Ambiguities in this idea permitted various degrees of control by voters over representatives, ranging from strict delegation to a fiduciary relationship subject to frequent accountability. Sometimes the two tendencies were

mixed, as when the town meeting of Boston in May 1764 at the height of the Stamp Act crisis delegated to their representatives in the provincial assembly "the power of acting in their public concerns in general as your own prudence shall direct you, always reserving to themselves the constitutional right of expressing their mind and giving you such instruction upon particular matters as they at any time shall judge proper." One part of the charge leads toward legislative discretion, the other toward popular sovereignty. Either makes government crucially dependent on the will of the voters. . . .

The National Question. When this failure had led to independence, the national question came suddenly and urgently to the fore. What was the source of the authority of the new government? Obviously, the consent of the people—that and nothing more. But was this consent given by one people or by several peoples, by the nation or by the states? The Declaration of Independence described itself in Jefferson's words as the act of "one people" and eleven years later the Constitution similarly declared that it was ordained and established by "We, the people." According to Abraham Lincoln, the unity of the nation asserted in these documents dated back to the time of the Continental Congress when the colonists chose to form the Union, which is, in his words, "older than any of the States, and, in fact . . . created the States" and "produced their independence and liberty."

This version of events provides the historical basis for the national theory of American federalism. According to that theory, a single sovereign power, the people of the United States, created both the federal and state governments, delegating to each a certain limited authority. In this theory of the juridical basis of the American polity popular sovereignty appears as a single national will acting as the constituent power. The compact theory, on the other hand, takes a different view of the same events and arrives at a different view of the Constitution and of federalism. According to this view, the colonies became separate, independent polities when they cast loose from Britain and only thereafter entered into an agreement to have a general government for certain limited purposes. From this theory justifications have been deduced for secession, interposition, or at least extensive "states' rights."

The national theory, I should say, is a superior interpretation of what actually happened, an interpretation incidentally which has been given further powerful support by recent historical research. The important thing, however, for the present inquiry into the original design of American federalism, is that the men who conceived and elaborated that design worked from the premises of the national theory. Their federalism presupposes their nationalism. In their view the constituent power was on people, the nation. What they sought to produce in the constitution of the new polity was a scheme by which that nation would act not only as the constituent power, but also as the continuous controlling and directing influence in the political life of the new polity. In seeking to give such effect to this idea of national democracy, they were consistently carrying out the belief in government by consent that had rationalized and impelled the resistance to Great Britain in prerevolutionary days. The problem of representation which had preoccupied the energies of that long struggle continued to be central to the shaping of the federal structure.

The Framers' Theory.   Theory had powerfully directed their labors of resistance and theory powerfully directed their labors of construction. In the later as in the earlier phase, the orienting ideology consisted of those same liberal democratic ideas that had come down from the seventeenth century. In their work of construction, however, the Americans also made wide use of "the new science of politics" which had blossomed in the early eighteenth century. This new study was by no means conceived as value-free, but was dominated by the new hope of the time, free government. Its main concern was how to protect liberty by dividing and balancing power within a polity. The premise of this concern and of its consequent technique was a certain distrust of human nature. Although many of these authors, as in the case of the Americans, had had a Protestant upbringing, I would not say that this distrust was Calvinist—it did not approach that black despair—nor even that it was distinctively Christian or biblical. It was more modern, more secular, a workable pessimism which saw a love of power in all men and feared any monopoly of the instruments of power, but which held that if control over these instruments were properly divided and balanced, power could be made to check power so that it would be used only for the common good. One technique was a separation of powers according to the "natural" functions of government or according to the ranks and orders of society. Another consisted in a division of powers between a general government and a number of provincial governments. It was, of course, this latter sort of balancing that the framers sought to achieve in their federal design.

That design was unique. At Philadelphia in 1787, it is generally recognized, the Americans invented federalism as it has come to be understood since that time. The scheme had no precedent. Its authors were not, as some have claimed, attempting to restore an allocation of powers between central and provincial governments like that the colonists had experienced in the days of "benign and salutary neglect" under the old empire before the Sugar Act. They were surely not trying to imitate the Dutch, Swiss or German regimes, a type of polity which they regarded as "the cause of incurable disorder and imbecility." Their new creation was theory-based. Yet even in drawing generously on the political science of their time, they did not follow their authorities slavishly. Indeed, their inventiveness consisted precisely in combining

elements taken from two incompatible constructions of, respectively, Montesquieu and Hume.

Montesquieu's contribution came principally from his famous discussion of the confederate republic in Books VIII and IX of *The Spirit of the Laws*. There he was trying to reconcile the conflicting conditions conducive respectively to liberty and to security. In conformity with the conventional view, he held that "republican government" could flourish only in a small state where "the public good" is "more obvious, better understood, and more within the reach of every citizen." In an extensive republic, on the other hand, although its defensive posture would be stronger, the public good would be "sacrificed to a thousand private views" and encroachments on liberty would be able to grow without arousing general resistance. Distance, size or—more properly—scale would present the man of ambition with his opportunity and his temptation. Montesquieu proposed to realize the respective advantages of smallness and largeness of scale without introducing their disadvantages by means of a confederate republic. Formed by "a convention" among a number of small republics, such a polity could amass defensive power without making itself vulnerable to the internal corruption of despotism, because the member states would retain the independent force to prevent the abuse of power by the general government. The territorial pluralism of these continuing small governments would counteract tendencies toward corruption in the wider polity.

Montesquieu's confederate republic alone was clearly not the model for the constitution makers at Philadelphia. It was rather the sort of regime which in their eyes had proved to be both inefficient and dangerous to liberty under the Articles of Confederation. Their radical transformation was to impose on it certain features of a unitary regime. For the sake of "stability and energy" they gave the general government a new instrument of power by enabling it to act directly on individuals. But their main concern was to add a further protection of "republican liberty" by providing for the representation of individuals in the federal legislature.

The significance of this new scheme of representation was given its classical exposition in Madison's Tenth Federalist. His idea is an adaptation of a proposal put forward by Hume in his essay on the "Idea of a Perfect Commonwealth." In that essay, first published in 1752, Hume sketched an elaborate system of representative government and against this background attacked the "common opinion" that republican government is more likely to survive in a small than a large polity. On the contrary, he argued, the "near habitation" of the citizens of a small polity will make even their division into small parties vulnerable to "the force of popular tides and currents." In the large representative republic, however, not only will the "higher magistrates" "refine" the opinions of the voters, but also the various parts will be less likely to unite against "the public interest." Madison improves on this model by stressing the diversity of social and economic interests that will be embraced in the more extensive republic. Thanks to the greater differentiation that goes with larger scale, the social pluralism of the general government will counteract tendencies toward a factional abuse of power in the subordinate governments.

The invention at Philadelphia transformed Montesquieu's model by integrating with it this Humean construction. The new unitary features meant that now the social pluralism of the nation as a whole would be represented in the general government, which, within limits, would be able to avert the dangers of faction within the states, while the continued existence of the states meant that, as in Montesquieu's model, territorial pluralism would constitute a safeguard against encroachments by the general government. It was a unified, internally coherent and highly original model of a new kind of government. This invention resulted from compromise, to be sure—not the compromise of stalemate, however, but of social learning.

Federalism As Representational. In the *Federalist* papers and the ratification debates, the new model was set forth and defended. It had a military version in which the possession of instruments of coercive force by each level held the balance for free government. "Power being almost always the rival of power," wrote Hamilton, "the general government will at all times stand ready to check the usurpations of the state governments, and these will have the same disposition towards the general government." His next sentence revealed the motor in the mechanism: "The people, by throwing themselves into either scale, will infallibly make it preponderate. If their rights are invaded by either, they can make use of the other as the instrument of redress." In short, the same force which, according to the national theory, had brought the Constitution into existence and formed its juridical foundation, the sovereign people, would continue to guarantee its free operation.

This military version of how the federal design would operate is hardly more than an historical curiosity today. But its authors were, of course, also thinking in larger terms and of a more political application. They expected the social pluralism of the general government to operate not only in emergencies, but also in day-to-day decision making. Nor did they see this function as merely negative—to prevent narrow and oppressive majorities from forming or acting. Their political science taught them that "the larger the society . . . the more duly capable it will be of self-government." They therefore expected that the majority coalitions which did form within the general government not only would respect "the rights of every class of citizens," but also would positively express "principles . . . of justice and the general good." The framers were not some sort of early-day laissez-fairists. Indeed, Turgot gave them a famous scolding for their interventionism. They lived in an age

of state-building and mercantilism and fully recognized the need for active government in their developing economy. They saw no need, however, to trade off liberty for development and, although by no means utopians, they had high hopes for their political engineering, believing that its processes of mutual balance and influence would not only break the violence of faction, but also produce decisions worthy of general assent.

In the *Federalist* papers and the ratification debates, discussion of the military aspects of the federal balance shade off into a more political version, which tells us a good deal about how the American system has actually worked and which is still vividly relevant to its operation today. "Notwithstanding the different modes in which [the federal and state governments] are appointed," Madison wrote in the 46th *Federalist*, "we must consider both of them as substantially dependent on the great body of the citizens of the United States. . . . The federal and the State governments are in fact but different agents and trustees of the people, constituted with different powers, and designed for different purposes." "The people" is "the ultimate authority," the "common superior" of both. Nor does he mean this only in the sense of juridical foundation or military balance. He is also concerned to show how the people, acting as the common electorate of all levels of government, bring state perspectives to bear on federal decisions and federal perspectives to bear on state decisions. The three main propositions in his analysis are that these perspectives will not merely reflect the immediate wishes of the voters, but will be shaped by the processes of self-government in which the voters take part; that the influence between levels will pass from state to general government, but also from general government to state government; and finally that the medium through which this influence will be transmitted will be the common electorate of the two sets of governments.

The essence of the invention of 1787 was the use of the same electorate to choose two sets of governments, each with constitutional protection. As in the military version of the new federal system, where the people were to maintain the balance for free government by casting their weight in one or the other scale, in this political version the medium of interaction was the common electorate. Governing himself through two different governments, the voter views the political world from two perspectives, one shaped by the social pluralism of the general government, the other shaped by the territorial pluralism of state government. In his political life, as a member of one nation, he does not separate from one another the two perspectives and the interests each elicits in him. His state perspective affects his choices and decisions in federal politics as his federal perspective affects his choices and decisions in state politics. One may call this process "representational federalism" because it gives representation in the general government to the territorial pluralism of the states and representation in the state governments to the social pluralism of the general government.

In framing and debating the new federal structure, Americans of the time were concerned with the same central problem that had stirred them to criticism, resistance and rebellion a generation before: the problem of representation. Now as then their interest in the allocation of specific powers between levels of government was secondary to this overriding concern. They did believe that certain government functions were more effectively exercised at one rather than the other level. Defense, for instance, was more properly a function of the general government. Yet, guided by their primary concern for liberty, they did not hesitate to divide authority over this function, giving important military powers to the states.

Federalism has often been advocated primarily as a means of accommodating levels of government to territorial diversity. The compact theory would lead one to expect this to be the major subject of debate during the framing and ratification of the Constitution. Supporters as well as critics did recognize that the "sentiments, habits, and customs" of the states were diverse and that, therefore, "a government which might be very suitable for one might not be agreeable to the other." Yet the great mass of utterance at Philadelphia and the ratifying conventions displays remarkably little concern with this fact. Even the most ardent champions of greater powers for the states gave little or no weight to the argument from territorial diversity. Luther Martin, for instance, did not ground his advocacy of state power in his identification with Maryland as a distinctive community or in its need for authority commensurate with its special values or way of life. When he attacked the new powers of the federal government, he, as much as Madison or Hamilton, saw liberty as his goal and the new science of politics as the means for reaching that goal. He differed from them only in clinging to the conventional wisdom of the time as put forward in an unalloyed version of Montesquieu's theory of the confederate republic. It is consistent with this ground of the differences among Americans of that day over the Constitution that a bill of rights, which protected the liberties most valued by their common ideology and which was, as John Hancock said, "in no wise local, but calculated to give security and ease alike to all the states," served to win over critics and produce the quick subsidence of opposition that followed ratification.

New Structures of Representational Federalism

In summary, my historical thesis is: that in making a democratic revolution, the American rebels created a nation and invented representational federalism as a means of governing their new national democracy.

A Rationale for the States.   The reason for looking at this history and especially at its theoretical component is that they tell us something important about how the American polity has actually worked and continues to work. This perspective, in the first place, throws light on what we can and cannot expect of the states today. Any modern polity will have one or more levels of government. The smaller governments may be designed simply as administrative districts under the central authority. They may be set up for an economic purpose, and, accordingly, endowed with powers and boundaries suited to a distinctive complex of agricultural, commercial or industrial activity. They may be so laid out as to match patterns of cultural differentiation, as in the case of linguistic boundaries or other indicators of diversity in community values.

None of these rationales, administrative, economic or cultural, makes sense of the American states, except occasionally and accidentally. Look at the map. It must make you wonder whether there could have been a United States, if the rectangle had not been invented. Typically, those boundaries were not laid out to fit some pre-existing community of value or complex of interests, nor has it been possible to adapt them to territorial diversities as these have emerged. Most of the boundaries were dictated by [an] Act of Congress, usually when the area was sparsely populated and had only the status of a territory. If the purpose of the states had been to provide a level of self-government functional to territorial diversity, then it would have been imperative, in this rapidly growing and developing society, that their boundaries be changed from time to time. On the contrary, however, our national policy toward federalism has been to freeze the boundaries of the states into a virtually unchangeable form by giving them constitutional protection.

Michael Reagan observes that the constitutional meaning of federalism still has importance in only one respect: the guarantee of the independent existence of the states. This may be so, but it does not mean that federalism is dead. Such a guarantee, to be sure, is dysfunctional to an administrative, economic or cultural role for the states. It is, however, highly functional and, I should say, indispensable to their political role in representational federalism. Even if state and federal power were completely overlapping, even if our society were perfectly homogeneous, it would still be necessary, in the light of the original design, that state government have its constitutionally protected existence. The rigidities of our federal system may often frustrate the purposes of public administration, economic efficiency and community living, but they make political sense as the foundation of a major and distinctive element of our representative system.

The Dual Role of Party.   Over the course of time, both state and general governments have performed in various ways the roles assigned them in this system by representational federalism. When one asks what specific forms these processes have taken, the answer, until very recently, I suggest, would be found mainly in the mode of operation of the major political parties. The original federal design endowed the voter with two basic roles, a federal role and a state role. Typically, any major American party has reflected this dualism. The territorial pluralism of the federal structure has had such great and obvious effect as to lead us often to speak of the parties as coalitions of state and local organizations. At the same time, we recognize that their participation in the politics of the general government draws them into a competition which addresses problems and appeals to group interests transcending state and local boundaries. In spite of the resulting territorial and social pluralism, each party is also national, as a body of voters possessing at all levels of government common symbols which focus sentiments of party identification and ideas of party principle. This affectual and cognitive identification is a bond of cohesion that helps make each party a forum within which federal and state perspectives mutually influence one another, instead of merely finding expression in separate spheres.

The politics of civil rights during the past generation provides striking illustration of how the Madisonian mechanism may work through the medium of party. I will merely suggest the outlines of this very complicated process. After World War II, the movement of southern blacks to Northern cities admitted them for the first time to effective political participation in the social pluralism of the more extensive republic. The competition of Republicans and Democrats for this vote led to intervention by the federal government to remedy the denial by state governments of rights generally enjoyed by American citizens. At the same time, within the Democratic party an interaction between federal and state levels was producing political changes tending toward the same result. Action by the national party organs supported and stimulated within some southern state parties the rise of loyalist groups favorable to civil rights. These groups fought the old leadership, won power in state parties and influence on state government and so were able in some degree to ease the acceptance of federal initiatives. Thanks to the party system the pluralism of the more extensive republic helped bring about a universalistic result. . . .

Comparative Perspectives

In spite of overpowering forces making for centralization, the modern state seems to be unable to do without territorial subunits. Nor are these mere branch offices of administration, but rather governmental units with a political capacity. Much has been said, but little done in any country about decentralizing power to them or enlarging their autonomy. They have been widely used, however, as vehicles for carrying out the programs of central governments and, at the same time, have taken an increasingly active role as agents of representation before, and indeed, within those central governments. In

other countries, both unitary and federal, the equivalent of the American intergovernmental lobby has appeared and flourishes. These varieties of topocratic representation are many and complex and light up major contrasts among the different versions of the modern state.

As we will want to look into the relation of technocratic representation to older processes of pressure group politics and functional representation, we shall also ask what are the conflicts and connections between topocratic representation and the older structures of territorial representation. In the U.S., for instance, the political relations of mayors and members of Congress are one of the great unexplored mysteries.

Moreover, whom does the topocrat represent when he formulates the presumed needs of his government before central authorities? He will commonly speak on behalf of groups among his constituents. He may know and be responsive to them. He might even have been chosen by them in part because he was expected to be a good lobbyist in the national capital. Yet he is subject not only to their wishes, but also to an array of influences proceeding from his position as the agent of a bureaucratic and political body. This governmental position will affect and may dominate his representative role.

I can communicate my unease at these technocratic and topocratic dilutions of the popular will by saying that the new structures have a strong connotation of corporate rather than personal representation. They do add real strengths to the modern state. But this may be at some cost to free government.

Critical Thinking

1. How are the physical boundaries of the U.S. states relevant to a discussion of America's national policy toward federalism?
2. Why was a military version of the Constitution a viable option for a federal design in 1787?
3. If the Founding Fathers had adopted just one political model—that of Montesquieu *or* that of Hume—which, if either, ideology would have had the greater chance of success as the basis for an American constitution?

Create Central

www.mhhe.com/createcentral

Internet References

Emory University School of Law
http://library.law.emory.edu/for-law-students/emory-law
-subject-guides/constitutional-and-statutory-research/
us-constitution

The National Archives and Records Administration
www.archives.gov

The National Governors Association
www.nga.org/portal/site/nga

From *American Political Science Review*, March 1978. Copyright © 1978 by American Political Science Association. Reprinted by permission.

Prepared by: James Newman, *University of Maryland University College*

Reforming Medicaid Waivers: The Governors' Council Perspective on Federalism Today

Governors' Council

Learning Outcomes

After reading this selection, you should be able to:

1. Explain the reasons why states want flexibility in implementing health care policies.

This article is a product of the Bipartisan Policy Center's Governors' Council. The purpose of the council is to "bring pragmatic state-based perspectives to national issues."

Key concept: state implementation of health care policies

Introduction

The federalist tenets at the heart of the U.S. Constitution have fuelled a dynamic debate about the balance of federal and state powers throughout our nation's history. Many of today's most complex and pressing challenges, from reviving the economy to controlling health care costs, are deeply entangled in the interplay between federal and state roles and responsibilities. As former state executives, we have each experienced the rewards and frustrations of working with the federal government. We have seen how federalism at its best marries the strength and resources of the federal government to the unique perspectives and capabilities of the states. But we have also seen a relationship that increasingly falls short of this ideal. Too often, policies adopted at the national level—though they may be well intended—result in federal over-reach and trigger unintended and undesired consequences. Too often, we have found the demands of federal agencies stifling state innovation. And we have seen firsthand how growing political dysfunction at the federal level adversely affects states and undermines the welfare of all our citizens.

It is precisely in times of economic hardship and social discontent that our nation needs federalism to work at its best. With states struggling through the third year of a jobless recovery and the federal government entering a period of unprecedented fiscal pressure, we see an opportunity to begin a fundamental realignment of the state-federal relationship. One area of particular opportunity and concern—for states and the federal government—is Medicaid. This is because Medicaid, which provided $401.4 billion in combined federal and state resources to finance health care for nearly 60 million people in 2010 alone, is by far the largest state-federal program in existence today.[1] By developing specific recommendations for improving the Medicaid waiver program, we hope to generate insights and provide a model for improving the state-federal relationship in ways that may be applicable to other areas of significant public policy importance as well.

This paper begins by describing some of the general challenges we see—from the perspective of former state executives—to the federalist relationship today. We then turn to a discussion of problems and options in the Medicaid program, particularly the Medicaid waiver process.

Federalism Today

Overall, federalism has served America well for more than two tumultuous centuries. Our system of government not only survived a devastating civil war, it enabled a large, diverse and geographically far flung population to enjoy long periods of political stability and prosperity, while also coming together to meet great challenges—from waging war to exploring space and building highways. Throughout, federalism has proved flexible and dynamic enough to keep America at the forefront of the economic, social and technological changes that have transformed modern life and the global economy.

Today, support for the basic idea of federalism remains strong and most Americans would endorse the proposition, first, that there are functions and powers that appropriately should and must be located at the federal level and, second, that the federal role should be limited to allow for maximum state and local control wherever possible. But it is also clear that the federal role has expanded steadily into areas not originally included among the enumerated powers. Today, a large share of federal resources is directed to broad-based social safety net programs; in addition, the federal government is actively engaged in delivering disaster relief, regulating on behalf of public health and safety, and promulgating education and technology policy. The largest federal budget items are Social Security and Medicare, which were established at a time when economic insecurity and access to medical care for elderly Americans were seen as major nationwide challenges that the states could not effectively address on their own.

In other areas, the federalist model has left states with primary responsibility for administering programs and policies even in areas that receive substantial amounts of federal funding. These include many programs for the non-elderly such as education, food stamps, welfare, Medicaid and job training. In theory, this division of responsibilities allows states to target resources and tailor programs that best serve the needs of their diverse populations, while also acting as the "laboratories of democracy" that Supreme Court Justice Louis Brandeis spoke of in 1932.[ii] The sequence Justice Brandeis envisioned, in which pioneer states enact legislation, other states follow suit with similar yet improved policies, and the whole process eventually prompts changes in federal policy, has played out in practice many times and across a wide range of issues. Thus, providing the flexibility needed to support state innovation is one of the most important strengths of a federalist system. The concern today is that the state-federal relationship in America is out of balance, and that the results of this imbalance—particularly in an age of increasingly constrained public resources—are eroding performance and public trust at all levels of government.

As governors from different parties, serving six very different states, we have worked with the federal government on a wide range of issues and under a wide range of circumstances. As a group, however, we have come to remarkably similar conclusions about the major challenges that confront our country and our federalist system of government today. From a state perspective, interactions with the federal government are increasingly dominated by three distinct challenges or concerns: (1) the impact of growing budget pressures at both the state and federal levels and the problem of unfunded mandates; (2) frustration with the inflexibility and bureaucracy associated with many federal policies and programs, particularly when it limits states' ability to innovate; and (3) growing dysfunction at the federal level, in terms of the most basic functions of government such as passing budgets on time. All of these challenges come together in the current Medicaid program. The remainder of this paper describes the need for Medicaid reform and recommends some concrete changes to the Medicaid waiver process. By looking in some detail at problems and opportunities in the Medicaid program, we hope to draw connections to larger issues of federalism and gain practical insights for improving the state-federal relationship in the future.

Medicaid

As noted in the introduction, Medicaid is the largest state-federal partnership program in existence. The Social Security Amendments of 1965 established Medicaid to provide health care services to low-income and high-need Americans, covering approximately 20 percent of today's U.S. population.[iii] It is a means-tested entitlement program jointly financed by the federal and state governments. While states are required to provide a basic set of health care benefits to certain eligible groups of individuals to receive federal matching dollars, state Medicaid programs and expenditures vary considerably. States, for example, have the authority to expand eligibility or benefits and to set provider reimbursement rates beyond federal requirements, producing various levels of coverage, access and costs.[iv] The federal matching rate, or the federal medical assistance percentage (FMAP), is calculated annually and reflects a state's per capita income level. On average, the federal government pays for 57 percent of state Medicaid expenditures. For FY 2013, state FMAP rates range from 50 percent (in 14 states) to 73.43 percent (in Mississippi).[v]

Since its inception, numerous legislative changes and thousands of new regulations have made the program increasingly rigid and complex. As in other programs, proliferating federal requirements and stipulations—despite being, in most cases, well intended or aimed at addressing a legitimate concern—have made it increasingly difficult for states to direct scarce resources in ways that allow them to maximize program benefits.

Medicaid is a significant burden on state budgets, representing an average of 16 percent of state general fund spending, second only to K-12 and higher education spending.[vi] As a result of the recent economic downturn, states experienced significant growth in Medicaid enrollment and spending in FY 2011. Meanwhile, a temporary, stimulus-based increase in federal assistance, which helped cover increased state Medicaid costs during the Great Recession, expired in June of 2011.[vii] As a result, state spending for FY 2012 jumped by 28.7 percent.[viii]

Looking forward, this growth trajectory is expected to continue. The Patient Protection and Affordable Care Act (PPACA), which was signed into law in 2010, will expand Medicaid coverage substantially: starting in 2014, nearly all individuals under age 65 with incomes up to 133 percent of the federal poverty line (about $14,856 for an individual and about $30,657 for a family of four in 2012) will be eligible for the Medicaid program.[ix] The number of people enrolled in Medicaid is projected to increase by 16 million by 2019. While the PPACA provides for 100 percent federal financing to cover newly eligible Medicaid recipients for 2014–2016, the federal share of costs for this mandated expansion will gradually decline, reaching a 90 percent FMAP for 2020 and beyond.[x] Additionally, any new enrollment among the previously eligible population prompted by awareness of the expansion will not be financed by the federal government.

Under growing budgetary pressure from rising Medicaid costs, states have been actively undertaking a number of cost-containment measures. Already, 18 states have reported eliminating, reducing or restricting benefits, 39 states lowered provider payments in 2011, and 46 are expected to do so in 2012.[xi] States are extremely concerned about their ability to manage costs going forward, particularly given the expansion in coverage that is mandated to occur in the next few years. As the National Governors Association has stated, "Plans for program expansion are deeply troubling for states that are already struggling with high Medicaid costs. Regulations that simply shift costs to the states are untenable and ultimately undermine the federal-state partnership as well as any national effort to expand coverage and access."[xii]

As state leaders struggle with budget deficits and reduced revenues, the need for additional flexibility in the Medicaid program is great.

Medicaid Waivers

Ensuring the Medicaid program's sustainability will require cooperation and compromise on behalf of both states and the federal government. As is the case with the health care system as a whole, innovation at the state, community and local levels is needed to address complex care financing and delivery challenges. The Medicaid waiver process offers a path forward for states seeking innovative solutions to pervasive problems.

Medicaid waivers allow states to test new strategies that could help improve care quality and lower costs for taxpayers.

The functionality of the Medicaid waiver process is a concern for many state leaders and is often singled out as a major stumbling block for states interested in innovating to reduce costs and improve outcomes among Medicaid recipients. There are three major types of waivers allowable in the current Medicaid law:

1. *Section 1915(b) Managed Care/Freedom of Choice Waivers.* Many states utilize managed care plans as a way to control rising health care costs. 1915(b) waivers allow states to enroll Medicaid beneficiaries in managed care plans, or exert state authority to control provider network options.
2. *Section 1915(c) Home and Community-Based Services Waivers.* Financing long-term care is a significant challenge for states. 1915(c) waivers allow states to move care out of costly institutional care settings and into communities.
3. *Section 1115 Research & Demonstration Projects.* These waivers allow the Secretary of Health and Human Services (HHS) to grant states broad exemptions from federal Medicaid requirements so that they can implement innovative demonstrations and pilot programs. Through Section 1115 waivers, states are able to expand eligibility to new categories of individuals, provide additional services and benefits, and implement novel health care delivery models.

States are also permitted to apply for concurrent 1915(b) and 1915(c) waivers.

Because Section 1115 waivers provide so much flexibility to state leaders, a streamlined Section 1115 waiver approval process is necessary to facilitate state innovation and progress. Currently, this process regularly takes well over a year and often necessitates countless meetings and telephone conversations. These waivers are subject to approval not only by HHS but also by the Office of Management and Budget (OMB), which must find that states' proposals are "neutral" with respect to the federal budget. To demonstrate budget neutrality, the state must project expenditures "with waiver" and "without waiver," and then defend its assumptions. When waivers are approved, they are generally approved for five years, though states can (and usually do) submit renewal requests to continue programs beyond this relatively short timeframe.

State Plan Amendments

States are also allowed to make smaller changes to their Medicaid program through amendments to their state plan. Each state has its own legislative language for Medicaid, which contains the state's unique plan for managing the program in compliance with minimum federal standards and rules. States can make changes to this through State Plan Amendments (SPA), provided these changes are "allowable" and do not conflict with federal rules.[xiii] The approval process for SPA is much faster than the waiver process, and the Centers for Medicare & Medicaid Services (CMS) recently initiated reforms to make the process faster and more efficient for states.[xiv]

Reforming the Process

We believe the waiver process can and should be improved. Common sense reforms will benefit leaders at both the state and federal level, and more importantly, continue to ensure that the Medicaid program is effective and sustainable in the future. Broadly, these reforms should include strategies to rapidly diffuse and adopt successful program reforms, greater federal transparency, the possibility of lengthened wavier extensions and renewals, and the development of clear, mutually understood timelines for the waiver approval process. The states and the federal government are all highly motivated to identify reforms that could improve health care quality while reducing costs, and must work together to remove barriers to innovation. We describe broad recommendations for improving the current waiver process below that will allow states to innovate and foster a more effective state-federal partnership.

Medicaid Waiver Recommendations

1. **Develop State Plan Amendment templates for effective Medicaid strategies.** Through the Deficit Reduction Act of 2005, CMS provided states

The following anecdotes help illustrate states' frustrations with the current waiver process.

In 2005, Vermont Governor Jim Douglas was seeking a waiver for a new preventive care initiative called Global Commitment to Health. After winning approval from HHS, Governor Douglas went to meet OMB officials. Outside the meeting room he encountered Florida Governor Jeb Bush, who was likewise paying a personal visit in search of a waiver. With the outcome for both states in doubt, Governor Douglas quipped that it would not bode well for Vermont's prospects if the president's own brother could not win OMB approval for a waiver.

In 2008, Tennessee sought a waiver from the federal government to shift the focus of its Medicaid program from nursing home care to home-based care. Even though this measure had broad support, was expected to produce cost savings, and portions of it had been successfully adopted by a number of other states, it still took more than a year for the federal bureaucracy to render a decision on Tennessee's waiver request.

with the tools to rapidly implement targeted program changes. For example, CMS provided state leaders with a pre-fabricated SPA template to create non-emergency medical transportation brokerage programs. Ensuring that low-income individuals are able to gain timely access to medical services can help prevent avoidable complications and encourage compliance with recommended treatments, ultimately lowering costs and improving beneficiary health. CMS should utilize a similar strategy to encourage the efficient dissemination of common sense reforms and best practices. One possible avenue for exploration would be combining the state public employee health care plan to select Medicaid populations into a common risk pool. The authority to implement this strategy already exists in statute, and offers an opportunity to spread risk and improve access to care.

2. **CMS should establish and circulate a detailed and transparent process for state-federal budget neutrality negotiations and waiver evaluations.** The recently released final regulation to increase the transparency of the waiver process is a commendable step forward in ensuring the waiver process is fair and efficient. The regulation includes many clear reporting requirements for states, but does not require corresponding transparent and detailed reporting requirements for the federal government. While we are not requesting that CMS make all internal deliberations or budget formulations public, it would be helpful to states if CMS established clear expectations and a consistent timeline for how the budget negotiation process will move forward. For example, it would be helpful if CMS ensured that all relevant parties were engaged at the beginning of the waiver approval process. Multiple layers of approvals create an inefficient and duplicative process for states. An obvious example is the late involvement of the OMB. Other additional parties, including the HHS Office of the General Counsel, similarly become involved late in the waiver approval process.

3. **CMS should design waiver templates that address time-sensitive and pertinent Medicaid challenges, supporting state efforts to quickly and effectively respond to changes in the marketplace attributable to provisions in the Affordable Care Act.** In the past, CMS has developed waiver templates that address specific needs of states. For example, CMS developed waiver templates to assist Medicare Part D implementation and HIFA waiver templates to increase Medicaid coverage. These templates offered states a simplified, streamlined and

expedited application and approval process that remained consistent with the goals of the Medicaid program. We encourage CMS to similarly standardize certain components of the waiver application process to provide states direction and reduce uncertainty as they look for creative and innovative ways to manage forthcoming changes in the Medicaid program. We believe CMS should provide templates that align with the goals, principles and/or provisions of the ACA. With limited resources at the state level, a more predictable waiver template would give states greater flexibility to reallocate resources. This may help states focus efforts on common challenges, such as addressing health care reform and dual eligibles and promoting new payment methods and innovative care delivery models.

4. **Establish a mechanism for converting successful waivers into permanent or semi-permanent state innovations in the Medicaid program.** A viable strategy must include clear guidelines and framework for approval, as well as any necessary statutory changes. The purpose of a waiver is to encourage innovation and allow states to serve as "laboratories of democracy" for testing new ideas and approaches. Implementing a process to make successful waivers more permanent is consistent with this notion. Permanent waivers are possible only if states and the federal government respect the fact that Medicaid is a partnership of shared accountability and resources. Permanent waivers are feasible in states with a long, well-established and documented history of successfully implemented innovation. Frequent waiver renewals are a burden on high performing state programs, and are an inefficient use of scarce resources for states as well as the federal government.

5. **HHS should make guidance and assistance provided to state leaders by the Medicaid State Technical Assistance Teams transparent and public.** In February 2011, HHS announced the creation of Medicaid State Technical Assistance Teams (MSTATs).[xv] The MSTATs are federal technical assistance teams dispatched to states to provide intensive and tailored assistance on day-to-day operations as well as on new initiatives. While we applaud the federal government's efforts to provide real-time assistance and guidance, we recommend that both the questions and answers be made transparent and available on Medicaid.gov. Many states are dealing with similar issues, and we believe state leaders would benefit from timely access to this information to support planning and decision making at the state level.

Conclusion

Several years into a period of prolonged economic weakness and instability, many Americans have lost faith in government and in the ability of state and federal decision makers alike to come to grips with a host of difficult challenges. Under these circumstances, it is not surprising that state-federal relations are under new strain. Today's challenges, however, create opportunities to put our federalist system on a new and stronger footing. If nothing else, the fiscal pressures currently being experienced at all levels of government will create powerful incentives for states and the federal government to work together more efficiently.

A good place to start exploring concrete improvements to the state-federal relationship is Medicaid. It has become clear that states need more flexibility to pursue their coverage and benefit goals in this program, while effectively managing costs. In this paper we recommend a number of reforms aimed at ensuring that the system for approving Medicaid waivers supports, rather than discourages, timely innovation and experimentation at the state level. We hope that these recommendations—focused on transparent, flexible, clear performance goals and shared responsibility—generate insights and provide a model for improving the state-federal relationship in ways that may be applicable to other areas of significant public policy importance as well.

In coming months, we will look to other policy areas for opportunities to improve the state-federal relationship. Solving the nation's problems with fewer resources is the reality for the foreseeable future. It is a reality—and a challenge—that could have some significant upsides if it spurs a thoughtful examination of how federalism could be made to work more effectively for the American people.

Endnotes

i.   Centers for Medicare and Medicaid Services. *National Health Expenditures 2010 Highlights*. Available at: https://www.cms.gov/NationalHealthExpendData/downloads/highlights.pdf.

ii. *New State Ice Co. v. Liebmann*, 285 U.S. 262 (1932). Justice Brandeis in a dissenting opinion said, "It is one of the happy incidents of a federal system that a single and courageous state may, if its citizens choose, serve as a laboratory and try novel social and economic experiments without risk to the rest of the country."

iii. "Health Policy Brief: Medicaid Reform." *Health Affairs*, January 12, 2012. Available at: http://www.healthaffairs.org/healthpolicybriefs/brief.php?brief_id=60.

iv. U.S. Congressional Research Service. *Medicaid: A Primer* (RL33202; July 15, 2010), by Elicia J. Herz.

v.   *Federal Register*. November 30, 2011 (Vol. 76, No. 230), pp 74061–74063, at http://www.gpo.gov/fdsys/pkg/FR-2011-11-30/pdf/2011-30860.pdf.

vi. "State Fiscal Conditions and Medicaid." Kaiser Commission on Medicaid and the Uninsured, February 2012. Available at: http://www.kff.org/medicaid/upload/7580-08.pdf.

vii.   Dept. of Health and Human Services. "Recovery Act Funded Programs." Available at: http://www.hhs.gov/recovery/programs/index.html.

viii. Smith, V., Gifford, K., Ellis, E., Rudowitz, R., and Snyder, L. "Moving Ahead Amid Fiscal Challenges: A Look at Medicaid Spending, Coverage and Policy Trends Results from a 50-State Medicaid Budget Survey for State Fiscal Years 2011 and 2012." Kaiser Commission on Medicaid and the Uninsured, October 2011. Available at: http://www.kff.org/medicaid/upload/8248.pdf.

ix.   Families USA. *2012 Annual Federal Poverty Guidelines*. Available at: http://www.familiesusa.org/resources/tools-for-advocates/guides/federal-poverty-guidelines.html.

x.   Holahan, J. and Headen, I. "Medicaid Coverage and Spending in Health Reform: National and State-by-State Results for Adults at or Below 133% FPL." Kaiser Commission on Medicaid and the Uninsured, May 2010. Available at: http://www.kff.org/healthreform/upload/medicaid-coverage-and-spending-in-health-reform-national-and-state-by-state-results-for-adults-at-or-below-133-fpl.pdf.

xi.   Smith, V., Gifford, K., Ellis, E., Rudowitz, R., and Snyder, L. "Moving Ahead Amid Fiscal Challenges: A Look at Medicaid Spending, Coverage and Policy Trends Results from a 50-State Medicaid Budget Survey for State Fiscal Years 2011 and 2012." Kaiser Commission on Medicaid and the Uninsured, October 2011." Available at: http://www.kff.org/medicaid/upload/8248.pdf.

xii.   National Governors Association. *HHS-27 Medicaid Reform Principles*. July 17, 2011. Retrieved from: http://www.nga.org/cms/home/federal-relations/nga-policy-positions/page-hhs-policies/col2-content/main-content-list/title_medicaid-reform-principles.html.

xiii.   Kaiser Family Foundation. "Federal Core Requirements and State Options in Medicaid: Current Policies and Key Issues." April 2011.

xiv.   Letter from Center for Medicaid, CHIP and Survey & Certification Director Cindy Mann to State Medicaid Directors and Health Officials. "Re: Revised State Plan Amendment Review Process." October 1, 2010. Available at: https://www.cms.gov/smdl/downloads/SMD10020.pdf.

xv.   Centers for Medicare and Medicaid Services. State Resource Center. Medicaid State Technical Assistance Teams. Retrieved from http://medicaid.gov/State-Resource-Center/Medicaid-State-Technical-Assistance/Medicaid-State-Technical-Assistance-Teams.html.

Critical Thinking

1.   What medical services should state government provide?
2.   What medical services should the federal government provide?
3.   Why is health care a contentious issue of public policy?

Create Central

www.mhhe.com/createcentral

Internet References

Defending the Public Sector without Being Defensive: Why Local Government Matters
http://icma.org/en/icma/knowledge_network/documents/kn/Document/303328
www.marketplace.org/topics/elections/why-local-elections-matter-more-your-personal-financeHolaha

From *Bipartisan Policy Center*, March 2013, pp. 1–12. Copyright © 2013 by Bipartisan Policy Center. Reprinted by permission.

The Dream, the Reality, and Some Solutions

Alice M. Rivlin

Learning Outcomes

After reading this selection, you should be able to:

1. Provide a general description of dual federalism.
2. Discuss the idea of shifting responsibilities from federal to state governments.
3. Understand why isolationism is no longer a rational option for the United States.

Alice M. Rivlin (b. 1931) has earned the reputation of integrating her sophisticated scholarly expertise and insights on economics and public policy with her extensive experiences in public service. Her book *Reviving the American Dream: The Economy, the States and the Federal Government* (Brookings Institution, 1992), from which the following selection is excerpted, has solidified this reputation. Rivlin received her M.A. and her Ph.D. from Radcliffe College. In her distinguished career, Rivlin has held numerous positions with the Brookings Institution in Washington, D.C., including research fellow, staff member of the Economics Studies Division, and senior staff economist. She is currently a senior fellow in the Economics Studies Program at the Brookings Institution. She was also the first director of the Congressional Budget Office as well as president of the American Economic Association. She served as deputy assistant secretary for program coordination, assistant secretary for planning and evaluation for the U.S. Department of Health, Education, and Welfare, and consultant to the U.S. House Committee on Education and Labor and to the U.S. Secretary of the Treasury.

Rivlin's scholarly writings have focused on American federalism and budgetary, fiscal, and taxation policies. Some of her other published works include *The Role of the Federal Government in Financing Higher Education* (Brookings Institution, 1961), *Systematic Thinking for Social Action* (Brookings Institution, 1971), *Economics Choices 1984* (Brookings Institution, 1984) and, coauthored with Joshua M. Wiener, *Caring for the Disabled Elderly: Who Will Pay?* (Brookings Institution, 1988). She has also been a frequent contributor to *The Progressive, New York Times Sunday Magazine,* and numerous political science and economics journals.

In *Reviving the American Dream,* Rivlin raises challenging questions about economic public policy and serious national economic problems, and she prescribes a reconfiguration of the responsibilities, roles, and relationships between the federal and state governments. She contends that the flexible and evolutionary nature of American federalism enables the political system to adapt to changing critical political and social needs. This book is considered a classic analysis of the American political economy, federalism, and public policy. It had a profound impact on contemporary scholarly thought and on the Clinton administration's vision of federalism, revision of major public programs (such as welfare reform), and the abolition of the federal budget deficit.

The basic objectives of Rivlin's prescribed fundamental revision of American federalism include the revitalization of the economy, an increase in governmental efficiency, and a restoration of Americans' trust in government. According to Rivlin, this reform proposal requires a devolution of public authority from the federal government to the state governments. This striking recommendation would dramatically reduce the federal government's direct involvement in major public programs and social services—including education, housing, highways, employment training, and economic development—and shift these responsibilities and initiatives to the state and local governments. Such a shift in responsibilities would enable the federal government to focus on critical national issues, such as the need to develop a comprehensive health insurance program, which would also limit escalating health costs. In addition, according to Rivlin's analysis, the complexity of contemporary global interdependence requires attention by the federal government.

Key Concept: a prescribed redesign of American federalism

The Case for Rethinking Federalism

The argument about which functions should be exercised by the federal government and which by the states has been going on for more than two hundred years. There are no "right" answers. The prevailing view shifts with changing perceptions of the needs of the country and the relative competence and responsiveness of the states and the federal government.

Until the 1930s, the federal government had limited powers and spent relatively little money except in time of war. Government services were not as extensive as they are now, and most were performed by states and their localities. In this period of "dual federalism," the powers of the federal government and the states were viewed as separate and distinct, not overlapping. Then, over the half century between 1930 and 1980, Americans laid increasing responsibilities on the central government. All levels of government grew, but the power, functions, and budget of the federal government grew most rapidly.

Americans turned to Washington for two distinct sets of reasons. First, the collapse of the economy in the Great Depression convinced many people of the need for national institutions to strengthen the economy and deal with problems that states could not be expected to handle on their own. The federal government created social security, set up the unemployment insurance system, developed river basins to control flooding and produce power, supported agricultural prices, strengthened banking and credit systems, and began regulating many economic activities.

Second, activists and reformers turned to Washington, especially in the 1960s, out of frustration with the way states and localities were performing their traditional functions. Compared with the federal government, states had limited capacities and resources. Their staffs were unsophisticated and unprofessional. Their legislatures, dominated by rural members, were unresponsive to city dwellers and minorities. Many state governments were overtly racist. Hence the federal government enacted a range of programs designed to influence the level and nature of state spending in areas that had traditionally been states' responsibilities, such as education, job training, health services, waste treatment, and housing. Many federal grants bypassed states entirely and went directly to local governments, especially big cities.

The surge of federal activities had many positive results, but it also diffused accountability and directed the energies of reformers toward Washington. Citizens concerned about improving state and local services began joining national organizations to lobby for federal money, rather than working at the state or local level. States and localities, even universities, established Washington offices, hired consultants, and acquired expertise in federal grantsmanship.

The proliferation of federal programs, projects, offices, and agencies in so many parts of the country made the federal government increasingly unmanageable. It resembled a giant conglomerate that has acquired too many different kinds of businesses and cannot coordinate its own activities or manage them all effectively from central headquarters.

Then the reaction set in. The flood of federal funds for state and local government crested in the late 1970s and ebbed in the 1980s. Tax cuts and defense spending increases created a huge federal budget deficit that precluded new federal domestic activities. States and cities had to rely more on their own resources. Moreover, the perception of superior federal competence, which had propelled Washington into many traditionally state areas, faded. Reforms gave states stronger governors, more representative legislatures, and more professional and sophisticated civil servants. Meanwhile, the federal government lost some of its former luster. The savings and loan debacle and scandals in defense procurement and housing programs undermined the presumption that the federal government managed more effectively than the states. The intertwining of state and local responsibilities and the diffusion of accountability remained, however.

In the 1990s the United States faces an urgent need to revitalize its economy and to get its political system off dead center and functioning responsively again. There are at least four reasons to think that reraising the fundamental questions of federalism—which level of government should do what and where the revenues should come from—would help in meeting these challenges.

The Impact of Global Interdependence

The first reason is that dramatic changes in the world are radically altering the tasks facing national governments. Rapid advances in the technology of transportation, communications, and weaponry have shrunk distances and intertwined the United States with the rest of the world, intimately and irreversibly. Goods, services, money, and people are flowing easily across oceans and borders. So are economic, political, and environmental problems.

Global interdependence requires international cooperation to solve common problems and some delegation of sovereignty to supranational authorities. The Gulf war and growing nuclear capacity in developing nations leave no doubt that stronger international controls are needed on sophisticated weapons. The rapidly thinning ozone layer dramatizes the stake that all nations have in controlling harmful atmospheric emissions.

Despite its political appeal, isolationism is no longer a viable option. If the United States is to protect its own citizens and help shape a more habitable world, it must take an active part in international partnerships focused on everything from chemical weapons to acid rain to narcotics traffic. These partnerships are already demanding increasing attention from both the executive and legislative branches of the federal government.

Global interdependence creates a paradox for the U.S. government. On the one hand, since both the president and Congress will be spending greater time and energy on international affairs, domestic policy will get less attention in Washington. At the same time, global interdependence makes domestic policy more important than ever. The United States needs rising productivity, a skilled labor force, and modern physical capital, both public and private, if it is to generate the improved standard of living necessary not only to foster domestic well-being, but also to play an effective role in international partnerships. The added complexity of Washington's international role strengthens the case for sorting out domestic responsibilities more clearly. Washington cannot do everything and should not try. The states should take responsibility for a larger and more clearly defined segment of the domestic agenda.

Top-Down and Bottom-Up Reform

A second and more important reason for rethinking the division of responsibilities is that some of the policies needed to revitalize the American economy require bottom-up community effort that cannot be imposed from the top down. They require experimentation and adaptation to local and regional conditions, and that can come only from the state and local level, not from Washington.

Improving education will take bottom-up reform. Presidential speeches and photo opportunities, national testing and assessment, federally funded experimental schools, even new grants spent in accordance with federal guidelines, can make only marginal contributions to fixing the schools. Education in America will not improve significantly until states and communities decide they want better schools. Making education more effective will take parents who care, committed teachers, community support, and accountable school officials. An "education president" can help focus media attention on schooling, but he risks diluting state and local responsibility by implying that Washington can actually produce change.

The popular federal Head Start program demonstrates that preschool education helps children from poor families cope better in school. The negative legacy of Head Start, however, is that states and communities have come to believe that the responsibility for preschool education lies with Washington, not with them. Change would come more rapidly if concerned citizens, parents, and educators worked to improve their own preschools instead of lobbying Washington to allocate more funds for Head Start.

Street crime, drug use, and teenage pregnancy are all examples of problems that the federal government can deplore but cannot fix. A resurgence of community concern and effort is needed. Social services, housing, community development, and most infrastructure also must be carefully adapted to the needs of particular places. Federal grants can help defray the costs, but at the price of confusing the issue of who is responsible and who needs to take action.

On the other hand, there are important public functions that Washington performs well and state and local governments cannot address effectively. First, there are inherently central responsibilities, like national defense and foreign affairs, for which the federal government must represent and defend the interests of the country as a whole. Second, there are activities whose benefits clearly spill over state lines—such as air traffic control, basic scientific research, and prevention of river pollution or acid rain. Individual states have little incentive to undertake these programs because so much of the benefit would go to people in other states. Third, there are programs whose workability depends on having a uniform national system, such as social security.

Social Security is perhaps the federal government's greatest domestic success. It is well administered and immensely popular. People are less resentful of social security taxes than other taxes, because they know what the money goes for and they expect benefits themselves. Because it involves tracking people over a lifetime, social security could not easily be handled by the states; too many people would move in and out of state systems and end up with conflicting and overlapping coverage.

The federal government is also best adapted to solving the double problem of controlling rapidly rising health costs and providing health insurance to the whole population. The U.S. health care system is the most expensive in the world, now consuming more than one-eighth of everything the nation produces, but it does not provide commensurate benefits. Millions of people are left out or inadequately insured. State-by-state efforts to expand insurance coverage and control medical costs are not likely to be successful. Sentiment is growing for some kind of national health insurance system that would provide universal coverage for basic health services and would control costs by setting reimbursement rates for doctors, hospitals, and other medical providers.

Another important role that the federal government is uniquely positioned to play at the moment is increasing national saving. Americans are saving by contributing to social security. The social security system is currently running significant annual surpluses because taxes collected exceed benefits paid out. These reserves will be needed to pay benefits to the large baby boom generation when its members retire. They ought to be used to help finance the productive investment needed to generate higher incomes in the future. At present, however, the social security surpluses are simply being lent to the rest of the government to offset part of the huge federal budget deficit. . . .

The Need for More Tax Revenue

The third reason for focusing on the assignment of tasks to federal and state governments is that all levels of government are in serious financial difficulties. Even if some services are cut back and others are run more efficiently, more revenues are needed to eliminate deficits at the federal, state, and local levels, to accomplish the productivity agenda, and to reform health care financing. If taxes must go up, it is important to consider which level of government will make best use of the revenues. . . .

The state fiscal crisis. Increasing the responsibilities of state and local governments is a dubious proposition because they too are in fiscal trouble. At first glance, their fiscal distress seems more temporary than that of the federal government. State and local governments generally suffer serious fiscal stress in recessions. Their revenues fall off as sales, income, and property values stop growing or decline while claims on their services continue to increase. Because, unlike the federal government, states and localities cannot normally borrow to cover operating expenses, they are forced to raise taxes and cut services as soon as their reserves are exhausted.

Even after the economy returns to moderate growth, however, there are reasons for pessimism about the prospects for state and local finance in the 1990s. The fiscal health of state and local governments declined in the second half of the 1980s. Pressures for spending outran revenues. The fiscal stress, especially in cities, reflected the growth in crime, drug addiction, AIDS, homelessness, and poverty, all of which continued to increase through the long recovery from the recession of the early 1980s. Moreover, a major villain of the federal budget drama appears again at the state and local level. Rising medical care costs, especially for medicaid, have put enormous pressure on state and local budgets that seems unlikely to abate.

Thus all levels of government will probably face continuing fiscal stress in the 1990s. Policies to revitalize the economy—increased public investment, a federal surplus, health financing reform—cannot be undertaken without more revenue at some level of government. The public seems angry and dissatisfied with government, however, and unwilling either to increase its support or to accept a lower level of services.

Dissatisfaction with Government

The fourth reason for questioning the jobs assigned to various levels of government in the 1990s is the American public's dissatisfaction with politics and politicians. Many Americans have "tuned out" political debate and stopped participating in elections. Polls reveal declining confidence in political leaders, rising skepticism that public officials care about the views of ordinary people, disgust at political campaigns, and cynicism about the democratic process.

There are many possible reasons for the disparagement of government: the need to blame someone for the stresses of a faltering economy, the influence of big money on political campaigns, the negativism of political advertising, and the insensitivity of politicians to the damage done to their collective image by even minor peccadillos such as getting parking tickets fixed. Some blame the ideological polarization of the major parties—the capture of the Republicans by ultraconservatives and the Democrats by extreme liberals—for leaving the pragmatic, middle-of-the-road majority without leadership.[1] Others point to the widening gulf between elites, who see public policy as a matter of technical control, and a general public that correctly perceives the elites' contempt for citizens' opinions.[2]

The blurring of state and federal roles contributes to cynicism about politics. For example, much of the rhetoric in the 1988 presidential campaign concerned issues over which presidents have little control—crime, drugs, education, child care, and industrial development. Voters care about these issues, but they also know that Washington is too remote from them to make a difference. Candidates for federal office undermine their credibility by implying these problems have national solutions and by refusing to address serious federal issues, such as the budget deficit.

Voters also appear more willing to pay taxes if they know that revenues will be used for identifiable services important to them. Polls show voters opposed to paying more taxes for undisclosed purposes but willing to pay for improved schools or increased environmental protection. In recent years the federal government's general revenues (other than social security and medicare payroll taxes) have declined as a percentage of GNP, while state and local revenues have increased substantially. Perhaps taxpayers are clearer about their need for state and local services and are more willing to pay for them than for the more remote services of the federal government. Despite substantial increases in payroll taxes for social security and medicare in recent decades, polls show these taxes are less unpopular than the federal income tax, presumably because taxpayers know what the payroll taxes buy and value the benefits. Hence the most feasible way to increase revenue may be to earmark new taxes for a particular federal benefit such as health insurance or for improved services at the state and local level.

Proposals for the Future

This focus on federalism suggests several quite drastic proposals aimed at reenergizing the American economy and restoring confidence in the political system. Their basic theme is that the federal and state governments should divide the jobs to be done and get moving.

- *The productivity agenda.* The states should take charge of the primary public investment needed to increase productivity and raise incomes, especially to improve education and skill training and modernize infrastructure.
- *Devolution.* The federal government should eliminate most of its programs in education, housing, highways, social services, economic development, and job training.
- *Common shared taxes.* With federal blessing, or even the assistance of the federal government, states should strengthen their revenue systems by cooperating in collecting common taxes to be shared among them on a formula basis.
- *Health care financing.* The federal government should adopt a plan that will ensure basic health insurance coverage for everyone and control the increase in health costs.

- *Federal budget surplus.* The federal government should run a surplus in its whole budget (counting social security), thus reducing federal debt service costs and adding to the pool of saving available to finance private investment.

These proposals fit together. State responsibility for the productivity agenda would sharpen the distinction between federal and state tasks, making it easier for citizens to understand what each level of government does and to blame the right set of officials for poor performance. Devolution would take whole areas of public spending out of the federal budget, making it easier to move that budget toward surplus. More important, making clear that the devolved functions belong to the states, not the federal government, would transfer pressure for increased spending in these areas from Washington to state capitals and help keep federal deficits from recurring.

The resulting fiscal pressure on states and localities would be alleviated in two ways. First, federal responsibility for health care financing, coupled with strong cost controls, would relieve states and localities of the escalating burden of medicaid and reduce the cost of other public medical care. Second, the adoption of one or more common shared taxes would improve the states' collective revenue-raising capacity.

One example of a common shared tax would be a uniform state sales tax (or value-added tax) collected at the same rate on the same items and shared on the basis of population. A uniform corporation income tax, collected along with the federal income tax and shared on a formula basis, would make tax compliance simpler for multistate corporations. A common state energy tax could reduce pollution and promote conservation as well as raising revenue.

The idea of states sharing common taxes is a radical departure from the American tradition that each state must go it alone [at] levying taxes. In other federal systems, tax sharing is more usual. In Germany, for example, the central government collects most of the taxes and shares the proceeds with the *Länder* (states). German taxpayers, individual and corporate, fill out only one income tax return, for both federal and state taxes. German firms pay a value-added tax whose proceeds are shared between the federal government and the states, with disproportionate shares going to the least affluent states to help equalize services.

As the American economy becomes more national and international, the case for more coordination of state taxation increases. People, companies, sales, and services move with greater ease across borders. One consequence is that states and localities have to worry about keeping their tax rates from getting out of line with those of other jurisdictions. Another is that more and more companies, and even individuals, owe taxes in multiple jurisdictions. The resulting complexity is costly for both taxpayers and tax collectors.

Like federal grants, common shared taxes could be designed to improve the relative position of the least affluent states. Unlike federal grants, however, they would not cause confusion about which level of government has responsibility for particular programs or impose federal rules and guidelines on state and local authorities.

To revive the American dream, citizens must find new energy and commitment to revitalize the myriad institutions that influence American life—families, businesses, schools, unions, churches, clubs, and government at all levels. They must be willing to experiment, restructure, and try new approaches to old and new problems. In the words of David Osborne and Ted Gaebler, they must even "reinvent government" by breaking out of old hierarchical patterns and empowering those closest to the problems to participate in finding solutions.[3]

A first step is to reexamine that peculiarly American institution, federalism. The current confusion of responsibilities between federal and state government is undermining confidence in government and impeding the implementation of policies needed to restore a healthy economy. Sorting out the roles more clearly could break the logjam, help both levels function more effectively, and improve both domestic and foreign policy.

Notes

1. E. J. Dionne, Jr., *Why Americans Hate Politics* (Simon and Schuster, 1991).
2. Daniel Yankelovich, *Coming to Public Judgment: Making Democracy Work in a Complex World* (Syracuse University Press, 1991).
3. David Osborne and Ted Gaebler, *Reinventing Government: How the Entrepreneurial Spirit Is Transforming the Public Sector* (Addison-Wesley, 1992).

Critical Thinking

1. For American education, what might be the greatest drawback to devolution of authority from the federal government to the state governments?
2. How relevant to the current form of U.S. federalism is the era of necessitated federal growth during the Great Depression of the 1930s?
3. If the idea of states sharing common taxes were to win popular interest, how feasible would it be to put such a plan in place?

Create Central

www.mhhe.com/createcentral

Internet References

The National Archives and Records Administration
www.archives.gov

The National Governors Association
www.nga.org/portal/site/nga

From *Reviving the American Dream: The Economy, the States and the Federal Government* by Alice M. Rivlin (Brookings Institution, 1992). Copyright © 1992 by Brookings Institution. Reprinted by permission.

Unit 4: Civil Liberties

Of the Liberty of Thought and Discussion

John Stuart Mill

Learning Outcomes

After reading this selection, you should be able to:

1. Discuss whether absolute certainty is ever a possibility.
2. Consider the detriment to truth when opinions are suppressed.
3. Regard open discourse as the only conduit to wisdom.

John Stuart Mill (1806–1873) was a classical liberal British political philosopher, logician, political economist, and social and political reformer. Classical liberalism refers to a political theory or ideology based upon a commitment to such fundamental normative principles or values as limited government, constitutionalism or rule of law, toleration, individualism, individual rights and freedoms, privacy, and voluntarism. Mill's philosophical work *On Liberty* (New American Library, 1968), from which the following selection is excerpted, had a profound impact upon the development of modern liberal democratic political thought in the United States.

Utilitarianism refers to an ethical or political theory that identifies an action or public policy as right or wrong, good or bad, just or unjust, based upon the consequences of such acts or policies, particularly in proportion to the degree of human happiness or societal benefit promoted. The greatest good for the greatest number is often cited as an ultimate or fundamental utilitarian moral principle. In *On Liberty* (1859), Mill's central argument and justification of liberty of thought and discussion is primarily utilitarian, in reflection of the desirable social consequences resulting from a policy of freedom of expression and the exposure of truth.

In the following selection, Mill defends freedom of thought and expression. He theorizes that the repression of any opinion or thought is bad policy, independent of the truth of such opinions or thoughts. Mill claims that the suppression of a true opinion deprives humanity from learning the truth.

In addition to the fundamental significance of freedom of thought and expression for a free democratic society, the American political system also has been influenced by Mill's defense of the self-development of the individual. Mill contends that an individual's acts should only be limited by the state or society if such acts are determined to cause injury to others.

Key Concept: freedom of thought and expression

The time, it is to be hoped, is gone by, when any defence would be necessary of the "liberty of the press" as one of the securities against corrupt or tyrannical government. No argument, we may suppose, can now be needed, against permitting a legislature or an executive, not identified in interest with the people, to prescribe opinions to them, and determine what doctrines or what arguments they shall be allowed to hear. This aspect of the question, besides, has been so often and so triumphantly enforced by preceding writers, that it needs not be specially insisted on in this place. Though the law of England, on the subject of the press, is as servile to this day as it was in the time of the Tudors, there is little danger of its being actually put in force against

political discussion, except during some temporary panic, when fear of insurrection drives ministers and judges from their propriety, and, speaking generally, it is not, in constitutional countries, to be apprehended, that the government, whether completely responsible to the people or not, will often attempt to control the expression of opinion, except when in doing so it makes itself the organ of the general intolerance of the public. Let us suppose, therefore, that the government is entirely at one with the people, and never thinks of exerting any power of coercion unless in agreement with what it conceives to be their voice. But I deny the right of the people to exercise such coercion, either by themselves or by their government. The power itself is illegitimate. The best government has no more title to it than the worst. It is as noxious, or more noxious, when exerted in accordance with public opinion, than when in opposition to it. If all mankind minus one were of one opinion, and only one person were of the contrary opinion, mankind would be no more justified in silencing that one person, than he, if he had the power, would be justified in silencing mankind. Were an opinion a personal possession of no value except to the owner; if to be obstructed in the enjoyment of it were simply a private injury, it would make some difference whether the injury was inflicted only on a few persons or on many. But the peculiar evil of silencing the expression of an opinion is, that it is robbing the human race; posterity as well as the existing generation; those who dissent from the opinion, still more than those who hold it. If the opinion is right, they are deprived of the opportunity of exchanging error for truth: if wrong, they lose, what is almost as great a benefit, the clearer perception and livelier impression of truth, produced by its collision with error.

It is necessary to consider separately these two hypotheses, each of which has a distinct branch of the argument corresponding to it. We can never be sure that the opinion we are endeavouring to stifle is a false opinion; and if we were sure, stifling it would be an evil still.

First: the opinion which it is attempted to suppress by authority may possibly be true. Those who desire to suppress it, of course deny its truth; but they are not infallible. They have no authority to decide the question for all mankind, and exclude every other person from the means of judging. To refuse a hearing to an opinion, because they are sure that it is false, is to assume that *their* certainty is the same thing as *absolute* certainty. All silencing of discussion is an assumption of infallibility. Its condemnation may be allowed to rest on this common argument, not the worse for being common.

Unfortunately for the good sense of mankind, the fact of their fallibility is far from carrying the weight in their practical judgment which is always allowed to it in theory; for while every one well knows himself to be fallible, few think it necessary to take any precautions against their own fallibility, or admit the supposition that any opinion, of which they feel very certain, may be one of the examples of the error to which they acknowledge themselves to be liable. Absolute princes, or others who are accustomed to unlimited deference, usually feel this complete confidence in their own opinions on nearly all subjects. People more happily situated, who sometimes hear their opinions disputed, and are not wholly unused to be set right when they are wrong, place the same unbounded reliance only on such of their opinions as are shared by all who surround them, or to whom they habitually defer; for in proportion to a man's want of confidence in his own solitary judgment, does he usually repose, with implicit trust, on the infallibility of "the world" in general. And the world, to each individual, means the part of it with which he comes in contact; his

party, his sect, his church, his class of society; the man may be called, by comparison, almost liberal and large-minded to whom it means anything so comprehensive as his own country or his own age. Nor is his faith in this collective authority at all shaken by his being aware that other ages, countries, sects, churches, classes, and parties have thought, and even now think, the exact reverse. He devolves upon his own world the responsibility of being in the right against the dissentient worlds of other people; and it never troubles him that mere accident has decided which of these numerous worlds is the object of his reliance, and that the same causes which make him a Churchman in London, would have made him a Buddhist or a Confucian in Peking. Yet it is as evident in itself, as any amount of argument can make it, that ages are no more infallible than individuals; every age having held many opinions which subsequent ages have deemed not only false but absurd; and it is as certain that many opinions now general will be rejected by future ages, as it is that many, once general, are rejected by the present.

The objection likely to be made to this argument would probably take some such form as the following. There is no greater assumption of infallibility in forbidding the propagation of error, than in any other thing which is done by public authority on its own judgment and responsibility. Judgment is given to men that they may use it. Because it may be used erroneously, are men to be told that they ought not to use it at all? To prohibit what they think pernicious, is not claiming exemption from error, but fulfilling the duty incumbent on them, although fallible, of acting on their conscientious conviction. If we were never to act on our opinions, because those opinions may be wrong, we should leave all our interests uncared for, and all our duties unperformed. An objection which applies to all conduct can be no valid objection to any conduct in particular. It is the duty of governments, and of individuals, to form the truest opinions they can; to form carefully, and never impose them upon others unless they are quite sure of being right. But when they are sure (such reasoners may say), it is not conscientiousness but cowardice to shrink from acting on their opinions, and allow doctrines which they honestly think dangerous to the welfare of mankind, either in this life or in another, to be scattered abroad without restraint, because other people, in less enlightened times, have persecuted opinions now believed to be true. Let us take care, it may be said, not to make the same mistake: but governments and nations have made mistakes in other things, which are not denied to be fit subjects for the exercise of authority: they have laid on bad taxes, made unjust wars. Ought we therefore to lay on no taxes, and, under whatever provocation, make no wars? Men and governments, must act to the best of their ability. There is no such thing as absolute certainty, but there is assurance sufficient for the purposes of human life. We may, and must, assume our opinion to be true for the guidance of our own conduct: and it is assuming no more when we forbid bad men to pervert society by the propagation of opinions which we regard as false and pernicious.

I answer, that it is assuming very much more. There is the greatest difference between presuming an opinion to be true, because, with every opportunity for contesting it, it has not been refuted, and assuming its truth for the purpose of not permitting its refutation. Complete liberty of contradicting and disproving our opinion is the very condition which justifies us in assuming its truth for purposes of action; and on no other terms can a being with human faculties have any rational assurance of being right.

When we consider either the history of opinion, or the ordinary conduct of human life, to what is it to be ascribed that the one and the other are no worse than they are? Not certainly to the inherent force of the human understanding; for, on any matter not self-evident, there are ninety-nine persons totally incapable of judging of it for one who is capable; and the capacity of the hundredth person is only comparative; for the majority of the eminent men of every past generation held many opinions now known to be erroneous, and did or approved numerous things which no one will now justify. Why is it, then, that there is on the whole a preponderance among mankind of rational opinions and rational conduct? If there really is this preponderance—which there must be unless human affairs are, and have always been, in an almost desperate state—it is owing to a quality of the human mind, the source of everything respectable in man either as an intellectual or as a moral being, namely, that his errors are corrigible. He is capable of rectifying his mistakes, by discussion and experience. Not by experience alone. There must be discussion, to show how experience is to be interpreted. Wrong opinions and practices gradually yield to fact and argument; but facts and arguments, to produce any effect on the mind, must be brought before it. Very few facts are able to tell their own story, without comments to bring out their meaning. The whole strength and value, then, of human judgment, depending on the one property, that it can be set right when it is wrong, reliance can be placed on it only when the means of setting it right are kept constantly at hand. In the case of any person whose judgment is really deserving of confidence, how has it become so? Because he has kept his mind open to criticism on his opinions and conduct. Because it has been his practice to listen to all that could be said against him; to profit by as much of it as was just, and expound to himself, and upon occasion to others, the fallacy of what was fallacious. Because he has felt, that the only way in which a human being can make some approach to knowing the whole of a subject, is by hearing what can be said about it by persons of every variety of opinion, and studying all modes in which it can be looked at by every character of mind. No wise man ever acquired his wisdom in any mode but this; nor is it in the nature of human intellect to become wise in any other manner. The steady habit of correcting and

completing his own opinion by collating it with those of others, so far from causing doubt and hesitation in carrying it into practice, is the only stable foundation for a just reliance on it: for, being cognisant of all that can, at least obviously, be said against him, and having taken up his position against all gainsayers—knowing that he has sought for objections and difficulties, instead of avoiding them, and has shut out no light which can be thrown upon the subject from any quarter—he has a right to think his judgment better than that of any person, or any multitude, who have not gone through a similar process.

It is not too much to require that what the wisest of mankind, those who are best entitled to trust their own judgment, find necessary to warrant their relying on it, should be submitted to by that miscellaneous collection of a few wise and many foolish individuals, called the public. The most intolerant of churches, the Roman Catholic Church, even at the canonisation of a saint, admits, and listens patiently to, a "devil's advocate." The holiest of men, it appears, cannot be admitted to posthumous honours, until all that the devil could say against him is known and weighed. If even the Newtonian philosophy were not permitted to be questioned, mankind could not feel as complete assurance of its truth as they now do. The beliefs which we have most warrant for have no safeguard to rest on, but a standing invitation to the whole world to prove them unfounded. If the challenge is not accepted, or is accepted and the attempt fails, we are far enough from certainty still; but we have done the best that the existing state of human reason admits of; we have neglected nothing that could give the truth a chance of reaching us: if the lists are kept open, we may hope that if there be a better truth, it will be found when the human mind is capable of receiving it; and in the meantime we may rely on having attained such approach to truth as is possible in our own day. This is the amount of certainty attainable by a fallible being, and this the sole way of attaining it. . . .

We have now recognised the necessity to the mental well-being of mankind (on which all their other well-being depends) of freedom of opinion, and freedom of the expression of opinion, on four distinct grounds; which we will now briefly recapitulate.

First, if any opinion is compelled to silence, that opinion may, for aught we can certainly know, be true. To deny this is to assume our own infallibility.

Secondly, though the silenced opinion be an error, it may, and very commonly does, contain a portion of truth; and since the general or prevailing opinion on any subject is rarely or never the whole truth, it is only by the collision of adverse opinions that the remainder of the truth has any chance of being supplied.

Thirdly, even if the received opinion be not only true, but the whole truth; unless it is suffered to be, and actually is, vigorously and earnestly contested, it will, by most of those who receive it, be held in the manner of a prejudice, with little comprehension or feeling of its rational grounds. And not only this, but, fourthly, the meaning of the doctrine itself will be in danger of being lost, or enfeebled, and deprived of its vital effect on the character and conduct; the dogma becoming a mere formal profession, inefficacious for good, but cumbering the ground, and preventing the growth of any real and heartfelt conviction, from reason or personal experience.

Before quitting the subject of freedom of opinion, it is fit to take some notice of those who say that the free expression of all opinions should be permitted, on condition that the manner be temperate, and do not pass the bounds of fair discussion. Much might be said on the impossibility of fixing where these supposed bounds are to be placed; for if the test be offence to those whose opinions are attacked, I think experience testifies that this offence is given whenever the attack is telling and powerful, and that every opponent who pushes them hard, and whom they find it difficult to answer, appears to them, if he shows any strong feeling on the subject, an intemperate opponent. But this, though an important consideration in a practical point of view, merges in a more fundamental objection. Undoubtedly the manner of asserting an opinion, even though it be a true one, may be very objectionable, and may justly incur severe censure. But the principal offences of the kind are such as it is mostly impossible, unless by accidental self-betrayal, to bring home to conviction. The gravest of them is, to argue sophistically, to suppress facts or arguments, to misstate the elements of the case, or misrepresent the opposite opinion. But all this, even to the most aggravated degree, is so continually done in perfect good faith, by persons who are not considered, and in many other respects may not deserve to be considered, ignorant or incompetent, that it is rarely possible, on adequate grounds, conscientiously to stamp the misrepresentation as morally culpable; and still less could law presume to interfere with this kind of controversial misconduct. With regard to what is commonly meant by intemperate discussion, namely invective, sarcasm, personality and the like, the denunciation of these weapons would deserve more sympathy if it were ever proposed to interdict them equally to both sides; but it is only desired to restrain the employment of them against the prevailing opinion: against the unprevailing they may not only be used without general disapproval, but will be likely to obtain for him who uses them the praise of honest zeal and righteous indignation. Yet whatever mischief arises from their use is greatest when they are employed against the comparatively defenceless; and whatever unfair advantage can be derived by any opinion from this mode of asserting it, accrues almost exclusively to received opinions. The worst offence of this kind which can be committed by a polemic is to stigmatise those who hold the contrary opinion as bad and immoral men. To calumny of this sort, those who hold any unpopular opinion are peculiarly exposed, because they are in general few and uninfluential, and nobody but themselves feels much interested in seeing justice

done them; but this weapon is, from the nature of the case, denied to those who attack a prevailing opinion: they can neither use it with safety to themselves, nor, if they could, would it do anything but recoil on their own cause. In general, opinions contrary to those commonly received can only obtain a hearing by studied moderation of language, and the most cautious avoidance of unnecessary offence, from which they hardly ever deviate even in a slight degree without losing ground: while unmeasured vituperation employed on the side of the prevailing opinion really does deter people from professing contrary opinions, and from listening to those who profess them. For the interest, therefore, of truth and justice, it is far more important to restrain this employment of vituperative language than the other; and, for example, if it were necessary to choose, there would be much more need to discourage offensive attacks on infidelity than on religion. It is, however, obvious that law and authority have no business with restraining either, while opinion ought, in every instance, to determine its verdict by the circumstances of the individual case; condemning every one, on whichever side of the argument he places himself, in whose mode of advocacy either want of candour, or malignity, bigotry, or intolerance of feeling manifest themselves; but not inferring these vices from the side which a person takes, though it be the contrary side of the question to our own; and giving merited honour to every one, whatever opinion he may hold, who has calmness to see and honesty to state what his opponents and their opinions really are, exaggerating nothing to their discredit, keeping nothing back which tells, or can be supposed to tell, in their favour. This is the real morality of public discussion: and if often violated, I am happy to think that there are many controversialists who to a great extent observe it, and a still greater number who conscientiously strive towards it.

Critical Thinking

1. What are some examples of social reform (such as the abolition of slavery) that validate Mill's view that "eminent men of every past generation held many opinions now known to be erroneous, and did or approved numerous things which no one will now justify"?
2. Identify a current social issue that is especially likely to generate a reform consistent with Mill's thesis.
3. Given the natural resonance of free thought and discussion with "Americanism," why is there a continuing rise in fundamentalism in the United States?

Create Central

www.mhhe.com/createcentral

Internet References

The American Civil Liberties Union
www.aclu.org

From *On Liberty* by John Stuart Mill (1859).

Gideon v. Wainwright

Hugo L. Black

Learning Outcomes

After reading this selection, you should be able to:

1. Describe the crime for which Clarence Earl Gideon was tried in a Florida state court.
2. Explain the rationale used to deny Gideon appointed counsel in Florida.
3. Identify the 1942 Supreme Court case whose facts and circumstances are nearly indistinguishable from *Gideon v. Wainwright*.

In the 1963 landmark decision *Gideon v. Wainwright* (372 U.S. 335), from which the following selection is taken, the U.S. Supreme Court expressed an opinion that had major constitutional and political consequences upon the interpretation of civil liberties and the application of the Bill of Rights to the state governments. Clarence Earl Gideon, a 51-year-old drifter with an extensive criminal record, was convicted of breaking into the Bay Harbor Poolroom in Panama City, Florida, with the intent of committing a misdemeanor, considered a felony under Florida law. Gideon appeared in court for his trial without an attorney and without the means to afford one, and he requested the trial court to appoint an attorney for him. The trial court judge rejected Gideon's request for legal counsel, referring to a Florida law that authorized the appointment of lawyers exclusively in capital cases (offenses punishable by death). Gideon served as his own defense counselor, and he was promptly found guilty by the jury and sentenced to five years in the Florida State Prison for petty larceny.

While in prison, Gideon became a "jail-house lawyer" and filed numerous unsuccessful lower-court actions disputing the constitutionality of his imprisonment and directed against Wainwright, the state director of corrections. Gideon's petition to the Florida Supreme Court was denied relief without opinion, but his poorly handwritten petition and case were accepted by the U.S. Supreme Court for review. Gideon argued that the trial judge's refusal to appoint legal counsel for him was a denial of rights guaranteed by the Sixth and Fourteenth Amendments.

Justice Hugo L. Black delivered the opinion of the Court. The opinion had a fundamental and profound impact upon state criminal cases by requiring state courts to appoint attorneys for all individuals accused of felony charges if they cannot afford counsel. Black argued that the Sixth Amendment right to counsel should be incorporated among the fundamental rights protected under the Fourteenth Amendment. Following the decision of this case, the Supreme Court expanded the rights of the accused, even requiring lawyers to be provided for individuals charged with offenses less severe than felonies in order to promote fair trials.

Key Concept: the right to counsel

*M*r. Justice Black delivered the opinion of the Court, saying in part:

Petitioner was charged in a Florida state court with having broken and entered a poolroom with intent to commit a misdemeanor. This offense is a felony under Florida law. Appearing in court without funds and without a lawyer, petitioner asked the court to appoint counsel for him, whereupon the following colloquy took place:

"The Court: Mr. Gideon, I am sorry, but I cannot appoint Counsel to represent you in this case. Under the laws of the State of Florida, the only time the Court can appoint Counsel to represent a Defendant is when that person is charged with a capital offense. I am sorry, but I will have to deny your request to appoint Counsel to defend you in this case."

"The Defendant: The United States Supreme Court says I am entitled to be represented by Counsel."

Put to trial before a jury, Gideon conducted his defense about as well as could be expected from a layman. He made an opening statement to the jury, cross-examined the State's witnesses, presented witnesses in his own defense, declined to testify himself, and made a short argument "emphasizing his innocence to the charge contained in the information filed in this case." The jury returned a verdict of guilty, and petitioner was sentenced to serve five years in the state prison. . . . Since 1942, when *Betts v. Brady* was decided by divided Court, the problem of a defendant's federal constitutional right to counsel in a state court has been a continuing source of controversy and litigation in both state and federal courts. . . .

The facts upon which Betts claimed that he had been unconstitutionally denied the right to have counsel appointed to assist him are strikingly like the facts upon which Gideon here bases his federal constitutional claim. Betts was indicted for robbery in a Maryland state court. On arraignment, he told the trial judge of his lack of funds to hire a lawyer and asked the court to appoint one for him. Betts was advised that it was not the practice in that county to appoint counsel for indigent defendants except in murder and rape cases. He then pleaded not guilty, had witnesses summoned, cross-examined the State's witnesses, examined his own, and chose not to testify himself. He was found guilty by the judge, sitting without a jury, and sentenced to eight years in prison. Like Gideon, Betts sought release by habeas corpus, alleging that he had been denied the right to assistance of counsel in violation of the Fourteenth Amendment. Betts was denied any relief, and on review this Court affirmed. It was held that a refusal to appoint counsel for an indigent defendant charged with a felony did not necessarily violate the Due Process Clause of the Fourteenth Amendment, which for reasons given the Court deemed to be the only applicable federal constitutional provision. The Court said:

"Asserted denial [of due process] is to be tested by an appraisal of the totality of facts in a given case. That which may, in one setting, constitute a denial of fundamental fairness, shocking to the universal sense of justice, may, in other circumstances, and in the light of other considerations, fall short of such denial."

Treating due process as "a concept less rigid and more fluid than those envisaged in other specific and particular provisions of the Bill of Rights," the Court held that refusal to appoint counsel under the particular facts and circumstances in the Betts Case was not so "offensive to the common and fundamental ideas of fairness" as to amount to a denial of due process. Since the facts and circumstances of the two cases are so nearly indistinguishable, we think the *Betts v. Brady* holding if left standing would require us to reject Gideon's claim that the Constitution guarantees him the assistance of counsel. Upon full reconsideration we conclude that *Betts v. Brady* should be overruled.

The Sixth Amendment provides, "In all criminal prosecutions, the accused shall enjoy the right . . . to have the Assistance of Counsel for his defence." We have construed this to mean that in federal courts counsel must be provided for defendants unable to employ counsel unless the right is competently and intelligently waived. Betts argued that this right is extended to indigent defendants in state courts by the Fourteenth Amendment. In response the Court stated that, while the Sixth Amendment laid down "no rule for the conduct of the States, the question recurs whether the constraint laid by the Amendment upon the national courts expresses a rule so fundamental and essential to a fair trial, and so, to due process of law, that it is made obligatory upon the States by the Fourteenth Amendment." In order to decide whether the Sixth Amendment's guarantee of counsel is of this fundamental nature, the Court in Betts set out and considered "[r]elevant data on the subject . . . afforded by constitutional and statutory provisions subsisting in the colonies and the States prior to the inclusion of the Bill of Rights in the national Constitution, and in the constitutional, legislative, and judicial history of the States to the present date." On the basis of this historical data the Court concluded that "appointment of counsel is not a fundamental right, essential to a fair trial." It was for this reason the Betts Court refused to accept the contention that the Sixth Amendment's guarantee of counsel for indigent federal defendants was extended to or, in the words of that Court, "made obligatory upon the States by the Fourteenth Amendment." Plainly, had the Court concluded that appointment of counsel for indigent criminal defendant was "a fundamental right, essential to a fair trial," it would have held that the Fourteenth Amendment requires appointment of counsel in a state court, just as the Sixth Amendment requires in a federal court.

We think the Court in Betts had ample precedent for acknowledging that those guarantees of the Bill of Rights which are fundamental safeguards of liberty immune from federal abridgment are equally protected against state invasion by the Due Process Clause of the Fourteenth Amendment. This same principle was recognized, explained and applied in *Powell v. Alabama* (1932), a case upholding the right of counsel, where the Court held that despite sweeping language to the contrary in *Hurtado v. California* (1884), the Fourteenth Amendment "embraced" those "fundamental principles of liberty and justice which lie at the base of all our civil and political institutions," even though they had been "specifically dealt with in another part of the federal Constitution." In many cases other than Powell and Betts, this Court has looked to the fundamental nature of original Bill of Rights guarantees to decide whether the Fourteenth Amendment makes them obligatory on the States. Explicitly recognized to be of this "fundamental nature" and therefore made immune from state invasion by the Fourteenth, or some part of it, are the First Amendment's freedoms of speech, press, religion, assembly, association, and petition for redress of grievances. For the same reason, though not always in precisely the same terminology, the Court has made obligatory on the States the Fifth Amendment's command that private property shall not be taken for public use without just compensation, the Fourth Amendment's prohibition of unreasonable searches and seizures, and the Eighth's ban on cruel and unusual punishment. On the other hand, this Court in *Palko v. Connecticut* (1937), refused to hold that the Fourteenth Amendment made the double jeopardy provision of the Fifth Amendment obligatory on the States. In so refusing, however, the Court, speaking through Mr. Justice Cardozo, was careful to emphasize that "immunities that are valid as against the federal government by force of the specific pledges of particular amendments have been found to be implicit in the concept of ordered liberty, and thus, through the Fourteenth Amendment, become valid as against the states" and that guarantees "in their origin . . . effective against the federal government alone" had by prior cases "been taken over from the earlier articles of the federal bill of rights and brought within the Fourteenth Amendment by a process of absorption."

We accept *Betts v. Brady's* assumption, based as it was on our prior cases, that a provision of the Bill of Rights which is "fundamental and essential to a fair trial" is made obligatory upon the States by the Fourteenth Amendment. We think the Court in Betts was wrong, however, in concluding that the Sixth Amendment's guarantee of counsel is not one of these fundamental rights. Ten years before *Betts v. Brady*, this Court, after full consideration of all the historical data examined in Betts, had unequivocally declared that "the right to the aid of counsel is of this fundamental character.". . . While the Court at the close of its Powell opinion did by its language, as this Court frequently does, limit its holding to the particular facts and circumstances of that case, its conclusions about the fundamental nature of the right to counsel are unmistakable. Several years later, in 1936, the Court reemphasized what it had said about the fundamental nature of the right to counsel in this language:

"We concluded that certain fundamental rights, safeguarded by the first eight amendments against federal action, were also safeguarded against state action by the due process of law clause of the Fourteenth Amendment, and among them the fundamental right of the accused to the aid of counsel in a criminal prosecution." *Grosjean v. American Press Co.* (1936).

And again in 1938 this Court said:

"[The assistance of counsel] is one of the safeguards of the Sixth Amendment deemed necessary to insure fundamental human rights of life and liberty. . . . The Sixth Amendment stands as a constant admonition that if the constitutional safeguards it provides be lost, justice will not 'still be done,'" *Johnson v. Zerbst* (1938). . . .

In light of these many other prior decisions of this Court, it is not surprising that the Betts Court, when faced with the contention that "one charged with crime, who is unable to obtain counsel, must be furnished counsel by the State," conceded that "[e]xpressions in the opinions of this court lend color to the argument. . . ."

The fact is that in deciding as it did—that "appointment of counsel is not a fundamental right, essential to a fair trial"—the Court in *Betts v. Brady* made an abrupt break with its own well-considered precedents. In returning to these old precedents, sounder we believe than the new, we but restore constitutional principles established to achieve a fair system of justice. Not only these precedents but also reason and reflection require us to recognize that in our adversary system of criminal justice, any person haled into court, who is too poor to hire a lawyer, cannot be assured a fair trial unless counsel is provided for him. This seems to us to be an obvious truth. Governments, both state and federal, quite properly spend vast sums of money to establish machinery to try defendants accused of crime. Lawyers to prosecute are everywhere deemed essential to protect the public's interest in an orderly society. Similarly, there are few defendants charged with crime, few indeed, who fail to hire the best lawyers they can get to prepare and present their defenses. That government hires lawyers to prosecute and defendants who have the money hire lawyers to defend are the strongest indications of the widespread belief that lawyers in criminal courts are necessities, not luxuries. The right of one charged with crime to counsel may not be deemed fundamental and essential for fair trials in some countries, but it is in ours. From the very beginning, our state and national constitutions and laws have laid great emphasis on procedural and substantive safeguards designed to assure fair trials before impartial tribunals in which every defendant stands equal before the law. This noble ideal cannot be realized if the poor man charged with crime has to face his accusers without a lawyer to assist him. A defendant's need for a lawyer is nowhere better stated than in the moving words of Mr. Justice Sutherland in *Powell v. Alabama*:

"The right to be heard would be, in many cases, of little avail if it did not comprehend the right to be heard by counsel. Even the intelligent and educated layman has small and sometimes no skill in the science of law. If charged with crime, he is incapable, generally, of determining for himself whether the indictment is good or bad. He is unfamiliar with the rules of evidence. Left without the aid of counsel he may be put on trial without a proper charge, and convicted upon incompetent evidence, or evidence irrelevant to the issue or otherwise inadmissable. He lacks both the skill and knowledge adequately to prepare his defense, even though he have a perfect one. He requires the guiding hand of counsel at every step in the proceedings against him. Without it, though he be not guilty, he faces the danger of conviction because he does not know how to establish his innocence."

The Court in *Betts v. Brady* departed from the sound wisdom upon which the Court's holding in *Powell v. Alabama* rested. Florida, supported by two other States, has asked that *Betts v. Brady* be left intact. Twenty-two States, as friends of the Court, argue that Betts was "an anachronism when handed down" and that it should now be overruled. We agree.

The judgment is reversed and the cause is remanded to the Supreme Court of Florida for further action not inconsistent with this opinion.

Reversed.

Mr. Justice Douglas, while joining the opinion of the Court, wrote a separate opinion, saying in part:

My Brother Harlan is of the view that a guarantee of the Bill of Rights that is made applicable to the States by reason of the Fourteenth Amendment is a lesser version of that same guarantee as applied to the Federal Government. Mr. Justice Jackson shared the view. But that view has not prevailed and rights protected against state invasion by the Due Process Clause of the Fourteenth Amendment are not watered-down versions of what the Bill of Rights guarantees.

*M*r. Justice Clark, concurring in the result, wrote a separate opinion.

U.S. Supreme Court, 1963.

Critical Thinking

1. Given that 22 states went on record in support of the *Gideon v. Wainright* decision in 1963, while three spoke out in opposition, would you expect the balance of support to be any different today, and why?

2. Has the right to counsel in all cases become too extreme, in that not even the most minor of offenses can be excluded?

3. Is there a point at which the Supreme Court's authority to reverse a previous Court's judgment calls into question the sanctity of the authority itself?

Create Central

www.mhhe.com/createcentral

Internet References

The American Civil Liberties Union
www.aclu.org

Lee v. Weisman

Anthony M. Kennedy et al.

Learning Outcomes

After reading this selection, you should be able to:

1. Cite the essence of the establishment clause of the First Amendment.
2. Discuss the Supreme Court's substantial lack of unity in *Lee v. Weisman*.

In the 1992 decision of *Lee v. Weisman* (112 S. Ct. 2649), from which the following selection is taken, the U.S. Supreme Court articulated an opinion that had fundamental constitutional and political ramifications upon the interpretation of civil liberties and the establishment of religion by government. The judgment of the Court was a landmark decision because of its interpretation of the establishment clause of the First Amendment of the Constitution; specifically, the Court found unconstitutional and banned the delivery of religious invocations and benediction prayers at public school graduation ceremonies.

The First Amendment consists of two statements regarding religion, the establishment clause and the free exercise clause. The establishment clause prohibits Congress from imposing religion upon citizens through legislation and from drafting legislation denying religious freedom. The free exercise clause prohibits states from passing legislation denying the free exercise of religious beliefs since the First Amendment has been applied to the state governments through the due process clause of the Fourteenth Amendment. A strict separation of church and state is derived from the establishment clause, which has required the creation of a secular state.

On behalf of his daughter Deborah, Daniel Weisman sued school board officials in the public middle and high schools of Providence, Rhode Island, for authorizing clergy-led benediction prayers and invocations at school graduation ceremonies. The federal district and appellate courts ruled that religious prayers and the citing of God during public school graduation ceremonies were in violation of the establishment clause. The school board appealed the decision to the U.S. Supreme Court. Justice Anthony M. Kennedy delivered the opinion of the Court, affirming the rulings of the lower courts. The following selection includes two concurring opinions and a dissenting opinion, indicating that there was substantial disagreement in this case. The Supreme Court remains deeply divided in articulating precise and explicit guidelines defining church-state relations, and it continues to struggle in its opinions to lower or raise the wall between church and state.

Key Concept: the establishment clause of the First Amendment

*J*ustice KENNEDY delivers the opinion of the Court.

This case does not require us to revisit the difficult questions dividing us in recent cases, questions of the definition and full scope of the principles governing the extent of permitted accommodation by the State for the religious beliefs and practices of many of its citizens. See *Allegheny County v. Greater Pittsburgh ACLU*, 492 U.S. 573 (1989); *Wallace v. Jaffree*, 472 U.S. 38 (1985); *Lynch v. Donnelly*, 465 U.S. 668 (1984). For without reference to those principles in other contexts, the controlling precedents as they relate to prayer and religious exercise in primary and secondary public schools compel the holding here that the policy of the city of Providence is an unconstitutional one. We can decide the case without reconsidering the general constitutional framework by which public schools' efforts to accommodate religion are measured. Thus we do not accept the invitation of petitioners and amicus the United States to reconsider our decision in *Lemon v. Kurtzman*, 403 U.S. 602 (1971). The government involvement with religious activity in this case is pervasive, to the point of creating a state-sponsored and state-directed religious exercise in a public school. Conducting this formal religious observance conflicts with settled rules pertaining to prayer exercises for students, and that suffices to determine the question before us.

The principle that government may accommodate the free exercise of religion does not supersede the fundamental limitations imposed by the Establishment Clause. It is beyond dispute that, at a minimum, the Constitution guarantees that government may not coerce anyone to support or participate in religion or its exercise, or otherwise act in a way which establishes a [state] religion or religious faith, or tends to do so. *Lynch*. The State's involvement in the school prayers challenged today violates these central principles. . . .

We need not look beyond the circumstances of this case to see the phenomenon at work. The undeniable fact is that the school district's supervision and control of a high school graduation ceremony places public pressure, as well as peer pressure, on attending students to stand as a group or, at least, maintain respectful silence during the Invocation and Benediction. This pressure, though subtle and indirect, can be as real as any overt compulsion. Of course, in our culture standing or remaining silent can signify adherence to a view or simple respect for the views of others. And no doubt some persons who have no desire to join a prayer have little objection to standing as a sign of respect for those who do. But for the dissenter of high school age, who has a reasonable perception that she is being forced by the State to pray in a manner her conscience will not allow, the injury is no less real. There can be no doubt that for many, if not most, of the students at the graduation, the act of standing or remaining silent was an expression of participation in the Rabbi's prayer. That was the very point of the religious exercise. It is of little comfort to a dissenter, then, to be told that for her the act of standing or remaining in silence signifies mere respect, rather than participation. What matters is that, given our social conventions, a reasonable dissenter in this milieu could believe that the group exercise signified her own participation or approval of it. . . .

The injury caused by the government's action, and the reason why Daniel and Deborah Weisman object to it, is that the State, in a school setting, in effect required participation in a religious exercise. It is, we concede, a brief exercise during which the individual can concentrate on joining its message, meditate on her own religion, or let her mind wander. But the embarrassment and the intrusion of the religious exercise cannot be refuted by arguing that these prayers, and similar ones to be said in the future, are of a de minimis character. To do so would be an affront to the Rabbi who offered them and to all those for whom the prayers were an essential and profound recognition of divine authority. And for the same reason, we think that the intrusion is greater than the two minutes or so of time consumed for prayers like these. . . .

Inherent differences between the public school system and a session of a State Legislature distinguish this case from *Marsh v. Chambers*, 463 U.S. 783 (1983). The considerations we have raised in objection to the invocation and benediction are in many respects similar to the arguments we considered in *Marsh*. But there are also obvious differences. The atmosphere at the opening of a session of a state legislature where adults are free to enter and leave with little comment and for any number of reasons cannot compare with the constraining potential of

the one school event most important for the student to attend. The influence and force of a formal exercise in a school graduation are far greater than the prayer exercise we condoned in *Marsh*. The *Marsh* majority in fact gave specific recognition to this distinction and placed particular reliance on it in upholding the prayers at issue there. Today's case is different. At a high school graduation, teachers and principals must and do retain a high degree of control over the precise contents of the program, the speeches, the timing, the movements, the dress, and the decorum of the students. In this atmosphere the state-imposed character of an invocation and benediction by clergy selected by the school combine to make the prayer a state-sanctioned religious exercise in which the student was left with no alternative but to submit. . . .

For the reasons we have stated, the judgment of the Court of Appeals is Affirmed.

*J*ustice BLACKMUN, with whom Justice STEVENS and Justice O'CONNOR join, concurring.

The Court holds that the graduation prayer is unconstitutional because the State "in effect required participation in a religious exercise." Although our precedents make clear that proof of government coercion is not necessary to prove an Establishment Clause violation, it is sufficient. Government pressure to participate in a religious activity is an obvious indication that the government is endorsing or promoting religion.

But it is not enough that the government restrain from compelling religious practices: it must not engage in them either. The Court repeatedly has recognized that a violation of the Establishment Clause is not predicated on coercion. The Establishment Clause proscribes public schools from "conveying or attempting to convey a message that religion or a particular religious belief is favored or preferred," *County of Allegheny v. ACLU* (1989), even if the schools do not actually "impose pressure upon a student to participate in a religious activity." *Westside Community Bd. of Ed. v. Mergens*, 496 U.S. 226 (1990) (KENNEDY, J., concurring).

There is no doubt that attempts to aid religion through government coercion jeopardize freedom of conscience. . . .

Our decisions have gone beyond prohibiting coercion, however, because the Court has recognized that "the fullest possible scope of religious liberty," *Schempp*, entails more than freedom from coercion. The Establishment Clause protects religious liberty on a grand scale; it is a social compact that guarantees for generations a democracy and a strong religious community—both essential to safeguarding religious liberty. . . .

*J*ustice SOUTER, with whom Justice STEVENS and Justice O'CONNOR join, concurring.

That government must remain neutral in matters of religion does not foreclose it from ever taking religion into account. The State may "accommodate" the free exercise of religion by relieving people from generally applicable rules that interfere with their religious callings. See, e.g., *Corporation of Presiding Bishop of Church of Jesus Christ of Latter-Day Saints v. Amos*, 483 U.S. 327 (1987); see also *Sherbert v. Verner*, 374 U.S. 398 (1963). Contrary to the views of some, such accommodation does not necessarily signify an official endorsement of religious observance over disbelief. . . .

Whatever else may define the scope of accommodation permissible under the Establishment Clause, one requirement is clear: accommodation must lift a discernible burden on the free exercise of religion. Concern for the position of religious individuals in the modern regulatory state cannot justify official solicitude for a religious practice unburdened by general rules; such gratuitous largesse would effectively favor religion over disbelief. By these lights one easily sees that, in sponsoring the graduation prayers at issue here, the State has crossed the line from permissible accommodation to unconstitutional establishment.

*J*ustice SCALIA, with whom the CHIEF JUSTICE, Justice WHITE, and Justice THOMAS join, dissenting.

From our Nation's origin, prayer has been a prominent part of governmental ceremonies and proclamations. The Declaration of Independence, the document marking our birth as a separate people, "appealed to the Supreme Judge of the world for the rectitude of our intentions" and avowed "a firm reliance on the protection of divine Providence." In his first inaugural address, after swearing his oath of office on a Bible, George Washington deliberately made a prayer a part of his first official act as President. . . . Such supplications have been a characteristic feature of inaugural addresses ever since. . . .

[A] tradition of Thanksgiving Proclamations—with their religious theme of prayerful gratitude to God—has been adhered to by almost every President. . . .

The Court presumably would separate graduation invocations and benedictions from other instances of public "preservation and transmission of religious beliefs" on the ground that they involve "psychological coercion." I find it a sufficient embarrassment that our Establishment Clause jurisprudence regarding holiday displays, has come to "require scrutiny more commonly associated with interior decorators than with the judiciary." *American Jewish Congress v. Chicago*, 827 F. 2d 120 (Easterbrook, J., dissenting). But interior decorating is a rock-hard science compared to psychology practiced by amateurs. A few citations of "research in psychology" that have no particular bearing upon the precise issue here, cannot disguise the fact that the Court has gone beyond the realm where judges know what they are doing. The Court's argument that state officials have "coerced" students to take part in the invocation and benediction at graduation ceremonies is, not to put too fine a point on it, incoherent.

The Court identifies two "dominant facts" that it says dictate its ruling that invocations and benedictions at public-school graduation ceremonies violate the Establishment Clause. Neither of them is in any relevant sense true.

The Court declares that students' "attendance and participation in the [invocation and benediction] are in a fair and real sense obligatory." But what exactly is this "fair and real sense"? According to the Court, students at graduation who want "to avoid the fact or appearance of participation," in the invocation and benediction are psychologically obligated by "public pressure, as well as peer pressure, . . . to stand as a group or, at least, maintain respectful silence" during those prayers. This assertion—the very linchpin of the Court's opinion—is almost as intriguing for what it does not say as for what it says. It does not say, for example, that students are psychologically coerced to bow their heads, place their hands in a Drer-like prayer position, pay attention to the prayers, utter "Amen," or in fact pray. (Perhaps further intensive psychological research remains to be done on these matters.) It claims only that students are psychologically coerced "to stand . . . or, at least, maintain respectful silence." Both halves of this disjunctive (both of which must amount to the fact or appearance of participation in prayer if the Court's analysis is to survive on its own terms) merit particular attention.

To begin with the latter: The Court's notion that a student who simply sits in "respectful silence" during the invocation and benediction (when all others are standing) has somehow joined—or would somehow be perceived as having joined—in the prayers is nothing short of ludicrous. We indeed live in a vulgar age. But surely "our social conventions" have not coarsened to the point that anyone who does not stand on his chair and shout obscenities can reasonably be deemed to have assented to everything said in his presence. Since the Court does not dispute that students exposed to prayer at graduation ceremonies retain (despite "subtle coercive pressures") the free will to sit, there is absolutely no basis for the Court's decision. It is fanciful enough to say that "a reasonable dissenter," standing head erect in a class of bowed heads, "could believe that the group exercise signified her own participation or approval of it." It is beyond the absurd to say that she could entertain such a belief while pointedly declining to rise.

But let us assume the very worst, that the nonparticipating graduate is "subtly coerced" . . . to stand! Even that half of the disjunctive does not remotely establish a "participation" (or an "appearance of participation") in a religious exercise. The Court acknowledges that "in our culture standing . . . can signify adherence to a view or simple respect for the views of others." (Much more often the latter than the former, I think, except perhaps in the proverbial town meeting, where one votes by standing.) But if it is a permissible inference that one who is standing is doing so simply out of respect for the prayers of others that are in progress, then how can it possibly be said that a "reasonable dissenter . . . could believe that the group exercise signified her own participation or approval"? Quite obviously, it cannot. I may add, more-over, that maintaining respect for the religious observances of others is a fundamental civic virtue that government (including the public schools) can and should cultivate—so that even if it were the case that the displaying of such respect might be mistaken for taking part in the prayer, I would deny that the dissenter's interest in avoiding even the false appearance of participation constitution-ally trumps the government's interest in fostering respect for religion generally.

The opinion manifests that the Court itself has not given careful consideration to its test of psychological coercion. For if it had, how could it observe, with no hint of concern or disapproval, that students stood for the Pledge of Allegiance, which immediately preceded Rabbi Gutterman's invocation? The government can, of course, no more coerce political orthodoxy than religious ortho-doxy. *West Virginia Board of Education v. Barnette*, 319 U.S. 624 (1943). Moreover, since the Pledge of Allegiance has been revised since *Barnette* to include the phrase "under God," recital of the Pledge would appear to raise the same Establishment Clause issue as the invocation and benediction. If students were psychologically coerced to remain standing during the invocation, they must also have been psychologically coerced, moments before, to stand for (and thereby, in the Court's view, take part in or appear to take part in) the Pledge. Must the Pledge there-fore be barred from the public schools (both from gradu-ation ceremonies and from the classroom)? In *Barnette* we held that a public-school student could not be compelled to recite the Pledge; we did not even hint that she could not be compelled to observe respectful silence—indeed, even to stand in respectful silence—when those who wished to recite it did so. Logically, that ought to be the next project for the Court's bulldozer. . . .

The deeper flaw in the Court's opinion does not lie in its wrong answer to the question whether there was state-induced "peer-pressure" coercion; it lies, rather, in the Court's making violation of the Establishment Clause hinge on such a precious question. The coer-cion that was a hallmark of historical establishments of religion was coercion of religious orthodoxy and of financial support by force of law and threat of penalty. Typically, attendance at the state church was required; only clergy of the official church could lawfully perform sacraments; and dissenters, if tolerated, faced an array of civil disabilities. . . .

Our religion-clause jurisprudence has become bedev-iled (so to speak) by reliance on formulaic abstractions that are not derived from, but positively conflict with, our long-accepted constitutional traditions. Foremost among these has been the so-called *Lemon* test, see *Lemon*

v. Kurtzman, 403 U.S. 602 (1971), which has received well-earned criticism from many members of this Court. The Court today demonstrates the irrelevance of *Lemon* by essentially ignoring it, and the interment of that case may be the one happy byproduct of the Court's otherwise lamentable decision. Unfortunately, however, the Court has replaced *Lemon* with its psycho-coercion test, which suffers the double disability of having no roots whatever in our people's historic practice, and being as infinitely expandable as the reasons for psychotherapy itself. . . .

The reader has been told much in this case about the personal interest of Mr. Weisman and his daughter, and very little about the personal interests on the other side. They are not inconsequential. . . .

The narrow context of the present case involves a com-munity's celebration of one of the milestones in its young citizens' lives, and it is a bold step for this Court to seek to banish from that occasion, and from thousands of similar celebrations throughout this land, the expression of grati-tude to God that a majority of the community wishes to make. The issue before us today is not the abstract philo-sophical question whether the alternative of frustrating this desire of a religious majority is to be preferred over the alternative of imposing "psychological coercion," or a feeling of exclusion, upon nonbelievers. Rather, the ques-tion is whether a mandatory choice in favor of the former has been imposed by the United States Constitution. As the age-old practices of our people show, the answer to that question is not at all in doubt. . . . For the foregoing reasons, I dissent.

Critical Thinking

1. Should respect for others' religious observances be consid-ered a fundamental civic virtue that government can and should cultivate?
2. Given the ruling in *Lee v. Weisman*, is it appropriate, or even constitutional, to condone the phrase "under God" in the recitation of the Pledge of Allegiance in public schools?
3. Is it necessarily remiss of the Supreme Court not to have fully regarded the "other side" of the case (i.e., the vast majority of graduation participants, who either supported or had no problem with the invocations and benedictions) as consequential?

Create Central

www.mhhe.com/createcentral

Internet References

The American Civil Liberties Union
www.aclu.org

Roe v. Wade

Harry A. Blackmun

Learning Outcomes

After reading this selection, you should be able to:

1. Discuss the "relatively recent vintage" of U.S. states' criminal abortion laws in 1973.
2. Describe the serious health concerns associated with illegal abortions.
3. Identify previous Supreme Court cases relevantly cited in *Roe v. Wade*.

In the 1973 landmark decision *Roe v. Wade* (410 U.S. 113), from which the following selection is taken, the U.S. Supreme Court expressed an opinion on probably the most controversial issue in American politics of the twentieth century. The Court's decision in this case had enormous constitutional and political implications for the interpretation of civil liberties. The reasoning of the U.S. Supreme Court reflected the classic decision that a woman's right to obtain an abortion is protected by the U.S. Constitution—specifically, that a linkage exists between the right to terminate a pregnancy and the constitutional right to privacy. Although the Constitution does not explicitly articulate a concept of privacy or its potential substantive range, Americans share a deep ideological commitment to such a right and assume its existence.

The Supreme Court's most comprehensive expression of the right to privacy was formulated in 1965 in a case filed by Planned Parenthood, *Griswold v. Connecticut* (381 U.S. 479). In this case, the Court found unconstitutional a Connecticut law banning the use of birth control methods. The *Griswold* decision provided a conceptual framework and an immediate Court precedent for *Roe v. Wade*.

Norma McCorvey was a poor, 21-year-old, pregnant carnival employee and the mother of one child. Since she was unable to obtain a legal abortion due to Texas's very strict law, McCorvey gave up her child for adoption. Under the pseudonym Jane Roe, McCorvey permitted Texas attorney Sarah Weddington to challenge the Texas statute before the U.S. Supreme Court in her behalf. Justice Harry A. Blackmun delivered the opinion of the Court, ruling that the Texas law violated a woman's constitutionally protected right to privacy, specifically, the right to terminate a pregnancy. The Court argued that the Fourteenth Amendment's guarantee of life, liberty, and property does not apply to an unborn fetus.

Pro-life organizations have vigorously fought to overturn *Roe v. Wade* and have lobbied state legislatures to impose stricter regulations on abortions. Although the Court has generally upheld *Roe v. Wade* and a woman's constitutional right to secure an abortion, recent decisions have greatly limited the scope of *Roe v. Wade* by permitting states to impose some restrictions.

Key Concept: privacy as a constitutional right

*M*r. Justice Blackmun delivered the opinion of the Court, saying in part: The principal thrust of appellant's attack on the Texas statutes is that they improperly invade a right, said to be possessed by the pregnant woman, to choose to terminate her pregnancy. Appellant would discover this right in the concept of personal "liberty" embodied in the Fourteenth Amendment's Due Process Clause; or in personal, marital, familial, and sexual privacy said to be protected by the Bill of Rights or its penumbras, see *Griswold v. Connecticut* (1965); *Eisenstadt v. Baird* (1972); (White, J., concurring); or among those rights reserved to the people by the Ninth Amendment, *Griswold v. Connecticut*

(Goldberg, J., concurring). Before addressing this claim, we feel it desirable briefly to survey, in several aspects, the history of abortion, for such insight as that history may afford us, and then to examine the state purposes and interests behind the criminal abortion laws.

*I*t perhaps is not generally appreciated that the restrictive criminal abortion laws in effect in a majority of States today are of relatively recent vintage. Those laws, generally proscribing abortion or its attempt at any time during pregnancy except when necessary to preserve the pregnant woman's life, are not of ancient or even of common law origin. Instead, they derive from statutory changes effected, for the most part, in the latter half of the 19th century. . . .

Three reasons have been advanced to explain historically the enactment of criminal abortion laws in the 19th century and to justify their continued existence. It has been argued occasionally that these laws were the product of a Victorian social concern to discourage illicit sexual conduct. Texas, however, does not advance this justification in the present case, and it appears that no court or commentator has taken the argument seriously. The appellants and amici contend, moreover, that this is not a proper state purpose at all and suggest that, if it were, the Texas statutes are overbroad in protecting it since the law fails to distinguish between married and unwed mothers.

A second reason is concerned with abortion as a medical procedure. When most criminal abortion laws were first enacted, the procedure was a hazardous one for the woman. This was particularly true prior to the development of antisepsis. Antiseptic techniques, of course, were based on discoveries by Lister, Pasteur, and others first announced in 1867, but were not generally accepted and employed until about the turn of the century. Abortion mortality was high. Even after 1900, and perhaps until as late as the development of antibiotics in the 1940's, standard modern techniques such as dilation and curettage were not nearly so safe as they are today. Thus it has been argued that a State's real concern in enacting a criminal abortion law was to protect the pregnant woman, that is, to restrain her from submitting to a procedure that placed her life in serious jeopardy.

Modern medical techniques have altered this situation. Appellants and various amici refer to medical data indicating that abortion in early pregnancy, that is, prior to the end of first trimester, although not without its risk, is now relatively safe. Mortality rates for women undergoing early abortions, where the procedure is legal, appear to be as low as or lower than the rates for normal childbirth. Consequently, any interest of the State in protecting the woman from an inherently hazardous procedure, except when it would be equally dangerous for her to forego it, has largely disappeared. Of course, important state interests in the area of health and medical standards do remain. The State has a legitimate interest in seeing to it that abortion, like any other medical procedure, is performed under circumstances that insure maximum safety for the patient. This interest obviously extends at least to the performing physician and his staff, to the facilities involved, to the availability of after-care, and to adequate provision for any complication or emergency that might arise. The prevalence of high mortality rates at illegal "abortion mills" strengthens, rather than weakens, the State's interest in regulating the conditions under which abortions are performed. Moreover, the risk to the woman increases as her pregnancy continues. Thus the State retains a definite interest in protecting the

woman's own health and safety when an abortion is proposed at a late stage of pregnancy.

The third reason is the State's interest—some phrase it in terms of duty—in protecting prenatal life. Some of the argument for this justification rests on the theory that a new human life is present from the moment of conception. The State's interest and general obligation to protect life then extends, it is argued, to prenatal life. Only when the life of the pregnant mother herself is at stake, balanced against the life she carries within her, should the interest of the embryo or fetus not prevail. Logically, of course, a legitimate State interest in this area need not stand or fall on acceptance of the belief that life begins at conception or at some other point prior to live birth. In assessing the State's interest, recognition may be given to the less rigid claim that as long as at least *potential* life is involved, the State may assert interests beyond the protection of the pregnant woman alone.

Parties challenging state abortion laws have sharply disputed in some courts the contention that a purpose of these laws, when enacted, was to protect prenatal life. . . .

It is with these interests, and the weight to be attached to them, that this case is concerned.

The Constitution does not explicitly mention any right of privacy. In a line of decisions, however, going back perhaps as far as *Union Pacific R. Co. v. Botsford* (1891), the Court has recognized that a right of personal privacy, or a guarantee of certain areas or zones of privacy, does exist under the Constitution. In varying contexts the Court or individual Justices have indeed found at least the roots of that right in the First Amendment, *Stanley v. Georgia* (1969); in the Fourth and Fifth Amendments, *Terry v. Ohio* (1968), *Katz v. United States* (1967) . . . ; in the penumbras of the Bill of Rights, *Griswold v. Connecticut* (1965); in the Ninth Amendment; or in the concept of liberty guaranteed by the first section of the Fourteenth Amendment, see *Meyer v. Nebraska* (1923). These decisions make it clear that only personal rights that can be deemed "fundamental" or "implicit in the concept of ordered liberty," *Palko v. Connecticut* (1937), are included in this guarantee of personal privacy. They also make it clear that the right has some extension to activities relating to marriage, *Loving v. Virginia* (1967), procreation, *Skinner v. Oklahoma* (1942), contraception, *Eisenstadt v. Baird* (1972). . . .

This right of privacy, whether it be founded in the Fourteenth Amendment's concept of personal liberty and restrictions upon state action, as we feel it is, or, as the District Court determined, in the Ninth Amendment's reservation of rights to the people, is broad enough to encompass a woman's decision whether or not to terminate her pregnancy. The detriment that the State would impose upon the pregnant woman by denying this choice altogether is apparent. Specific and direct harm medically diagnosable even in early pregnancy may be involved. Maternity, or additional offspring, may force upon the woman a distressful life and future. Psychological harm may be imminent. Mental and physical health may be taxed by child care. There is also the distress, for all concerned, associated with the unwanted child, and there is the problem of bringing a child into a family already unable, psychologically and otherwise, to care for it. In other cases, as in this one, the additional difficulties and continuing stigma of unwed motherhood may be involved. All these are factors the woman and her responsible physician necessarily will consider in consultation. . . .

We therefore conclude that the right of personal privacy includes the abortion decision, but that this right is not unqualified and must be considered against state interests in regulation.

Where certain "fundamental rights" are involved, the Court has held that regulation limiting these rights may be justified only by a "compelling state interest," *Kramer v. Union Free School District* (1969), *Shapiro v. Thompson* (1969), . . . and that legislative enactments must be narrowly drawn to express only the legitimate state interests at stake. *Griswold v. Connecticut* (1965). . . .

*T*he District Court held that the appellee failed to meet his burden of demonstrating that the Texas statute's infringement upon Roe's rights was necessary to support a compelling state interest. . . . Appellee argues that the State's determination to recognize and protect prenatal life from and after conception constitutes a compelling state interest. As noted above, we do not agree fully with either formulation.

A. The appellee and certain amici argue that the fetus is a "person" within the language and meaning of the Fourteenth Amendment. In support of this they outline at length and in detail the well-known facts of fetal development. If this suggestion of personhood is established, the appellant's case, of course, collapses, for the fetus' right to life is then guaranteed specifically by the Amendment. The appellant conceded as much on reargument. On the other hand, the appellee conceded on reargument that no case could be cited that holds that a fetus is a person within the meaning of the Fourteenth Amendment.

The Constitution does not define "person" in so many words. Section 1 of the Fourteenth Amendment contains three references to "person." The first, in defining "citizens," speaks of "persons born or naturalized in the United States." The word also appears both in the Due Process Clause and in the Equal Protection Clause. "Person" is used in other places in the Constitution. . . . But in nearly all these instances, the use of the word is such that it has application only postnatally. None indicates, with any assurance, that it has any possible prenatal application. All this, together with our observation, that throughout the major portion of the 19th century prevailing legal abortion practices were far freer than they are today, persuades us that the word "person," as used in the Fourteenth Amendment, does not include the unborn. . . .

B. The pregnant woman cannot be isolated in her privacy. She carries an embryo and, later, a fetus, if one accepts the medical definitions of the developing young in the human uterus. . . . The situation therefore is inherently different from marital intimacy, or bedroom possession of obscene material, or marriage, or procreation, or education, with which Eisenstadt, Griswold, Stanley, Loving, Skinner, Pierce, and Meyer were respectively concerned. As we have intimated above, it is reasonable and appropriate for a State to decide that at some point in time another interest, that of health of the mother or that of potential human life, becomes significantly involved. The woman's privacy is no longer sole and any right of privacy she possesses must be measured accordingly.

Texas urges that, apart from the Fourteenth Amendment, life begins at conception and is present throughout pregnancy, and that, therefore, the State has a compelling interest in protecting that life from and after conception. We need not resolve the difficult question of when life begins. When those trained in the respective disciplines of medicine, philosophy, and theology are unable to arrive at any consensus, the judiciary, at this point in the development of man's knowledge, is not in a position to speculate as to the answer.

It should be sufficient to note briefly the wide divergence of thinking on this most sensitive and difficult question. . . .

*I*n view of all this, we do not agree that, by adopting one theory of life, Texas may override the rights of the pregnant woman that are at stake. We repeat, however, that the State does have an important and legitimate interest in preserving and protecting the health of the pregnant woman, whether she be a resident of the State or a nonresident who seeks medical consultation and treatment there, and that it has still another important and legitimate interest in protecting the potentiality of human life. These interests are separate and distinct. Each grows in substantiality as the woman approaches term and, at a point during pregnancy, each becomes "compelling." . . .

*T*o summarize and to repeat:
1. A state criminal abortion statute of the current Texas type, that excepts from criminality only a *life saving* procedure on behalf of the mother, without regard to pregnancy stage and without recognition of the other interests involved, is violative of the Due Process Clause of the Fourteenth Amendment.

(a) For the stage prior to approximately the end of the first trimester, the abortion decision and its effectuation must be left to the medical judgment of the pregnant woman's attending physician.

(b) For the stage subsequent to approximately the end of the first trimester, the State, in promoting its interest in the health of the mother, may, if it chooses, regulate the abortion procedure in ways that are reasonably related to maternal health.

(c) For the stage subsequent to viability the State, in promoting its interest in the potentiality of human life, may, if it chooses, regulate, and even proscribe, abortion except where it is necessary, in appropriate medical judgment, for the preservation of the life or health of the mother.

2. The State may define the term "physician," as it has been employed in the preceding numbered paragraphs of this Part XI of this opinion, to mean only a physician currently licensed by the State, and may proscribe any abortion by a person who is not a physician as so defined.

In *Doe v. Bolton* procedural requirements contained in one of the modern abortion statutes are considered. That opinion and this one, of course, are to be read together. . . .

Mr. Chief Justice Burger concurred.

Mr. Justice Douglas concurred. . . .

Mr. Justice Rehnquist, dissenting, said in part:

. . . I have difficulty in concluding, as the Court does, that the right of "privacy" is involved in this case. Texas by the statute here challenged bars the performance of a medical abortion by a licensed physician on a plaintiff such as Roe. A transaction resulting in an operation such as this is not "private" in the ordinary usage of that word. . . .

If the Court means by the term "privacy" no more than that the claim of a person to be free from unwanted state regulation of consensual transactions may be a form of "liberty" protected by the Fourteenth Amendment, there is no doubt that similar claims have been upheld in our earlier decisions on the basis of that liberty. I agree with the statement of Mr. Justice Stewart in his concurring opinion that the "liberty," against deprivation of which without due process the Fourteenth Amendment protects, embraces more than the rights found in the Bill of Rights. But that liberty is not guaranteed absolutely against deprivation, but only against deprivation without due process of law. The test traditionally applied in the area of social and economic legislation is whether or not a law such as that challenged has a rational relation to a valid state objective. . . . But the Court's sweeping invalidation of any restrictions on abortion during the first trimester is impossible to justify under that standard, and the conscious weighing of competing factors which the Court's opinion apparently substitutes for the established test is far more appropriate to a legislative judgment than to a judicial one.

The Court eschews the history of the Fourteenth Amendment in its reliance on the "compelling state interest" test. . . . But the Court adds a new wrinkle to this test by transposing it from the legal considerations associated with the Equal Protection Clause of the Fourteenth Amendment to this case arising under the Due Process Clause of the Fourteenth Amendment. Unless I misapprehend the consequences of this transplanting of the "compelling state interest test," the Court's opinion will accomplish the seemingly impossible feat of leaving this area of the law more confused than it found it.

While the Court's opinion quotes from the dissent of Mr. Justice Holmes in Lochner v. New York (1905), the result it reaches is more closely attuned to the majority opinion of Mr. Justice Peckham in that case. As in Lochner and similar cases applying substantive due process standards to economic and social welfare legislation, the adoption of the compelling state interest standard will inevitably require this Court to examine the legislative policies and pass on the wisdom of these policies in the very process of deciding whether a particular state interest put forward may or may not be "compelling." . . .

The fact that a majority of the States, reflecting after all the majority sentiment in those States, have had restrictions on abortions for at least a century is a strong indication, it seems to me, that the asserted right to an abortion is not "so rooted in the traditions and conscience of our people as to be ranked as fundamental," *Snyder v. Massachusetts* (1934). . . .

Mr. Justice White, with whom Mr. Justice Rehnquist joins, dissented.

Critical Thinking

1. What is the likelihood that, in revisiting the *Roe v. Wade* decision, any sitting Supreme Court will ever produce a unanimous opinion?
2. How crucial to the abortion debate is the right to privacy?
3. In future deliberations at the Supreme Court level, how much consideration should be given to the fact that Norma McCorvey ("Roe") is now an outspoken pro-lifer who has petitioned for the overturning of *Roe v. Wade*?

Create Central

www.mhhe.com/createcentral

Internet References

The American Civil Liberties Union
www.aclu.org

Supreme Court of the United States, 1973.

Unit 5: Civil Rights

Prepared by: James Newman, *University of Maryland University College*

Grutter v. Bollinger et al.

Sandra Day O'Connor

Learning Outcomes

After reading this selection, you should be able to:

1. Understand the argument for using affirmative action to create diversity.
2. Explain why the notion of affirmative action is used in contemporary society.

This case upholds affirmative action policies of the University of Michigan Law School. The case supports the notion a Law School may have a compelling interest in promoting class diversity. It also supports the notion of using race conscious admission policies to advantage applicants of 'underrepresented minority groups.' This ruling does not overturn a previous ruling, Regents of the University of California v. Bakke in that setting quotas for applicants is not permitted.

Key concept: affirmative action

The University of Michigan Law School (Law School), one of the Nation's top law schools, follows an official admissions policy that seeks to achieve student body diversity through compliance with *Regents of Univ. of Cal.* v. *Bakke,* 438 U.S. 265. Focusing on students' academic ability coupled with a flexible assessment of their talents, experiences, and potential, the policy requires admissions officials to evaluate each applicant based on all the information available in the file, including a personal statement, letters of recommendation, an essay describing how the applicant will contribute to Law School life and diversity, and the applicant's undergraduate grade point average (GPA) and Law School Admission Test (LSAT) score. Additionally, officials must look beyond grades and scores to so-called "soft variables," such as recommenders' enthusiasm, the quality of the undergraduate institution and the applicant's essay, and the areas and difficulty of undergraduate course selection. The policy does not define diversity solely in terms of racial and ethnic status and does not restrict the types of diversity contributions eligible for "substantial weight," but it does reaffirm the Law School's commitment to diversity with special reference to the inclusion of African-American, Hispanic, and Native-American students, who otherwise might not be represented in the student body in meaningful numbers. By enrolling a "critical mass" of underrepresented minority students, the policy seeks to ensure their ability to contribute to the Law School's character and to the legal profession.

When the Law School denied admission to petitioner Grutter, a white Michigan resident with a 3.8 GPA and 161 LSAT score, she filed this suit, alleging that respondents had discriminated against her on the basis of race in violation of the Fourteenth Amendment, Title VI of the Civil Rights Act of 1964, and 42 U.S.C. § 1981; that she was rejected because the Law School uses race as a "predominant" factor, giving applicants belonging to certain minority groups a significantly greater chance of admission than students with similar credentials from disfavored racial groups; and that respondents had no compelling interest to justify that use of race. The District Court found the Law School's use of race as an admissions factor unlawful. The Sixth Circuit reversed, holding that Justice Powell's opinion in *Bakke* was binding precedent establishing diversity as a compelling state interest, and that the Law School's use of race was narrowly tailored because race was merely a "potential 'plus' factor" and because the Law School's program was virtually identical to the Harvard admissions program described approvingly by Justice Powell and appended to his *Bakke* opinion.

Held: The Law School's narrowly tailored use of race in admissions decisions to further a compelling interest in obtaining the educational benefits that flow from a diverse student body is not prohibited by the Equal Protection Clause, Title VI, or § 1981. Pp. 322–344.

(a) In the landmark *Bakke* case, this Court reviewed a medical school's racial set-aside program that reserved 16 out of 100 seats for members of certain minority groups. The decision produced six separate opinions, none of which commanded a majority. Four Justices would have upheld the program on the ground that the government can use race to remedy disadvantages cast on minorities by past racial prejudice. 438 U.S., at 325. Four other Justices would have struck the program down on statutory grounds. *Id.,* at 408. Justice Powell, announcing the Court's judgment, provided a fifth vote not only for invalidating the program, but also for reversing the state court's injunction against any use of race whatsoever. In a part of his opinion that was joined by no other Justice, Justice Powell expressed his view that attaining a diverse student body was the only interest asserted by the university that survived scrutiny. *Id.,* at 311. Grounding his analysis in the academic freedom that "long has been viewed as a special concern of the First Amendment," *id.,* at 312, 314, Justice Powell emphasized that the " 'nation's future depends upon leaders trained through wide exposure' to the ideas and mores of students as diverse as this Nation." *Id.,* at 313. However, he also emphasized that "[i]t is not an interest in simple ethnic diversity, in which a specified percentage of the student body is in effect guaranteed to be members of selected ethnic groups," that can justify using race. *Id.,* at 315. Rather, "[t]he diversity that furthers a compelling state interest encompasses a far broader array of qualifications and characteristics of which racial or ethnic origin is but a single though important element." *Ibid.* Since *Bakke,* Justice Powell's opinion has been the touchstone for constitutional analysis of race-conscious admissions policies. Public and private universities across the Nation have modeled their own admissions programs on Justice Powell's views. Courts, however, have struggled to discern whether Justice Powell's diversity rationale is binding precedent. The Court finds it unnecessary to decide this issue because the Court endorses Justice Powell's view that student body diversity is a compelling state interest in the context of university admissions. Pp. 322–325.

(b) All government racial classifications must be analyzed by a reviewing court under strict scrutiny. *Adarand Constructors, Inc.* v. *Peña,* 515 U.S. 200, 227. But not all such uses are invalidated by strict scrutiny. Race-based action necessary to further a compelling governmental interest does not violate the Equal Protection Clause so long as it is narrowly tailored to further that interest. *E.g., Shaw* v. *Hunt,* 517 U.S. 899, 908. Context matters when reviewing such action. See *Gomillion* v. *Lightfoot,* 364 U.S. 339, 343–344. Not every decision influenced by race is equally objectionable, and strict scrutiny is designed to

provide a framework for carefully examining the importance and the sincerity of the government's reasons for using race in a particular context. Pp. 326–327.

(c) The Court endorses Justice Powell's view that student body diversity is a compelling state interest that can justify using race in university admissions. The Court defers to the Law School's educational judgment that diversity is essential to its educational mission. The Court's scrutiny of that interest is no less strict for taking into account complex educational judgments in an area that lies primarily within the university's expertise. See, *e.g., Bakke,* 438 U.S., at 319, n. 53 (opinion of Powell, J.). Attaining a diverse student body is at the heart of the Law School's proper institutional mission, and its "good faith" is "presumed" absent "a showing to the contrary." *Id.,* at 318–319. Enrolling a "critical mass" of minority students simply to assure some specified percentage of a particular group merely because of its race or ethnic origin would be patently unconstitutional. *E.g., id.,* at 307. But the Law School defines its critical mass concept by reference to the substantial, important, and laudable educational benefits that diversity is designed to produce, including cross-racial understanding and the breaking down of racial stereotypes. The Law School's claim is further bolstered by numerous expert studies and reports showing that such diversity promotes learning outcomes and better prepares students for an increasingly diverse work force, for society, and for the legal profession. Major American businesses have made clear that the skills needed in today's increasingly global marketplace can only be developed through exposure to widely diverse people, cultures, ideas, and view-points. High-ranking retired officers and civilian military leaders assert that a highly qualified, racially diverse officer corps is essential to national security. Moreover, because universities, and in particular, law schools, represent the training ground for a large number of the Nation's leaders, *Sweatt* v. *Painter,* 339 U.S. 629, 634, the path to leadership must be visibly open to talented and qualified individuals of every race and ethnicity. Thus, the Law School has a compelling interest in attaining a diverse student body. Pp. 327–333.

(d) The Law School's admissions program bears the hallmarks of a narrowly tailored plan. To be narrowly tailored, a race-conscious admissions program cannot "insulat[e] each category of applicants with certain desired qualifications from competition with all other applicants." *Bakke,* 438 U.S., at 315 (opinion of Powell, J.). Instead, it may consider race or ethnicity only as a " 'plus' in a particular applicant's file"; *i.e.,* it must be "flexible enough to consider all pertinent elements of diversity in light of the particular qualifications of each applicant, and to place them on the same footing for consideration, although not necessarily according them the same weight," *id.,* at 317. It follows that universities cannot establish quotas for members of certain racial or ethnic groups or put them on separate admissions tracks. See *id.,* at 315–316. The Law School's admissions program, like the Harvard plan approved by Justice Powell, satisfies these requirements. Moreover, the program is flexible enough to ensure that each applicant is evaluated as an individual and not in a way that makes race or ethnicity the defining feature of the application. See *id.,* at 317. The Law School engages in a highly individualized, holistic review of each applicant's file, giving serious consideration to all the ways an applicant might contribute to a diverse educational environment. There is no policy, either *de jure* or *de facto,* of automatic acceptance or rejection based on any single "soft" variable. *Gratz* v. *Bollinger, ante,* p. 244, distinguished. Also, the program adequately ensures that all factors that may contribute to diversity are meaningfully considered alongside race. Moreover, the Law School frequently accepts nonminority applicants with grades and test scores lower than underrepresented minority applicants (and other nonminority applicants) who are rejected. The Court rejects the argument that the Law School should have used other race-neutral means to obtain the educational benefits of student body diversity, *e.g.,* a lottery system or decreasing the emphasis on GPA and LSAT scores. Narrow tailoring does not require exhaustion of every conceivable race-neutral alternative or mandate that a university choose between maintaining a reputation for excellence or fulfilling a commitment to provide educational opportunities to members of all racial groups. See, *e.g., Wygant* v. *Jackson Bd. of Ed.,* 476 U.S. 267, 280, n. 6. The Court is satisfied that the Law School adequately considered the available alternatives. The Court is also satisfied that, in the context of individualized consideration of the possible diversity contributions of each applicant, the Law School's race-conscious admissions program does not unduly harm nonminority applicants. Finally, race-conscious admissions policies must be limited in time. The Court takes the Law School at its word that it would like nothing better than to find a race-neutral admissions formula and will terminate its use of racial preferences as soon as practicable. The Court expects that 25 years from now, the use of racial preferences will no longer be necessary to further the interest approved today. Pp. 333–343.

(e) Because the Law School's use of race in admissions decisions is not prohibited by the Equal Protection Clause, petitioner's statutory claims based on Title VI and § 1981 also fail. See *Bakke, supra,* at 287 (opinion of Powell, J.); *General Building Contractors Assn., Inc.* v. *Pennsylvania,* 458 U.S. 375, 389–391. Pp. 343–344.

Critical Thinking

1. How are minority groups defined?
2. Should race and ethnicity be primary criteria of defining underrepresented status?

Create Central

www.mhhe.com/createcentral

Additional Resources

Bankston, Carl (2006). "*Grutter v. Bollinger*: Weak Foundations?" Ohio State Law Journal 67 (1): 1–13.

Devins, Neal (2003). "Explaining *Grutter v. Bollinger*" University of Pennsylvania Law Review 152 (1): 347–383.

Internet References

Regents of the University of *California v. Bakke*
www.oyez.org/cases/1970–1979/1977/1977_76_811

O'Connor, Sandra Day. United States Supreme Court, 2003.

The Pursuit of Fairness
A History of Affirmative Action

Terry H. Anderson

Learning Outcomes

After reading this selection, you should be able to:

1. Provide a general overview of the history of affirmative action.
2. Discuss the implications of the watershed rulings of "the Michigan cases."
3. Address the issue of a George W. Bush Administration divided over affirmative action.

Affirmative action is considered by many political science scholars as one of the most divisive and contentious issues in American politics in the past several decades. In the following selection, which is excerpted from Terry H. Anderson's classic historical analytical study of affirmative action entitled *The Pursuit of Fairness* (Oxford University Press, 2004), Anderson recounts the decline of the successful impact of affirmative action programs particularly in minority student enrollment in various academic programs at the most prestigious universities. Anderson recalls how this decline was evident especially towards the end of President Bill Clinton's presidency in the late 1990s.

In particular, Anderson investigates this transformation in the viability of affirmative action through the lens of American public opinion and the electorate's shift in its perception of alternative domestic public policy issues as more highly salient than affirmative action. In an attempt to be proactive in the historical context of terrorism on American soil on September 11, 2001, the George W. Bush administration initiated a dramatic shift in national priorities and considered military and national security policies to trump domestic policies, including affirmative action. Furthermore, this selection examines the George W. Bush administration's reaction and position to affirmative action, particularly in the context of college admissions and reveals a restrained rejection—although a nuanced and limited approach—in conjunction with several legal challenges and court rulings, most prominently the watershed rulings of the Michigan cases (i.e., *Gratz v. Bollinger*, and *Grutter v. Bollinger*).

Anderson (b. 1946) received his M.A. from the University of Missouri and his Ph.D. from Indiana University. He is currently a professor of history at Texas A&M University. Anderson's scholarly research area of specialization and expertise has included the study of modern U.S. history. He has earned numerous honors and grants, including being awarded a Fulbright to be in China (1994–1995). He is author of many scholarly publications, including *The Sixties* (Third Edition, Pearson Longman, 2006) and *The Movement and the Sixties* (Oxford University Press, 1995).

Key Concept: the historical evolution and contemporary status of affirmative action

While Bill Clinton was preoccupied fighting for his political life, the demise of affirmative action was observed at select venues in the nation. The Supreme Court had refused to hear a lawsuit against California's Proposition 209, making it clear that the future of the policy would be left up to voters, or regents, as the University of California decision and the *Hopwood* case was having an immediate impact. In 1997 the percentage of black, Latino, and Native American undergraduates at Berkeley had been more than 23 percent; the next year it had plummeted to just over 10 percent, while those percentages at UCLA dropped from about 20 to less than 13. Berkeley and UCLA law schools witnessed a more significant decline, as the number of blacks admitted declined over 80 percent, while Hispanic admissions dropped in half. At the University of Texas Law School where African American and Hispanic students had made up about 75 of the 500 incoming students, the number dropped to 30: only four were blacks. "It took us 30 years to get here," said Mexican American student Diana Saldana, "and it took them 24 hours to dismantle any progress we have made."

With jobs plentiful and a hot stock market, citizens lost interest in the affirmative action debate. This became obvious during the 2000 election where both presidential candidates, Texas Governor George W. Bush and Vice President Al Gore Jr., avoided civil rights issues. There was good reason for that, for opinion polls demonstrated voters were most interested in health-care topics, such as HMOs and prescription drug costs for the elderly, and with such issues as school violence, while they were least concerned about immigration, defense, and affirmative action. Polls also demonstrated that majorities of both blacks and whites felt that race relations were "generally good" in the nation, and more than 80 percent said the same thing about their own neighborhoods. And when asked, "In order to make up for past discrimination, do you favor or oppose programs that make special efforts to help minorities get ahead?" 46 percent of whites favored, 44 percent opposed, meaning that there was little political reason to run a campaign for or against affirmative action, especially since opposition had not helped Bob Dole. . . .

The age of diversity became even more apparent that year in the 2000 census. For the first time officials allowed individuals to identify themselves as being of more than one race, and the resulting snapshot of the nation revealed more than ever that race no longer could be measured in black and white, but in living color. The incredible increase of interracial couples since 1970, and their kids, was changing the face of America. In California, mixed parents gave birth to one out of every seven babies. Interracial marriages had soared during the last generation. In 2000, about half of native-born Asians and 40 percent of Hispanics, ages 25 to 34, had married someone of another race. While still small in comparison, the number of black–white marriages increased seven times since 1960; about 8 percent of black husbands had white wives, including such prominent people as Justice Clarence Thomas and Ward Connerly, who was of African, Indian, French, and Irish descent. "Yet," Connerly declared, "I have reporters call me African American! What does that mean?" To confuse matters almost half of all Hispanics checked "white" or "other" as their race on the census form, and during the next two years this fastest-growing population supplanted African Americans as the largest minority group in the nation. . . .

The results of the 2000 census raised profound questions about affirmative action, but the circumstances of the 2000 election meant difficulties for the new president. Bush received no honeymoon period, had mediocre public support, and struggled during his first eight months—until September 11. Like the Oklahoma City bombing, the shocking terrorist attacks boosted the president's approval ratings. It also refocused his agenda away from domestic to foreign affairs and resulted in the subsequent wars in and occupations of Afghanistan and Iraq. Except for homeland security and tax cuts, domestic issues took a back seat to military action.

Back home on the civil rights front, the administration took a moderate approach. Although the Justice and Labor secretaries had stated their opposition to affirmative action while favoring outreach programs, the administration did not slash enforcement or the budgets of the EEOC or OFCCP. As in the late 1990s the EEOC continued cutting the time of resolution of cases and boosting the use of mediation. The administration surprised some observers by supporting federal set-asides mandated by the Disadvantaged Business Enterprise Program. Officials filed an *amicus* brief in *Adarand v. Mineta*, citing "extensive evidence of public and private discrimination," declaring the program "narrowly tailored," to which the Supreme Court agreed, dismissing the case and allowing federal set-asides to continue. Meanwhile, the president's call for "affirmative access" never materialized, until it resurfaced two years later during discussions about the suits against the University of Michigan. Press secretary Ari Fleischer attempted to define it as seeking "ways to encourage diversity and to do so in a way that does not rely on either quotas or racial preferences . . . which have a tendency to divide people."

Federal courts remained interested in affirmative action and they continued to chip away at various programs. A three-judge panel, Reagan and Bush appointees, unanimously found that the Federal Communications Commission's program to increase job opportunities and ownership for women and minorities in the broadcasting industry "ultimately does not withstand constitutional review." The new rules made clear that a company's record in hiring women and minorities no longer would be a factor in deciding whether to renew a broadcaster's license. Another court ruled the University of Georgia's admission policy, which gave minorities an extra half point in the process, was "naked racial balancing" and unconstitutional. By 2002 Georgia banned affirmative action in college admissions, while most other states continued their programs, leaving the nation with a patchwork quilt of admission practices—until the Michigan cases.

"Many civil rights lawyers agree that the University of Michigan could be the Alamo of affirmative action," wrote *Time*, "the place where they make their last stand."

During spring 2003 the Ann Arbor campus became the epicenter of the national debate. More than 3,000 organizations filed over 60 briefs supporting the university, including briefs from over 110 members of Congress, 70 from Fortune 500 companies, and almost 30 from former military and civilian leaders of the armed forces. U.S. Army General Norman Schwarzkopf, commander in the 1991 Persian Gulf War, even argued that the policy was mandatory at the military academies for recruiting minority officer candidates. Only a few cases in history had seen so many *amicus* briefs, even more than *Bakke*. Leading Democrats running for their party's presidential nomination in 2004, Senator John Kerry, Congressman Dick Gephardt, former Vermont governor Howard Dean, former NATO commander General Wesley Clark, all supported the university.

President Bush took the opposite side, asking the court to declare the admission system unconstitutional, supporting affirmative access and the state percentage plans to guarantee admission. He declared his support for "diversity of all kinds" but stated that Michigan's admission policy was "fundamentally flawed . . . divisive, unfair and impossible to square with our Constitution." That provoked a vicious attack on the president. "It wasn't his SAT scores," wrote Michael Kinsley, "or his C grades, but "bloodlines and connections" that got him into Yale. Bush, who graduated near the bottom of his college class, nevertheless was accepted by Harvard, demonstrating that he "may be the most spectacular affirmative action success story of all time." "When It Comes to Hypocrisy," added a *Newsday* columnist, "He's Brilliant!"

During the firestorm the administration's two most prominent African Americans, Colin Powell and Condoleezza Rice, declared that they supported affirmative action in college admissions: The Bush administration was as divided as the nation.[1]

Both cases concerned reverse discrimination. In 1995 high school senior Jennifer Gratz applied to the University of Michigan. She had a 3.76 GPA, good test scores, had been a student council leader, math tutor, blood drive organizer, cheerleader, and homecoming queen. During the process she learned that some of her minority classmates, who had lower grades, had been accepted, but she had been placed on the waiting list. According to the university, Gratz was evaluated in a group of more than 400 students with similar academic qualifications. The university admitted every qualified minority applicant, in this case 46 of them, and 121 whites, but not Gratz, who eventually attended the Dearborn campus. "I was treated unfairly because of my skin color," she maintained, and in 1997 she and another white applicant, Patrick Hamacher, sued the university and the case became *Gratz v. Bollinger.*

Barbara Grutter, in her 40s and a mother of two, applied to the University of Michigan law school with a 3.8 GPA and 161 on the LSAT, but she was rejected in 1997. "We have always conscientiously taught our children that discrimination is wrong," she said, "morally wrong and illegal. . . . Is what I'm teaching them a platitude, or is it real?" She charged that she was rejected because the law school used race as the "predominant" factor in its selection process and that the school had "no compelling interest to justify their use of race in the admissions process." The case became *Grutter v. Bollinger.*

Both sides based their cases on *Bakke.* The Center for Individual Rights, a nonprofit law group in Washington which had sued for Cheryl Hopwood, filed both lawsuits against U.M. The center claimed that the university's use of racial preferences violated the equal protection clause of the Fourteenth Amendment and Title VI of the 1964 Civil Rights Act. U.M. declared that *Bakke* ruled that diversity could be a compelling governmental interest; the university did not claim that it had a history of discrimination and that its policy was a remedy for the past.

Every year about 25,000 apply for a freshman class of about 5,500 at the University of Michigan. To deal with this mass of applicants, the university had established a system with 150 possible points. Almost all students needed 100 for admission, 99 to 90 was admit or postpone, 89 to 75 was delay or postpone. The largest number of points was given for high school grades. Each black, Hispanic, and Native American applicant automatically got 20 points, as did out-of-state minority applicants, all athletes, and those from residents from "economically disadvantaged" backgrounds or predominately minority high schools. Because minorities did not do as well on standardized tests as Asians and whites, SAT scores were discounted and could add up to twelve points; Michigan residents got ten points; from two to ten points on the quality of the high school; four points for parental legacies; up to five points for artistic talent; and a few more points for advanced placement or honors courses in high school and for geographical areas in the state underrepresented in the student body. All things equal, 20 points meant a minority with a 3.0 high school GPA automatically equaled a white applicant with 4.0. In other words, being a minority earned 8 points more than scoring a perfect 1600 on the SAT. The university admitted virtually every "qualified" minority. A white student with a 3.2 GPA and a SAT of 1000 would be rejected; a black or Hispanic would be admitted, even those with even lower grades and scores.

The result was diversity—and disgust. While there were about 8 percent blacks in the student body, 14 percent in the state, there were twice as many Hispanics present than the state's demographics and 10 times more Asian Americans. In a state about 83 percent white, the student body was about 25 percent minority. The University of Michigan did not look like Michigan. That was good, declared the former university president Lee Bollinger, an advocate of diversity. "A classroom that does not have a significant representation from members of different races produces an impoverished discussion," he claimed. Many debated that idea, while some minority students felt isolated, noting little interracial socializing. "One of the reasons I chose to come to U.M. is their boastful reputation on diversity," said a black sophomore. "But . . . this campus is extremely segregated." Many white parents in small towns and working-class Detroit suburbs were irritated because their kids no longer could get accepted to the campus in Ann Arbor. Affirmative action was "the No. 1 economic and social issue" said a state senator representing those Detroit districts. Everyone knew someone "who has suffered a loss due to minority preferences." Various state polls between 1998 and 2002 found that only a quarter of those interviewed supported the university's admission policy, between half and two-thirds were opposed, and the remainder were undecided.

The Michigan law school used a different, more flexible system. It received about 5,000 applicants a year for 350 places, and a committee examined each applicant's GPA, LSAT score, undergraduate college records, personal statement, and recommendations to assess the individual's potential contributions. The policy aimed to achieve "racial and ethnic diversity" by including blacks, Hispanics, and Native Americans, "who without this commitment might not be represented in our student body in meaningful numbers." Admission officers had testified that they used no points, and no numerical targets, for admitting students, while they stated that they felt that it was important to have a "critical mass" or a "meaningful representation" of minority students and not just tokens who felt isolated in the classroom. They stated that the number of minorities in each incoming class varied from year to year, but without the policy only about 4 percent of those students admitted for fall 2000 would have been minorities, instead of the current 14 percent. Surveys demonstrated that there was no significant difference between the races in passing bar examinations.

In *Gratz* and *Grutter* the Sixth U.S. Circuit Court of Appeals supported the university, allowing the affirmative action program—contradicting the Fifth U.S. Circuit Court's ruling in the *Hopwood* decision. That prompted a showdown at the Supreme Court. Accepting the case Justice Sandra Day O'Connor aimed to resolve the judicial disagreement "on a question of national importance. . . . Whether diversity is a compelling interest that can justify the narrowly tailored use of race in selecting applicants for admission to public universities."

In *Gratz*, Chief Justice Rehnquist wrote for the majority. He noted that the *Adarand* decision established that "all racial classifications . . . must be strictly scrutinized" and that meant college admission policies had to be "narrowly tailored measures that further compelling governmental interest." Rehnquist then referred to Justice Powell's opinion in *Bakke* that "race or ethnic background may be deemed a 'plus' in a particular applicant's file," but that such an admission system had to be "flexible enough to consider all pertinent elements of diversity in light of the particular qualifications of each applicant." He pointed out that an applicant with artistic talent that "rivaled that of Monet or Picasso" would "receive, at most, five points," while "every single underrepresented minority applicant . . . automatically received 20 points for submitting an application." Moreover, applicants with the same GPA and test scores "were subject to different admissions outcomes based upon their racial or ethnic status. An in-state or out-of-state minority applicant with Gratz's scores" would have been admitted. The Court ruled 6 to 3 against the university's admission policy; it was "not narrowly tailored to achieve . . . compelling interest in diversity" and too much like a quota and therefore unconstitutional.

In *Grutter*, Justice O'Connor wrote for the majority. She noted that Justice Powell's opinion in *Bakke* was the "touchstone for constitutional analysis of race-conscious admission policies" at both public and private universities and that he approved the use of race for only one reason: "the attainment of a diverse student body." She wrote that the "critical mass" was not "some specified percentage," a quota. "That would amount to outright racial balancing, which is patently unconstitutional." She continued that the law school used a "highly individualized, holistic review" of each applicant's file with "no mechanical, predetermined diversity 'bonuses' based on race or ethnicity," and that the school frequently accepted white students with grades and test scores lower than minority applicants, demonstrating that its policy considered other diversity factors besides race. To her, the question was whether the admission policy use of race was justified by state interest. "Today," she declared, "we hold that the Law School has a compelling interest in attaining a diverse student body." She concluded:

> It has been 25 years since Justice Powell first approved the use of race to further an interest in student body diversity. . . . Since that time, the number of minority applicants with high grades and test scores has indeed increased. We expect that 25 years from now, the use of racial preferences will no longer be necessary to further the interest approved today.

By one vote, 5 to 4, the court upheld affirmative action for college admissions—and it also upheld *Adarand, Richmond, Bakke,* as it overturned *Hopwood.* Narrowly tailored affirmative action policies were constitutional only if they could withstand strict scrutiny, and in education, only as *one of many* factors to bring about a diverse student body. O'Connor noted that numerous academic studies, along with briefs submitted by corporations and the armed forces, demonstrated that benefits derived from a diverse student body and workforce "are not theoretical but real," including the "military's ability to fulfill its principle mission to provide national security." That statement was written in a post-September 11 environment when U.S. armed forces were engaged in Afghanistan and Iraq.

"This is a wonderful, wonderful day," exclaimed University of Michigan president Mary Sue Coleman. "We're very, very excited and very pleased," as was the civil rights community. Curiously, President Bush praised the decision, stating that the Court struck a "careful balance" between campus diversity and equal protection. Conservative columnist Michelle Malkin described the ruling as, "Go ahead and trample the 14th Amendment's equal protection clause. Just don't make it so damn obvious." Ward Connerly flew to the campus and, flanked by the plaintiffs, pledged to get the necessary signatures to put an antipreference proposition on the Michigan ballot in November 2004. "Our crusade will not end with the state of Michigan," he declared, as his organization considered similar initiatives for Arizona, Colorado, Missouri, Oregon, and Utah.[2]

*T*he Michigan cases closed another chapter—the demise of affirmative action. During the 1990s problems had emerged. Set-asides had too much fraud while the issue of original intent had been complicated by surging immigration. The concept of race itself was becoming increasingly blurry, raising serious questions about who, if anyone, should receive preferences. As for set-asides, the Court mandated strict scrutiny first for cities in *Richmond* and then federally in *Adarand*. After the first decision some 230 state and local authorities suspended their programs, reevaluated them, and by 1995 about 100 remained. In response to *Adarand*, the Clinton administration also decreased the federal program and tightened the criteria for participation. On campus, admission systems that allotted points based on race were tossed out, and colleges revised their processes, but not toward the "class-based" affirmative action. Social scientists had discredited that system because surveys demonstrated that there were not enough poor blacks and Latinos who actually graduated from high school; that policy would eventually result in fewer minorities in college and more poor whites. Voters, governors, or attorneys general in California, Florida, Georgia, Mississippi, Texas, and Washington banned all or part of their state's programs, and some established percentage plans for college admissions.

Yet this was not the end of affirmative action in the nation, most states, college admissions, or the private sector. Some Republicans had tried to end the policy in the first half of 1995, and Bob Dole had run against it in 1996. That stand won Dole few votes and it divided his party. Attempts to place ballot initiatives in more states stalled as citizens lost interest. President Clinton had been right. Giving his landmark speech in 1995, he used a simple phrase, "mend it, don't end it," and that had popular appeal. Before the Michigan decisions, opinion polls found that Americans approved 2 to 1 of "programs designed to increase the number of black and minority students"; the same people disapproved 3 to 1 of "giving preferential treatment" to minorities and that included a *majority* of minority respondents. What 30 years earlier President Lyndon Johnson had called "a hand up," President Nixon had labeled a "little extra start," Justice Powell said was a "plus," and what Justice Sandra Day O'Connor referred to as "some sort of bonus" had become the definition of affirmative action. That type of program had become part of the social fabric—and most Americans considered that fair.[3]

Notes

1. EEOC Combined Annual Reports Fiscal Years 1999–2001, AP article, 7 February 2003; *Adarand* case see WP, 11 August 2001; Fleischer, White House Press Release, 15 January 2003; FCC in NYT, 17 January 2001; U. Georgia in WP, 4 December 2002; *Time*, 23 August 1999, 48; background of Michigan case in *Chronicle of Higher Education*, 28 February 2003; Kinsley in *Time*, 27 January 2003, 70; hypocrisy in Newsday, 17 January 2003; Bush's grades in NYT, 18, 19 June 2000.
2. Gratz background in *Time*, 10 November 1997, 52–54; comment in AP article, 1 April 2003; Grutter see NYT, 11 May 1999 and *New Yorker*, 18 December 2000, 46ff.; U.M. 150 point system see *Detroit Free Press*, 23 June 2003, WP, 5 December 1997, Newsweek, 29 December 1997, 76; for system and Bollinger, state senator see *Chronicle of Higher Education*, 30 October 1998; state polls, 9 July 2003; impact of diversity on education is debated, see Holzer and Neumark, "Assessing Affirmative Action," *Journal of Economic Literature* (September 2000): 553–54, 559; black sophomore in WP, *1 April 2003, and bar surveys in Time*, 23 August 1999, 48; Rehnquist and O'Connor from their opinions; Coleman in CNN press release, 23 June, Malkin in *Houston Chronicle*, 26 June, and Connerly in *Chronicle of Higher Education*, 9 July, all 2003.
3. Decline of set-aside plans see *U.S. News*, 26 June 1995, 39; for why class-based will not work see Thomas J. Kane, "Misconceptions in the Debate over Affirmative Action in College Admissions," Chapter 2, and Jerome Karabel, "No Alternative," Chapter 3, Orfield, *Chilling Admissions*; polls in WP, *24 June, and New Republic*, 3 February 14, both 2003. Orfield, Gary, and Edward Miller, eds. Chilling Admissions: The Affirmative Action Crisis and the Search for Alternatives (Cambridge, Mass., 2000).

Critical Thinking

1. Can the ongoing growth in America's inter-racialism be reliably factored into a predicted obsolescence of affirmative action?
2. Although often seen as understandable, is the back-seating of domestic issues a necessary consequence of such attention demands as foreign wars and national security?
3. In a showcase of American civil-rights milestones, what prominence should be given to the establishment of affirmative action?

Create Central

www.mhhe.com/createcentral

Internet References

The American Civil Liberties Union
www.aclu.org

From *The Pursuit of Fairness: A History of Affirmative Action* by Terry H. Anderson (Oxford University Press, 2004). Copyright © 2004 by Oxford University Press. Reprinted by permission.

Korematsu v. United States

Hugo L. Black

Learning Outcomes

After reading this selection, you should be able to:

1. Discuss the wartime threat to America's West Coast in 1942.
2. Describe the general content of and rationale behind Civilian Exclusion Order No. 34.

In the 1944 case *Korematsu v. United States* (323 U.S. 214), from which the following selection is taken, the U.S. Supreme Court articulated an opinion on a divisive racial issue in American domestic and defense policy during World War II. The Court's decision in this case had fundamental constitutional and political consequences upon the interpretation of civil rights. In particular, the judgment of the Court was a landmark decision in that it reinterpreted the equal protection clause of the Fourteenth Amendment and the government's authority to override conventional civil rights of American citizens. The equal protection clause forbids any state to deny equal protection of the laws to any individual within its jurisdiction. The Court, however, specifically found constitutional President Franklin Roosevelt's policy of compulsory mass evacuation and internment of 135,000 citizens of Japanese descent during World War II so as to promote American national defense and safety.

Roosevelt had issued an executive order authorizing the construction of military or defense areas from which particular American citizens could be excluded in order to avoid potential sabotage or espionage. (It is interesting to note that not one Japanese American citizen was ever found guilty of either of these crimes.) Toyosaburo Korematsu, an American citizen of Japanese descent, refused to leave his California home and was subsequently convicted in a federal district court for violating the exclusion order. After his conviction was upheld by a circuit court of appeals, Korematsu brought the case to the U.S. Supreme Court. The Court has consistently overturned laws that distinguish between citizens upon the criterion of race. However, the Court's ruling in *Korematsu v. United States* was a rare exception to this principle, as the Court deliberately sustained a government policy (i.e., evacuation and internment) that promoted discrimination upon the criterion of race and, in effect, denied the application of the equal protection clause of the Fourteenth Amendment to a particular minority group of American citizens. Justice Hugo L. Black delivered the opinion of the Court.

In 1988 Congress formally apologized to the survivors and passed legislation that provided $20,000 in compensation to all former camp inhabitants or their survivors.

Key Concept: the evacuation and internment of Japanese American citizens

*M*r. Justice Black delivered the opinion of the Court, saying in part:

The petitioner, an American citizen of Japanese descent, was convicted in a federal district court for remaining in San Leandro, California, a "Military Area," contrary to Civilian Exclusion Order No. 34 of the Commanding General of the Western Command, U.S. Army, which directed that after May 9, 1942, all persons of Japanese ancestry should be excluded from that area. No question was raised as to petitioner's loyalty to the United States. The Circuit Court of Appeals affirmed, and the importance of the constitutional question involved caused us to grant certiorari.

It should be noted, to begin with, that all legal restrictions which curtail the civil rights of a single racial group are immediately suspect. That is not to say that all such restrictions are unconstitutional. It is to say that courts must subject them to the most rigid scrutiny. Pressing public necessity may sometimes justify the existence of such restrictions; racial antagonism never can.

In the instant case prosecution of the petitioner was begun by information charging violation of an Act of Congress, of March 21, 1942, which provides that ". . . whoever shall enter, remain in, leave, or commit any act in any military area or military zone prescribed, under the authority of an Executive order of the President, by the Secretary of War, or by any military commander designated by the Secretary of War, contrary to the restrictions applicable to any such area or zone or contrary to the order of the Secretary of War or any such military commander, shall, if it appears that he knew or should have known of the existence and extent of the restrictions or order and that his act was in violation thereof, be guilty of a misdemeanor and upon conviction shall be liable to a fine of not to exceed $5,000 or to imprisonment for not more than one year, or both, for each offense."

Exclusion Order No. 34, which the petitioner knowingly and admittedly violated was one of a number of military orders and proclamations, all of which were substantially based upon Executive Order No. 9066. That order, issued after we were at war with Japan, declared that "the successful prosecution of the war requires every possible protection against espionage and against sabotage to national-defense material, national-defense premises, and national-defense utilities. . . ."

One of the series of orders and proclamations, a curfew order, which like the exclusion order here was promulgated pursuant to Executive Order 9066, subjected all persons of Japanese ancestry in prescribed West Coast military areas to remain in their residences from 8 p.m. to 6 a.m. As is the case with the exclusion order here, that prior curfew order was designed as a "protection against espionage and against sabotage." In *Kiyoshi Hirabayashi v. United States* [1943], we sustained a conviction obtained for violation of the curfew order. The Hirabayashi conviction and this one thus rest on the same 1942 Congressional Act and the same basic executive and military orders, all of which orders were aimed at the twin dangers of espionage and sabotage.

The 1942 Act was attacked in the Hirabayashi case as an unconstitutional delegation of power; it was contended that the curfew order and other orders on which it rested were beyond the war powers of the Congress, the military authorities and of the President, as Commander in Chief of the Army; and finally that to apply the order against none but citizens of Japanese ancestry amounted to a constitutionally prohibited discrimination solely on account of race. To these questions, we gave the serious consideration which their importance justified. We upheld the curfew order as an exercise of the power of the government to take steps necessary to prevent espionage and sabotage in an area threatened by Japanese attack.

In the light of the principles we announced in the Hirabayashi case, we are unable to conclude that it was beyond the war power of Congress and the Executive to exclude those of Japanese ancestry from the West Coast war area at the time they did. True, exclusion from the area in which one's home is located is a far greater deprivation than constant confinement to the home from 8 p.m. to 6 a.m. Nothing short of apprehension by the proper military authorities of the gravest imminent danger to the public safety can constitutionally justify either. But exclusion from a threatened area, no less than curfew, has a definite and close relationship to the prevention of espionage and sabotage. The military authorities, charged with the primary responsibility of defending our

shores, concluded that curfew provided inadequate protection and ordered exclusion. They did so, as pointed out in our Hirabayashi opinion, in accordance with Congressional authority to the military to say who should, and who should not, remain in the threatened areas.

In this case the petitioner challenges the assumptions upon which we rested our conclusions in the Hirabayashi case. He also urges that by May 1942, when Order No. 34 was promulgated, all danger of Japanese invasion of the West Coast had disappeared. After careful consideration of these contentions we are compelled to reject them.

Here, as in the Hirabayashi case, ". . . we cannot reject as unfounded the judgment of the military authorities and of Congress that there were disloyal members of that population, whose number and strength could not be precisely and quickly ascertained. We cannot say that the war-making branches of the Government did not have ground for believing that in a critical hour such persons could not readily be isolated and separately dealt with, and constituted a menace to the national defense and safety, which demanded that prompt and adequate measures be taken to guard against it."

Like curfew, exclusion of those of Japanese origin was deemed necessary because of the presence of an unascertained number of disloyal members of the group, most of whom we have no doubt were loyal to this country. It was because we could not reject the finding of the military authorities that it was impossible to bring about an immediate segregation of the disloyal from the loyal that we sustained the validity of the curfew order as applying to the whole group. In the instant case, temporary exclusion of the entire group was rested by the military on the same ground. The judgment that exclusion of the whole group was for the same reason a military imperative answers the contention that the exclusion was in the nature of group punishment based on antagonism to those of Japanese origin. That there were members of the group who retained loyalties to Japan has been confirmed by investigations made subsequent to the exclusion. Approximately five thousand American citizens of Japanese ancestry refused to swear unqualified allegiance to the United States and to renounce allegiance to the Japanese Emperor, and several thousand evacuees requested repatriation to Japan.

We uphold the exclusion order as of the time it was made and when the petitioner violated it. . . . In doing so, we are not unmindful of the hardships imposed by it upon a large group of American citizens. . . . But hardships are part of war, and war is an aggregation of hardships. All citizens alike, both in and out of uniform, feel the impact of war in greater or lesser measure. Citizenship has its responsibilities as well as its privileges, and in time of war the burden is always heavier. Compulsory exclusion of large groups of citizens from their homes, except under circumstances of direst emergency and peril, is inconsistent with our basic governmental institution. But when under conditions of modern warfare our shores are threatened by hostile forces, the power to protect must be commensurate with the threatened danger. . . .

It is said that we are dealing here with the case of imprisonment of a citizen in a concentration camp solely because of his ancestry, without evidence or inquiry concerning his loyalty and good disposition towards the United States. Our task would be simple, our duty clear, were this a case involving the imprisonment of a loyal citizen in a concentration camp because of racial prejudice. Regardless of the true nature of the assembly and relocation centers—and we deem it unjustifiable to call them concentration camps with all the ugly connotations that term implies—we are dealing specifically with nothing but an exclusion order. To cast this case into outlines of racial prejudice, without reference to the real military dangers which were presented, merely confuses the issue. Korematsu was not excluded from the Military Area because of hostility to him or his race. He was excluded because we are at war with the Japanese Empire, because the properly constituted military authorities feared an invasion of our West Coast and felt constrained to take proper security measures, because they decided that the military urgency of the situation demanded that all citizens of Japanese ancestry be segregated from the West Coast temporarily, and finally, because Congress, reposing its confidence in this time of war in our military leaders—as inevitably it must—determined that they should have the power to do just this. There was evidence of disloyalty on the part of some, the military authorities considered that the need for action was great, and time was short. We cannot—by availing ourselves of the calm perspective of hindsight—now say that at that time these actions were unjustified.

Affirmed.

Critical Thinking

1. Should the fact that not one Japanese American was ever found guilty of sabotage or espionage color an assessment of Civilian Exclusion Order No. 34?

2. Do hardships of war, as cited in *Korematsu*, necessarily justify conditional exemptions in constitutional rights?

3. In the debates over racial profiling since the terrorist attacks of September 11, 2001, does the history of Japanese American evacuation and internment provide a reasonable parallel?

Create Central

www.mhhe.com/createcentral

Internet References

The American Civil Liberties Union
www.aclu.org

U.S. Supreme Court, 1944.

Presidential Power, Judicial Deference, and the Status of Detainees in an Age of Terrorism by Otis H. Stephens Jr.

89

Presidential Power, Judicial Deference, and the Status of Detainees in an Age of Terrorism

Otis H. Stephens, Jr.

Learning Outcomes

After reading this selection, you should be able to:

1. Explain the distinction between a law-enforcement model and a military-justice model.
2. Identify the classes of U.S.-held detainees, as categorized since 9/11 (September 11, 2001).
3. Describe the Nazi saboteur incident that occurred on the East Coast of the United States in 1942.

The terrorism perpetrated on American soil on September 11, 2001 became a critical historical moment in the evolution of American constitutional and political ideological thought and served as a strong stimulus for profoundly reflecting on the appropriate balance between national security and civil liberties. As a constitutional law scholar, Otis H. Stephens, Jr. articulates a sophisticated interpretation of this contemporary divisive constitutional and political philosophical issue investigating in particular the rights of detainees suspected of terrorism. The following selection is from his "Presidential Power, Judicial Deference, and the Status of Detainees in an Age of Terrorism," in David B. Cohen and John W. Wells, eds., *American National Security and Civil Liberties in an Era of Terrorism* (Palgrave Macmillan, 2004).

Stephens, Jr. is a highly respected constitutional law scholar whose expertise has been widely recognized by the publication of such books as *The Supreme Court and Confessions of Guilt* (University of Tennessee Press, 1973) and, coauthored with Gregory J. Rathjen, *The Supreme Court and the Allocation of Constitutional Power* (W. H. Freeman Co., 1980). Stephens, Jr., (b. 1936) received his M.A. from the University of Georgia, his Ph.D. from Johns Hopkins University, and his J.D. from the University of Tennessee. He is the Alumni Distinguished Service Professor of political science and resident scholar of constitutional law in the College of Law at the University of Tennessee-Knoxville.

Stephens, Jr. contends that a dramatic transformation in the American criminal justice paradigm and procedural rules for the prosecution of alleged terrorists from a "*law enforcement model*" to a "*military justice model*" resulted directly and with great urgency from the horrific acts of terrorism against the United States. A significant increase in the war powers of the contemporary American president as commander in chief—largely authorized by congress—occurred in conjunction with this fundamental juridical change in treating alleged terrorists. In the following selection, Stephens, Jr. recounts how President Bush's order for military tribunals had a legal precedent set by President Franklin D. Roosevelt's military orders aimed at potential sabotage during World War II. Stephens, Jr. scrutinizes the legal arguments articulated in numerous court cases focused on the presidential authorization of military tribunals and the detention of suspected terrorists, including American citizens identified and detained as "enemy combatants." Furthermore, the constitutionality of the Bush administration's implementation of the "*military justice model*" is discussed in the context of its critics who claim that the customary principles and procedures of American criminal justice are applicable even in dealing with suspected terrorists.

Key Concept: American criminal justice and the rights of detainees in the context of the war on terror

Introduction

The murderous attacks of September 11, 2001 marked a turning point in America's escalating war on terrorism. Prior to that date, suspected terrorists had typically been prosecuted in accordance with a law enforcement model based on the well-defined procedures of the American criminal justice system. For example, in accordance with the *law enforcement model*, Ramzi Yousef, the mastermind behind the 1993 bombing of the World Trade Center, was tried and convicted in 1998 in United States District Court.[1] After 9/11, however, the emphasis changed abruptly, and the procedural rules associated with criminal trials began to yield to claims of military exigency in the war on terrorism. The expanded use of presidential power in the immediate aftermath of 9/11 reflects this basic shift to a *military justice model*.

Responding to widespread fear and anger, as well as demands for retaliation and protection from future attacks, on September 14, 2001, President George W. Bush proclaimed a "Declaration and National Emergency by Reason of Certain Terrorist Attacks."[2] Congress promptly adopted a joint resolution authorizing the president to use "all necessary and appropriate force" against the 9/11 terrorists and those who harbored them.[3] Then in October 2001, the president initiated military operations in Afghanistan (Operation Enduring Freedom) resulting a few months later in the overthrow of the Taliban regime and the destruction of many of the Al Qaeda cells and training camps operating in that country. Meanwhile, on November 13, 2001, citing the previously noted joint resolution and his constitutional and statutory authority as commander in chief, President Bush issued a sweeping military order authorizing the detention of non-U.S. citizens suspected of committing or otherwise being involved in acts of international terrorism against "the United States, its citizens, national security, foreign policy, or economy. . . ."[4] The order also provided for the trial of such detainees before military tribunal "for violations of the laws of war and other applicable laws. . . ." Pursuant to this order as implemented by the secretary of defense, at least 640 noncitizen detainees have reportedly been imprisoned at Guantanamo Bay, Cuba, where they remain awaiting formal charges.

Three additional classes of detainees have figured prominently in the post–September 11 War on Terror: 1) *INS detainees*: aliens taken into custody by the Immigration and Naturalization Service; 2) *criminal detainees*: typically American citizens charged with involvement in terrorist activities; and 3) *material witness detainees*: persons detained following the issuance of a material witness warrant to secure their testimony before a grand jury. . . .

President Bush's order establishing military tribunals closely paralleled President Franklin D. Roosevelt's proclamations pertaining to the Nazi saboteur incident in the summer of 1942.[5] In mid-June of that year, eight German soldiers, after receiving extensive training in the techniques of sabotage, were transported by submarine to the east coast of the United States, four coming ashore on Long Island and four in Florida. They landed secretly at night and buried their uniforms along with explosives presumably intended for use in the destruction of various war facilities and other property. Dressed in civilian clothing, they attempted to conceal their identity as they mingled with the population and traveled to New York City, Chicago, and other urban centers. Before any acts of destruction were undertaken,

two of the saboteurs had second thoughts and provided the Federal Bureau of Investigation with information about the ill-conceived plot. Before the end of June, all of the saboteurs were incarcerated.

In an attempt to reassure a civilian population still reeling from the devastating attack on Pearl Harbor, Roosevelt issued two military orders on July 2, 1942. The first of these provided that enemies entering this country for purposes including sabotage were subject to the laws of war and the jurisdiction of military tribunals. The order further provided that "such persons shall not be privileged to seek any remedy or maintain any proceeding directly or indirectly, or have any such remedy or proceeding sought in their behalf, in the courts of the United States, or of its States, territories, and possessions. . . ."

In the second order, Roosevelt set up a military tribunal for trial of the Nazi saboteurs, relying on his authority as "President and as Commander in Chief of the Army and Navy, under the Constitution and statutes of the United States, and more particularly the Thirty-Eighth Article of War. . . ." Convictions by this seven-member tribunal required a two-thirds vote. The order sought to preclude judicial review by providing that "The record of the trials, including any judgment or sentence, shall be transmitted directly to [the President] for [his] action thereon."

This hastily created military commission, operating in strict secrecy, proceeded immediately to the trial of the saboteurs. The procedure followed by the commission did not include many of the constitutional protections guaranteed in civil trials. Nevertheless, the saboteurs were provided with able defense counsel consisting of legally trained military officers. The defense argued that the president had exceeded his constitutional powers by barring the defendants from the civil courts and by ordering their trials before a military commission. They also argued that the commission had not been established in accordance with the existing provisions of the Articles of War. Defense counsel was also concerned that the president retained the sole power to review the commission's decision. They feared that the trial would be rushed to conclusion and sentences carried out without notice or time to permit a constitutional challenge in the Supreme Court.

The District Court for the District of Columbia denied petitioners applications for habeas corpus.[6] By complicated steps involving issuance of writs of habeas corpus and certiorari, the Supreme Court justices, who were scattered throughout the country during their summer recess, were individually contacted and rushed back to Washington. In a special term convened for this case only, they heard oral arguments on July 29 and 30 and rendered a brief per curiam decision on July 31 in *Ex Parte Quirin* denying defendants' applications for leave to file petitions for habeas corpus. The Court concluded that the "alleged offenses . . . could be tried by a military commission, that the commission was lawfully constituted, and that the petitioners were lawfully held for trial."[7]

Undeterred by these events, the military trial proceeded, the defendants were speedily convicted, and in early August 1942, six of the eight defendants were executed in Washington, D.C.

Military Tribunals Since 9/11

Relying heavily on the precedent established in *Ex parte Quirin*, President Bush's military order of November 13, 2001 authorized military tribunals to depart from "the principles of law and the rules of evidence generally recognized in the trial of criminal cases in the United States District Courts."[8] As justification for this departure from the law enforcement model, President Bush emphasized his determination "that an extraordinary emergency exists for national defense purposes, that this emergency constitutes an urgent and compelling government interest, and that issuance of this order is necessary to meet this emergency."[9] The order granted the secretary of defense broad authority to establish and implement regulations. Under this authority, a number of regulations were adopted in early 2002 restoring certain procedural guarantees. These include the right to privately retained counsel and a provision requiring a unanimous vote of the commission for imposition of the death penalty. For other convictions and sentences, a two-thirds vote of the commission, as provided in the original order, remains intact. Like Roosevelt's 1942 proclamations, Bush's military order sought to preclude judicial review of convictions and sentences. The order provided for "review and final decision" by the president or the secretary of defense as his designee. The November 13 military order has been the subject of heated debate among legal scholars, civil liberties groups, and other interested parties.[10]

As previously noted, several hundred non-U.S. citizens have been detained and imprisoned at Guantanamo Bay, Cuba, under the president's November 13 order. A number of unsuccessful efforts have been made by, and on behalf of, these persons to challenge the constitutionality of their detention. For example, in *Coalition of Clergy v. Bush*, the Ninth U.S. Circuit Court of Appeals affirmed an order dismissing a habeas corpus petition on the ground that the clergy, lawyers, and law professors bringing the action were not proper "next friends" of the detainees.[11]

Al Odah v. U.S involved three separate actions brought by nationals from Kuwait, Australia, and Great Britain, in the D.C. District Court, challenging the legality and conditions of their confinement. From adverse judgments, these individuals sought review in the Court of Appeals for the District of Columbia. On March 11, 2003, Judge Randolph, writing for a three-judge panel, delivered an opinion holding that the "privilege of litigation" does not extend to aliens in military custody outside the territory of the United States.[12] The court relied heavily on the Supreme Court's 1950 decision in *Johnson v. Eisentrager*.[13] That case arose from the convictions of

twenty-one German nationals by an American military tribunal in China for having engaged in military activity against the United States after the surrender of Germany on May 8, 1945, but before the surrender of Japan the following August. After their convictions, these individuals were repatriated to Germany and confined in the U.S. army prison at Landsberg. They petitioned the United States District Court for the District of Columbia for writs of habeas corpus to review the legality of their detention. Their case ultimately reached the Supreme Court. Speaking through Justice Jackson, the Court ruled that the "privilege of litigation" had not been extended to these prisoners. It is important to note that the petitioners in *Al Odah*, like the German prisoners in *Eisentrager*, had at no relevant time been within the territorial jurisdiction of the United States.

Al Odah and his fellow petitioners argued that under the existing lease agreement between the United States and Cuba, Guantanamo Bay is in essence a territory of the United States and that the government exercises sovereignty over this territory. Judge Randolph noted that for a variety of reasons, including the fact that Guantanamo Bay is neither a state nor an insular possession, that United States does not exercise sovereignty over this military base. In short, the court held that the detainees were in the same position as the prisoners in *Eisentrager*. Since the courts were not open to them, they could not "seek release based on violations of the Constitution or treaties of federal law. . . ." By denying jurisdiction, the court thus avoided dealing with the question of the president's constitutional authority to issue the November 13 order. On a separate issue, the District of Columbia Circuit disagreed with the Ninth Circuit by ruling that relatives who were assisting the petitioners in this litigation qualified as "next friends" available to file the lawsuit. The court reasoned that these relatives, unlike the clergy, lawyers, and law professors in the Ninth Circuit case, had a "significant relationship" with the detainees.

Reacting strongly to the court's denial of jurisdiction, attorneys for the petitioners vowed to seek either en banc review in the Court of Appeals or a petition for certiorari in the Supreme Court. Critics maintain that the court's opinion sets a dangerous precedent since its reasoning is not limited to times of war. They argue that the decision allows U.S. officials to detain any noncitizen abroad in times of peace as well as war without judicial review. By contrast, Justice Department officials welcomed the decision as "an important victory in the war on terrorism. . . . In times of war, the President must be able to protect our nation from enemies who seek to harm innocent Americans."[14]

The *Al Odah* decision illustrates the lengths to which American courts will go to avoid constitutional questions that relate to the president's exercise of war powers. As in other cases discussed below, this posture of judicial deference indicates that most judges are inclined to take a realistic view of the limits of judicial policymaking in this area. Judicial deference, however, is not synonymous with abdication. The Supreme Court may yet have occasion to address the constitutionality of the president's November 13th order. Whether it should address this substantive issue or treat it as a "political question" remains a perplexing problem.

Detention of United States Citizens Since 9/11

In the post–September 11 era, courts have not reached agreement in deciding cases involving U.S. citizens designated as enemy combatants. In *Hamdi v. Rumsfeld*, the Fourth Circuit Court of Appeals has in effect adhered to the military justice model.[15] On the other hand, the United States District for the Southern District of New York in *Padilla v. Rumsfeld* has opted, at least to some extent, for the criminal justice model. These distinct approaches are examined in the following paragraphs.[16]

Yaser Esam Hamdi was captured by American forces while fighting for the Taliban in Afghanistan in the fall of 2001.[17] Initially detained at Guantanamo Bay, Hamdi was removed to the Naval Brig in Norfolk, Virginia, in April 2002, when authorities learned that he was a United States citizen. There he remains awaiting the filing of criminal charges by the government. A federal public defender and a private citizen filed "next friend" habeas petitions on Hamdi's behalf in May 2002. In June, Hamdi's father, Esam Fouad Hamdi, as "next friend," also filed for habeas corpus. After resolving the question of who had standing to bring a habeas petition on Hamdi's behalf, the court appointed the public defender to represent him, required the government to allow Hamdi unmonitored access to counsel, and ordered the government to answer the habeas petition. Thus began a complicated series of proceedings in the U.S. District Court for the Eastern District of Virginia and the Fourth Circuit Court of Appeals. On remand from the Fourth Circuit Court of Appeals, the District Court, on August 16, 2002, held that Hamdi was entitled to due process of law and certified for appeal the question of whether a declaration by Under Secretary of Defense Michael Mobbs was sufficient "to establish that continuing military detention did not violate [the] detainee's due process rights."[18]

Ultimately, on January 8, 2003, the Fourth Circuit remanded the case with directions to dismiss Hamdi's habeas corpus petition. Chief Judge J. Harvey Wilkinson, writing for a three-judge panel, held that the Mobbs declaration was a "sufficient basis upon which to conclude that the Commander in Chief [had] constitutionally detained Hamdi pursuant to the war powers entrusted to him by the United States Constitution."[19] In addition, the court held that Hamdi's detention was authorized by Congress; that he did not have a right under the Geneva Convention to a formal hearing to determine his status as enemy belligerent; and that the district court's order

impermissibly conflicted with the constitutional war-making powers of the president and Congress.

As in the *Al Odah* case, involving noncitizen detainees, the court in *Hamdi* emphasized the necessity of extreme judicial deference in relation to military authority. . . .

Throughout his opinion, Judge Wilkinson adheres to the military justice model. Although he recognizes that judicial review "does not disappear during wartime," he leaves no doubt that, in his view, the judiciary is in no position to second-guess military judgments.

By contrast, in considering Jose Padilla's challenge to detention as an "enemy combatant," Federal District Judge Michael Mukasey accorded greater weight to procedural requirements. An American citizen by birth, Padilla was arrested in Chicago on May 8, 2002, by Department of Justice officers on a material witness warrant issued by the United State District Court for the Southern District of New York to secure his testimony before a grand jury. Padilla was promptly removed from Chicago to New York, where he was detained by the Justice Department at the Metropolitan Detention Center. He appeared before the District Court on May 15 and attorney Donna R. Newman was appointed to represent him. On May 22, Padilla, represented by Newman, moved to vacate the warrant. On June 9, the government notified the court that it was withdrawing the subpoena and the court vacated the warrant. The government at that time disclosed that President Bush had designated Padilla an "enemy combatant" and had directed Secretary of Defense Donald Rumsfeld to detain him. The Defense Department immediately took custody of Padilla and transferred him to the Consolidated Naval Brig in Charleston, South Carolina.[20] It was alleged that Padilla had conspired with senior Al Qaeda members in Afghanistan for the purpose of building and detonating a radioactive "dirty bomb." He remains imprisoned at Charleston, and criminal charges have yet to be filed against him.

On June 11, Newman filed a petition for habeas corpus, challenging the lawfulness of Padilla's detention and seeking an order permitting him to consult counsel. At this point, Padilla had no direct access to the court. Thus, Newman acted for him as "next friend." On December 4, 2002, Judge Mukasey ruled that Newman, as Padilla's attorney, had standing as "next friend"; that the secretary of defense, rather than the president, was the proper respondent; that the District Court in New York retained jurisdiction to hear the case; that President Bush had authority to order Padilla's detention despite his United States citizenship; that Padilla could consult with counsel while pursuing his petition; and that the "some evidence" standard applied in determining whether Padilla was lawfully detained. Mukasey acknowledged that the government could invoke enemy combatant law and classify citizens as enemy combatants even in the absence of a declaration of war. This authority is derived from the president's constitutional power as commander in chief: "Even assuming that a court can pronounce when a 'war' exists, in the sense that word is used in the

Presidential Power, Judicial Deference, and the Status of Detainees in an Age of Terrorism by Otis H. Stephens Jr.

93

Constitution . . . a formal declaration of war is not necessary in order for the executive to exercise its constitutional authority to prosecute an armed conflict—particularly when, as on September 11, the United States is attacked."[21] In reaching this conclusion, the court relied heavily both on *Ex Parte Quirin* (1942) and *The Prize Cases* (1863).[22] In the latter, the Supreme Court rejected a challenge to the president's power to impose a blockade, an act of war, on the secessionist states. It made no difference to a majority of the Justices that the Union had not formally declared war on the Confederacy. While acknowledging that the president has no power to initiate or declare a war, the Court recognized that "war may exist without a declaration on either side. . . ." When another country imposes war on the United States, the president "does not initiate that war, but is bound to accept the challenge without waiting for any special legislative authority. . . ."[23] Judge Mukasey added that even if Congressional authority were "deemed necessary," such authority was provided by the joint resolution of Congress passed in the immediate aftermath of 9/11. Although Mukasey discussed the nebulous concepts of "lawful combatant," "unlawful combatant," and "enemy combatant," he again deferred to the president's judgment in placing Padilla in the latter category. In short, Mukasey regarded the exercise of presidential power to detain enemy aliens as a political question and refused to speculate on whether and when such power might be limited.[24]

Apart from the question of presidential power, Judge Mukasey did recognize Padilla's right to challenge his detention by means of a habeas corpus petition. To facilitate the exercise of this right, Mukasey concluded that Padilla would be permitted to consult with counsel. Since no criminal charges had been brought against Padilla, his right to counsel did not derive from the Constitution's Sixth Amendment. Nor was the court willing to invoke the self-incrimination clause or the due process clause of the Fifth Amendment in support of Padilla's contentions. Rather, Padilla's right to counsel was grounded in the habeas corpus statutes. Although recognizing that these statutes "do not explicitly provide a right to counsel for a petitioner in Padilla's circumstances," Judge Mukasey concluded that certain provisions permitted the appointment of counsel if the court determines that "the interests of justice so require."[25] Mukasey asserted that: "It would frustrate the purpose of the procedure Congress established in habeas corpus cases, and of the remedy itself, to leave Padilla with no practical means whatever for following that procedure."[26] Mukasey distinguished Padilla's situation from that of Hamdi (who was not accorded the right to counsel), pointing out that Padilla initially had access to counsel after his capture but before his designation as an enemy combatant. In conclusion, the court directed Secretary of Defense Rumsfeld "to permit Padilla to consult with counsel solely for the purpose of submitting to the court facts bearing upon his petition. . . ." Mukasey allowed access to counsel on the

condition that "Padilla [would not] use his attorneys for the purpose of conveying information to others."[27]

On March 11, 2003, after hearing the government's motion to reconsider various aspects of the order implementing the December 4, 2002, decision, Judge Mukasey reaffirmed Padilla's right to consult counsel.[28] The judge issued rulings on further procedural motions by Padilla and the government on April 9, 2003.[29]

Conclusion

Over the years, American courts have, with few exceptions, been unwilling to limit the president's war-making power. The Supreme Court has recognized broad "inherent" executive power in the field of foreign policy—sometimes maintaining that this power transcends the Constitution itself.[30] In spite of a strong inclination toward judicial deference, however, the Supreme Court and lower courts as well have nurtured the principle of judicial review. Even in the aftermath of 9/11, courts seem unwilling to relinquish this ultimate authority.

Since the World War II era, the constitutional rights of criminal defendants, as well as First Amendment freedoms of expression, have undergone major expansion. Even though some trimming back has occurred during the Rehnquist era, individuals enjoy far greater constitutional protections in these areas than during any previous period in American history. Americans have become accustomed to exercising their greatly expanded rights and liberties. This fact may help to explain the growing public debate over governmental limitations on such freedoms since 9/11. No significant debate of this kind occurred during World War II, as exemplified by the wide public approval of Franklin Roosevelt's handling of the Nazi saboteur case.[31] Even the forcible "relocation" of approximately 120,000 Americans of Japanese ancestry aroused only mild protests at the time. Moreover, in the Supreme Court's widely publicized decision on this issue, a majority of the Justices gave their stamp of constitutional approval to the government's action.[32]

Many critics of the Bush administration's war on terrorism are deeply concerned about the extent to which the procedural requirements of the criminal justice system have been brushed aside. These persons are not convinced that the traditional law enforcement model is inadequate to deal with the threat of international terrorism. As they see it, the criminal justice system has become just another casualty in the war on terrorism. On the other hand, defenders of the president's antiterrorism policies accept his assertion that we are at war with Al Qaeda. They believe that the military model is far more appropriate than the law enforcement model in dealing with detainees suspected of having ties with Al Qaeda. They reject the view that the American justice system is threatened by limiting the terrorists' access to criminal courts.

Notes

1. For background, see Stephen Dycus, et al., *National Security Law* (New York: Aspen Publishers, 2002), pp. 826–827.
2. Proclamation 7463, "Declaration of National Emergency by Reason of Certain Terrorist Attacks" (September 14, 2001). Available at www.whitehouse.gov/news/releases/2001/09/20010914–4.html.
3. "Sense Of Congress Regarding Terrorist Attacks," Pub. L. No. 107–40, 115 Stat. 224 (2001).
4. "Military Order of November 13, 2001—Detention, Treatment, and Trial of Certain Non-Citizens in the War against Terrorism," (November 13, 2001), 66 Federal Register No. 222, pp. 57833–6.
5. For general background on the Nazi saboteur episode, see Alex Abella and Scott Gordon, *Shadow Enemies: Hitler's Secret Terrorist Plot against the United States* (Guilford, CT: Globe Pequot Press, 2003), and Carl Brent Swisher, *The Supreme Court in Modern Role*, rev. ed. (New York: New York University Press, 1965), 118–22.
6. Noted in *Ex parte Quirin,* 317 U.S. 1 (1942): 18.
7. Swisher, *The Supreme Court in Modern Role*, p. 120.
8. "Military Order of November 13, 2001," Section 1(f).
9. Ibid., Section 1(g).
10. Many legal scholars and civil liberties groups have been highly critical of the November 13 military order. For example, see Neal K. Katyal and Laurence H. Tribe, "Waging War, Deciding Guilt: Trying the Military Tribunals," *Yale Law Journal* 111 (2002) and Jordan Paust, "Antiterrorism Military Commissions: Courting Illegality," *Michigan Journal of International Law* 23 (fall 2001). On the other hand, a number of scholars have defended the constitutionality of Bush's order. See, for example, Ruth Wedgwood, "Al Qaeda, Terrorism, and Military Commissions," *American Journal of International Law* 96 (2002) and Ronald J. Seivert, "War on Terrorism or Global Law Enforcement Operation?" *Notre Dame Law Review* 78 (2003). For a balanced appraisal concluding that the president's order is constitutional under *Ex parte Quirin,* but that it is inconsistent with international law, of which the laws of war are a subcategory, see Christopher M. Evans, "Terrorism on Trial: The President's Authority to Order the Prosecution of Suspected Terrorists by Military Commission," *Duke Law Journal* 51 (2002).
11. *Coalition of Clergy v. Bush,* 310 F.3d. 1153 (2002).
12. *Al Odah v. United States,* 321 F.3d 1134 (2003).
13. *Johnson v. Eisentrager,* 339 U.S. 763 (1950).
14. *American Bar Association E-Report,* e-mail report to ABA members, sent March 14, 2003.
15. *Hamdi v. Rumsfeld,* 316 F.3d 450 (2003).
16. *Padilla v. Bush,* 233 F.Supp.2d 564 (2002).
17. For a detailed account of the *Hamdi* litigation, see Nickolas A. Kacprowski, "Stacking the Deck against Suspected Terrorists: The Dwindling Procedural Limits on the Government's Power to Indefinitely Detain United States Citizens as Enemy Combatants," *Seattle Law Review* 26 (2003): 651.
18. See case history in *Hamdi v. Rumsfeld,* 316 F.3d 450 (2003), pp. 460–3.
19. *Hamdi,* p. 459.
20. See *Padilla v. Bush,* 233 F.Supp. 2d 564.
21. Ibid., p. 589.
22. *The Prize Cases,* 67 U.S. 635 (1863).
23. Ibid., p. 668.
24. U.S. District Court Judge Mukasey discusses the distinctions in combatant status: "The laws of war draw a fundamental distinction between lawful and unlawful combatants. Lawful combatants may be held as prisoners of war, but are immune from criminal prosecution by their captors for belligerent acts that do not constitute war crimes. . . . Four criteria generally determine the conditions an armed force and its members must meet in order to be considered lawful combatants: 1) To be commanded by a person responsible for his subordinates; 2) To have a fixed distinctive emblem recognizable at a distance; 3) To carry arms openly; and 4) To conduct their operations in accordance with the laws and customs of War. . . . Those who do not meet those criteria, including saboteurs and guerrillas, may not claim prisoner of war status. . . . Although in the past unlawful combatants were often summarily executed, such Draconian measures have not prevailed in modern times in what some still refer to without embarrassment as the civilized world. . . . Rather, as recognized in *Quirin,* unlawful combatants generally have been tried by military commissions. . . . Although unlawful combatants, unlike prisoners of war, may be tried and punished by military tribunals, there is no basis to impose a requirement that they be punished. Rather, their detention for the duration of hostilities is supportable—again, logically and legally—on the same ground that the detention of prisoners of war is supportable: to prevent them from rejoining the enemy. . . . The President designated Padilla an 'enemy combatant' based on his alleged association with al Qaeda and on an alleged plan undertaken as part of that association. The point of the protracted discussion immediately above is simply to support what should be an obvious conclusion: when the President designated Padilla an 'enemy combatant,' he necessarily meant that Padilla was an unlawful combatant, acting as an associate of a terrorist organization whose operations do not meet the four criteria necessary to confer lawful combatant status on its members and adherents." *Padilla v. Bush,* pp. 592–593.
25. Ibid., p. 600. See also 18 U.S.C. Sect. 3006A(2)(B) (2000).
26. Ibid., p. 602.
27. Ibid., p. 605.
28. *Padilla v. Rumsfeld,* 243 F. Supp. 2d 42 (2003).
29. 2003 WL 18581570.
30. E.g., see *U.S. v Curtiss-Wright Export Corporation,* 299 U.S. 304 (1936).
31. For a perceptive comparison of popular attitudes then and now, see Jack Goldsmith and Cass R. Sunstein, "Military Tribunals and Legal Culture: What A Difference Sixty Years Make," *Constitutional Commentary* 19 (2002): 261.
32. See *Korematsu v. United States,* 323 U.S. 214 (1944). But see also of *Ex parte Endo,* 323 U.S. 283 (1944) ordering the release of a relocation center detainee whose "loyalty" to the United States had been confirmed. See also Patrick O. Gudridge, "Remember Endo?" *Harvard Law Review* 116 (2003): 1933.

Critical Thinking

1. Is history likely to regard the judicial deference under President George W. Bush following 9/11 on a par with the circumstances of presidential power as assumed by FDR following the attack on Pearl Harbor?

Presidential Power, Judicial Deference, and the Status of Detainees in an Age of Terrorism by Otis H. Stephens Jr.

95

2. How important to the debate on "privilege of litigation" is the observation that in neither *Al Odah* (2002) nor *Eisentrager* (1950) were the petitioners within the territorial jurisdiction of the United States at any relevant time?
3. Assess the following facts, which occurred after this selection was written: In 2006, Congress upheld President Bush's authority to designate certain people as "enemy combatants," deprived of habeas corpus; in 2008, the Supreme Court ruled this unconstitutional.

Create Central

www.mhhe.com/createcentral

Internet References

The American Civil Liberties Union
www.aclu.org

From *American National Security and Civil Liberties in an Era of Terrorism* by David B. Cohen and John W. Wells, eds. (Palgrave Macmillan, 2004). Copyright © 2004 by David B. Cohen and John W. Wells. Reprinted by permission.

Unit 6: Interest Groups

Federalist, No. 10

James Madison

Learning Outcomes

After reading this selection, you should be able to:

1. Cite Madison's definition of a "faction."
2. Discuss the human inclination to fall into mutual animosities.
3. Analyze the difference between a republic and a democracy.

The *Federalist Papers* are a collection of 85 essays written by James Madison (1751–1836), Alexander Hamilton (1757–1804), and John Jay (1745–1829) under the pseudonym "Publius." American government scholars agree that these papers reveal in a systematic and comprehensive way the intentions of the framers of the U.S. Constitution as they designed a Federalist legal framework in conjunction with a representative, or popular, form of government. Since there existed a strong Anti-Federalist partisan sentiment in New York, the authors thought that a massive printing of these essays written in powerful political rhetoric would persuade many to vote for ratification of the Constitution. However, some scholars argue that the *Federalist Papers* had only a minor impact on the successful ratification of the Constitution. Their enduring value is in their comprehensive analysis of the configuration of the institutions and processes of the new government.

Madison's *Federalist*, No. 10 (1788) is the most frequently cited of all the *Federalist Papers*. It is recognized by political science scholars as America's unique contribution to political theory. In the following selection from *Federalist*, No. 10, Madison analyzes a prescribed set of solutions to the fundamental governmental problem of maintaining a delicate balance between the establishment of a representative government and popular majority rule, and the simultaneous fulfillment of individual and minority rights and freedoms.

The primary goal of *Federalist*, No. 10 is to demonstrate how a "well-constructed Union" can "break and control the violence of faction" or limit "the mischiefs of faction." Madison defines *factions* as competitive economic special interest groups that often conflict with the interests of other citizens or the public good of the entire community or nation. Factions naturally evolve in any society due to the unequal distribution of property and the natural inclination of individuals to join private voluntary associations due to self-interested human nature. Instead of abolishing factions, which would destroy individual liberty, Madison recommends regulating the excesses of factions through a Federalist division of public authority and a republican, or representative, form of government.

Madison correctly projected that the division of governmental powers among several branches; the levels of federal, state, and local governments; the numerous checks and balances in the Constitution; and the intense competition between the factions themselves would all assist to limit or work against the negative and dangerous effects of factions.

Key Concept: the regulation of factions

Among the numerous advantages promised by a well-constructed Union, none deserves to be more accurately developed than its tendency to break and control the violence of faction. The friend of popular governments never finds himself so much alarmed for their character and fate as when he contemplates their propensity to this dangerous vice. He will not fail, therefore, to set a due value on any plan which, without violating the principles to which he is attached, provides a proper cure for it. The instability, injustice, and confusion introduced into the public councils have, in truth, been the mortal diseases under which popular governments have everywhere perished, as they continue to be the favorite and fruitful topics from which the adversaries to liberty derive their most specious declamations. The valuable improvements made by the American constitutions on the popular models, both ancient and modern, cannot certainly be too much admired; but it would be an unwarrantable partiality to contend that they have as effectually obviated the danger on this side, as was wished and expected. Complaints are everywhere heard from our most considerate and virtuous citizens, equally the friends of public and private faith and of public and personal liberty, that our governments are too unstable, that the public good is disregarded in the conflicts of rival parties, and that measures are too often decided, not according to the rules of justice and the rights of the minor party, but by the superior force of an interested and Overbearing majority. However anxiously we may wish that these complaints had no foundation, the evidence of known facts will not permit us to deny that they are in some degree true. It will be found, indeed, on a candid review of our situation, that some of the distresses under which we labor have been erroneously charged on the operation of our governments; but it will be found, at the same time, that other causes will not alone account for many of our heaviest misfortunes; and, particularly, for that prevailing and increasing distrust of public engagements and alarm for private rights which are echoed from one end of the continent to the other. These must be chiefly, if not wholly, effects of the unsteadiness and injustice with which a factious spirit has tainted our public administration.

By a faction I understand a number of citizens, whether amounting to a majority or minority of the whole, who are united and actuated by some common impulse of passion, or of interest, adverse to the rights of other citizens, or to the permanent and aggregate interests of the community.

There are two methods of curing the mischiefs of faction: the one, by removing its causes; the other, by controlling its effects.

There are again two methods of removing the causes of faction: the one, by destroying the liberty which is essential to its existence; the other, by giving to every citizen the same opinions, the same passions, and the same interests.

It could never be more truly said than of the first remedy that it was worse than the disease. Liberty is to faction what air is to fire, an aliment without which it instantly expires. But it could not be a less folly to abolish liberty, which is essential to political life, because it nourishes faction than it would be to wish the annihilation of air, which is essential to animal life, because it imparts to fire its destructive agency.

The second expedient is as impracticable as the first would be unwise. As long as the reason of man continues fallible, and he is at liberty to exercise it, different opinions will be formed. As long as the connection subsists between his reason and his self-love, his Opinions and his passions will have a reciprocal influence on each other; and the former will be objects to which the latter will attach themselves. The diversity in the faculties of men, from which the rights of property originate, is not less an insuperable obstacle to a uniformity of interests. The protection of these faculties is the first object of government. From the protection of different and unequal faculties of acquiring property, the possession of different degrees and kinds of property immediately results; and from the influence of these on the sentiments and views of the respective proprietors ensues a division of the society into different interests and parties.

The latent causes of faction are thus sown in the nature of man; and we see them everywhere brought into different degrees of activity, according to the different circumstances of civil society. A zeal for different opinions concerning religion, concerning government, and many other points, as well of speculation as of practice; an attachment to different leaders ambitiously contending for preeminence and power; or to persons of other descriptions whose fortunes have been interesting to the human passions, have, in turn, divided mankind into parties, inflamed them with mutual animosity, and rendered them much more disposed to vex and oppress each other than to cooperate for their common good. So strong is this propensity of mankind to fall into mutual animosities that where no substantial occasion presents itself the most frivolous and fanciful distinctions have been sufficient to kindle their unfriendly passions and excite their most violent conflicts. But the most common and durable source of factions has been the various and unequal distribution of property. Those who hold and those who are without property have ever formed distinct interests in society. Those who are creditors, and those who are debtors, fall under a like discrimination. A landed interest, a manufacturing interest, a mercantile interest, a moneyed interest, with many lesser interests, grow up of necessity in civilized nations, and divide them into different classes, actuated by different sentiments and views. The regulation of these various and interfering interests forms the principal task of modern legislation and involves the spirit of party and faction in the necessary and ordinary operations of government.

No man is allowed to be a judge in his own cause, because his interest would certainly bias his judgment, and, not improbably, corrupt his integrity. With equal, nay with greater reason, a body of men are unfit to be both judges and parties at the same time; yet what are many of the most important acts of legislation but so many judicial determinations, not indeed concerning the rights of single persons, but concerning the rights of large bodies of citizens? And what are the different classes of legislators but advocates and parties to the causes which they determine? Is a law proposed concerning private debts? It is a question to which the creditors are parties on one side and the debtors on the other. Justice ought to hold the balance between them. Yet the parties are, and must be, themselves the judges; and the most numerous party, or in other words, the most powerful faction must be expected to prevail. Shall domestic manufacturers be encouraged, and in what degree, by restrictions on foreign manufacturers? are questions which would be differently decided by the landed and the manufacturing classes, and probably by neither with a sole regard to justice and the public good. The apportionment of taxes, on the various descriptions of property is an act which seems to require the most exact impartiality; yet there is, perhaps, no legislative act in which greater opportunity and temptation are given to a predominant party to trample on the rules of justice. Every shilling with which they overburden the inferior number is a shilling saved to their own pockets.

It is in vain to say that enlightened statesmen will be able to adjust these clashing interests and render them all subservient to the public good. Enlightened statesmen will not always be at the helm. Nor, in many cases, can such an adjustment be made at all without taking into view indirect and remote considerations, which will rarely prevail, over the immediate interest which one party may find in disregarding the rights of another or the good of the whole.

The inference to which we are brought is that the *causes* of faction cannot be removed and that relief is only to be sought in the means of controlling its *effects*.

If a faction consists of less than a majority, relief is supplied by the republican principle, which enables the majority to defeat its sinister views by regular vote. It may clog the administration, it may convulse the society; but it will be unable to execute and mask its violence under the forms of the Constitution. When a majority is included in a faction, the form of popular government, on the other hand, enables it to sacrifice to its ruling passion or interest both the public good and the rights of other citizens. To secure the public good and private rights against the danger of such a faction, and at the same time to preserve the spirit and the form of popular government, is then the great object to which our inquiries are directed. Let me add that it is the great desideratum by which alone this form of government can be rescued from the opprobrium under which it has so long labored and be recommended to the esteem and adoption of mankind.

By what means is this object attainable? Evidently by one of two only. Either the existence of the same passion or interest in a majority at the same time must be prevented, or the majority, having such coexistent passion or interest, must be rendered, by their number and local situation, unable to concert and carry into effect schemes of oppression. If the impulse and the opportunity be suffered to coincide, we well know that neither moral nor religious motives can be relied on as an adequate control. They are not found to be such on the injustice and violence of individuals, and lose their efficacy in proportion to the number combined together, that is, in proportion as their efficacy becomes needful.

From this view of the subject it may be concluded that a pure democracy, by which I mean a society consisting of a small number of citizens, who assemble and administer the government in person, can admit of no cure for the mischiefs of faction. A common passion or interest will, in almost every case, be felt by a majority of the whole; a communication and concert results from the form of government itself; and there is nothing to check the inducements to sacrifice the weaker party or an obnoxious individual. Hence it is that such democracies have ever been spectacles of turbulence and contention; have

ever been found incompatible with personal security or the rights of property; and have in general been as short in their lives as they have been violent in their deaths. Theoretic politicians, who have patronized this species of government, have erroneously supposed that by reducing mankind to a perfect equality in their political rights, they would at the same time be perfectly equalized and assimilated in their possessions, their opinions, and their passions.

A republic, by which I mean a government in which the scheme of representation takes place, opens a different prospect and promises the cure for which we are seeking. Let us examine the points in which it varies from pure democracy, and we shall comprehend both the nature of the cure and the efficacy which it must derive from the Union.

The two great points of difference between a democracy and a republic are: first, the delegation of the government, in the latter, to a small number of citizens elected by the rest; secondly, the greater number of citizens and greater sphere of country over which the latter may be extended.

The effect of the first difference is, on the one hand, to refine and enlarge the public views by passing them through the medium of a chosen body of citizens, whose wisdom may best discern the true interest of their country and whose patriotism and love of justice will be least likely to sacrifice it to temporary or partial considerations. Under such a regulation it may well happen that the public voice, pronounced by the representatives of the people, will be more consonant to the public good than if pronounced by the people themselves, convened for the purpose. On the other hand, the effect may be inverted. Men of factious tempers, of local prejudices, or of sinister designs, may, by intrigue, by corruption, or by other means, first obtain the suffrages, and then betray the interests of the people. The question resulting is, whether small or extensive republics are most favorable to the election of proper guardians of the public weal; and it is clearly decided in favor of the latter by two obvious considerations.

In the first place it is to be remarked that however small the republic may be the representatives must be raised to a certain number in order to guard against the cabals of a few; and that however large it may be they must be limited to a certain number in order to guard against the confusion of a multitude. Hence, the number of representatives in the two cases not being in proportion to that of the constituents, and being proportionally greatest in the small republic, it follows that if the proportion of fit characters be not less in the large than in the small republic, the former will present a greater option, and consequently a greater probability of a fit choice.

In the next place, as each representative will be chosen by a greater number of citizens in the large than in the small republic, it will be more difficult for unworthy candidates to practise with success the vicious arts by which elections are too often carried; and the suffrages of the people being more free, will be more likely to center on men who possess the most attractive merit and the most diffusive and established characters.

It must be confessed that in this, as in most other cases, there is a mean, on both sides of which inconveniencies will be found to lie. By enlarging too much the number of electors, you render the representative too little acquainted with all their local circumstances and lesser interests; as by reducing it too much, you render him unduly attached to these, and too little fit to comprehend and pursue great and national objects. The federal Constitution forms a happy combination in this respect; the great and aggregate interests being referred to the national, the local and particular to the State legislatures.

The other point of difference is the greater number of citizens and extent of territory which may be brought within the compass of republican than of democratic government; and it is this circumstance principally which renders factious combinations less to be dreaded in the former than in the latter. The smaller the society, the fewer probably will be the distinct parties and interests composing it; the fewer the distinct parties and interests, the more frequently will a majority be found of the same party; and the smaller the number of individuals composing a majority, and the smaller the compass within which they are placed, the more easily will they concert and execute their plans of oppression. Extend the sphere and you take in a greater variety of parties and interests; you make it less probable that a majority of the whole will have a common motive to invade the rights of other citizens; or if such a common motive exists, it will be more difficult for all who feel it to discover their own strength and to act in unison with each other. Besides other impediments, it may be remarked that, where there is a consciousness of unjust or dishonorable purposes, communication is always checked by distrust in proportion to the number whose concurrence is necessary.

Hence, it clearly appears that the same advantage which a republic has over a democracy in controlling the effects of faction is enjoyed by a large over a small republic—is enjoyed by the Union over the States composing it. Does this advantage consist in the substitution of representatives whose enlightened views and virtuous sentiments render them superior to local prejudices and to schemes of injustice? It will not be denied that the representation of the Union will be most likely to possess these requisite endowments. Does it consist in the greater

security afforded by a greater variety of parties, against the event of any one party being able to outnumber and oppress the rest? In an equal degree does the increased variety of parties comprised within the Union increase this security. Does it, in fine, consist in the greater obstacles opposed to the concert and accomplishment of the secret wishes of an unjust and interested majority? Here again the extent of the Union gives it the most palpable advantage.

The influence of factious leaders may kindle a flame within their particular States but will be unable to spread a general conflagration through the other States. A religious sect may degenerate into a political faction in a part of the Confederacy; but the variety of sects dispersed over the entire face of it must secure the national councils against any danger from that source. A rage for paper money, for an abolition of debts, for an equal division of property, or for any other improper or wicked project, will be less apt to pervade the whole body of the Union than a particular member of it, in the same proportion as such a malady is more likely to taint a particular county or district than an entire State.

In the extent and proper structure of the Union, therefore, we behold a republican remedy for the diseases most incident to republican government. And according to the degree of pleasure and pride we feel in being republicans ought to be our zeal in cherishing the spirit and supporting the character of federalists.

Critical Thinking

1. Why is the distinction between a republic and a democracy relevant to the regulation of factions?
2. If Madison were with us today, would he make a favorable assessment of the Constitution's ability to limit "the mischiefs of factions"?

Create Central

www.mhhe.com/createcentral

Internet References

The Democratic National Committee (DNC)
www.democrats.org

The Federal Election Commission
www.fec.gov

The Republican National Committee (RNC)
www.rnc.org

From *Federalist*, no. 10, 1788.

The Changing Nature of Interest Group Politics

Burdett A. Loomis and Allan J. Cigler

Learning Outcomes

After reading this selection, you should be able to:

1. Recognize the development of special-interest groups as a highly significant trend.
2. Perceive the impact of the 1970s federal election campaign reforms upon the proliferation of political action committees (PACs).
3. Identify the chief beneficiaries of the trend in interest group politics.

The book *Interest Group Politics* established editors Burdett A. Loomis and Allan J. Cigler as leading scholars of American interest group politics and theory. By focusing on the behavior of political interest groups, interest group theory expresses a set of assumptions about the development and implementation of public policy. According to this perspective, adopted by Loomis and Cigler, intense competition among organized special interests results in some policy output. The authors also contend that interest groups that are successful in influencing governmental decisions tend to rely upon contemporary technological developments (e.g., cable television and computer-based operations).

Loomis (b. 1945) received his M.A. and Ph.D. from the University of Wisconsin. He has taught at Indiana University, Knox College, and the University of Kansas, where he served as chairman of the political science department from 1986 to 1989. His research has focused on legislative politics, political parties, and interest groups. His other published works include *Setting Course: A Congressional Management Guide* (American University, 1984) and *The New American Politician* (Basic Books, 1988).

Cigler (b. 1943) received his M.A. from the University of Maryland and his Ph.D. from Indiana University. A professor of political science at the University of Kansas, Cigler's research interests have included political behavior, political parties and interest groups, elections, and public opinion. He has written numerous scholarly articles for various political science journals, and he is the coeditor, with William P. Browne, of *U.S. Agricultural Groups: Institutional Profiles* (Greenwood Press, 1990).

In the following selection from the fifth edition of *Interest Group Politics* (CQ Press, 1998), Loomis and Cigler focus on fundamental developments that have occurred in interest group political behavior during the past few decades. In particular, they emphasize the most significant changes in the character, function, and impact of political interest groups. The authors discuss the development of special, or single-issue, interest groups (e.g., the National Rifle Association [NRA] and Mothers Against Drunk Driving [MADD]) as a highly significant trend. Loomis and Cigler also analyze the impact of federal election campaign finance reform legislation in the early 1970s upon the proliferation of political action committees (PACs).

Key Concept: the contemporary nature and influence of political interest groups

*F*rom James Madison to Madison Avenue, political interests have played a central role in American politics. But this great continuity in our political experience has been matched by the ambivalence with which citizens, politicians, and scholars have approached interest groups. James Madison's warnings on the dangers of faction echo in the rhetoric of reformers ranging from Populists and Progressives near the turn of the century to the so-called public interest advocates of today.

If organized special interests are nothing new in American politics, can today's group politics nevertheless be seen as having undergone some fundamental changes? Acknowledging that many important, continuing trends do exist, we seek to place in perspective a broad series of changes in the nature of modern interest group politics. Among the most substantial of these developments are:

1. A great proliferation of interest groups since the early 1960s
2. A centralization of group headquarters in Washington, D.C., rather than in New York City or elsewhere
3. Major technological developments in information processing that promote more sophisticated, more timely, and more specialized communication strategies, such as grassroots lobbying
4. The rise of single-issue groups
5. Changes in campaign finance laws (1971, 1974) and the ensuing growth of political action committees (PACs), and more recently, the growth of independent campaign expenditures by some interests
6. The increased formal penetration of political and economic interests into the bureaucracy (advisory committees), the presidency (White House group representatives), and the Congress (caucuses of members)
7. The continuing decline of political parties' abilities to perform key electoral and policy-related activities
8. The increased number, activity, and visibility of public-interest groups, such as Common Cause and the Ralph Nader-inspired public interest research organizations
9. The growth of activity and impact by institutions, including corporations, universities, state and local governments, and foreign interests
10. A continuing rise in the amount and sophistication of group activity in state capitals, especially given the devolution of some federal programs and substantial increases in state budgets. . . .

Contemporary Interest Group Politics

Several notable developments mark the modern age of interest group politics. Of primary importance is the large and growing number of active groups and other interests. The data here are sketchy, but one major study found that most current groups came into existence after World War II and that group formation has accelerated substantially since the early 1960s.[1] Also since the 1960s groups have increasingly directed their attention toward the center of power in Washington, D.C., as the scope of federal policy making has grown, and groups seeking influence have determined to "hunt where the ducks are." As a result, the 1960s and 1970s marked a veritable explosion in the number of groups lobbying in Washington.

A second key change is evident in the composition of the interest group universe. Beginning in the late 1950s political participation patterns underwent some significant transformations. Conventional activities such as voting declined, and political parties, the traditional aggregators and articulators of mass interests, became weaker. Yet at all levels of government, evidence of citizen involvement has been apparent, often in the form of new or revived groups. Particularly impressive has been the growth of citizens' groups—those organized around an idea or cause (at times a single issue) with no occupational basis for membership. Fully 30 percent of such groups have formed since 1975, and in 1980 they made up more than one-fifth of all groups represented in Washington.[2]

In fact, a participation revolution has occurred in the country as many citizens have become active in an ever-increasing number of protest groups, citizens' organizations, and special interest groups. These groups often comprise issue-oriented activists or individuals who seek collective material benefits. The free-rider problem has proven not to be an insurmountable barrier to group formation, and many new interest groups do not use selective material benefits to gain support. Still, since the late 1970s, the number of these groups has remained relatively stable, and they have become well-established in representing the positions of consumers, environmentalists, and other public interest organizations.[3]

Third, government itself has had a profound effect on the growth and activity of interest groups. Early in this century, workers found organizing difficult because business and industry used government-backed injunctions to prevent strikes. By the 1930s, however, with the prohibition of injunctions in private labor disputes and the rights of collective bargaining established, most governmental actions directly promoted the growth of labor unions. In recent years changes in the campaign finance laws have led to an explosion in the number of PACs, especially among business, industry, and issue-oriented groups. Laws facilitating group formation certainly have contributed to group proliferation, but government policy in a broader sense has been equally responsible.

Fourth, not only has the number of membership groups grown in recent decades, but a similar expansion has occurred in the political activity of many other interests such as individual corporations, universities, churches, governmental units, foundations, and think tanks.[4] Historically, most of these interests have been satisfied with representation by trade or professional associations. Since the mid-1960s, however, many have chosen to employ their own Washington representatives. Between 1961 and 1982, for example, the number of corporations with Washington offices increased tenfold.[5] The chief beneficiaries of this trend are Washington-based lawyers, lobbyists, and public relations firms. The number of attorneys in the nation's capital, taken as a rough indicator of lobbyist strength, tripled between

1973 and 1983, and the growth of public relations firms was dramatic. The lobbying community of the 1990s is large, increasingly diverse, and part of the expansion of policy domain participation, whether in agriculture, the environment, or industrial development. Overall, political scientist James Thurber has calculated that, as of the early 1990s, 91,000 lobbyists and people associated with lobbying were employed in the Washington, D.C., area.[6] As of 1993, the *Encyclopedia of Associations* listed approximately 23,000 organizations, up more than 50 percent since 1980 and almost 40 percent since 1955.[7] . . .

The Growth of Interest Groups

Although it may be premature to formulate a theory that accounts for spurts of growth,[8] we can identify several factors fundamental to group proliferation in contemporary politics. Rapid social and economic changes, powerful catalysts for group formation, have developed new interests (for example, the recreation industry) and redefined traditional ones (for example, higher education). The spread of affluence and education, coupled with advanced communication technologies, further contributes to the translation of interests into formal group organizations. Postindustrial changes have generated a large number of new interests, particularly among occupational and professional groups in the scientific and technological arenas. For instance, genetic engineering associations have sprung up in the wake of recent DNA discoveries, to say nothing of the growing clout and sophistication of the computer industry, from Microsoft's Bill Gates on down.

Perhaps more important, postindustrial changes have altered the pattern of conflict in society and created an intensely emotional setting in which groups rise or fall in status. Ascending groups, such as members of the new professional–managerial–technical elite, have both benefited from and supported government activism; they represent the new cultural liberalism, politically cosmopolitan and socially permissive. At the same time, rising expectations and feelings of entitlement have increased pressures on government by aspiring groups and the disadvantaged. The 1960s and early 1970s witnessed wave after wave of group mobilization based on causes ranging from civil rights to women's issues to the environment to consumer protection.

Abrupt changes and alterations in status, however, threaten many citizens. Middle America, perceiving itself as downwardly mobile, has grown alienated from the social, economic, and cultural dominance of the postindustrial elites, on one hand, and resentful toward government attempts to aid minorities and other aspiring groups, on the other. The conditions of a modern, technologically based culture also are disturbing to more traditional elements in society. Industrialization and urbanization can uproot people, cutting them loose from

familiar life patterns and values and depriving them of meaningful personal associations. Fundamentalist elements feel threatened by various technological advances (such as use of fetal tissue for medical research) as well as by the more general secular liberalism and moral permissiveness of contemporary life. In the 1990s, the growth of the Christian Coalition, both nationally and locally, has profoundly affected both electoral and legislative politics by mobilizing citizens and activists. In addition, the growth of bureaucracy, in and out of government, antagonizes everyone at one time or another.

Postindustrial threats are felt by elites as well. The nuclear arms race and its potential for mass destruction fostered the revived peace movement of the 1980s and its goal of a freeze on nuclear weapons. In addition, the excesses and errors of technology, such as oil spills and toxic waste disposal, have led to group formation among some of the most advantaged and ascending elements of society.

Illustrating the possibilities is the growth since the mid-1980s of the animal rights movement. Although traditional animal protection organizations such as the Humane Society have existed for decades, the past fifteen years have "spawned a colorful menagerie of pro-animal offspring" such as People for Ethical Treatment of Animals (PETA), Progressive Animal Welfare Society (PAWS), Committee to Abolish Sport Hunting (CASH), and the Animal Rights Network (ARN). Reminiscent of the 1960s, there is even the Animal Liberation Front, an extremist group that engages in direct actions that sometimes include violence.[9] Membership in the organizations that make up the animal rights movement has increased rapidly; founded in 1980, PETA grew from 20,000 in 1984 to 250,000 in 1988 and 370,000 by 1994.[10] One estimate places the number of animal rights organizations at 400, representing approximately ten million members.[11]

One major goal of these groups is to stop, or greatly retard, scientific experimentation on animals. Using a mix of protest, lobbying, and litigation, the movement has contributed to the closing of several animal labs, including the Defense Department's Wound Laboratory and a University of Pennsylvania facility involved in research on head injuries. In 1988 Trans-Species, a recent addition to the animal rights movement, forced the Cornell University Medical College to give up a $600,000 grant, which left unfinished a fourteen-year research project in which cats were fed barbiturates.[12]

As the most visible of the animal rights groups, PETA embarked on an intensive campaign in the early 1990s to influence children's attitudes and values toward society's treatment of animals. Using a seven-foot mascot, Chris P. Carrot, to spread its message, PETA organizers have sought to visit public schools throughout the Midwest. Although some of their message is noncontroversial (for example, children should eat their vegetables), they also argue aggressively against consuming meat. Chris P. Carrot thus carries a placard stating, "Eat your veggies, not your friends," More prosaically, PETA produces publications denouncing hunting, trapping, and other practices that abuse animals. . . .

It is not surprising that threats to those involved in activities that PETA protests have spawned countermobilizations, as, for instance, in the growth of an anti-animal rights movement. In the forefront of such actions are organizations that support hunting as a sport. They must contend with a public that has become increasingly hostile to hunting; a 1993 survey reported that 54 percent of Americans were opposed to hunting, with the youngest respondents (ages 18 to 29) expressing the most negative sentiments.[13] In addition, farm and medical groups have mobilized against the animal rights movements, and a number of new organizations have been formed. Such groups range from the incurably ill for Animal Research (iiFAR), representing those who hope for medical breakthroughs in biomedical research, to the Foundation for Animal Health, organized by the American Medical Association in hopes of diverting funds away from animal rights groups.

The most visible group in the animal rights countermobilization, Putting People First (PPF), claimed more than 35,000 members and one hundred local chapters within one year of its formation. As well as its individual members, PPF counted hunting clubs, trapping associations, rodeos, zoos, circuses, veterinary hospitals, kennels/stables, and carriage horse companies among its membership. Taking a page from animal rights' public relations activities, PPF has begun a Hunters for the Hungry campaign that has provided 160,000 pounds of venison to economically disadvantaged families in the South. To PPF, the animal rights movement has declared war on much of America and is "seeking to destroy a way of life—to tell us we can no longer believe in the Judeo-Christian principles this country was founded on. They insist every form of life is equal: humans and dogs and slugs and cockroaches." PPF leaders see the organization as speaking for "the average American who eats meat and drinks milk, benefits from medical research, wears leather, wool, and fur, hunts and fishes, and owns a pet and goes to the zoo."[14]

The intensity of conflict between the animal rights advocates and their opponents typifies the deep cultural divisions of the postindustrial era. Similar differences affect many other key issues, from gun control to education (school choice) to immigration policy. Moreover, many of these conflicts do not lend themselves to compromise, whether because of vast policy differences or group leaders' desire to keep "hot" issues alive as a way to increase membership.

Although postindustrial conflicts generate the issues for group development, the spread of affluence also systematically contributes to group formation and maintenance. In fact, affluence creates a large potential for "checkbook" membership. Issue-based groups have done especially well. Membership in such groups as

PETA and Common Cause might once have been considered a luxury, but the growth in discretionary income has placed the cost of modest dues within the reach of most citizens. For a $15 to $25 membership fee, people can make an "expressive" statement without incurring other organizational obligations. Increasing education also has been a factor in that "organizations become more numerous as ideas become more important."[15]

Reform groups and citizens' groups depend heavily upon the educated, suburban–urban, white middle-class for their membership and financial base. A Common Cause poll, for example, found that members' mean family income was $17,000 above the national average and that 43 percent of members had an advanced degree.[16] Animal rights groups display a similar membership profile, although they are disproportionately composed of college-educated, urban, professional women.[17] Other expressive groups, including those on the political Right, have been aided as well by the increased wealth of constituents and the community activism that result from education and occupational advancement.

Groups can overcome the free-rider problem by finding a sponsor who will support the organization and reduce its reliance upon membership contributions. During the 1960s and 1970s private sources (often foundations) backed various groups. Jeffrey Berry's 1977 study of eighty-three public interest organizations found that at least one-third received more than half of their funds from private foundations, and one in ten received more than 90 percent of its operating expenses from such sources.[18] Jack Walker's 1981 study of Washington-based interest groups confirmed many of Berry's earlier findings, indicating that foundation support and individual grants provide 30 percent of all citizens' group funding.[19] Such patterns produce many staff organizations with no members, raising major questions about the representativeness of the new interest group universe. Finally, groups themselves can sponsor other groups. The National Council of Senior Citizens (NCSC), for example, was founded by the AFL-CIO, which helped recruit members from the ranks of organized labor and still pays part of NCSC's expenses.

Patrons often are more than just passive sponsors who respond to group requests for funds. In many instances, group mobilization comes from the top down, rather than the reverse. The patron—whether an individual such as General Motors' heir Stewart Mott or the peripatetic conservative Richard Mellon Scaife, an institution, another group, or government entity—may serve as the initiator of group development, to the point of seeking entrepreneurs and providing a forum for group pronouncements.

Postindustrial affluence and the spread of education also have contributed to group formation and maintenance through the development of a large pool of potential group organizers. This group tends to be young, well educated, and from the middle-class, caught up in a movement for change and inspired by ideas or doctrine.

The 1960s was a period of opportunity for entrepreneurs, as college enrollments skyrocketed and powerful forces such as civil rights and the antiwar movement contributed to an idea orientation in both education and politics. Communications-based professions—from religion to law to university teaching—attracted social activists, many of whom became involved in the formation of groups. . . .

Compounding the effects of the growing number of increasingly active groups are changes in what organizations can do, largely as a result of contemporary technology. On a grand scale, technological change produces new interests, such as cable television and the silicon chip industry, which organize to protect themselves as interests historically have done. Beyond this, communications breakthroughs make group politics much more visible than in the past. Civil rights activists in the South understood this, as did many protesters against the Vietnam War. Of equal importance, however, is the fact that much of what contemporary interest groups do derives directly from developments in information-related technology. Many group activities, whether fundraising or grassroots lobbying or sampling members' opinions, rely heavily on computer-based operations that can target and send messages and process the responses.

Although satellite television links and survey research are important tools, the technology of direct mail has had by far the greatest impact on interest group politics. With a minimum initial investment and a reasonably good list of potential contributors, any individual can become a group entrepreneur. These activists literally create organizations, often based on emotion-laden appeals about specific issues, from Sarah Brady's Handgun Control to Randall Terry's Operation Rescue.[20] To the extent that an entrepreneur can attract members and continue to pay the costs of direct mail, he or she can claim—with substantial legitimacy—to articulate the organization's positions on the issues, positions probably defined initially by the entrepreneur.

In addition to helping entrepreneurs develop organizations that require few (if any) active members, information technology also allows many organizations to exert considerable pressure on elected officials. The Washington-based interests increasingly are turning to grassroots techniques to influence legislators. Indeed, after the mid-1980s these tactics had become the norm in many lobbying efforts, to the point that they were sometimes discounted as routine and "manufactured" by groups and consultants.

Communications technology is widely available but expensive. In the health care debate, most mobilized opinion has come from the best-financed interests, such as insurance companies, the drug industry, and the medical profession. Money remains the mother's milk of politics. Indeed, one of the major impacts of technology may be to inflate the costs of political action, whether for candidates engaged in increasingly expensive election campaigns or in public lobbying efforts that employ specifically targeted advertisements and highly sophisticated grassroots efforts. . . .

Contemporary Practices

Modern lobbying emphasizes information, often on complex and difficult subjects. Determining actual influence is, as one lobbyist noted, "like finding a black cat in the coal bin at midnight,"[21] but we can make some assessments about the overall impact of group proliferation and increased activity.

First, more groups are engaged in more forms of lobbying than ever before—both classic forms, such as offering legislative testimony, and newer forms, such as mounting computer-based direct mail campaigns to stir up grassroots support.[22] As the number of new groups rises and existing groups become more active, the pressure on decision makers—especially legislators—mounts at a corresponding rate. Thus, a second general point can be made: Congressional reforms that opened up the legislative process during the 1970s have provided a much larger number of access points for today's lobbyists. Most committee (and subcommittee) sessions, including the mark-ups at which legislation is written, remain open to the public, as do many conference committee meetings. More roll-call votes are taken, and congressional floor action is televised. Thus, interests can monitor the performance of individual members of Congress as never before. This does nothing, however, to facilitate disinterested decision making or foster graceful compromises on most issues.

In fact, monitoring the legions of Washington policy actors has become the central activity of many groups. As Robert Salisbury recently observed, "Before [organized interests] can advocate a policy, they must determine what position they wish to embrace. Before they do this, they must find out not only what technical policy analysis can tell them but what relevant others, inside and outside the government, are thinking and planning."[23] Given the volume of policy making, just keeping up can represent a major undertaking.

The government itself has encouraged many interests to organize and articulate their demands. The rise of group activity thus leads us to another level of analysis: the impact of contemporary interest group politics on society. Harking back to Lowi's description of interest group liberalism, we see the eventual result to be an immobilized society, trapped by its willingness to allow interests to help fashion self-serving policies that embody no firm criteria of success or failure. For example, even in the midst of the savings and loan debacle, the government continued to offer guarantees to various sectors, based not on future promise but on past bargains and continuing pressures.

The notion advanced by Olson that some such group-related stagnation affects all stable democracies makes the prognosis all the more serious. In summary form,

Olson argued that the longer societies are politically stable, the more interest groups they develop; the more interest groups they develop, the worse they work economically.[24] The United Automobile Workers' protectionist leanings, the American Medical Association's fight against intervention by the Federal Trade Commission into physicians' business affairs, and the insurance industry's successful prevention of FTC investigations all illustrate the possible linkage between self-centered group action and poor economic performance—that is, higher automobile prices, doctors' fees, and insurance premiums for no better product or service.[25]

In particular, the politics of Social Security demonstrate the difficulties posed by a highly mobilized, highly representative set of interests. Virtually everyone agrees that the Social Security system requires serious reform; at the same time, many groups of elderly citizens (with the AARP among the most moderate) have resisted changes that might reduce their benefits over time. In the end, the Social Security system will have to be restructured to maintain its viability, but particular interests pose serious obstacles to pursuing the more general welfare of society as a whole.

Conclusion

The ultimate consequences of the growing number of groups, their expanding activities both in Washington and in state capitals, and the growth of citizens' groups remain unclear. From one perspective, such changes have made politics more representative than ever before. Although most occupation-based groups traditionally have been well organized in American politics, many other interests have not. Population groupings such as African Americans, Hispanics, and women have mobilized since the 1950s and 1960s; even animals and the unborn are well represented in the interest group arena, as is the broader "public interest," however defined.

Broadening the base of interest group participation may have truly opened up the political process, thus curbing the influence of special interests. For example, agricultural policy making in the postwar era was almost exclusively the prerogative of a tight "iron triangle" composed of congressional committee and subcommittee members from farm states, government officials representing the agriculture bureaucracy, and major agriculture groups such as the American Farm Bureau. Activity in the 1970s by consumer and environmental interest groups changed agricultural politics, making it more visible and lengthening the agenda to consider such questions as how farm subsidies affect consumer purchasing power and how various fertilizers, herbicides, and pesticides affect public health.

From another perspective, more interest groups and more openness do not necessarily mean better policies or ones that genuinely represent the national interest. "Sunshine" and more participants may generate greater

complexity and too many demands for decision makers to process effectively. Moreover, the content of demands may be ambiguous and priorities difficult to set.

Finally, elected leaders may find it practically impossible to build the kinds of political coalitions necessary to govern effectively, especially in an era of divided government.

This second perspective suggests that the American constitutional system is extraordinarily susceptible to the excesses of minority faction—in an ironic way a potential victim of the Madisonian solution of dealing with the tyranny of the majority. Decentralized government, especially one that wields considerable power, provides no adequate controls over the excessive demands of special interest politics. Decision makers feel obliged to respond to many of these demands, and "the cumulative effect of this pressure has been the relentless and extraordinary rise of government spending and inflationary deficits, as well as the frustration of efforts to enact effective national policies on most major issues."[26]

In sum, the problem of contemporary interest group politics is one of representation. For particular interests, especially those that are well defined and adequately funded, the government is responsive to the issues of their greatest concern. But representation is not just a matter of responding to specific interests or citizens; the government also must respond to the collective needs of a society, and here the success of individual interests reduces the possibility of overall responsiveness. The very vibrancy and success of contemporary groups contribute to a society that finds it increasingly difficult to formulate solutions to complex policy questions.

Notes

1. Jack L. Walker, "The Origins and Maintenance of Interest Groups in America," *American Political Science Review* 77 (June 1983): 390–406; for a conservative critique of this trend, see James T. Bennett and Thomas Di Lorenzo, *Destroying Democracy* (Washington, D.C.: Cato Institute, 1986). See also many of the articles in *The Politics of Interests,* ed. Mark P. Petracca (Boulder, Colo.: Westview, 1992).
2. Walker, "Origins and Maintenance of Interest Groups," 16.
3. Robert H. Salisbury, "Interest Representation and the Dominance of Institutions," *American Political Science Review* 78 (March 1984): 64–77.
4. See Jeffery Berry, "The Power of Citizen Groups," unpublished manuscript.
5. Gregory Colgate, ed., *National Trade and Professional Associations of the United States 1982* (Washington, D.C.: Columbia Books, 1984).
6. Cited in Kevin Phillips, *Arrogant Capital* (Boston: Back Bay/Little, Brown, 1995), 43.
7. Jonathan Rauch, *Democlerosis* (New York: Times Books, 1994), 39.
8. But see Virginia Gray and David Lowery, *The Population Ecology of Interest Representation* (Ann Arbor: University of Michigan Press, 1996).
9. Kevin Kasowski "Showdown on the Hunting Ground," *Outdoor America* 51 (Winter 1986): 9.

10. Sarah Lyall, "Scientist Gives Up Grant to Do Research on Cats," *The New York Times*, November 21, 1988, A12.
11. Lauristan R. King and Kimberly Stephens, "Politics and the Animal Rights Movement" (Paper delivered at the annual meeting of the Southern Political Science Association, Tampa, Florida, 1991).
12. Lyall, "Scientist Gives Up Grant."
13. "Americans Divided on Animal Rights," *Los Angeles Times*, December 17, 1993. This national survey of 1,612 adults also found that 50 percent opposed the wearing of fur.
14. Phil McCombs, "Attack of the Omnivore," *Washington Post*, March 27, 1992, B1, B4.
15. James Q. Wilson, *Political Organizations* (New York: Basic Books, 1973), 201.
16. Andrew S. McFarland, *Common Cause* (Chatham, N.J.: Chatham House, 1984), 48–49.
17. King and Stephens, "Politics and the Animal Rights Movement," 15.
18. Jeffrey M. Berry, *Lobbying for the People* (Princeton, N.J.: Princeton University Press, 1977), 72.
19. Walker, "Origins and Maintenance of Interest Groups," 400.
20. Sarah Brady, wife of former White House press secretary James Brady, organized Handgun Control after her husband was wounded in John Hinckley's 1981 attack on Ronald Reagan. Randall Terry formed Operation Rescue, which seeks to shut down abortion clinics through direct action (for example, blocking entrances), after concluding that other prolife groups were not effective in halting abortions.
21. Quoted in "A New Era: Groups and the Grass Roots," by Burdett A. Loomis, in *Interest Group Politics* 2d ed., ed. Allan J. Cigler and Burdett A. Loomis (Washington, D.C.: CQ Press, 1983), 184.
22. Kay Lehman Schlozman and John T. Tierney, "More of the Same: Washington Pressure Group Activity in a Decade of Change," *Journal of Politics* 45 (May 1983): 18.
23. Robert H. Salisbury, "The Paradox of Interest Groups in Washington—More Groups and Less Clout," in *The New American Political System*, 2d ed., ed. Anthony King (Washington, D.C.: American Enterprise Institute, 1990), 225–226.
24. For an expansion of this argument, see Rausch, *Democlerosis*.
25. Robert J. Samuelson's description in *National Journal*, September 25, 1982, 1642.
26. Everett Carll Ladd, "How to Tame the Special Interest Groups," *Fortune*, (October 1980), 6.

Critical Thinking

1. How does the intensity of conflict between animal-rights advocates and their opponents typify the cultural divisions of the postindustrial era?
2. Even though satellite television links and survey research are important tools, why has the technology of direct mail had by far the greatest impact on interest-group politics?
3. Since the 1990s, when this selection was written, has the authors' prediction that interest-group liberalism will eventually bring about "an immobilized society" come any closer to realization?

Create Central

www.mhhe.com/createcentral

Internet References

The Democratic National Committee (DNC)
www.democrats.org

The Federal Election Commission
www.fec.gov

The Republican National Committee (RNC)
www.rnc.org

From *Interest Group Politics*, 5th ed. by Burdett A. Loomis and Allan J. Cigler (CQ Press, 1998). Copyright © 1998 by CQ Press, a division of Congressional Quarterly Inc. Reprinted by permission.

Unit 7: Political Parties

New Campaign Techniques and the American Party System

Larry Sabato

Learning Outcomes

After reading this selection, you should be able to:

1. Discuss the influence of independent professional political consultants.
2. Identify the prominent role of pollsters.
3. Assess the functions and authority of political action committees (PACs).

Larry Sabato is a contemporary scholar of campaign politics, electoral behavior, and political interest group analysis. He has researched the roles of the mass media, political consultants, and political action committees (PACs) in modern political campaigns and elections. His extensive publications have also focused on the impact of campaign finance reform legislation on contemporary elections. Sabato's classic work *The Rise of Political Consultants: New Ways of Winning Elections* (Basic Books, 1981) was recognized as an innovative study of modern political campaigns and elections. The following selection is from Sabato's "New Campaign Techniques and the American Party System," in Vernon Bogdanor, ed., *Parties and Democracy in Britain and America* (Praeger, 1984).

Sabato (b. 1952) has taught at Oxford University, and he has been a professor of government and foreign affairs at the University of Virginia for most of his professional career. Sabato was a Rhodes Scholar and a Danforth Fellow, and he is the author of 12 books and monographs, most of which focus on political campaigns and elections, the impact of the media on elections, political interest groups, state government and politics, and Virginia politics and government.

In the following selection, Sabato offers a detailed historical review and analysis of the most significant developments that have occurred among political parties and in electoral behavior. He claims that the political power and influence of political parties and party leaders have greatly declined in recent decades. Independent professional political consultants have become competitors of party leaders and political party organizations. The critical electoral functions once performed efficiently by political parties are presently provided by political consultants. Political consultants are individuals that remain independent of formal party organizations but are employed by candidates because of their professional expertise on contemporary campaign strategies such as polling, media advertising, and computerized direct-mail requests for campaign contributions. PACs have also become rivals of political parties, as they often perform basic electoral functions such as recruiting political candidates, developing the candidates' political skills, designing campaign strategies, organizing campaign staffs, and soliciting campaign contributions.

Key Concept: political parties and contemporary campaign methods

The political parties have been weakened by a multitude of circumstances, and in many respects the influence party leaders once wielded in election campaigns now is exercised by independent political consultants, just as the vital electoral roles once performed almost exclusively by parties are now available to anyone who masters the new campaign technologies such as polling, media advertising, and direct mail. The growth of political consultancy and the development of advanced campaign techniques were combined with the new election finance laws that hurt the parties, favored the prospering consultants, and encouraged the mushrooming of party-rivaling political action committees. . . .

From Party Polls to Political Consultants

. . . To understand the transformation of the parties within the American electoral system, it is important first to understand how the perception that the electorate has of them has changed over the years. Martin P. Wattenberg has recently argued[1] that American voters have *not* grown more alienated from the parties (contrary to journalistic myth). Rather, voters have become more neutral in their evaluations of the parties. Why has this happened? As Wattenberg explains it:

> The reason for party decline has not been that people no longer see any important differences between the parties. . . . Rather the problem which the parties must face is that they are considered less relevant in solving the most important domestic and foreign policy issues of the day. *In the voters' minds, the parties are losing their association with the candidates and the issues which the candidates claim to stand for.* [Emphasis added.]

That association between parties and candidates is weakening partly because the parties have ceased to be very important in the process of electing their candidates. Since candidates are not beholden to the party for their elections, they are not responsive to the party's needs or platform once in office.

As the parties have moved to the sidelines, independent political consultants have rushed forward to replace them.[2] Pollster Patrick Caddell clearly identified the alternate nonparty route that consultants have provided to willing politicians:

> Parties traditionally provided the avenue by which candidates reached voters. What we've done with media, what we've done with polling, and what we've done with direct organizational techniques is that we have provided candidates who have the resources (and that's the important thing, the resources), the ability to reach the voters and have a direct contact with the electorate without regard to party or party organization.[3]

The value of consultants to candidates is perhaps best described by the technologies at the consultants' command. The design and production of media advertising is among the essential skills that consultants offer political aspirants. It is difficult to find a contested race for major office in the United States today which does not feature television and radio commercials, and even campaigns for minor posts such as city councilor and state legislator often employ professional advertising. Quite simply, the paid media advertisements (together with the "free" media of press coverage) have replaced the political party as the middleman between candidate and voter. The candidate no longer depends so heavily on party workers to present his case to voters in his constituency; television can do it more directly and efficiently. The media consultant who can design effective and pleasing advertisements is thus worth his weight in gold to the modern candidate.

Equally prominent in modern campaigns is another kind of political consultant, the pollster. At every stage of the campaign the pollster, his survey data in hand and his role as *vox populi* [voice of the people] foremost in mind, aids the candidate and staff in crucial decisions—whether to run at all, how to run, what issues

to emphasize and which ones to avoid, which aspects of his opponent's platform and personality are vulnerable, and so on. In doing so, the pollster substitutes for party leaders, since it was exactly this kind of advice that the party kingpins used to dispense and their candidates used to follow. Once again, the new technology replaces the political party as the middleman between candidate and voter. Office seekers formerly depended on party workers to convey to them grassroots sentiment and the opinions of average voters in the constituency. Now random-sample surveys can perform the same chore, but with relative certainty and with a wealth of semiprecise detail that party wheel-horses could only guess at. For example, it would be difficult even for a modern-day George Washington Plunkitt to know which television shows are watched by a population sub-group targeted by the campaign. Simple crosstabulations of standard survey questions used by the political pollsters reveal this, and more, today. While the process of polling has many weaknesses[4] and is rarely as error-free as the unwittingly arrogant disclaimer accompanying most surveys suggests—"this poll is accurate to within a margin of error of plus or minus 4 percent"—survey sampling is usually more accurate and normally more directly useful than the surmises of party leaders. Candidates know it, and that is why polling consultants like Jimmy Carter's Patrick Caddell and Ronald Reagan's Richard Wirthlin have had far more influence on the course of their client's campaigns than have party chiefs. It should be noted, too, that the pollster's dominance has recently been extended to governance as well as campaigning. Caddell, for instance, clearly had major influence on a number of President Carter's decisions (including his crucial 1979 Camp David domestic summit and subsequent "crisis of confidence" speech[5]). Wirthlin's frequent polling studies on a wide range of subjects are reportedly closely studied by President Reagan and his key aides; Wirthlin himself is a frequent White House visitor. . . .

Even the political party's greatest remaining strength, its precinct organization and network of volunteers, is being duplicated by independent consultants.[6] Some consultants use a technique called "Instant Organization" (IO), which utilizes paid callers to ring up voters from centralized banks of telephones. Using various tested scripts, block captains are recruited and office volunteers solicited. Subsequent mail and telephone contracts, as well as get-togethers with the candidate and his surrogate, keep the "instant" volunteers motivated.

The Relationship of Consultants to the Political Parties

The consultants and their new campaign technologies have, then, increasingly been replacing the parties as the middlemen between candidate and voter. If the relationship between the consultants and the parties is a symbiotic or mutually reinforcing one, little harm—and potentially much good—is done. Unfortunately for the political parties, few consultants are vitally interested in the health of the party system. It is fair to describe most political consultants as businessmen, not party ideologues. There are exceptions, and a few are fierce partisans, having had their political baptism as party functionaries and occasionally having had years of direct party employment. One of these, Robert Odell, is inclined to take on just about any Republican in his direct-mail firm because, "Democrats do little or nothing that I respect and Republicans do nearly everything I respect." Striking a rare pose for a private consultant, Odell declares, "The most important goal for me is to make the Republican party effective." Matt Reese holds the Democratic party in similar esteem, observing only half in jest that he is "a partisan without apology. I don't even *like* Republicans, except for Abraham Lincoln." And few professionals have shown as long and abiding a concern for a political party as Stuart Spencer and his partner, Bill Roberts, who both began their political careers as volunteers for the Republican party in California. Their consulting shop actually developed around the GOP and was encouraged by the party. Spencer explained that he and Roberts "wanted to be an extension of the party, a management tool that the party could use," and they viewed each of their early consultant outings as "an opportunity for the Republican party."

The greatest number of consultants, though, are simply not committed in any real sense to a political party. Michael Kaye, for instance, proclaims himself to be an Independent and the parties to be "bull."

Yet, for all of the danger supposedly involved in crossing party lines, consultants seem to yield frequently to the temptation. Democrat Peter Hart conducted Republican U.S. Senate nominee John Heinz's surveys in Pennsylvania in 1976 (and claimed he was told he could not take polls for Jimmy Carter as a consequence). Media consultant David Garth has been "all over the lot," as one of his detractors termed his tendency to take moderate-to-liberal Democrats and Republicans indiscriminately, and it was a surprise to no one in the profession when GOP Congressman John Anderson tapped Garth to help with his 1980 Independent presidential bid. Another Democratic-leaning liberal firm, Craver, Matthews, Smith, and Company, took on Anderson's direct-mail program. The now-defunct firm of Baus and Ross in California secured the accounts of Richard Nixon, Barry Goldwater, and Edmund G. "Pat" Brown, Sr., within a few years of one another. The survey firm of D.M.I. not only worked for both Democrats and Republicans, it actually polled both sides of the same congressional election district in 1966. Vincent Breglio, the D.M.I. vice president, took one side, and President Richard Wirthlin took the other. They ran the research independent of one another and provided consulting services to each side without crossing communications. Apparently the candidates were rather trusting souls who reportedly agreed to this outrageous arrangement

(although it was quite a useful one for the firm's "win ratio"). D.M.I. converted permanently to Republicanism in 1967 when Michigan Governor George Romney asked the firm to join his presidential effort on condition that it work only for the GOP. Convinced that the move was good for business, Wirthlin and Breglio made the switch over the objections of the Democratic members of the firm, who nevertheless stayed. . . .

Even though virtually all consultants identify with one of the parties (primarily for business purposes, as Michael Kaye suggested), most of them are at least passively hostile to the parties, some of them openly contemptuous. At times consultants can sound like the evangelical populists they often portray their candidates to be, railing against the evils of boss rule. "Really the only major function of the political party structure these days is to nominate the candidates for president, and my personal feeling is that we'd all be better off if this responsibility also were placed in the hands of the people," consultant Joe Napolitan has written.[7] Media consultant Bob Goodman, in tones echoed time and again by his fellow independent professionals, lauds consultants for unshackling candidates, putting them beyond the reach of the petty party barons:

> We have enabled people to come into a party or call themselves independent Democrats or Republicans and run for office without having to pay the dues of being a party member in a feudal way. Meaning kiss the ass of certain people and maybe down the line they'll give you a shot at public office.

Parties are usually viewed as one more obstacle in the way of the client's election. "In most places the party operation does not do a great deal to help a candidate get elected the first time, and [it] is more of a hassle than it's worth," concludes GOP media consultant Douglas Bailey. Many party-consultant relationships are marked by sharp conflict, explained by Napolitan as the result of party workers' jealousy of consultants, who "have replaced organization regulars in making important campaign decisions" and who are possible usurpers of "what they [party workers] consider their rights to patronage."[8]

A natural consequence of the consultant's antagonism toward the party is his willingness to run his candidates apart from, or even against, their party label. It was difficult to know whether GOP nominee John Heinz was a Democrat or Republican in his 1976 Pennsylvania Senate race, since media consultant David Garth fashioned his advertising campaign around an antiparty theme: "If you think Pennsylvania needs an *Independent* senator, elect John Heinz." One of Garth's spots actually featured a glowing "endorsement" of Heinz's character by Jimmy Carter (delivered in March of 1975), to further confuse the voter. Scrambling labels may seem unfortunate to those concerned about the role of party in elections, but at least the party is not under direct attack, a common tactic in party primaries. Milton Shapp, for instance, won the Democratic nomination for the Pennsylvania governorship in 1966 in a major upset, thanks to Joe Napolitan's "Man Against the Machine" theme.[9] . . .

The Growth of Political Action Committees

Possibly the most far-reaching change wrought by FECA was in its legitimizing the use of corporate funds to establish and administer Political Action Committees (PACs). Labor unions already had that right, and the PAC had long been an essential political tool for organized labor. Now business and trade interests could benefit as well.

Once the floodgates were opened, the growth of corporate and trade PACs was nothing short of phenomenal.

Just between 1976 and 1978, the number of PACs rose from 1,242 to 1,938 and by 1982 PACs totaled 3,371. Their total spending increased from $30.1 million in 1976 to $127.7 million in 1980 and on to $190.4 million in 1982.[10] New business PACs comprised by far the largest share of the growth. In 1978, for instance, when all PACs accounted for $34.1 million of the $199 million in contributions received by congressional candidates, one researcher estimated that business and business-related groups outspent labor by better than two to one.[11] Between 1976 and 1978, corporate PAC gifts to candidates more than doubled, while labor's PAC donations showed only a 25% gain.[12] Business and trade PACs, which at first favored incumbents (and thus gave more to Democratic candidates), have gradually moved to the GOP's banner.

Of far greater concern to the political parties is another increasingly prominent form of political action committee: the ideological PAC. The National Committee for an Effective Congress (NCEC) on the left and the Committee for the Survival of a Free Congress (CSFC) on the right are typical examples. Both provide organizational assistance to ideologically compatible candidates, irrespective of party. The NCEC is much the elder of the two and was founded in 1948. It describes itself as a "bipartisan progressive" group dedicated to civil rights, civil liberties, and internationalism. Rather than giving money, the NCEC provides specific services, such as the hiring and paying of the campaign manager, polling, targeting, and organizing. In a normal election year the NCEC will assist in some way up to 60 House candidates and a dozen Senate contenders. Russell Hemenway, executive director of the NCEC, sees his organization as a substitute for the Democratic National Committee, which "provides almost no services to candidates," and for political consultants who "are looking for campaigns that can pay hefty bills."

Many of the same goals are shared by the CSFC, which has sought to imitate somewhat the NCEC and the AFL–CIO's Committee on Political Education (COPE). "I make no secret of the fact that I admire their [COPE's] operations and have to some extent modeled our committee on the labor groups" says CSFC director Paul Weyrich.[13] Founded in 1974 with financial support from Joseph Coors, the conservative Colorado brewer, the CSFC plays a central role in the so-called "New Right," along with Richard Viguerie's direct-mail outfit and other political committees, such as Sen. Jesse Helms' Congressional Club and the National Conservative PAC.[14] Like the NCEC, the CSFC helps candidates assemble a skilled campaign team, usually contributing about $500 a month to pay the salary of a field organizer. The CSFC acts almost like a political party, recruiting candidates, refining candidates' political abilities, performing electoral organizational chores, devising strategy, and constructing campaign staffs. An extensive five-day "candidate school" is held by the CSFC four to six times every two years, and it is attended by prospective congressional contenders and campaign managers from the conservative wings of both parties, who pay a registration fee of $500 per person. The schools enlist incumbent congressmen and consultants as instructors and are organized around problem-solving groups that enable the CSFC directors to evaluate each political candidate's performance. At the end of the course, a simulated election is held, which sometimes serves as an informal primary of sorts since more than one candidate from the same district attends. In 1978, three Republican House contenders from the same Wisconsin constituency attended the CSFC school, and the PAC decided that one of them, Toby Roth, was clearly superior (and the most conservative). After the school's adjournment, Roth received the group's blessing, and he went on to win his party's nomination and to defeat an incumbent Democratic congressman in November.

Ideological PACs are proliferating and strengthening. In 1981–82, the six largest conservative PACs raised a combined total of $29.4 million, up by 25% from the previous election cycle.[15] Liberal PACs did less well, raising about $9.4 million, but five of the six top groups were new-formed in reaction to the conservative PACs' 1980 election successes—and the comparable liberal total was a scant $400,000.[16]

In explaining the explosive growth of all forms of PACs, most (but not all) roads lead to FECA. The 1974 lifting of the ban on corporate funding of PACs was crucial, and the tighter public disclosure requirements, by revealing the previously obscured extent of each corporation's involvement in politics, have produced a "keep up with the Joneses" mentality among business and trade association circles. FECA's $1,000 limitation on individual contributions and its more permissive $5,000 PAC limit encourage candidates to rely on PACs as a more generous source of funds. Also having an effect on the extent and pace of PAC expansion is a growing group of political consultants, who specialize in assisting PAC formation and activity. The professionals are finding PAC consulting to be more stable, continuous, and profitable than candidate work, and almost all consultants have advised at least one or a few PACs from time to time.

Even though PACs are clearly party rivals, both parties seem to be resigned to the age of PACs. Like Willie Sutton who robbed banks "because that's where they keep the money," the parties have begun to direct their attentions to the overflowing PAC treasuries and have hired consultants to ensure that they get their fair share of PAC money. The GOP assists its candidates in soliciting PACs, helping its nominees to secure appointments with PAC officials and directing them toward committees that are likely to donate to them. Behind the facade of cooperation, however, lies the inescapable incompatibility and competitiveness between parties and PACs. Many political action committees are slowly but surely developing into rival institutions that raise money, develop memberships, recruit candidates, organize campaigns, and influence officeholders just as the parties do (or are supposed to do). PACs already outfinance the parties, partly because they drain away potential gifts to them, permitting supporters to tell the Democratic or Republican committee that they have already given at the office. PACs also outspend the parties by a large margin. While the two parties were contributing $21.9 million to their congressional nominees in 1982, for instance, PACs mustered $83.1 million in congressional contributions.

PACs are not organized along party lines and are never likely to be. In the words of one PAC official, "We believe you have to be pretty cold-blooded concerning your giving policy. You simply have to support candidates who support you . . . regardless of party or philosophy."[17] The ideological PACs, of course, make no pretense about their aims. Most of them view the parties with undisguised hostility, attacking them for a lack of ideological clarity and working to defeat the more moderate choices of party leaders in primaries. Paul Weyrich of CSFC proudly cites the case of Republican right-wing political novice Gordon Humphrey of New Hampshire, a former airline pilot who upset incumbent Democratic U.S. Senator Thomas McIntyre in 1978. The GOP senatorial campaign committee gave assistance to Humphrey's more moderate primary opponent, but CSFC helped to engineer a primary victory for him. Now, reports Weyrich, "Gordon is less than enthusiastic about the party," which suits CSFC just fine. It is easy to agree with Weyrich's observation that "both political parties would have an all-night celebration if we were to go out of business." The problem for the parties can be succinctly stated: Groups like CSFC are in no danger of going out of business. In fact, they are flourishing.

Notes

1. Martin P. Wattenberg, "The Decline of Political Partisanship in the United States: Negativity or Neutrality?" *American Political Science Review* 75 (1981): 941–50.
2. Much of the following discussion of consultants and their technologies is derived from Sabato, *The Rise of Political Consultants* (New York: Basic Books, 1981).
3. This quotation, and the others of political consultants that follow, are taken from the author's personal interviews conducted in 1979 and 1980.

4. Ibid., pp. 92–102.
5. Ibid., pp. 74–75.
6. Ibid., pp. 200–4.
7. Joseph Napolitan, *The Election Game and How to Win It* (New York: Doubleday, 1972), pp. 17–18.
8. Ibid.
9. See ibid., pp. 162–208. Shapp lost the general election that year but came back to win the statehouse in 1970.
10. See *National Journal*, February 27, 1982, p. 391, and *Congressional Quarterly Weekly*, April 10, 1982, pp. 814–23; 1982 figures are from FEC press release "1981–82 PAC Giving Up 51%," April 29, 1983.
11. See Edwin M. Epstein, "An Irony of Electoral Reform: The Business PAC Phenomenon," *Regulation* (May/June, 1979): 35–41. Also see FEC release of April 29, 1983 (ibid.).
12. Labor's figures do not, however, include separate spending for registration, get-out-the-vote, and other activities, which may amount to as much as $20 million in an election year.
13. See Paul M. Weyrich, "The New Right: PACs and Coalition Politics," in Michael J. Malbin (ed.), *Parties, Interest Groups, and Campaign Finance Laws* (Washington, D.C.: American Enterprise Institute, 1980), pp. 68–81.
14. *National Journal*, October 23, 1976, p. 1514, and January 5, 1980, p. 20. See also *Congressional Quarterly Weekly*, December 24, 1977, p. 2652.
15. See FEC release of April 29, 1983. See also *National Journal*, January 21, 1978, pp. 33–92, and March 20, 1982, pp. 500–1; *Congressional Quarterly Weekly*, February 27, 1982, p. 482, and March 6, 1982, pp. 499–505. The latter article closely examines the Helms group, which in 1981 became the country's largest PAC.
16. Ibid.
17. As quoted in *Campaigning Reports*, vol. 1, no. 6 (August 9, 1979): 10.

Critical Thinking

1. Can the political culture in America ever revert to a climate in which PACs are not campaign necessities?
2. Of the consultant, the pollster, and the PAC, which wields the most decisive sword in undermining the strength of the traditional American party system?
3. Given that this selection is from a book published in 1984, how has the substance of Sabato's thesis held up over the past 30 years?

Create Central

www.mhhe.com/createcentral

Internet References

The Democratic National Committee (DNC)
www.democrats.org

The Federal Election Commission
www.fec.gov

The Republican National Committee (RNC)
www.rnc.org

From *Parties and Democracy in Britain and America* by Vernon Bogdanor, ed. (Praeger, 1984), pp. 185–192, 196–199. Copyright © 1984 by Larry Sabato. Reprinted by permission of Greenwood Press - ABC-CLIO, LLC.

Strengthening the National Parties

James L. Sundquist

Learning Outcomes

After reading this selection, you should be able to:

1. Provide a general description of the Madisonian model for organizing government.
2. Give a brief history of the binding caucus.
3. Describe the concept of a responsible-party model.

In 1950 the American Political Science Association's Committee on Political Parties identified American political parties as weak, decentralized organizations without coherent sets of beliefs or principles and without strong party loyalty or consensus on fundamental positions or policies. The committee strongly recommended that the parties should be transformed into two highly-centralized, disciplined organizations. These organizations should then construct two national councils to generate and articulate each national party's policies and platforms and to serve as a means of transition toward a more responsible two-party system. The proposed council would also attempt to influence congressional and presidential politics by making recommendations on party candidates and by sharing in the policy-making power of both national institutions. A disciplined, responsible party system is a model of political parties that conforms to the theory of majoritarian democracy by compelling the party leadership in government to comply directly to majority public opinion. In a responsible party government, political parties articulate identifiable and coherent policies to the electorate, and the victorious party attempts to implement its agenda while in office. This type of party system also assumes that the electorate will vote for candidates because of party policies and will hold the governing party accountable for its decisions.

James L. Sundquist (b. 1915) is recognized as an outstanding scholar of political parties, electoral behavior, federalism, and intergovernmental relations. He received his M.S. from Syracuse University, and he is a senior fellow emeritus of the Brookings Institution. His publications include *The Decline and Resurgence of Congress* (Brookings Institution, 1981) and *Constitutional Reform and Effective Government* (Brookings Institution, 1986).

The following selection is an excerpt from Sundquist's "Strengthening the National Parties," in A. James Reichley, ed., *Elections American Style* (Brookings Institution, 1987). In it, Sundquist examines the inadequacies of contemporary American parties and gives his recommendations for strengthening the parties. He also analyzes the historical evolution of American political parties, and he contends that a responsible party system is unlikely in the American political system. The Madisonian model for organizing government became dominant in the American political system and was intentionally designed to impede the formation and power of factions or parties. In particular, the principle of separation of powers designed by the U.S. Constitution's framers and the creation of a bicameral Congress are perceived by Sundquist as fundamental barriers to the strengthening of political parties. Although Sundquist is skeptical of the development of a responsible party system, his reform proposals for increasing the discipline and power of parties have influenced many scholars.

Key Concept: the responsible party model

*P*olitical parties have always occupied an ambiguous position in American public life. They are profoundly mistrusted—yet accepted. Their constant maneuvering for petty advantage is reviled and ridiculed, but millions of people call themselves either Democrats or Republicans and cherish the ideals of their party with a religious fervor. Parties have been credited with such supreme achievements as saving the Union and rescuing the country from the Great Depression. But they have also been accused of placing partisan advantage ahead of the national good, of failing to conceive far-sighted programs, of running away from problems and responsibilities, and sometimes of deep and pervasive corruption. . . .

The Madisonian Model: A System without Parties

The Constitution that emerged from the Convention of 1787 made no place for parties. At that time, only the faint forerunners of modern political parties had appeared anywhere in the world. Factions had taken shape within legislative bodies in both the American states and in England, but they were not formally organized, and political organizations formed by citizens of the new states for purposes of particular elections were still local and rudimentary. Insofar as the Constitution's framers at Philadelphia referred to these groupings at all, they condemned them. They were usually termed factions or cabals rather than parties, and they were denounced as responsible for the "corruption" and "intrigue" of legislative bodies.

Accordingly, in designing the institutions of the new government, the men of 1787 deliberately sought to erect barriers against the development and influence of parties. Indeed, the basic tripartite structure of the government, as well as the division of the legislative branch into two houses, can be seen as having that essential purpose. The framers scattered power in order to forestall the evils of concentration in any individual or group, that is, in any one faction or party. They feared that a transient popular majority might be able to seize the House of Representatives and try to impose its will on the country, but they designed the Senate as a body of elder statesmen with long, overlapping terms who would rise above factionalism, and conceived the presidency, possessed of a veto in the legislative process, as the very embodiment of the nonpartisan ideal. . . .

The Responsible-Party Model

The opposing model for organizing a government recognizes not only the inevitability but the necessity of parties and assigns them the role that they everywhere seek and come naturally to assume. This is the model that has been adopted in various forms by most of the other advanced democracies of the world, and it is the one that inspires the recommendations of such contemporary American reformist groups as the CPR and the CCS.

In this model, political parties are formed because groups of people, each sharing a philosophy and a set of goals, desire governmental power in order to carry out their programs. In competition with one another, they present their programs to the people in an open and free election. The party or coalition that wins the support of a majority of the people gains control of the government and enacts its program. The minority party or parties form an opposition, with power to criticize, debate, and delay but not to block. After a few years the voters in another election render a verdict on the majority's stewardship. If they approve what has been done, they

return the ruling party or coalition to office. If they disapprove, they turn the incumbents out and entrust power to an opposition party or combination of parties. At all times, one of the parties, or a combination, is responsible for the government, possesses authority commensurate with its responsibility (subject to check by the judiciary if it exceeds its constitutional powers), and is fully accountable for whatever the government (except for the judiciary) does. In the metaphors of political science textbook writers, the political party is the tie that binds, the glue that fastens, the bridge or the web that unites the disparate institutions that make up the government. Without parties, democracy on a national scale simply could not work. . . .

The Obstacles to Strengthening Parties

The fundamental barrier to strengthening political parties is the survival in popular culture of the Madisonian model. Rejected almost unanimously by the country's political elite for two centuries, the Madisonian ideal of a factionless government has never lost its hold on the public. Factionalism is derided, and wherever possible averted, in the multitude of private organizations with which individual citizens are familiar. Why then, they ask, must politicians divide into factions that spend their energies in recrimination and petty squabbling rather than getting together to do what is best for the country?

The machines that were the target of antiparty legislation nearly a century ago have by now virtually disappeared, and the strongest political organizations in the country are those held together not by public jobs and other forms of patronage but by ideology and philosophy. Yet the antiparty rhetoric of the Progressive era still rings loudly in political campaigns. Both Jimmy Carter and Ronald Reagan trumpeted their antiestablishment sentiments, and candidates at every level still find their road to victory by running against a party organization wherever one exists—the "man against the machine." So advocates of stronger parties must struggle against the widespread and often prevailing view that powerful party organizations are more a menace than a boon.

A second obstacle, related to the first, is the self-interest of individual politicians. A stronger party is by definition one with a stronger center, possessing some institutional means of fostering unity and cohesion. But . . . the individual politician who does not aspire to national leadership usually finds more to lose than to gain by strengthening the center. With a loose, decentralized structure the state or local leader can follow the national party and its leaders when their policies are popular at home or defy them when they are not. The self-interest of thousands of politicians is a centrifugal force within the party structure that is operative constantly; centripetal political forces develop now and then, but most of the time they are overbalanced.

Recent Progress Toward Stronger Parties

Yet advocates of stronger parties are the beneficiaries of one profound trend in American politics and one series of deliberate actions, and both of these give hope.

The promising trend is that the two major parties have both become, and are still becoming, more homogeneous ideologically. This trend is the simple consequence of the party realignment that began in the 1930s and has been working its way, gradually but inexorably, through the political system. Simply put, the minority wings, once strong enough to disrupt the internal unity of the two parties, have been dying out. The "four-party system" James MacGregor Burns condemned a generation ago for producing "the deadlock of democracy" is now much more nearly a genuine two-party system.[1]

First to fade were the progressive Republicans. The progressive wing of the GOP, which spanned the generations from Theodore Roosevelt through the La Follettes and George Norris to Nelson Rockefeller and George Romney, was powerful enough as recently as twenty years ago to contest seriously for the presidential nomination. But the progressive Republicans are now an ineffectual remnant. Their counterparts, the conservative Democrats, have been vanishing as well, although more slowly. Virtually confined to the South since the New Deal era, they have from the 1960s been gradually losing their base there to the burgeoning Republican party. As conservative Democrats have ended their careers one by one—usually through retirement rather than defeat—their successors have typically been either conservative Republicans or Democrats cut in the mold of their national party. Thus Republicans occupy the seats once held by such archconservative senators as Harry F. Byrd and A. Willis Robertson of Virginia and James O. Eastland of Mississippi, while new Democratic senators arriving from the South tend to be moderates, such as Terry Sanford of North Carolina and Bob Graham of Florida, or even bear the liberal label, like Wyche Fowler of Georgia. A corresponding transformation has taken place in both parties in the House.

The deliberate actions are those taken by congressional Democrats . . . to impose discipline on party dissenters. Any article on strengthening political parties written earlier than [the mid-1960s] would have opened and closed with a call for destruction of the seniority system in the Congress. That has now been accomplished on the Democratic side. As long as seniority was automatically honored, any Democrat, no matter

how out of step with the majority of the party in Congress, could acquire all the plenary power of a committee chairmanship through mere longevity. Through that device some of the Senate and House committees most crucial to the enactment of the Democratic party's program were turned over to conservative Democrats who voted regularly with the Republicans against the majority of their own party. Sooner or later the situation was bound to prove intolerable. Finally the revolution occurred: liberals in the House forced through the party caucus a series of rules changes that not only scrapped seniority but reduced the arbitrary power of committee chairmen. The revolt was solidified in 1975 when the caucus deposed three chairmen. And it has continued to exercise disciplinary power. In 1987 the caucus voted to remove Les Aspin of Wisconsin from the chairmanship of the House Armed Services Committee, reversing itself only after Aspin humbly promised to accept its guidance on major questions of military policy. The caucus has also assumed, and exercised, the power to instruct the Democratic committee majorities to bring specific measures to the House floor.

With this power of discipline, the caucus has been revived as an instrument for building policy consensus. In their drive to assert control over party policy, the liberals won a demand for regular monthly party caucuses plus additional meetings on petition of fifty members—a dramatic departure from the once-every-two-years tradition that had prevailed for a quarter of a century. The caucus has proved to be an effective consensus-building mechanism, particularly in the long and acrimonious debate over the Vietnam War when the passion of the antiwar Democratic majority eventually persuaded some reluctant senior party figures to abandon their support. Since then it has expressed itself on a wide range of measures, including the issues of defense policy that led to Aspin's pledge of conformity. In early February 1987 the caucus denounced the Reagan administration's resumption of underground nuclear testing and urged the administration instead to begin negotiations with the Soviet Union for an agreement banning such tests.

Institutional change has occurred less formally in the clublike Senate, but the arbitrary power of Democratic committee chairmen has been effectively curtailed there as well. Within the committee structures in both houses, democratic norms now prevail.

Finally, the new Democratic party rule that guarantees seats in the quadrennial presidential nominating convention to 80 percent of the party's members of Congress may prove to be an important move in the direction of greater party cohesion. While most members will no doubt be guided by the sentiment of their states' voters as expressed in primaries and caucuses, and while they are unlikely to vote as a bloc in any case, their influence will be enhanced. In a close convention contest a determined network of House and Senate leaders could conceivably be decisive in selecting a nominee experienced in dealing with Congress, as opposed to an outsider like Jimmy Carter whose misfortunes in his relationships with the legislators and the rest of the party establishment spurred the rules revision.

So, whenever the next Democratic president is elected, advocates of responsible-party government may yet expect to see a close approximation to their model. Given reasonable luck in the presidential nominating lottery, today's more homogeneous Democratic party should be able to attain a degree of cohesion under presidential leadership that observers of the party system have not seen—except for the honeymoon years of Lyndon Johnson—in half a century.

Perhaps that cohesion will provide a satisfactory enough version of responsible-party government. But if additional measures to strengthen parties could be taken, the possibilities are worth considering. Any such measures, however, are sure to be difficult. If they were easy, they would already have been adopted, for those who lead the two national parties would assuredly prefer to lead stronger organizations.

The Limited Opportunities for Further Action

The first obvious possibility for further action is for the majorities in Congress to impose party discipline not merely to get measures out of committee but to get them passed. The means to that end is the binding caucus, which both houses last used with full effectiveness in the first Congress of the Wilson administration, in 1913–14. Through that device two-thirds of the Democratic caucus could bind the entire membership to vote with the majority. When the rule was invoked, however, the Democrats laid themselves open to attack by the Republican opposition and its supporters in the media and elsewhere, as well as by independents revolted by the spectacle of coercion. Rule by "King Caucus" developed into a major political issue. Chastened by the public reaction and by intraparty opposition as well, Senate Democrats abandoned the device after the Wilson era. The House party discarded it, too, after a brief revival in the early New Deal period. Any proposal for its reintroduction would undoubtedly arouse an even more adverse response in today's climate of political individualism, which makes the suggestion futile at the outset.

Another instrument employed by strong parties in other countries also appears beyond consideration in the United States. That is control by the national party, in one or another degree, over the selection of candidates for the national legislature. On reflection, it has to appear anomalous that anyone, no matter how ideologically opposed to the program and philosophy of the

Democratic or Republican party, may run for Congress as the party's candidate, take his or her seat with the party upon election, and receive choice committee assignments as a matter of right from the party caucus. Yet neither party has ever developed mechanisms at any level for screening candidacies. Even to design such a mechanism would be difficult. Some have suggested that the copyright laws be made the vehicle, with only persons authorized by the national party allowed to use the party label. But the idea of national control of nominations has too antidemocratic a ring—smacking, like the binding caucus, of thought control—ever to acquire noticeable support. In emergencies, like the one that developed in Illinois in 1986 when two unacceptable candidates won Democratic nominations for state office, the party can devise extraordinary remedies, as the Democrats did in that case by organizing a temporary new party. Moreover, the principal reason for advocating control of candidacies disappeared on the Democratic side when the seniority system was scrapped, for while a dissenter can win committee assignments, he or she can now be denied on ideological grounds the power of a chairmanship. This, if the issue arises, would be the easier solution for the GOP as well.

In its 1950 report the American Political Science Association Committee on Political Parties proposed creation of a national council in each party to set party policy as a means for moving toward a more responsible two-party system. The council, to consist of about fifty members from both inside and outside government, would draft the preliminary party platform and, after its adoption by the convention, interpret it. The council would also make recommendations "in respect to congressional candidates," and perhaps presidential candidates as well. But any such proposal also founders on the rock of self-interest. Why would a president and leading legislators who had won governmental office through arduous election campaigns voluntarily share their policymaking power with outsiders and submit to their restraints? That was the experience when the Democratic National Committee, influenced by the APSA committee report, established its Democratic Advisory Council after the 1956 election. The party's congressional leaders simply declined to join. The council issued well-considered policy pronouncements, but it spoke for only a segment of the party and could not serve its purpose as an institution to unify the party.

There remains one other instrument of discipline: money. Dependent as legislators are on campaign contributions, the power to grant or deny financial assistance can in theory be a powerful disciplinary tool. The national Republican party in recent years has demonstrated the capacity to raise and distribute an enormous treasury. The Democrats' capability is by no means comparable, but it has been improving. Is money a potential means, then, for tightening party discipline within Congress to achieve responsible-party government?

In theory, yes. In practice, probably not to a significant degree. Because discretionary power over congressional campaign funds would be a powerful device to achieve central control, the resistance that arises against central control of any aspect of party organization would in this case be commensurately potent. But even if discretion were granted to the national party committees, their self-interest would steer them away from exercising it as an instrument of party discipline. The overriding objective of the national party in congressional campaigns is to win a majority of seats. To this end, the party's self-interest is to support any candidate with a chance of victory, and to support most generously the candidates in the closest races, where additional spending is most likely to pay off in victories. In the heat of a campaign the national party officials making money decisions do not ask about the voting regularity of a party's incumbents or extract voting promises from nonincumbents. They ask only about election prospects. They take polls and are guided by the numbers.

So it is that in these days of Republican opulence no complaints have been heard that the national party has been using its funds in a discriminatory fashion to penalize legislators who have deviated from the Reagan party line. After the 1986 election the party was proud to announce that it had "maxed out" on every candidate, that is, given the maximum amount permissible by law to its nominee in every race. No one was disciplined. Indeed, one true believer in party discipline, Patrick J. Buchanan, the White House director of communications, could complain after the election that President Reagan had been "travelling the nation as no other president before him, fighting to save the Senate for . . . Republicans, throwing his arm around men—some of whom had cut-and-run on him in every major engagement he has fought since he came to the White House."[2]

In any case, cash contributions to congressional campaigns by national party committees are now so tightly limited by law that the potential for monetary discipline is not great. In House campaigns a party committee is treated as just another political action committee limited to contributing the same $5,000 a race (in Senate contests the ceiling is $17,500). Compared with what the array of PACs can put into closely contested races, these sums are a pittance, particularly in the case of the senior members of key committees who—if any member needed discipline—might need it the most. Any major influence by party committees has to be exerted indirectly, through advice given by party officials to friendly PACs, rather than directly through the party's own funds.

The limits on party contributions could, of course, be raised by new legislation, but the Democrats are hardly likely to use their Senate and House majorities to enhance the advantage that the richer Republican party would get

from freer spending. And if a large share of congressional campaign funds were to come from the public treasury, that would not change matters either. In the bill introduced in January 1987 as S. 2 by Democratic Senators David L. Boren of Oklahoma and Robert C. Byrd of West Virginia, the majority leader, the public funds would be distributed among candidates by formula, with the party not even serving as a channel.

Money, then, is not likely to become the powerful centralizing force within the parties that at first sight might appear possible. The handling of money has yielded to, and been conformed to, the prevailing pattern of decentralization in the party structure. And it is likely to remain that way, no matter how the sums at the disposal of the parties might be increased. The members of Congress who would write any public financing law and who already have the decisive voice in determining the national parties' policies for distributing congressional campaign funds will see to that.

Deliberate attempts, then, to strengthen political parties run counter to deep-seated public attitudes, to the self-interest of the politicians who would have to initiate change, and to the structure of governmental and political institutions, including the electoral system. The feasible actions have already been taken—notably the crucial decisions in the 1970s to assert majority rule within the congressional parties. There is a solid basis for hope, however, in political trends beyond the influence of even the political elite itself—the continuing realignment of the party system that is producing the homogeneity on which party cohesion and strength at the governmental level must rest.

If, when one party again wins single-party control of the presidency and Congress, it succeeds in coping effectively with the problems of the country, the value of the responsible-party concept will have been demonstrated and the model will win a wider public acceptance. More people will then see the role of parties as those who believe in the responsible party model see it—as institutions crucially necessary to formulate governmental programs, to enact and execute those programs, and to account for them to the electorate afterward.

Only such a period of success can provide the necessary popular support for institutional changes that will further the same ends. In the meantime, such changes of any consequence will simply have to wait.

Notes

1. Burns, *The Deadlock of Democracy* (Prentice-Hall, 1963).
2. *Washington Post*, December 8, 1986.

Critical Thinking

1. How indisputable is the assertion that America's adoption of political parties was both inevitable and necessary?

2. What objections would be most predictable if a reintroduction of the binding caucus were proposed today?
3. Can anything short of successful single-party control of the presidency and Congress restore the value of the responsible-party concept?

Create Central

www.mhhe.com/createcentral

Internet References

The Democratic National Committee (DNC)
www.democrats.org

The Federal Election Commission
www.fec.gov

The Republican National Committee (RNC)
www.rnc.org

From *Elections American Style* by James L. Sundquist (Brookings Institution, 1987). Copyright © 1987 by Brookings Institution. Reprinted by permission.

Unit 8: Electoral Politics

The Voice of the People: An Echo

V. O. Key, Jr.

Learning Outcomes

After reading this selection, you should be able to:

1. Assess what election returns can and cannot tell us about the voters.
2. Discuss the first stages in the 1930s of the modern electoral studies.

V. O. Key, Jr., is considered one of the most influential American political scientists of the twentieth century. He has demonstrated expertise in such diverse areas of study as public opinion and polling analysis, political parties and electoral behavior, state politics (particularly southern states), and interest group theory. Key's book *The Responsible Electorate: Rationality in Presidential Voting, 1936–1960* (Harvard University Press, 1966), from which the following selection is excerpted, is a study of the nature of the American electorate and party organizations. This work relies extensively upon public opinion or polling data and reflects Key's scientific detachment and scrupulous approach, which became a model of precise research emulated by many other contemporary political scientists.

In the following selection, Key analyzes the electorate's voting behavior across party lines and public policy preferences in presidential elections between 1936 and 1960. Key uses this data analysis and historical study of presidential elections to refute the common presumption that American voters are primarily influenced by subjective, nonrational factors (e.g., a candidate's personality). In sharp contrast to this assumption of electoral behavior, Key claims that the general electorate is much more responsible and rational in their voting behavior. He contends that the data he collected indicate that voters are generally consistent in their evaluation of the performance of incumbent presidents based upon their successful implementation of policies. This linkage between the voters' policy preferences and electoral decisions to support or reject incumbents is referred to by Key as retrospective voting.

Key (1908–1963), who received his Ph.D. from the University of Chicago, taught at Johns Hopkins University; Yale University, where he was the Alfred Cowles Professor of Government and served as chairman of the Department of Political Science; and Harvard University, where he was the Jonathan Trumbull Professor of American History and Government. Key is the author of numerous publications, including *The Initiative and the Referendum in California* (University of California Press, 1939) and *Public Opinion and American Democracy* (Alfred A. Knopf, 1962). In 1949 he received the prestigious Woodrow Wilson Foundation Award from the American Political Science Association for his book *Southern Politics* (Alfred A. Knopf, 1949).

Key Concept: the rational voter

In his reflective moments even the most experienced politician senses a nagging curiosity about why people vote as they do. His power and his position depend upon the outcome of the mysterious rites we perform as opposing candidates harangue the multitudes who finally march to the polls to prolong the rule of their champion, to thrust him, ungratefully, back into the void of private life, or to raise to eminence a new tribune of the people. What kinds of appeals enable a candidate to win the favor of the great god, The People? What circumstances move voters to shift their preferences in this direction or that? What clever propaganda tactic or slogan led to this result? What mannerism of oratory or style of rhetoric produced another outcome?

What band of electors rallied to this candidate to save the day for him? What policy of state attracted the devotion of another bloc of voters? What action repelled a third sector of the electorate?

The victorious candidate may claim with assurance that he has the answers to all such questions. He may regard his success as vindication of his beliefs about why voters vote as they do. And he may regard the swing of the vote to him as indubitably a response to the campaign positions he took, as an indication of the acuteness of his intuitive estimates of the mood of the people, and as a ringing manifestation of the esteem in which he is held by a discriminating public. This narcissism assumes its most repulsive form among election winners who have championed intolerance, who have stirred the passions and hatreds of people, or who have advocated causes known by decent men to be outrageous or dangerous in their long-run consequences. No functionary is more repugnant or more arrogant than the unjust man who asserts, with a color of truth, that he speaks from a pedestal of popular approbation.

It thus can be a mischievous error to assume, because a candidate wins, that a majority of the electorate shares his views on public questions, approves his past actions, or has specific expectations about his future conduct. Nor does victory establish that the candidate's campaign strategy, his image, his television style, or his fearless stand against cancer and polio turned the trick. The election returns establish only that the winner attracted a majority of the votes—assuming the existence of a modicum of rectitude in election administration. They tell us precious little about why the plurality was his.

For a glaringly obvious reason, electoral victory cannot be regarded as necessarily a popular ratification of a candidate's outlook. The voice of the people is but an echo. The output of an echo chamber bears an inevitable and invariable relation to the input. As candidates and parties clamor for attention and vie for popular support, the people's verdict can be no more than a selective reflection from among the alternatives and outlooks presented to them. Even the most discriminating popular judgment can reflect only ambiguity, uncertainty, or even foolishness if those are the qualities of the input into the echo chamber. A candidate may win despite his tactics and appeals rather than because of them. If the people can choose only from among rascals, they are certain to choose a rascal.

Scholars, though they have less at stake than do politicians, also have an abiding curiosity about why voters act as they do. In the past quarter of a century they have vastly enlarged their capacity to check the hunches born of their curiosities. The invention of the sample survey—the most widely known example of which is the Gallup poll—enabled them to make fairly trustworthy estimates of the characteristics and behaviors of large human populations. This method of mass observation revolutionized the study of politics—as well as the management of political campaigns. The new technique permitted large-scale tests to check the validity of old psychological and sociological theories of human behavior. These tests led to new hunches and new theories about voting behavior, which could, in turn, be checked and which thereby contributed to the extraordinary ferment in the social sciences during recent decades.

The studies of electoral behavior by survey methods cumulate into an imposing body of knowledge which conveys a vivid impression of the variety and subtlety of factors that enter into individual voting decisions. In their first stages in the 1930's the new electoral studies chiefly lent precision and verification to the working maxims of practicing politicians and to some of the crude theories of political speculators. Thus, sample surveys established that people did, indeed, appear to vote their pocketbooks. Yet the demonstration created its embarrassments because it also established that exceptions to the rule were numerous. Not all factory workers, for example, voted alike. How was the behavior of the deviants from "group interest" to be explained? Refinement after refinement of theory and analysis added complexity to the original simple explanation. By introducing a bit of psychological theory it could be demonstrated that factory workers with optimistic expectations tended less to be governed by pocketbook considerations than did those whose outlook was gloomy. When a little social psychology was stirred into the analysis, it could be established that identifications formed early in life, such as attachments to political parties, also reinforced or resisted the pull of the interest of the moment. A sociologist, bringing to play the conceptual tools of his trade, then could show that those factory workers who associate intimately with like-minded persons on the average vote with greater solidarity than do social isolates. Inquiries conducted with great ingenuity along many such lines have enormously broadened our knowledge of the factors associated with the responses of people to the stimuli presented to them by political campaigns.[1]

Yet, by and large, the picture of the voter that emerges from a combination of the folklore of practical politics and the findings of the new electoral studies is not a pretty one. It is not a portrait of citizens moving to considered decision as they play their solemn role of making and unmaking governments. The older tradition from practical politics may regard the voter as an erratic and irrational fellow susceptible to manipulation by skilled humbugs. One need not live through many campaigns to observe politicians, even successful politicians, who act as though they regarded the people as manageable fools. Nor does a heroic conception of the voter emerge from the new analyses of electoral behavior. They can be added up to a conception of voting not as a civic decision but as an almost purely deterministic act. Given knowledge of certain characteristics of a voter—his occupation, his residence, his religion, his national origin, and perhaps certain of his attitudes—one can predict with a high probability the direction of his vote. The actions of persons are made to appear to be only predictable and automatic responses to campaign stimuli.

Most findings of the analysts of voting never travel beyond the circle of the technicians; the popularizers, though, give wide currency to the most bizarre—and most dubious—theories of electoral behavior. Public-relations experts share in the process of dissemination as they sell their services to politicians (and succeed in establishing that politicians are sometimes as gullible as businessmen). Reporters pick up the latest psychological secret from campaign managers and spread it through a larger public. Thus, at one time a goodly proportion of the literate population must have placed some store in the theory that the electorate was a pushover for a candidate who projected an appropriate "father image." At another stage, the "sincere" candidate supposedly had an overwhelming advantage. And even so kindly a gentleman as General Eisenhower was said to have an especial attractiveness to those of authoritarian personality within the electorate.

Conceptions and theories of the way voters behave do not raise solely arcane problems to be disputed among the democratic and antidemocratic theorists or questions to be settled by the elegant techniques of the analysts of electoral behavior. Rather, they touch upon profound issues at the heart of the problem of the nature and workability of systems of popular government. Obviously the perceptions of the behavior of the electorate held by political leaders, agitators, and activists condition, if they do not fix, the types of appeals politicians employ as they seek popular support. These perceptions—or theories affect the nature of the input to the echo chamber, if we may revert to our earlier figure, and thereby control its output. They may govern, too, the kinds of actions that governments take as they look forward to the next election. If politicians perceive the electorate as responsive to father images, they will give it father images. If they see voters as most certainly responsive to nonsense, they will give them nonsense. If they see voters as susceptible to delusion, they will delude them. If they see an electorate receptive to the cold, hard realities, they will give it the cold, hard realities.

In short, theories of how voters behave acquire importance not because of their effects on voters, who may proceed blithely unaware of them. They gain significance because of their effects, both potentially and in reality, on candidates and other political leaders. If leaders believe the route to victory is by projection of images and cultivation of styles rather than by advocacy of policies to cope with the problems of the country, they will project images and cultivate styles to the neglect of the substance of politics. They will abdicate their prime function in a democratic system, which amounts, in essence, to the assumption of the risk of trying to persuade us to lift ourselves by our bootstraps.

Among the literary experts on politics there are those who contend that, because of the development of tricks for the manipulation of the masses, practices of political leadership in the management of voters have moved far toward the conversion of election campaigns into obscene parodies of the models set up by democratic idealists. They point to the good old days when politicians were deep thinkers, eloquent orators, and farsighted statesmen. Such estimates of the course of change in social institutions must be regarded with reserve. They may be only manifestations of the inverted optimism of aged and melancholy men who, estopped from hope for the future, see in the past a satisfaction of their yearning for greatness in our political life.

Whatever the trends may have been, the perceptions that leadership elements of democracies hold of the modes of response of the electorate must always be a matter of fundamental significance. Those perceptions determine the nature of the voice of the people, for they determine the character of the input into the echo chamber. While the output may be governed by the nature of the input, over the longer run the properties of the echo chamber may themselves be altered. Fed a steady diet of buncombe, the people may come to expect and to respond with highest predictability to buncombe. And those leaders most skilled in the propagation of buncombe may gain lasting advantage in the recurring struggles for popular favor.

The perverse and unorthodox argument of this little book is that voters are not fools. To be sure, many individual voters act in odd ways indeed; yet in the large the electorate behaves about as rationally and responsibly as we should expect, given the clarity of the alternatives presented to it and the character of the information available to it. In American presidential campaigns of recent decades the portrait of the American electorate that develops from the data is not one of an electorate strait-jacketed by social determinants or moved by subconscious urges triggered by devilishly skillful propagandists. It is rather one of an electorate moved by concern about central and relevant questions of public policy, of governmental performance, and of executive personality. Propositions so uncompromisingly stated inevitably represent overstatements. Yet to the extent that they can be shown to resemble the reality, they are propositions of basic importance for both the theory and the practice of democracy.

To check the validity of this broad interpretation of the behavior of voters, attention will center on the movements of voters across party lines as they reacted to the issues, events, and candidates of presidential campaigns between 1936 and 1960. Some Democratic voters of one election turned Republican at the next; others stood pat. Some Republicans of one presidential season voted Democratic four years later; others remained loyal Republicans. What motivated these shifts, sometimes large and sometimes small, in voter affection? How did the standpatters differ from the switchers? What led them to stand firmly by their party preference of four years earlier? Were these actions governed by images, moods, and other irrelevancies; or were they expressions of judgments about the sorts of questions that, hopefully, voters will weigh as they responsibly cast their ballots? On these matters evidence is available that is impressive in volume, if not always so complete or so precisely relevant as hindsight would wish. If one perseveres through the analysis of this extensive body of information, the proposition that the voter is not so irrational a fellow after all may become credible.

Notes

1. The principal books are: Paul F. Lazarsfeld, Bernard Berelson, and Hazel Gaudet, *The People's Choice* (New York: Duell, Sloan and Pearce, 1944); Angus Campbell, Gerald Gurin, and Warren E. Miller, *The Voter Decides* (Evanston, Ill.: Row, Peterson, 1954); Bernard R. Berelson, Paul F. Lazarsfeld, and William N. McPhee, *Voting* (Chicago: University of Chicago Press, 1954); Angus Campbell, Philip

E. Converse, Warren E. Miller, and Donald E. Stokes, *The American Voter* (New York: Wiley, 1960). The periodical literature is almost limitless. The footnotes in Robert E. Lane's *Political Life* (Glencoe, Ill.: Free Press, 1959) constitute a handy guide to most of it.

Critical Thinking

1. How have the measures to profile the electorate evolved since 1960?
2. Does the proliferation of online information and interactivity put the rationality of today's voter at risk, or does it in fact preserve and promote it?

3. Why might be the long-term consequences detrimental to the public if a candidate ascribes his or her victory to all the wrong reasons?

Create Central

www.mhhe.com/createcentral

Internet References

Project Vote Smart
www.votesmart.org/index.htm

From *The Responsible Electorate: Rationality in Presidential Voting 1936–1960* by V. O. Key, Jr. (Harvard University Press, 1966). Copyright © 1966 by The President and Fellows of Harvard University. Reprinted by permission.

Critical Elections and the Mainsprings of American Politics

Walter Dean Burnham

Learning Outcomes

After reading this selection, you should be able to:

1. Identify the key components of Burnham's cyclical theory of national elections.
2. Describe the basic characteristics of critical realignment.

Walter Dean Burnham's classic study *Critical Elections and the Mainsprings of American Politics* (W. W. Norton, 1970), from which the following selection is taken, is a political analysis and historical overview of American voting behavior.

Burnham (b. 1930) received his M.A. and Ph.D. from Harvard University. He has taught at Kenyon College, Haverford College, Washington University, and the Massachusetts Institute of Technology. He is currently a professor of government at the University of Texas at Austin. In addition to his fellowship at the Center for Advanced Study in the Behavioral Sciences, Burnham has received a Social Science Research Council Fellowship, a grant from the National Science Foundation, and a Guggenheim Fellowship. His expertise and research areas of specialization have included presidential politics, political parties, and electoral behavior. Burnham is coauthor and coeditor, with William N. Chambers, of *The American Party System* (Oxford University Press, 1967) and the author of *Presidential Ballots, 1836–1892* (Johns Hopkins University Press, 1955). He has also published numerous scholarly articles in professional journals of American government.

Burnham used quantitative techniques and presidential and congressional electoral voting data to confirm his cyclical theory of national elections. Using the categories of national election analysis first constructed by V. O. Key, Jr., and several other political scientists at the Survey Research Center at the University of Michigan, Burnham contends that national elections can be scientifically studied through an understanding of the political party identification of the electorate. These national elections conform to a pattern or sequence of recurring events.

A "maintaining election" is the most common type of election and one that preserves the previously established majority party identification of the electorate. It promotes stability and preserves the status quo as far as the existent party balance of power is concerned. In a "deviating election," the electorate's party identification remains stable, although the majority party loses the election. This type of election represents only a temporary shift in party power, and it occurs when a highly charismatic or popular presidential candidate of the minority party seeks office. The "realigning election," or "critical election," is very rare in American party history, as the electorate dramatically changes its party identification, and the majority party that loses in that election becomes the minority party. Burnham cites several classic examples of critical realignments that resulted in a shift of the party balance of power over a long period of time. Most of Burnham's analysis is focused on this type of election, which occurs because of some economic crisis and often results in a decline in voting participation.

Key Concept: "realigning elections"

Toward a Definition of Critical Realignment

For many decades it has been generally recognized that American electoral politics is not quite "all of a piece" despite its apparent diverse uniformity. Some elections have more important long-range consequences for the political system as a whole than others, and seem to "decide" substantive issues in a more clear-cut way. There has long been agreement among historians that the elections of those of 1800, 1828, 1860, 1896, and 1932, for example, were fundamental turning points in the course of American electoral politics.

Since the appearance in 1955 of V. O. Key's seminal article, "A Theory of Critical Elections," political scientists have moved to give this concept quantitative depth and meaning. In his article, Key isolated New England data in order to demonstrate the differential impact of a compressing sectionalism in the 1890's and of a class-ethnic polarity which emerged in the 1928–36 period.[1] . . .

[T]he authors of *The American Voter* developed a typology of elections which included realigning elections—although, of course, on the basis of historical evidence rather than on grounds then observable in survey-research data.[2] Also writing in 1960, E. E. Schattschneider—employing little data but fertile insight—addressed our attention to the utility of viewing the structure of politics brought into being by realignments as systems of action: in the aftermath of realignment, not only voting behavior but institutional roles and policy outputs undergo substantial modifications.[3]

Work done by a number of scholars during the 1960's has fleshed out our empirical knowledge of some of the processes associated with critical realignment. For example, evidence has been brought forward that the adjustments of the 1890's were accompanied and followed by significant transformations in the rules of the game and in the behavioral properties of the American electorate. It has also been suggested that each era between realignments can be described as having its own "party system," even if the formal names of the major parties which form most of its organizational base happen to remain unchanged. A Schattschneiderian analysis has very recently been applied to California for the 1890–1910 period and found to work quite well.[4]

At the same time, there has been rather little effort directed to the task of exploring these phenomena in terms of their implications for effective analysis of American politics across time and space. While Key entitled his seminal article "A Theory of Critical Elections," and while both he and Schattschneider clearly regarded realignments of fundamental analytical importance, one is impressed with how little theorizing has been forthcoming in this area. One reason for this paucity may well be an annoying incompleteness in certain key ranges of data analysis; this often leaves us in controversy not only as to the implications of the facts of change, but even as to the structure of those facts themselves.

It now seems time to attempt at least an interim assessment of the structure, function, and implications of critical realignments for the American political process. Such an effort is motivated in particular by the author's view that critical realignments are of fundamental importance not only to the system of political action called "the American political process" but also to the clarifications of some aspects of its operation. It seems particularly important in a period of obvious political upheaval not only to identify these phenomena and place them in time, but to integrate them into a larger (if still very modest) theory of movement in American politics.

Such a theory must inevitably emphasize the elements of stress and abrupt transformation in our political life at the expense of the consensual, gradualist perspectives

which have until recently dominated the scholar's vision of American political processes and behavior. For the realignment phenomenon focuses our attention on "the dark side of the moon." It reminds us that politics as usual in the United States is not politics as always; that there are discrete types of voting behavior and quite different levels of voter response to political stimuli, depending on what those stimuli are and at what point in time they occur; and that American political institutions and leadership, once defined (or redefined) in a "normal phase" of our politics, seem to become part of the very conditions that threaten to overthrow them.

The work of survey research over the past generation has heavily confirmed what earlier students and practitioners of politics in the United States noted: once a stable pattern of voting behavior and of generalized leadership recruitment has been established, it tends to continue over time with only short-term deviations. As is well known, for example, party identification in the 1952–64 period showed only the most glacial movement, in sharp contrast to the actual partisan outcomes of elections. . . .

It is enough to say for the present that any working definition of the concept "critical realignment" must, practically speaking, eliminate both deviating election situations—even landslides such as Theodore Roosevelt's in 1904 or Warren Harding's in 1920—and gradual secular realignments. It must also emphasize that while there are large historical, territorial, and stratification differences in the stability of "stable phases," they reveal comparatively far more of a component of political inertia at the mass base than do realigning eras.

In its "ideal-typical" form, the critical realignment differs from stable alignments eras, secular realignments, and deviating elections in the following basic ways.

1. The critical realignment is characteristically associated with short-lived but very intense disruptions of traditional patterns of voting behavior. Majority parties become minorities; politics which was once competitive becomes noncompetitive or, alternatively, hitherto one-party areas now become arenas of intense partisan competition; and large blocks of the active electorate—minorities, to be sure, but perhaps involving as much as a fifth to a third of the voters—shift their partisan allegiance.

2. Critical elections are characterized by abnormally high intensity as well.

a. This intensity typically spills over into the party nominating and platform-writing machinery during the upheaval and results in major shifts in convention behavior from the integrative "norm" as well as in transformations in the internal loci of power in the major party most heavily affected by the pressures of realignment. Ordinarily accepted "rules of the game" are flouted; the party's processes, instead of performing their usual integrative functions, themselves contribute to polarization.

b. The rise in intensity is associated with a considerable increase in ideological polarizations, at first within one or more of the major parties and then between them. Issue distances between the parties are markedly increased, and elections tend to involve highly salient issue-clusters, often with strongly emotional and symbolic overtones, far more than is customary in American electoral politics. One curious property of established leadership as it drifts into the stress of realignment seems to be a tendency to become more rigid and dogmatic, which itself contributes greatly to the explosive "bursting stress" of realignment. Federalist leadership just before 1801 stands in marked contrast to the Jeffersonian afterward, for example. The same may be said (perhaps less certainly) of the inherited inner-circle political style of a John Quincy Adams as the antideferential democratic revolution got under way; of the inflexible leadership of a James Buchanan in 1857–61, which effectively foreclosed a middle-of-the-road northern Democratic alternative to the Republicans; of the rigid defense of the status quo waged by Grover Cleveland and Herbert Hoover in our two greatest depressions; and of Lyndon Johnson's unhappy second administration.

c. The rise in intensity is also normally to be found in abnormally heavy voter participation for the time. This significant increase in political mobilization is not always or uniformly present, to be sure. It is particularly true of realigning cycles with a strong sectional thrust that the areas which are propelled most strongly to one party or the other tend to be those in which turnout does not increase much, or even declines. Similarly, while increases in participation during the 1928–36 period were very heavy in most of the country, they were slight or nonexistent in the South, because the restrictive structure of local politics which had been created at the turn of the century was not disturbed until long after World War II. Moreover, the net effect of the New Deal realignment was to make the South even more lopsidedly Democratic than it had been before. With such exceptions, however, there has still been a general tendency toward markedly increased participation during realigning eras.

3. Historically speaking, at least, national critical realignments have not occurred at random. Instead, there has been a remarkably uniform periodicity in their appearance. A variety of measures can be employed to examine this periodic phenomenon. Sudden shifts in the relationship between percentages for a given political party in one election and the next can be easily detected through autocorrelation and may present strong evidence of realignment.[5] . . .

4. It has been argued, with much truth, that American political parties are essentially constituent parties.[6] That is to say, the political-party subsystem is sited in a socioeconomic system of very great heterogeneity and diversity. For a variety of reasons this party system has tended to be preoccupied with performing the functions of integration and "automatic" aggregation of highly diverse and often antagonistic subgroupings in the population to the near exclusion of concern for development of "modern" mass organization in the European sense. It is neither structured nor widely perceived as a cohesive policy link between voters and officials. The conditions in which our political parties operate, and their normal operating styles and limitations, have produced not a little anguish among an older generation of political scientists who grew to professional maturity during the New Deal and who rightly saw the structure and functioning of our major political parties as a major obstacle to the realization of democratic accountability.[7] It has been well said that "electorally, American parties represent outcomes *in general*; parties seldom shape or represent outcomes *in particular*."[8]

Critical realignments emerge directly from the dynamics of this constituent-function supremacy in American politics in ways and with implications which will be analyzed subsequently. Here we will only note that since they involve constitutional readjustments in the broadest sense of the term, they are intimately associated with and followed by transformations in large clusters of policy. This produces correspondingly profound alternations in policy and influences the grand institutional structures of American government. In other words, realignments are themselves constituent acts: they arise from emergent tensions in society which, not adequately controlled by the organization or outputs of party politics as usual, escalate to a flash point; they are issue-oriented phenomena, centrally associated with these tensions and more or less leading to resolution adjustments; they result in significant transformations in the general shape of policy; and they have relatively profound aftereffects on the roles played by institutional elites.[9] They are involved with redefinitions of the universe of voters, political parties, and the broad boundaries of the politically possible.

To recapitulate, then, eras of critical realignment are marked by short, sharp reorganizations of the mass coalitional bases of the major parties which occur at periodic intervals on the national level; are often preceded by major third-party revolts which reveal the incapacity of "politics as usual" to integrate, much less aggregate, emergent political demand; are closely associated with abnormal stress in the socioeconomic system; are marked by ideological polarizations and issue-distances between the major parties which are exceptionally large by normal standards; and have durable consequences as constituent acts which determine the outer boundaries of policy in general, though not necessarily of policies in detail. . . .

The Periodicity of American Critical Realignments

The precise timing of the conditions which conduce to realignment is conditioned heavily by circumstance, of course: the intrusion of major crises in society and economy with which "politics as usual" in the United States cannot adequately cope, and the precise quality and bias of leadership decisions in a period of high political tension, cannot be predicted in specific time with any accuracy. Yet a broadly repetitive pattern of oscillation between the normal inertia of mass electoral politics and the ruptures of the normal which realignments bring about is clearly evident from the data. So evident is this pattern that one is led to suspect that the truly "normal" structure of American electoral politics at the mass base is precisely this dynamic, even dialectic polarization between long-term inertia and concentrated bursts of change in this open system of action. It may well be that American political institutions, including the major political parties, are so organized that they have a chronic, cumulative tendency toward underproduction of other than currently "normal" policy outputs. They may tend persistently to ignore, and hence not to aggregate, emergent political demand of a mass character until a boiling point of some kind is reached. . . .

[C]ritical realignment emerges as decisively important in the study of the dynamics of American politics. It is as symptomatic of political nonevolution in this country as are the archaic and increasingly rudimentary structures of the political parties themselves. But even more importantly, critical realignment may well be defined as the chief tension-management device available to so peculiar a political system. Historically it has been the chief means through which an underdeveloped political system can be recurrently brought once again into some balanced relationship with the changing socioeconomic system, permitting a restabilization of our politics and a redefinition of the dominant Lockian political formula in terms which gain overwhelming support from the current generation. Granted the relative inability of our political institutions to make gradual adjustments along vectors of *emergent* political demand, critical realignments have been as inevitable as they have been necessary to the normal workings of American politics. Thus once again there is a paradox: the conditions which decree that coalitional negotiation, bargaining, and incremental, unplanned, and gradual policy change become the dominant characteristic of American politics in its normal state also decree that it give way to abrupt, disruptive change with considerable potential for violence. So central has this dialectic been to the workings of our "Tudor polity" across time that the disappearance of one of its key elements, the critical realignment, could only mean that the most fundamental turning point in the entire history of this political system has occurred.

Such a dynamically oriented frame of reference presupposes a holistic view of American politics which is radically different from that which until very recently has tended to dominate the professional literature. The models of American political life and political processes with which we are most familiar emphasize the well-known attributes of pluralist democracy. There are not stable policy majorities. Intense and focused minorities with well-defined interests exert influence on legislation and administrative rule making out of all proportion to their size. The process involves gradual, incremental change secured after bargaining has been completed among a wide array of interested groups who are prepared to accept the conditions of bargaining. It is true that such descriptions apply to a "politics as usual" which is an important fragment of political reality in the United States, but to describe this fragment as the whole of that reality is to assume an essentially ideological posture whose credibility can be maintained only by ignoring the complementary dynamics of American politics as a whole. The study of the electoral process and its relationship to the effectiveness of the system's integration of the demands made of it and to the political elites chosen through it provides an important key for a broader understanding.

The reality of this process taken as a whole seems quite different from the pluralist vision. It is one shot through with escalating tensions, periodic electoral upheavals, and repeated redefinitions of the rules and outcomes-in-general of the political game, as well as redefinitions—by no means always broadening ones—of those who are in fact permitted to play it. One very basic characteristic of American party politics which emerges from a contemplation of critical realignments is a profound incapacity of established political leadership to adapt itself sequentially—or even incrementally?—to emergent political demand generated by the losers in our stormy socioeconomic transformations. American political parties are not action instrumentalities of definable and broad social collectivities; as organizations they are, consequently, interested in control of offices but not of government in the broader sense of which we have been speaking. It follows from this that once successful routines are established or reestablished for winning office, there is no motivation among party leaders to disturb the routines of the game. These routines are disturbed not by adaptive change within the party-policy system, but by the application of overwhelming external force.

Notes

1. V. O. Key, Jr., "A Theory of Critical Elections," 17 *Journal of Politics*, pp. 3–18 (1955).
2. Angus Campbell *et al., The American Voter* (New York: Wiley & Sons, 1960), pp. 531–38.
3. E. E. Schattschneider, *The Semisovereign People* (New York: Holt, Rinehart & Winston, 1960), especially pp. 78–96.
4. Michael Rogin, "California Populism and the 'System of 1896,' " 22 *Western Political Quarterly*, pp. 179–96 (1969).

5.	Gerald Pomper, "Classification of Presidential Elections," 29 *Journal of Politics*, pp. 535–66 (1967); and Walter Dean Burnham, "American Voting Behavior and the 1964 Election," 12 *Midwest Journal of Political Science*, pp. 1–40 (1968).
6.	Theodore J. Lowi, "Party, Policy, and Constitution" in William N. Chambers and Walter Dean Burnham (eds.), *The American Party Systems* (New York: Oxford University Press, 1967), pp. 238–76.
7.	The *locus classicus* here is, of course, the report of the ASPA's Committee on Political Parties, *Toward a More Responsible Two-Party System* (1950).
8.	Lowi, *op. cit.*, p. 263.
9.	The most obviously plausible example of synchronization of institutional-role and policy-output change with critical realignment is the Supreme Court of the United States. The literature is voluminous if frequently inferential, and the subject merits a more explicit relational treatment that it has received. For an excellent account of elite attitudes under the pressure of the crisis of the 1890's and the enormous impetus this gave to judicial creativity in this period, see Arnold M. Paul, *Conservative Crisis and the Rule of Law* (Ithaca, N.Y.: Cornell University Press, 1960).

Critical Thinking

1.	How do the 2008 election and 2012 reelection of Barack Obama figure into Burnham's cyclical theory?
2.	Within the cyclical view, which type of election would seem to be of the greatest benefit to the general populace?
3.	How are the attributes of pluralist democracy affected by periods of critical realignment?

Create Central

www.mhhe.com/createcentral

Internet References

Project Vote Smart
www.votesmart.org/index.htm

From *Critical Elections and the Mainsprings of American Politics* by Walter Dean Burnham (W.W. Norton, 1970). Copyright © 1970 by W.W. Norton. Reprinted by permission.

Prepared by: James Newman, *University of Maryland University College*

The Money Crisis

How Citizens United Undermines Our Elections and the Supreme Court

Russ Feingold

Learning Outcomes

After reading this selection, you should be able to:

1. Identify laws regulating financing of elections.

Russ Feingold served as a United States Senator from 1993 until 2011. The Democratic Senator from Wisconsin is known for his work with Arizona Republican Senator John McCain on the Bipartisan Campaign Reform Act of 2002, also known as the McCain-Feingold Act.

Key concept: the influx of money creates an imbalance of influence in our democratic society

$\mathcal{A}$s we draw closer to the November election, it becomes clearer that this year's contest, thanks to the Supreme Court's 2010 *Citizens United* decision, will be financially dominated by big money, including, whether directly or indirectly, big money from the treasuries of corporations of all kinds. Without a significant change in how our campaign finance system regulates the influence of corporations, the American election process, and even the Supreme Court itself, face a more durable, long-term crisis of legitimacy.

For years, our political process was governed by an underlying principle: large organizations, primarily corporations, were not allowed to buy their way into elections. For 100 years, our laws reflected this principle.

First, Congress passed the Tillman Act in 1907, which prohibited corporations from using their treasuries to influence federal elections.[1] Signed by President Theodore Roosevelt, the legislation recognized what had become abundantly clear: corporate influence corrupts elections. Later, under the Taft-Hartley Act of 1947, Congress extended the same prohibition to labor unions.[2] For generations, these regulations provided the bedrock of our election law that followed, including the landmark Bipartisan Campaign Reform Act passed in 2003. And for several election cycles, between 2004 and 2008, our

system seemed headed towards more fair and transparent elections. But *Citizens United* changed everything.

Soft Money, Regulation, and a New Road to Corruption

Unfortunately, in the early 1990s, Democratic lawyers and strategists exploited a loophole created by the FEC in the late 1970s. They created "soft money" writ large—a system that allowed the solicitation of unlimited contributions to the political parties from corporations, labor unions, and individuals. This system was corrupting—Senators would solicit gigantic, unregulated contributions from the same corporations that had legislation pending on the Senate floor. Both parties were guilty. By the peak of the 2002 cycle, combined soft money raised from both Republican and Democratic committees reached nearly $500,000,000.[3]

After many years of work, and on the heels of the infamous Enron scandal, Senator John McCain and I won our battle and closed the soft money loophole with the enactment of the Bipartisan Campaign Reform Act ("BCRA"), better known as the McCain-Feingold bill.[4] The law's most significant provision, which remains the law of the land today, prohibits parties from raising (and elected officials from soliciting) unlimited contributions.

Almost immediately, the same corporate interests that fought McCain-Feingold set to work to dismantle it. In what was clearly an orchestrated effort by opponents of campaign reform,[5] a group called *Citizens United* produced a movie savaging the record of then-Senator Clinton. Ostensibly intended to educate the public about conservative concerns regarding Clinton's run for the presidency, the film was little more than a legal vehicle to challenge some of the common-sense restrictions enacted by the BCRA. Specifically, the creators of the film sought to challenge the BCRA's requirement that electioneering communications—commonly known as "phony issue ads" that attack a candidate in the days before the election, but don't explicitly advocate voting for or against that candidate—be subject to the same disclosure requirements and contribution limits as other campaign ads.

The Court was presented with a narrow question from petitioners: should the McCain-Feingold provision on electioneering communications (either thirty days before a primary election or sixty days before a general election) apply to this movie about Hillary Clinton? The movie, of course, was not running as a normal television commercial; instead, it was intended as a long-form, "on demand" special.

Yet Chief Justice Roberts apparently wanted a much broader, sweeping outcome, and it is now clear that he manipulated the Court's process to achieve that result.[6] Once only a question about an "on-demand" movie, the majority in *Citizens United* ruled that corporations and unions could now use their general treasuries to influence elections directly. Despite giving strenuous assurances during his confirmation hearing to respect settled law, Roberts now stands responsible for the most egregious upending of judicial precedent in a generation. As now-retired Justice John Paul Stevens wrote in his dissent to the majority in *Citizens United*: "[F]ive Justices were unhappy with the limited nature of the case before us, so they changed the case to give themselves an opportunity to change the law."[7]

So while the most significant portion of McCain-Feingold remains law, *Citizens United* created a framework for corruption parallel to "soft money."

The most notorious byproduct of *Citizens United* is certainly the super PAC. Super PACs, now ubiquitous across the political spectrum, can collect unlimited funds from corporations and individuals, and then spend that money to elect or defeat candidates for office, so long as that work is not "coordinated" with the candidate campaigns themselves. In practical terms, super PACs can now legally use barely-disclosed money from corporate treasuries to produce blisteringly negative television ads attacking candidates and elected officials directly. The super PAC supporting Governor Mitt Romney's candidacy, for example, spent more than $50 million in the first three months of 2012 in the pursuit of the presidential nomination.[8]

The *Citizens United* decision also has had an effect on the perceived legitimacy of our elections—increasing skepticism about the campaign finance system. When the public sees the Supreme Court overturn 100 years of settled law, a cynicism sets in. And when the groups created by *Citizens United* dominate our elections with hundreds of millions of dollars of unregulated money, many may begin to believe that the average participant's small contribution is irrelevant, and that the average person's vote is grossly outweighed by the gigantic contributions now allowed.

The Rise of Internet Politics and the Lessons of 2008

It was not always this way; it was not even this way recently. For three election cycles, in 2004, 2006, and 2008, our system of campaign financing began to take shape in a way that channeled citizen participation and provided incentive for candidates to turn to the democratic support of online activists and small-dollar contributors.

This turn toward online organizing began with the presidential campaign of Howard Dean during the 2004 election, and came to fruition with then-candidate Obama's use of online fundraising and organizing during the primary and general election of the 2008 cycle. The change resulted from two coinciding factors: the changed regulatory environment following the passage of the BCRA, and the technological advances the Internet afforded campaigns and party committees.

The effect of the change in law was immediate. For example, the national Democratic Party raised an unprecedented amount of money from small-dollar donors in 2004, the first election since the BCRA entered into effect. But the true innovation didn't occur until 2008, when then-Senator Obama's campaign invested the time and resources to fully embrace the ability of technology to organize supporters online. Not only did the campaign raise a historic amount in small-dollar contributions, they created a new platform for supporter engagement— an in-house social network called my.barackobama.com. The new platform allowed supporters to create their own profiles, track the volunteer time they dedicated to the campaign, and raise money on their own from their personal network of friends and families.[9] The results were staggering: over 2,000,000 profiles were created on the platform and 30,000 offline events were planned. In total, Obama raised $500,000,000 online.[10]

But as candidates for office were given incentive to connect more directly with average voters and donors, they also found themselves more publicly accountable to those whose support they sought. In the summer of 2008, then-Senator Obama faced a tough vote—whether to support legal immunity for telecommunications companies that assisted the Bush administration's illegal, warrantless wiretapping program. Originally, then-Senator Obama opposed immunity, and favored accountability for those who had helped President Bush break the law, the Foreign Intelligence Surveillance Act (FISA).

When a new bill came up in the Senate, then-Senator Obama decided to support the legislation, which essentially swept the conduct into the bounds of law retroactively. Quickly, a new phenomenon occurred: the social network created to build supporter enthusiasm and translate it into volunteer time and donations had now become a loud platform for dissent. "Senator Obama Please Vote NO on Telecom Immunity—Get FISA Right" quickly became the largest group on the my.barackobama.com social network.

Within weeks of the group's creation—and subsequent media coverage—then-Senator Obama responded personally, by posting a message to the group explaining (although not changing) his position on the FISA bill.[11]

The 2008 election cycle, however, saw at least one ongoing major flaw in its campaign finance system: a completely neutered enforcement agency. The Federal Election Commission has been fatally flawed since the time of its creation—any administrative law professor will point out that a law enforcement commission with an even number of commissioners is probably designed specifically not to enforce the law at all. And in 2008, the Commission was especially feeble: for the first half of that year, the FEC could claim only two seated commissioners. In effect, campaign laws were simply not enforced.[12]

Since 2008, despite having a full roster of commissioners, the FEC still remains ineffective, as even Democratic violators go unpunished as conservative commissioners remain unwilling, philosophically, to enforce any campaign finance law.[13]

The Deep Threat of *Citizens United*

The corrupt entities created by *Citizens United* threatened to erase the gains we've enjoyed since the Bipartisan Campaign Reform Act. Now, instead of small-dollar, online donors, the most prominent actors in the 2012 election cycle are unnamed corporations and a small group of influential—primarily conservative—billionaires.

And the public is noticing. A recent poll conducted jointly between the *Washington Post* and ABC News found a staggering reality: nearly seven in ten registered voters believe that super PACs, the prominent vehicle used to channel unlimited funds into our elections, should be illegal.[14]

Public disapproval extends to the Court itself, and that sentiment is bipartisan. A recent survey conducted by the Pew Research Center found that public favorability of the Court dropped a full six percentage points (from 58% approval to 52%) since 2010, the year the Court handed down *Citizens United*.[15] And unlike public opinion during the George W. Bush administration, which saw a split in approval along party lines—Democrats disapproved far more often—now, both Democrats and Republicans disapprove. Pew found another striking figure: among self-identified independents, the Court's approval rating

is down twelve points since 2009 (from 64% approval to 52%).

While this drop in public faith in the Court is undoubtedly attributable to many factors, including the nomination of new Justices, it's clear that a large majority of Americans oppose the *Citizens United* decision and disagree with the Court's assertion that corporations should enjoy similar First Amendment rights as individuals.[16] This concern about corporate influence began to manifest itself in the past year, most notably in the form of legitimate, earnest protest of Wall Street.

Now-retired Justice John Paul Stevens, in his stinging ninety-page dissent in *Citizens United*, recognized the danger in the majority's departure from precedent regarding corporate regulation:

At bottom, the Court's opinion is thus a rejection of the common sense of the American people, who have recognized a need to prevent corporations from undermining self-government since the founding, and who have fought against the distinctive corrupting potential of corporate electioneering since the days of Theodore Roosevelt.[17]

It's also true that Congress can and must do more to reform our elections. Possible legislative steps include passing strong disclosure legislation, fixing our now broken system of presidential public financing, and replacing the dysfunctional Federal Election Commission with a true enforcement agency.

Ultimately, however, it is the Supreme Court that must find its way back to the path we began in 2004, 2006 and 2008, when candidates for office were given an incentive to seek the support of small-dollar contributors, if only from necessity.

The Court has a clear opportunity. A new challenge from Montana, based on that state's historic anti-corruption laws, could allow the Supreme Court to reconsider its decision in *Citizens United*, and at least two justices have hinted that the 2010 ruling is untenable. In granting a stay of a Montana Supreme Court decision upholding that state's anticorruption laws, Justice Ginsburg, writing with Justice Breyer, found the pulse of the chaos *Citizens United* has wrought: "Montana's experience, and experience elsewhere since this Court's decision in *Citizens United v. Federal Election Commission*, make it exceedingly difficult to maintain that independent expenditures by corporations 'do not give rise to corruption or the appearance of corruption.' "[18]

Justice Ginsburg is correct. Today's framework for corruption cannot stand.

Notes

1. Ch. 420, Pub. L. No. 59–36, 34 Stat. 864 (1907) (codified as amended at 2 U.S.C. § 441b(a) (2006)).
2. Ch. 120, sec. 304, § 313, 61 Stat. 136, 159 (1947) (codified as amended at 2 U.S.C. § 441b(a) (2006)).
3. David B. Magleby, *Political Parties and the Financing of the 2008 Elections, in* Financing the 2008 Election 210, 214 (David B. Magleby & Anthony Corrado, eds., 2011).

4. Pub. L. No. 107–155, 116 Stat. 81 (2002) (codified primarily in scattered sections of 2 and 47 U.S.C.).

5. Philip Rucker, Citizens United *used 'Hillary: The Movie' to take on McCain-Feingold*, Wash. Post (Jan. 22, 2010), www.washingtonpost.com/wp-dyn/content/article/2010/01/21/AR2010012103582.html.

6. *See* Jeffrey Toobin, *Money Unlimited: How Chief Justice John Roberts Orchestrated the* Citizens United *Decision*, New Yorker, May 21, 2012, at 36, *available at* www.newyorker.com/reporting/2012/05/21/120521fa_fact_toobin.

7. Citizens United v. FEC, 130 S. Ct. 876, 932 (2010) (Stevens, J., concurring in part and dissenting in part).

8. *See Independent Spending Totals*, N.Y. Times, http://elections.nytimes.com/2012/campaign-finance/independent-expenditures/totals (last visited May 30, 2012).

9. Sarah Lai Stirland, *Propelled by Internet*, Barack Obama Wins Presidency, Wired (Nov. 4, 2008, 8:25 PM), www.wired.com/threatlevel/2008/11/propelled-by-in.

10. Jose Antonio Vargas, *Obama Raised Half a Billion Online*, Wash. Post: Clickocracy (Nov. 20, 2008, 8:00 PM), http://voices.washingtonpost.com/44/2008/11/20/obama_raised_half_a_billion_on.html.

11. Barack Obama, *My Position on FISA*, Huffington Post (July 3, 2008, 5:05 PM), www.huffingtonpost.com/barack-obama/my-position-on-fisa_b_110789.html; *see also Response from Barack on FISA and Discussion with Policy Staff*, Joe Rospars's Blog (July 3, 2008, 4:32 PM), https://my.barackobama.com/page/community/post/rospars/gGxsZF.

12. *See Senate Confirms New FEC Commissioners, Ending Long Partisan Standoff*, CBSNews (June 26, 2009, 5:15 PM), www.cbsnews.com/2100-501743_162-4206600.html.

13. *See* Jesse Zwick, *Broken Federal Election Commission Fails to Enforce Campaign-Finance Laws*, Wash. Indep. (Sept. 28, 2010, 4:36 PM), http://washingtonindependent.com/98816/broken-federal-election-commission-fails-to-enforce-campaign-finance-laws.

14. Chris Cillizza & Aaron Blake, *Poll: Voters Want Super PACs To Be Illegal*, Wash. Post (Mar. 13, 2012, 7:00 AM ET), www.washingtonpost.com/blogs/the-fix/post/poll-voters-want-super-pacs-to-be-illegal/2012/03/12/gIQA6skT8R_blog.html.

15. Pew Research Ctr., Supreme Court Favorability Reaches New Low 1 (2012), *available at* www.people-press.org/files/legacy-pdf/5-1-12%20Supreme%20Court%20Release.pdf.

16. Press Release, Democracy Corps, Greenberg Quinlan Rosner Research, & Pub. Campaign Action Fund, *Two Years After* Citizens United, *Votes Fed Up With Money in Politics* (Jan. 19, 2012), *available at* http://campaignmoney.org/files/DemCorpPCAFmemoFINAL.pdf.

17. Citizens United v. FEC, 130 S. Ct. 876, 979 (2010) (Stevens, J., concurring in part and dissenting in part).

18. Order Granting Stay in Pending Case, Am. Tradition P'ship v. Bullock, No. 11-1179 (Feb. 17, 2012) (citation omitted).

Critical Thinking

1. Should donations to campaigns be limited?
2. Should limits on campaign spending exist?
3. Does limiting spending on campaigns unduly infringe on a person's right to redress government of grievances?

Create Central

www.mhhe.com/createcentral

Internet References

Obama Raised Half a Billion Online
http://voices.washingtonpost.com/44/2008/11/20/obama_raised_half_a_billion_on.html

Independent Spending Totals
http://elections.nytimes.com/2012/campaign-finance/independent-expenditures/totals

OpenSecrets.org
www.opensecrets.org

From *Stanford Law Review*, June 14, 2012. Copyright © 2012 by Stanford Law Review. Reprinted by permission.

Unit 9: The Media and Public Opinion

From Cronkite's Complaint to Orwell's Oversight

Michael Parenti

Learning Outcomes

After reading this selection, you should be able to:

1. Describe the influential role of the press in image politics.
2. Recognize the media's power to ignore political views outside the two-party system.
3. Discuss the control of media owners over the content of news coverage.

Michael Parenti (b. 1933) has been a spokesperson for the American ideological left for the last 30 years. His book *Inventing Reality: The Politics of the Mass Media* (St. Martin's Press, 1986), from which the following selection is excerpted, is a study of the impact of mass media on public opinion in the American political context.

Parenti's work has been interpreted as a classic study of political elitism because Parenti emphasizes the conservative nature of the mass media in its uncritical support of established governmental and private powers and interests in American society. The political theory, or perspective, of political elitism is an interpretation of the division of power in the United States, which claims that a minority of the population representing the leadership of corporate, military, and governmental institutions makes the most significant policies for society. Parenti contends that in the American political system there is a concentration of power among an unelected elite who represent their own private interests and ignore the public interest.

In the following selection, Parenti argues that the contemporary mass media conform to the policy objectives of the dominant governmental and corporate leadership in the United States. In electoral campaigns, the media emphasizes trivial issues concerning candidates rather than issues of substantive significance for the electorate. As a consequence, according to Parenti, the electorate remains passive, apathetic, and unlikely to mobilize around serious policy considerations. In addition, media political coverage focuses on the two major parties as the legitimate competitors in the electoral arena, while denying the significance of any substantive challenge of a minor or third party. Parenti concludes that the news media designs the political world for American citizens by controlling the public issue agenda.

Parenti received his M.A. from Brown University and his Ph.D. from Yale University. He has taught at numerous colleges and universities, including the State University of New York at Stony Brook and at Albany, Cornell University, and American University. He is the author of many innovative studies on American government, including *Democracy for the Few* (St. Martin's Press, 1974) and *Power and the Powerless* (St. Martin's Press, 1978). He has also been an active contributor of scholarly articles to various journals and periodicals, such as *Commonweal*, *The Progressive*, and *Society*.

Key Concept: the media's impact upon public discourse

Image Politics

The press sees the established governmental leadership as essential to the maintenance of social order; and it gives more credence to public officials, corporate representatives, church leaders and university officers than it does to protesters, taxpayers, consumers, workers, parishioners, and students.

The foremost leader in the United States is the president, "who is viewed as the ultimate protector of order."[1] A systematic examination of twenty-five years of presidential news in *The New York Times* and *Time* magazine, as well as ten years of CBS broadcasts, reveals a "consistent pattern of favorable coverage of the President," with sympathetic stories outnumbering critical ones by two to one.[2] More often than not, a president's viewpoint, especially if it has no liberal slant, is transmitted by the press with no opposing set of facts. Thus when President Reagan claimed credit for the 1982 extension of the Voting Rights Act and for appointing more minority members and females to administrative posts and waging a more vigorous enforcement of civil rights than previous administrations, the press faithfully reported his claims without pointing out that in fact he had threatened to veto the Voting Rights Act (and only signed it because it passed both houses by veto-proof majorities) and had actually cut back on minority and female appointments and on civil rights enforcement.[3] And in the 1984 campaign when President Reagan asserted he would "never" attack Social Security, most of the major media gave top play to his statement without noting that in previous years he had repeatedly attacked Social Security, equating it and other entitlement programs with welfare—which he hated. . . .

By focusing on "human interest" trivia, on contest rather than content, the media make it difficult for the public to give intelligent expression to political life and to mobilize around the issues. Thus the media have—intentionally or not—a conservative effect on public discourse. Given short shrift are the concerns of millions of people regarding nuclear arms escalation, Pentagon spending, tax reform, war in Central America, unemployment, and poverty. The democratic input, the great public debate about the state of the Union and its national policies, the heightening of political consciousness and information levels—all the things democratic electoral campaigns are supposed to foster—are crowded off the stage by image politics.

Not only during election campaigns but just about on every other occasion the news media prefer surface to substance, emphasizing the eye-catching visuals, the attention-catching "special angle" report, and the reassuring and comforting stories, while slighting the deeper, more important but politically more troublesome and more controversial themes. There is so much concentration on surface events that we often have trouble grasping the content of things, so much focus on action and personality that we fail to see the purposive goal of the action. For instance, during 1981, President Reagan dismantled major portions of forty years of domestic social legislation, initiated enormous tax cuts for rich individuals and corporations, dramatically escalated an already huge military spending program, and launched a series of cold-war confrontations against the Soviet Union—all policies of great import. However, the theme that predominated in most of the stories about those crucial actions was whether Reagan was "winning" or "losing" in his contests with Congress, the bureaucracy, labor, and foreign governments. Thus momentous political issues were reduced to catchy but trivial questions about Reagan's political "score card," his efficacy as a leader, and his personal popularity.[4]

Monopoly Politics

Such as it is, media electoral coverage is lavishly bestowed on the two major parties, while minor parties are totally ignored or allotted but a few minutes, if that, over the entire campaign. Thus the media help perpetuate the procapitalist, two-party monopoly.

In recent contests, presidential candidates of the Communist Party, the Citizens Party, the Socialist Workers Party, the Workers World Party, and others did all the things presidential candidates are supposed to do. They met thousands of voters on street corners, spoke on college campuses and at voter forums, issued position papers and press releases, traveled around the country, and probably spoke directly to more people than did the major candidates. But on election day, most voters had never heard of them. Deprived of mass media coverage, a third party cannot reach the voting masses. Most people remain unaware not only of its candidates but of its programs, issues, and critiques of status quo politics. . . .

Media exposure confers legitimacy on one's candidacy. By giving elaborate national coverage only to Republicans and Democrats, news organizations are letting us know that these are the only ones worth considering. Candidates who are not taken seriously by the media swiftly discover that they are not taken seriously by many voters. Even when they make face-to-face contact with live audiences and with voters on street corners, they still lack legitimacy as candidates for national office, being more a curiosity than a serious choice. People may like what third-party candidates say, because often they are the only ones saying anything, but they usually won't vote for someone who doesn't have a chance. Since third-party candidates are not in the news, they are considered to be not really in the race; and since they are not in the race, this justifies treating them as if they are not news. . . .

Do the Media Manage Our Minds?

Are the media independent of government influence? If not, what is the nature of that influence? Are the media dominated by particular class interests? If so, does this dominance carry over into news content? Does control of news content translate into propaganda? Does propaganda translate into indoctrination of the public mind? And does indoctrination translate into support for politics? These questions guide the present inquiry: let us run through them again, a little more slowly.

1. In the United States a free press is defined as one unhampered by repressive laws. As we shall find, government interference with the news is not the only or even the major problem. More often the danger is that the press goes along willingly with officialdom's view of things at home and abroad, frequently manifesting a disregard for accuracy equal to that of policymakers. To be sure, questions are sometimes raised and criticisms voiced, but most of these are confined to challenging the *efficacy* of a particular policy rather than its underlying interests especially if the interests are powerful ones.

2. The newspeople who participate in the many forums on freedom of the press usually concentrate on threats to the press from without, leaving untouched the question of coercion from within, specifically from media owners. Are the media free from censorial interference by their owners? Does ownership translate into actual control over information, or does responsibility for the news still rest in the hands of journalists and editors who are free to report what they want—limited only by professional canons of objectivity? As we shall see, the working press, including newspaper editors and television news producers and even the top media executives are beholden to media owners and corporate advertisers. More specifically, the owners exercise control through the power to hire and fire, to promote and demote anyone they want and by regularly intervening directly into the news production process with verbal and written directives.

3. But does control over media content and personnel translate into ruling class propaganda? Even if we allow that owners ultimately determine what is or is not publicized, can it be assumed that the end product serves their interests and gives only their viewpoint? I will argue that, except for momentary departures, a capitalist ideological perspective regarding events at home and abroad rather consistently predominates. The system of control works, although not with absolute perfection and is not devoid of items that might at times be discomforting to the rich and powerful.

4. A final concern: Does ruling class propaganda translate into indoctrination of the public? It might be argued that even if the news is cast in a capitalist ideological mold, the public does not swallow it and has ways of withstanding the propaganda. The news may be manipulated by the press lords, but are we manipulated by the news? It is this last question I want to deal with here at some length. For if the press exercises only an inconsequential influence over the public, then we are dealing with a tempest in a teapot and are being unduly alarmist about "mind management."

Early studies of the media's impact on voting choices found that people seemed surprisingly immune from media manipulation. Campaign propaganda usually reinforced the public's preferences rather than altered them. People exposed themselves to media appeals in a selective way, giving more credence and attention to messages that bolstered their own views. Their opinions and information intake also were influenced by peers, social groups, and community, so the individual did not stand without a buffer against the impact of the media. The press, it was concluded, had only a "minimal effect."[5]

At first glance, these findings are reassuring: People seem fairly self-directed in their responses to the media and do not allow themselves to be mindlessly directed. Democracy is safe. But troublesome questions remain. If through "selective exposure" and "selective attention" we utilize the media mainly to reinforce our established predispositions, where do the predispositions themselves come from? We can point to various socializing agencies: family, school, peer groups, work place—and the media themselves. Certainly some of our internalized political predispositions come from the dominant political culture that the media have had a hand in shaping—and directly from earlier exposure to the media themselves.

Our ability to discriminate is limited in part by how we have been conditioned by previous media exposures. The selectivity we exercise is not an autonomous antidote to propaganda but may feed right into it, choosing one or another variation of the same establishment offering. Opinions that depart too far from the mainstream are likely to be rejected out of hand. In such situations, our "selectivity" is designed to *avoid* information and views that contradict the dominant propaganda, a propaganda we long ago implicitly embraced as representative of "the nature of things." Thus, an implanted set of conditioned responses are now mistakenly identified as our self-generated political perceptions, and the public's selective ingestion of the media's conventional fare is wrongly treated as evidence of the "minimal effect" of news organizations.

In addition, more recent empirical evidence suggest that, contrary to the earlier "minimal effects" theory, the news media are able to direct our attention to certain issues and shape our opinions about them. One study found that "participants exposed to a steady stream of news about defense or about pollution came to believe that defense or pollution were more consequential problems."[6] Other studies found that fluctuations in public concern for problems like civil rights, Vietnam, crime, and inflation over the last two decades reflected variations in the attention paid to them by the major media.[7]

Theorists who maintain that the media have only a minimal effect on campaigns ought to try convincing those political candidates who believe they survive and perish because of media exposure or the lack of it. And as we saw earlier, the inability to buy media time or attract press coverage consigns third-party candidates to the dim periphery of American politics. The power to ignore political viewpoints other than the standard two-party offerings is more than minimal, it is monumental. Media exposure frequently may be the single most crucial mobilizer of votes, even if certainly not the only one.

If much of our informational and opinion intake is filtered through our previously established mental predilections, these predilections are often not part of our conscious discernment but of our unexamined perceptual conditioning—which brings us back to an earlier point: *Rather than being rational guardians against propaganda, our predispositional sets, having been shaped by prolonged exposure to earlier outputs of that same propaganda, may be active accomplices. . . .*

If the press cannot mold our every opinion, it can frame the perceptual reality around which our opinions take shape. Here may lie the most important effect of the news media: they set the issue agenda for the rest of us, choosing what to emphasize and what to ignore or suppress, in effect, organizing much of our political world for us. *The media may not always be able to tell us what to think, but they are strikingly successful in telling us what to think about.*[8]

Along with other social, cultural, and educational agencies, the media teach us tunnel vision, conditioning us to perceive the problems of society as isolated particulars, thereby stunting our critical vision. Larger causalities are reduced to immediately distinct events, while the linkages of wealth, power, and policy go unreported or are buried under a congestion of surface impressions and personalities. There is nothing too essential and revealing that cannot be ignored by the American press and nothing too trivial and superficial that cannot be accorded protracted play.

In sum, the media set the limits on public discourse and public understanding. They may not always mold opinion but they do not always have to. It is enough that they create opinion visibility, giving legitimacy to certain views and illegitimacy to others. The media do the same to substantive issues that they do to candidates, raising some from oblivion and conferring legitimacy upon them, while consigning others to limbo. This power to determine the issue agenda, the information flow, and the parameters of political debate so that it extends from ultra-right to no further than moderate center, is if not total, still totally awesome.

Notes

1. Herbert Gans, "The Message Behind the News," *Columbia Journalism Review,* January/February 1979, p. 45.
2. Michael Grossman and Martha Kumar, *Portraying the President* (Baltimore: Johns Hopkins University Press, 1981).
3. The above facts and figures are from James Nathan Miller, "Ronald Reagan and the Techniques of Deception," *Atlantic Monthly,* February 1984, pp. 62–68.
4. W. Lance Bennett, *News, The Politics of Illusion* (New York: Longman, 1983), pp. 9–10.
5. P. Lazarsfeld, B. Berelson, and H. Gaudet, *The People's Choice* (New York: Columbia University Press, 1948); C. I. Hovel et al., *Experiments on Mass Communication* (Princeton, N.J.: Princeton University Press, 1949).
6. S. Iyengar, M. Peters, and D. Kinder, "Experimental Demonstrations of the 'Not-So-Minimal' Consequences of Television News Programs," *American Political Science Review,* 76, December 1982, p. 852.
7. G. R. Funkhouser, "The Issues of the Sixties," *Public Opinion Quarterly,* 37, pp. 62–75; Michael MacKuen and Steven Coombs, *More than News* (Beverly Hills, Calif.: Sage Publications, 1981); also the essay by MacKuen therein.
8. The point was first made by B. Cohen, *The Press and Foreign Policy* (Princeton, N.J.: Princeton University Press, 1963), p. 16; a similar point is made in Maxwell McCombs and Donald Shaw, *The Emergence of American Political Issues: the Agenda-Setting Function of the Press* (St. Paul, Minn.: West, 1977), p. 5.

Critical Thinking

1. If it is true that the media "are strikingly successful in telling us what to think about," what might be our best defense against such manipulation?
2. Does the Internet have the capacity to help make an appreciable dent in the two-party monopoly long perpetuated by traditional media?

Create Central

www.mhhe.com/createcentral

Internet References

Encyclopedia Britannica
www.britannica.com/EBchecked/topic/482436/public-opinion/258760/The-mass-media

From *Inventing Reality: The Politics of the Mass Media* by Michael Parenti (St. Martin's Press, 1986). Copyright © 1986 by St. Martin's Press. Reprinted by permission.

Unit 10: Congress

The Electoral Incentive

David R. Mayhew

Learning Outcomes

After reading this selection, you should be able to:

1. Identify the three basic types of reelection-related activities.
2. Describe the difference between safe and marginal congressional districts.
3. Define the term "particularized benefits."

David R. Mayhew (b. 1937) has been recognized as an expert on Congress for the past three decades. His book *Congress: The Electoral Connection* (Yale University Press, 1974), from which the following selection has been excerpted, is considered a classic investigation of congressional motivation and behavior. The book has filled a gap in the contemporary literature on Congress and has shifted the theoretical focus of legislative research to emphasize the linkage between congressional elections and congressional public policy making.

In *Congress*, Mayhew argues that all members of Congress are primarily and continuously motivated and pressured by the impulse to be reelected, and they act accordingly. This is true regardless of whether they are representatives from safe congressional districts (i.e., lacking much party competition, rivalry, or turnover) or marginal congressional districts (i.e., marked by intensive party competition, rivalry, and turnover). Mayhew contends that the three basic types of political behavior that enable congresspersons to be successful include advertising, credit claiming, and position taking.

"Advertising" is expressed as any act, through any forum or medium and conveyed in messages with minimal substance, to publicize a candidate's positive image to the electorate. "Credit claiming" refers to a congressperson creating the perception among constituents of being personally responsible for providing desirable governmental programs or services or concrete benefits. Finally, "position taking" is a congressperson's public expression of a particular policy position or value judgment on policy priorities perceived to be of serious interest to one's constituents. This is concretely expressed in a congressperson's legislative voting record.

Mayhew received his Ph.D. from Harvard University. He is currently the Sterling Professor of Political Science at Yale University. His areas of expertise and research have included legislative politics, political parties, and interest groups. *Congress: The Electoral Connection* won *The Washington Monthly* Political Book Award in 1974. Mayhew is also the author of *Placing Parties in American Politics* (Princeton University Press, 1986) and *Divided We Govern* (Yale University Press, 1991).

Key Concept: congressional incumbent electoral strategies

Whether they are safe or marginal, cautious or audacious, congressmen must constantly engage in activities related to reelection. There will be differences in emphasis, but all members share the root need to do things—indeed, to do things day in and day out during their terms. The next step here is to present a typology, a short list of the *kinds* of activities congressmen find it electorally useful to engage in. The case will be that there are three basic kinds of activities. . . .

One activity is *advertising*, defined here as any effort to disseminate one's name among constituents in such a fashion as to create a favorable image but in messages having little or no issue content. A successful congressman builds what amounts to a brand name, which may have a generalized electoral value for other politicians in the same family. The personal qualities to emphasize are experience, knowledge, responsiveness, concern, sincerity, independence, and the like. Just getting one's name across is difficult enough; only about half the electorate, if asked, can supply their House members' names. It helps a congressman to be known. . . . A vital advantage enjoyed by House incumbents is that they are much better known among voters than their November challengers. They are better known because they spend a great deal of time, energy, and money trying to make themselves better known. There are standard routines—frequent visits to the constituency, nonpolitical speeches to home audiences, the sending out of infant care booklets and letters of condolence and congratulation. Of 158 House members questioned in the mid-1960s, 121 said that they regularly sent newsletters to their constituents,[1] 48 wrote separate news or opinion columns for newspapers; 82 regularly reported to their constituencies by radio or television, 89 regularly sent out mail questionnaires.[2] . . . [C]ongressional advertising is done largely at public expense. Use of the franking privilege has mushroomed in recent years; in early 1973 one estimate predicted that House and Senate members would send out about 476 million pieces of mail in the year 1974, at a public cost of $38.1 million—or about 900,000 pieces per member with a subsidy of $70,000 per member.[3] By far the heaviest mailroom traffic comes in Octobers of even-numbered years. There are some differences between House and Senate members in the ways they go about getting their names across. House members are free to blanket their constituencies with mailings for all boxholders; senators are not. But senators find it easier to appear on national television—for example, in short reaction statements on the nightly news shows. Advertising is a staple congressional activity, and there is no end to it. For each member there are always new voters to be apprised of his worthiness and old voters to be reminded of it.

A second activity may be called *credit claiming*, defined here as acting so as to generate a belief in a relevant political actor (or actors) that one is personally responsible for causing the government, or some unit thereof, to do something that the actor (or actors) considers desirable. The political logic of this, from the congressman's point of view, is that an actor who believes that a member can make pleasing things happen will no doubt wish to keep him in office so that he can make pleasing things happen in the future. The emphasis here is on individual accomplishment (rather than, say, party or governmental accomplishment) and on the congressman as doer (rather than as, say, expounder of constituency views). Credit claiming is highly important to congressmen, with the consequence that much congressional life is a relentless search for opportunities to engage in it.

Where can credit be found? If there were only one congressman rather than 535, the answer would in principle be simple enough. Credit (or blame) would attach in Downsian fashion to the doings of the government as a whole. But there are 535. Hence it becomes necessary for each congressman to try to peel off pieces of governmental accomplishment for which he can believably generate a sense of responsibility. For the average congressman the staple way of doing this is to traffic in what may be called "particularized benefits." Particularized governmental benefits, as the term will be used here, have two properties: (1) Each benefit is given out to a specific individual, group, or geographical constituency, the recipient unit being of a scale that allows a single congressman to be recognized (by relevant political actors and other congressmen) as the claimant for the

benefit (other congressmen being perceived as indifferent or hostile). (2) Each benefit is given out in apparently ad hoc fashion (unlike, say, social security checks) with a congressman apparently having a hand in the allocation. A particularized benefit can normally be regarded as a member of a class. That is, a benefit given out to an individual, group, or constituency can normally be looked upon by congressmen as one of a class of similar benefits given out to sizable numbers of individuals, groups, or constituencies. Hence the impression can arise that a congressman is getting "his share" of whatever it is the government is offering. . . .

In sheer volume the bulk of particularized benefits come under the heading of "casework"—the thousands of favors congressional offices perform for supplicants in ways that normally do not require legislative action. High school students ask for essay materials, soldiers for emergency leaves, pensioners for location of missing checks, local governments for grant information, and on and on. Each office has skilled professionals who can play the bureaucracy like an organ—pushing the right pedals to produce the desired effects.[4] But many benefits require new legislation, or at least they require important allocative decisions on matters covered by existent legislation. Here the congressman fills the traditional role of supplier of goods to the home district. It is a believable role; when a member claims credit for a benefit on the order of a dam, he may well receive it. Shiny construction projects seem especially useful. In the decades before 1934, tariff duties for local industries were a major commodity.[5] In recent years awards given under grant-in-aid programs have become more useful as they have become more numerous. Some quests for credit are ingenious; in 1971 the story broke that congressmen had been earmarking foreign aid money for specific projects in Israel in order to win favor with home constituents.[6] It should be said of constituency benefits that congressmen are quite capable of taking the initiative in drumming them up; that is, there can be no automatic assumption that a congressman's activity is the result of pressures brought to bear by organized interests. . . .

How much particularized benefits count for at the polls is extraordinarily difficult to say. But it would be hard to find a congressman who thinks he can afford to wait around until precise information is available. The lore is that they count—furthermore, given home expectations, that they must be supplied in regular quantities for a member to stay electorally even with the board. Awareness of favors may spread beyond their recipients, building for a member a general reputation as a good provider. "Rivers Delivers." "He Can Do More for Massachusetts." . . .

The third activity congressmen engage in may be called *position taking*, defined here as the public enunciation of a judgmental statement on anything likely to be of interest to political actors. The statement may take the form of a roll call vote. The most important classes of judgmental statements are those prescribing American governmental ends (a vote cast against the war; a statement that "the war should be ended immediately") or governmental means (a statement that "the way to end the war is to take it to the United Nations"). The judgments may be implicit rather than explicit, as in: "I will support the president on this matter." But judgments may range far beyond these classes to take in implicit or explicit statements on what almost anybody should do or how he should do it: "The great Polish scientist Copernicus has been unjustly neglected"; "The way for Israel to achieve peace is to give up the Sinai." The congressman as position taker is a speaker rather than a doer. The electoral requirement is not that he make pleasing things happen but that he make pleasing judgmental statements. The position itself is the political commodity. Especially on matters where governmental responsibility is widely diffused it is not surprising that political actors should fall back on positions as tests of incumbent virtue. For voters ignorant of congressional processes the recourse is an easy one. . . .

The ways in which positions can be registered are numerous and often imaginative. There are floor addresses ranging from weighty orations to mass-produced "nationality day statements." There are speeches before home groups, television appearances, letters, newsletters, press releases, ghostwritten books, *Playboy* articles, even interviews with political scientists. On occasion congressmen generate what amount to petitions; whether or not to sign the 1956 Southern Manifesto defying school desegregation rulings was an important decision for southern members. Outside the roll call process the congressman is usually able to tailor his positions to suit his audiences. A solid consensus in the constituency calls for ringing declarations; for years the late Senator James K. Vardaman (D., Miss.) campaigned on a proposal to repeal the Fifteenth Amendment. Division or uncertainty in the constituency calls for waffling; in the late 1960s a congressman had to be a poor politician indeed not to be able to come up with an inoffensive statement on Vietnam ("We must have peace with honor at the earliest possible moment consistent with the national interest"). On a controversial issue a Capitol Hill office normally prepares two form letters to send out to constituent letter writers—one for the pros and one (not directly contradictory) for the antis. . . .

Probably the best position-taking strategy for most congressmen at most times is to be conservative—to cling to their own positions of the past where possible and to reach for new ones with great caution where necessary. Yet in an earlier discussion of strategy the suggestion was made that it might be rational for members in electoral danger to resort to innovation. The form of innovation available is entrepreneurial position taking, its logic being that for a member facing defeat with his old array of positions it makes good sense to gamble on some new ones. It may be that congressional marginals fulfill an important function here as issue pioneers—experimenters who test out new issues and thereby show other

politicians which ones are usable. An example of such a pioneer is Senator Warren Magnuson (D., Wash.), who responded to a surprisingly narrow victory in 1962 by reaching for a reputation in the area of consumer affairs.[7] Another example is Senator Ernest Hollings (D., S.C.), a servant of a shaky and racially heterogeneous southern constituency who launched "hunger" as an issue in 1969—at once pointing to a problem and giving it a useful nonracial definition. One of the most successful issue entrepreneurs of recent decades was the late Senator Joseph McCarthy (R., Wis.); it was all there—the close primary in 1946, the fear of defeat in 1952, the desperate casting about for an issue, the famous 1950 dinner at the Colony Restaurant where suggestions were tendered, the decision that "Communism" might just do the trick.[8]

The effect of position taking on electoral behavior is about as hard to measure as the effect of credit claiming. Once again there is a variance problem; congressmen do not differ very much among themselves in the methods they use or the skills they display in attuning themselves to their diverse constituencies. All of them, after all, are professional politicians. . . .

There can be no doubt that congressmen believe positions make a difference. An important consequence of this belief is their custom of watching each other's elections to try to figure out what positions are salable. Nothing is more important in Capitol Hill politics than the shared conviction that election returns have proven a point. Thus the 1950 returns were read not only as a rejection of health insurance but as a ratification of McCarthyism. When two North Carolina nonsigners of the 1956 Southern Manifesto immediately lost their primaries, the message was clear to southern members that there could be no straying from a hard line on the school desegregation issue. Any breath of life left in the cause of school bussing was squeezed out by House returns from the Detroit area in 1972. . . .

These, then, are the three kinds of electorally oriented activities congressmen engage in—advertising, credit claiming, and position taking.

Notes

1. These and the following figures on member activity are from Donald G. Tacheron and Morris K. Udall, *The Job of the Congressman* (Indianapolis: Bobbs-Merrill, 1966), pp. 281–288.

2. On questionnaires generally see Walter Wilcox, "The Congressional Poll—and Non-Poll," in Edward C. Dreyer and Walter A. Rosenbaum (eds.), *Political Opinion and Electoral Behavior* (Belmont, Calif.: Wadsworth, 1966), pp. 390–400.

3. Norman C. Miller, "Yes, You Are Getting More Politico Mail: And It Will Get Worse," *Wall Street Journal*, March 6, 1973, p. 1.

4. On casework generally see Kenneth G. Olson, "The Service Function of the United States Congress," pp. 337–74 in American Enterprise Institute, *Congress: The First Branch of Government* (Washington, D.C.: American Enterprise Institute for Public Policy Research, 1966).

5. The classic account is in E. E. Schattschneider, *Politics, Pressures, and the Tariff* (New York: Prentice-Hall, 1935).
6. "Israeli Schools and Hospitals Seek Funds in Foreign-Aid Bill," *The New York Times*, October 4, 1971, p. 10.
7. David Price, *Who Makes the Laws?* (Cambridge Mass.: Schenkman, 1972), p. 29.
8. Robert Griffith, *The Politics of Fear: Joseph R. McCarthy and the Senate* (New York: Hayden, 1970), p. 29.

Critical Thinking

1. Given that, as far back as 1974, the public cost for House and Senate members' postage was $38.1 million, should limits be imposed on congressional franking privileges?
2. If members of Congress exploit the ignorance of voters by engaging in "position taking," who is more to blame: the politician or the voter?

Create Central

www.mhhe.com/createcentral

Internet References

C-SPAN
www.c-span.org

United States House of Representatives
www.house.gov

United States Senate
www.senate.gov

The White House
www.whitehouse.gov

From *Congress: The Electoral Connection* by David R. Mayhew (Yale University Press, 1974). Copyright © 1974 by Yale University. Reprinted by permission.

Prepared by: James Newman, *University of Maryland University College*

Why Is Congress So Partisan?

Lee Hamilton

Learning Outcomes

After reading this selection, you should be able to:

1. Describe the challenges presented to Congress from increasing partisanship.
2. Understand the impact of Congressional district lines on partisanship.

Lee Hamilton is the Director of the Center on Congress at Indiana University. The Center is a non-partisan educational institution seeking increase awareness and understanding of Congress. From 1965 to 1999 he served Indiana in the U.S. House. While in Congress, he was Chairman of the Joint Committee on the Organization of Congress and worked to promote integrity and efficiency in the institution.

He is currently a member of the President's Intelligence Advisory Board, the President's Homeland Security Advisory Council, the CIA External Advisory Board, and the U.S. Department of Homeland Security Task Force on Preventing the Entry of Weapons of Mass Effect on American Soil.

At Indiana University, Hamilton is a Professor of Practice in the School for Public and Environmental Affairs, is a Distinguished Scholar in the School of Global and International Studies, and serves as Co-Chair for IU's International Engagement Advisory Board.

Key concept: divisiveness in Congress

Early in my career in the U.S. House, I trekked over to the Senate side one day to watch a debate between Hubert Humphrey and Barry Goldwater, two of the great ideological warriors of the era. I don't recall the issue, but I do remember the heat they generated as they went at each other hammer and tongs. They were knowledgeable, passionate, and deeply committed to their vastly different points of view.

I remember just as keenly what happened after they'd tried to eviscerate each other rhetorically: They joked together as they left the floor, heading off to have a drink.

I have a hard time imagining such a scene in today's Washington, where a moment of camaraderie like that might be viewed with deep suspicion, as though personal friendship somehow undercuts ideological integrity. In the intensely partisan atmosphere that reigns today on Capitol Hill, it is much less common for two legislators to pursue their beliefs with such intensity of purpose, yet remain fast friends or work together when their interests coincide.

Americans of all stripes have noticed this, too, and they don't like it. The partisanship that divides Congress, and its members' apparent inability to transcend their divisions, is one important reason the institution's public standing is at historic depths.

How did we get here? In part, the answers lie in a series of long-term political trends that have converged to create this current unhappy mood.

For one thing, computers have enabled state legislators—or members of Congress eager to dictate to them—to draw congressional district lines that create safely Democratic or Republican districts. The result is that politicians running for the U.S. House don't have to appeal to the center to win, they need to appeal to the core of their parties' supporters.

This has happened at the same time that the parties themselves have moved toward their ideological extremes, pushed by the interest groups that fund and try to influence them. As members become spokesmen for particular points of view, their positions take on a harder edge, since they are playing to potential campaign funders or to an interest group whose supporters' votes they need at election time. The upshot is that moderate Democrats and Republicans are the exception in office these days, not the rule.

The sad truth, though, is that the electorate, too, is divided, which manifests itself at the moment in a Congress that is narrowly controlled by one party and faces a President of the other. Over the last decade, each party has been struggling to become the majority party, and so every vote on Capitol Hill has taken on heavily partisan implications, since the leadership hopes that by taking the position it does—and forcefully encouraging rank-and-file members to go along—it will pick up a few extra seats at the next election. This invites partisan struggle.

These political trends have been cemented by changes within Congress. If it is hard to find moderates there, it is even harder to find institutionalists—people who worry about the role of Congress as a separate and independent branch of government and who focus on strengthening Congress as an institution. Preoccupation with partisanship and political calculation erodes Congress' role as a deliberative body; "debate" these days is generally two sets of talking points hammering at each other, rather than a genuine effort to reach consensus on the best course for the American people to follow.

Even something as mundane as the congressional schedule now works in favor of partisanship. As their time on Capitol Hill has come to focus on committee hearings, floor debate and other opportunities for confrontation, and as their weekends now are often taken up with travel back to their states to meet with constituents, members of Congress in recent years have found far fewer opportunities to develop the kinds of friendships that cross party lines—and that produced such close friends as Humphrey and Goldwater.

These are all deep-seated trends, and they are not easy to reverse. My hope, oddly enough, lies in the low standing Congress currently enjoys. For all its faults, it does respond to public pressure, and if enough Americans let their members know that they're unhappy with the intense partisanship they see, change will come.

Perhaps it will be a move in some states to abandon partisan redistricting and move to some more neutral way of drawing lines; perhaps it will simply be a change in attitude and a greater emphasis on Capitol Hill on careful deliberation and comity, or greater respect for the institution of the Congress. Whatever the case, even little moves in the right direction would be an improvement over the situation as it stands today.

Critical Thinking

1. Is the legitimacy of Congress decreasing due to increasing partisanship?
2. What can be done to reduce partisanship?

Create Central

www.mhhe.com/createcentral

Internet References

Why Congress is so partisan, in two charts (Aaron Blake)
www.washingtonpost.com/blogs/the-fix/wp/2012/08/21/the-nasty-things-democrats-and-republicans-say-about-each-other

Why Congress is so partisan, in two charts (Chris Cillizza)
www.washingtonpost.com/blogs/the-fix/wp/2012/12/12/why-congress-is-so-partisan-in-2-charts

From *Center on Congress at Indiana University*, August 17, 2007. Copyright © 2007 by The Center on Congress. Reprinted by permission.

Unit 11: The Presidency

The Powers of the Presidency

Clinton Rossiter

Learning Outcomes

After reading this selection, you should be able to:

1. Enumerate the multiple roles of the U.S. president.
2. Discuss why "chief executive" may be the most troublesome of all the president's roles.
3. Explain how the presidency can at times become a sort of "third House of Congress."

Clinton Rossiter (1917–1970), an American historian and political scientist, is the author of *The American Presidency* (Harcourt, Brace, 1960), from which the following selection has been excerpted. The book focuses on the historical development of the modern presidency and its unique characteristics and powers.

Rossiter's work begins with a political analysis of the enormous and complex tasks, responsibilities, and burdens of the modern presidency. Beginning with Franklin D. Roosevelt, the American presidency has involved expanded powers and duties. Rossiter uses historical case studies to elaborate on the most significant presidential roles, or "hats" that modern presidents wear. He focuses on the formal constitutional responsibilities of the president, including such important functions as chief of state, chief executive, commander in chief, chief diplomat, and chief legislator. Rossiter also elaborates on the president's roles as chief of party, voice of the people, protector of the peace, manager of prosperity, and world leader.

Rossiter received his M.A. and Ph.D. from Princeton University. He was the John L. Senior Professor of American Institutions at Cornell University for several years. He authored several influential books, such as *The Seedtime of the Republic: The Origin of the American Tradition of Political Liberty* (Harcourt, Brace, 1953), for which he won the Bancroft Prize, the Woodrow Wilson Foundation Award of the American Political Science Association, and the prize of the Institute of Early American History and Culture; *Parties and Politics in America* (Cornell University Press, 1960); and *Conservatism in America* (Vintage Books, 1962), for which he received the Charles Austin Beard Memorial Prize. *The American Presidency* has been translated into 30 languages and has often been used as a standard text in the study of that topic in colleges and universities. Rossiter also served as a consultant to the Ford Foundation and the Rockefeller Foundation.

Key Concept: presidential functions

This presentation must begin with a careful accounting of those tasks we call upon the President to perform, for if there is any one thing about him that strikes the eye immediately, it is the staggering burden he bears for all of us. Those who cherish Gilbert and Sullivan will remember Pooh-Bah, the "particularly haughty exclusive person" in *The Mikado* who filled the offices of "First Lord of the Treasury, Lord Chief Justice, Commander-in-Chief, Lord High Admiral, Master of the Buckhounds, Groom of the Back Stairs, Archbishop of Titipu, and Lord Mayor, both acting and elect." We chuckle at the fictitious Pooh-Bah; we can only wonder at the real one that history has made of the American President. He has at least three jobs for every one of Pooh-Bah's, and they are not performed with the flick of a lacquered fan. At the risk of being perhaps too analytical, let me review the functions of the modern

President. These, as I interpret them, are the major roles he plays in the sprawling drama of American government.

First, the President is Chief of State. He remains today, as he has always been, the ceremonial head of the government of the United States, and he must take part with real or apparent enthusiasm in a range of activities that would keep him running and posing from sunrise to bedtime if he were not protected by a cold-blooded staff. Some of these activities are solemn or even priestly in nature; others, through no fault of his own, are flirtations with vulgarity. The long catalogue of public duties that the Queen discharges in England, the President of the Republic in France, and the Governor-General in Canada is the President's responsibility in this country, and the catalogue is even longer because he is not a king, or even an agent of one, and is therefore expected to go through some rather undignified paces by a people who think of him as a combination of scoutmaster, Delphic oracle, hero of the silver screen, and father of the multitudes.

As figurehead rather than working head of our government, he greets distinguished visitors from all parts of the world, lays wreaths on the tomb of the Unknown Soldier and before the statue of Lincoln, makes proclamations of thanksgiving and commemoration, bestows medals on flustered pilots, holds state dinners for the diplomatic corps and the Supreme Court, lights the nation's Christmas tree, buys the first poppy from the Veterans of Foreign Wars, gives the first crisp banknote to the Red Cross, throws out the first ball for the Senators (the harmless ones out at Griffith Stadium), rolls the first egg for the Easter Bunny, and in the course of any month greets a fantastic procession of firemen, athletes, veterans, Boy Scouts, Campfire Girls, boosters, hog callers, exchange students, and heroic school children. The annual United Fund Drive could not possibly get under way without a five-minute telecast from the White House; Sunday is not Sunday if the President and his lady skip church; a public-works project is not public until the President presses a silver key in Washington and explodes a charge of dynamite in Fort Peck or Hanford or the Tennessee Valley....

The President, in short, is the one-man distillation of the American people just as surely as the Queen is of the British people; he is, in President Taft's words, "the personal embodiment and representative of their dignity and majesty."...

The second of the President's roles is that of Chief Executive. He reigns, but he also rules; he symbolizes the people, but he also runs their government. "The true test of a good government is its aptitude and tendency to produce a good administration," Hamilton wrote in *The Federalist*, at the same time making clear that it would be the first duty of the proposed President to produce this "good administration." For reasons that I shall touch upon later, the President (and I mean any President, no matter how happily he may wallow in the details of administration) has more trouble playing this role successfully than he does any of the others. It is, in fact, the one major area of presidential activity in which his powers are simply not equal to his responsibilities. Yet the role is an important one, and we cannot savor the fullness of the President's duties unless we recall that he is held primarily and often exclusively accountable for the ethics, loyalty, efficiency, frugality, and responsiveness to the public's wishes of the two and a third million Americans in the national administration.

Both the Constitution and Congress have recognized his authority to supervise the day-to-day activities of the executive branch, strained and restrained though this supervision may often be in practice. From the Constitution, explicitly or implicitly, he receives the twin powers of appointment and removal, as well as the primary

duty, which no law or plan or circumstance can ever take away from him, to "take care that the laws be faithfully executed." He alone may appoint, with the advice and consent of the Senate, the several thousand top officials who run the government; he alone may remove, with varying degrees of abruptness, those who are not executing the laws faithfully—or, in the case of all those Secretaries and generals and attorneys directly under his command, not executing them in a manner consistent with his own policies.

It is the power of removal—the "gun behind the door"—that makes it possible for the President to bend his "team" to his will. More to the point, this power is the symbol and final sanction of his position as Chief Executive, and no official in the administration, not even the most nonpartisan chairman of the most independent regulatory commission, is entirely immune to a fatal attack of presidential displeasure....

The President's third major function is one he could not escape if he wished, and several Presidents have wished it mightily. The Constitution designates him specifically as "Commander-in-Chief of the Army and Navy of the United States, and of the militia of the several States when called into the actual service of the United States." In peace and war he is the supreme commander of the armed forces, the living guarantee of the American belief in "the supremacy of the civil over military authority."

In time of peace he raises, trains, supervises, and deploys the forces that Congress is willing to maintain, and he has a great deal to say about the size and make-up of these forces. With the aid of the Secretary of Defense, the Secretaries of the three services, the Joint Chiefs of Staff, and the members of the National Security Council—every one of these men his personal choice—he looks constantly to the state of the nation's defenses. He is never for one day allowed to forget that he will be held accountable by people, Congress, and history for the nation's readiness to meet an enemy assault....

But this, the power of command, is only a fraction of the vast responsibility the modern President draws from the Commander in Chief clause. The framers of the Constitution, to be sure, took a narrow view of the authority they had granted. "It would amount," Hamilton wrote offhandedly in *The Federalist*, "to nothing more than the supreme command and direction of the military and naval forces, as first General and Admiral of the Confederacy." This view of presidential power as something purely military foundered on the hard facts of the first of our modern wars. Faced by an overriding necessity for harsh, even dictatorial action, Lincoln used the Commander in Chief clause, at first gingerly, in the end boldly, to justify an unprecedented series of measures that cut deeply into the accepted liberties of the people and the routine pattern of government. Wilson added another cubit to the stature of the wartime

Presidency by demanding that Congress give him those powers over the economy about which there was any constitutional doubt, and Franklin Roosevelt, who had read about Lincoln and lived with Wilson, carried the wartime Presidency to breath-taking heights of authority over the American economy and social order. The creation and staffing of a whole array of emergency boards and offices, the seizure and operation of more than sixty strike-bound or strike-threatened plants and industries, and the forced evacuation of 70,000 American citizens of Japanese descent from the West Coast are three startling and prophetic examples of what a President can do as Commander in Chief to stiffen the home front in support of the fighting forces. It is important to recall that Congress came to Roosevelt's aid in each of these series of actions by passing laws empowering him to do what he had done already or by fixing penalties for violating the orders of his subordinates. Congress, too, likes to win wars, and Congressmen are more likely to needle the President for inactivity and timidity than to accuse him of acting too swiftly and arbitrarily.

Now that total war, which ignores the old line between battlefield and home front, has been compounded by the absolute weapon, which mocks every rule we have ever tried to honor, we may expect the President to be nothing short of a "constitutional dictator" in the event of war. The next wartime President, who may well be our last, will have the right, of which Lincoln spoke with feeling, to take "any measure which may best subdue the enemy," and he alone will be the judge of what is "best" for the survival of the republic. We have placed a shocking amount of military power in the President's keeping, but where else, we may ask, could it possibly have been placed?

𝒩ext, the President is Chief Diplomat. Although authority in the field of foreign relations is shared constitutionally among three organs—President, Congress, and, for two special purposes, the Senate—his position is paramount, if not indeed dominant. In 1799 John Marshall, no particular friend of executive power, spoke of the President as "the sole organ of the nation in its external relations, and its sole representative with foreign nations." In 1936 Justice Sutherland, no particular friend of executive power and even less of Franklin D. Roosevelt, put the Court's stamp of approval on "the very delicate, plenary and exclusive power of the President as the sole organ of the government in the field of international relations." . . .

The field of foreign relations can be conveniently if somewhat inexactly divided into two sectors: the formulation of policy and the conduct of affairs. The first of these is a joint undertaking in which the President proposes, Congress disposes, and the wishes of the people prevail in the end. The President's leadership is usually vindicated. Our most ancient and honored policy is significantly known as the *Monroe* Doctrine; our leading

policies of recent years have been the *Truman* Doctrine and the *Eisenhower* Doctrine. From Washington's Proclamation of Neutrality in 1793 to Eisenhower's decision to stand fast in Berlin in 1959, the President has repeatedly committed the nation to decisive attitudes and actions abroad, more than once to war itself. Occasionally Congress has compelled him to abandon a policy already put forward, as it did in the case of Grant's plans for Santo Domingo, or has forced distasteful policies upon him, as it did upon Madison in 1812 and McKinley in 1898. Nevertheless, a stubborn President is hard to budge, a crusading President hard to thwart. The diplomatic lives of the two Roosevelts are proof enough of these assertions. Mr. Truman was not exaggerating much when he told an informal gathering of the Jewish War Veterans in 1948: "I make American foreign policy." . . .

𝒯he President's duties are not all purely executive in nature. He is also intimately associated, by Constitution and custom, with the legislative process, and we may therefore consider him to be the Chief Legislator. Congress has a wealth of strong and talented men, but the complexity of the problems they are asked to solve by a people who assume that all problems are solvable has made *external* leadership a requisite of effective operation. The President alone is in a political, constitutional, and practical position to provide such leadership, and he is therefore expected, within the limits of constitutional and political propriety, to guide Congress in much of its lawmaking activity. Indeed, since Congress is no longer organized to guide itself, not even under such tough-minded leaders as Senator Johnson and Speaker Rayburn, the refusal or inability of the President to point out the way results in weak or, at best, stalemated government.

Success in the delicate area of executive-legislative relations depends on several variables: the political complexion of President and Congress, the state of the Union and of the world around us, the vigor and tact of the President's leadership, and the mood of Congress, which is generally friendly near the beginning of a President's term and rebellious near the end. Yet even the President whose announced policy is to "restore our hallowed system of the separation of powers" and leave Congress strictly alone (Coolidge is a capital example, one not likely to be repeated) must exercise his constitutional option to veto or not to veto about a thousand times each session, must discourse once a year on the state of the Union and occasionally recommend "such measures as he shall judge necessary and expedient," must present the annual budget, and must make some effort to realize at least the less controversial promises in his party's platform. "After all," Mr. Eisenhower told a press conference in 1959, "the Constitution puts the President right square into the legislative business." In the hands of a Wilson or a Roosevelt, even at times in the hands of an Eisenhower, the Presidency becomes a sort of prime ministership or "third House of Congress," and the chief concern of the

President is to push for the enactment of his own or his party's legislative desires.

Upon many of our most celebrated laws the presidential imprint is clearly stamped. Each of these was drafted in the President's offices, introduced and supported by his friends, defended in committee by his aides, voted through by a party over which every form of discipline and persuasion was exerted, and then made law by his signature. . . .

Even the President who lacks a congressional majority must go through the motions of leadership. The Republicans in the Eightieth Congress always waited politely for Mr. Truman's proposals on labor, taxes, inflation, civil rights, and education, however scant the regard they intended to pay them. The Democrats, if we may believe the protests of Speaker Rayburn and Senator Johnson, were impatient to hear President Eisenhower's proposals and to feel the lash of his leadership. In any case, the chief responsibility for bridging the constitutional gulf between executive and legislature now rests irrevocably with the President. His tasks as leader of Congress are difficult and delicate, yet he must bend to them steadily or be judged a failure. The President who will not give his best thoughts to guiding Congress, more so the President who is temperamentally or politically unfitted to "get along with Congress," is now rightly considered a national liability.

Chief of State, Chief Executive, Commander in Chief, Chief Diplomat, Chief Legislator—these functions make up the strictly constitutional burden of the President. As Mr. Truman himself allowed in several of his folksy sermons on the Presidency, they form an aggregate of power that would have made Caesar or Genghis Khan or Napoleon bite his nails with envy. Yet even these are not the whole weight of presidential responsibility. I count at least five additional functions that have been piled on top of the original load.

The first of these is the President's role as Chief of Party, one that he has played by popular demand and to a mixed reception ever since the administration of Thomas Jefferson. However sincere Washington's abhorrence of "factions" may have been, his own administration and policies spawned our first two parties, and their arrival upon the scene altered the character of the Presidency radically. No matter how fondly or how often we may long for a President who is above the heat of political strife, we must acknowledge resolutely his right and duty to be the leader of his party. He is at once the least political and most political of all heads of government.

The value of this function has been attested by all our first-rate Presidents. Jackson, Lincoln, Wilson, and the two Roosevelts were especially skillful party leaders. By playing the politician with unashamed zest the first of these gave his epic administration a unique sense of cohesion, the second rallied doubting Republican leaders and their followings to the cause of the Union, and

the other three achieved genuine triumphs as catalysts of congressional action. . . .

Yet [the President] is, at the same time if not in the same breath, the Voice of the People, the leading formulator and expounder of public opinion in the United States. While he acts as political leader of some, he serves as moral spokesman for all. . . .

The President is the American people's one authentic trumpet, and he has no higher duty than to give a clear and certain sound. "Words at great moments of history are deeds," Clement Attlee said of Winston Churchill on the day the latter stepped down in 1945. The strong and imaginative President can make with his own words the kind of history that Churchill made in 1940 and 1941. When the events of 1933 are all but forgotten, we shall still recall Roosevelt's words, "The only thing we have to fear is fear itself."

In the memorable case of *In re Neagle* (1890), which still makes good reading for those who like a touch of horse opera in their constitutional law, Justice Samuel Miller spoke with a feeling of the "peace of the United States"—a happy condition, it would appear, of domestic tranquillity and national prosperity that is often broken by violent men and forces and just as often restored by the President. Perhaps the least known of his functions is the mandate he holds from the Constitution and the laws, but even more positively from the people of the United States, to act as Protector of the Peace. The emergencies that can disturb the peace of the United States seem to grow thicker and more vexing every year, and hardly a week now goes by that the President is not called upon to take forceful steps in behalf of a section or city or group or enterprise that has been hit hard and suddenly by disaster. Generally, it is for state and local authorities to deal with social and natural calamities, but in the face of a riot in Detroit or floods in New England or a tornado in Missouri or a railroad strike in Chicago or a panic in Wall Street, the people turn almost instinctively to the White House and its occupant for aid and comfort. . . .

There is at least one area of American life, the economy, in which the people of this country are no longer content to let disaster fall upon them unopposed. They now expect their government, under the direct leadership of the President, to prevent a depression or panic and not simply to wait until one has developed before putting it to rout. Thus the President has a new function, which is still taking shape, that of Manager of Prosperity. . . .

In order to grasp the full import of the last of the President's roles, we must take him as Chief Diplomat, Commander in Chief, and Chief of State, then thrust him onto a far wider stage, there to perform before a much more numerous and more critical audience. For the modern President is, whether we or our friends abroad like it or not, marked out for duty as a World Leader.

The President has a much larger constituency than the American electorate: his words and deeds in behalf of our own survival as a free nation have a direct bearing upon the freedom and stability of at least several score other countries. . . .

Having engaged in this piecemeal analysis of the Presidency, I hasten to fit the pieces back together into a seamless unity. For that, after all, is what the Presidency is, and I hope this exercise in political taxonomy has not obscured the paramount fact that it is a single office filled by a single man. I feel something like a professor of nutritional science who has just ticked off the ingredients of a wonderful stew. The members of the audience may be clear in their minds about the items in the pot, but they have not the slightest notion of what the final product looks like or tastes like or will feel like in their stomachs. The Presidency, too, is a wonderful stew whose unique flavor cannot be accounted for simply by making a list of its ingredients. It is a whole greater than and different from the sum of its parts, an office whose power and prestige are something more than the arithmetical total of all its functions. The President is not one kind of official during one part of the day, another kind during another part—administrator in the morning, legislator at lunch, king in the afternoon, commander before dinner, and politician at odd moments that come his weary way. He is all these things all the time, and any one of his functions feeds upon and into all the others. He is a more exalted Chief of State because he is also Voice of the People, a more forceful Chief Diplomat because he commands the armed forces personally, a more effective Chief Legislator because the political system forces him to be Chief of Party, a more artful Manager of Prosperity because he is Chief Executive.

Critical Thinking

1. As Rossiter observes, we have placed a shocking amount of military power in the president's keeping, but where else could it possibly have been placed?
2. If the president's role as "manager of prosperity" was a new function still taking shape in the 1950s, what can be said of this role today, 10 administrations later?
3. What makes the expression "leader of the free world" an appropriate (or inappropriate) title for the president of the United States?

Create Central

www.mhhe.com/createcentral

Internet References

C-SPAN
www.c-span.org

United States House of Representatives
www.house.gov

United States Senate
www.senate.gov

The White House
www.whitehouse.gov

From *The American Presidency* by Clinton Rossiter (Harcourt Brace, 1960). Copyright © 1960 by Clinton Rossiter. Copyright renewed 1988 by Mary Crane Rossiter, Caleb S. Rossiter, and Winton G. Rossiter. Reprinted by permission of Cengage Learning.

Prepared by: James Newman, *University of Maryland University College*

Inaugural Address by President Barack Obama

Barack Obama

Learning Outcomes

After reading this selection, you should be able to:

1. Understand our nation's strengths and challenges.
2. Discuss the common threads that unite Americans, according to the president.

Barack Obama is the 44th president of the United States. His January 20, 2009, inauguration marked the first occasion an African American became president of the United States. Shortly after his inauguration, he won the Nobel Peace Prize. Prior to his election to the presidency, he served in the Illinois state senate and as a U.S. Senator. His first term was noted as one of the most economically challenging times since the Great Depression. Managing a fragile economic recovery and reducing the number of troops stationed in Iraq and Afghanistan were primary concerns in his first term.

The inaugural address carries a theme of economic fairness. Notions of equity in opportunity and fairness were debated in Congress and in the media as the economic recovery impacted individuals differently. In the address President Obama makes a case for his notion of equity and fairness. As is often found in presidential addresses, national unity and pride is a common thread in the address.

Key concept: President Obama discusses current challenges of the nation

THE PRESIDENT: Vice President Biden, Mr. Chief Justice, members of the United States Congress, distinguished guests, and fellow citizens:

*E*ach time we gather to inaugurate a President we bear witness to the enduring strength of our Constitution. We affirm the promise of our democracy. We recall that what binds this nation together is not the colors of our skin or the tenets of our faith or the origins of our names. What makes us exceptional—what makes us American—is our allegiance to an idea articulated in a declaration made more than two centuries ago:

"We hold these truths to be self-evident, that all men are created equal; that they are endowed by their Creator with certain unalienable rights; that among these are life, liberty, and the pursuit of happiness."

Today we continue a never-ending journey to bridge the meaning of those words with the realities of our time. For history tells us that while these truths may be self-evident, they've never been self-executing; that while freedom is a gift from God, it must be secured by His people here on Earth. The patriots of 1776 did not fight to replace the tyranny of a king with the privileges of a few or the rule of a mob. They gave to us a republic, a government of, and by, and for the people, entrusting each generation to keep safe our founding creed.

And for more than two hundred years, we have.

Through blood drawn by lash and blood drawn by sword, we learned that no union founded on the principles of liberty and equality could survive half-slave and half-free. We made ourselves anew, and vowed to move forward together.

Together, we determined that a modern economy requires railroads and highways to speed travel and commerce, schools and colleges to train our workers.

Together, we discovered that a free market only thrives when there are rules to ensure competition and fair play.

Together, we resolved that a great nation must care for the vulnerable, and protect its people from life's worst hazards and misfortune.

Through it all, we have never relinquished our skepticism of central authority, nor have we succumbed to the fiction that all society's ills can be cured through government alone. Our celebration of initiative and enterprise, our insistence on hard work and personal responsibility, these are constants in our character.

But we have always understood that when times change, so must we; that fidelity to our founding principles requires new responses to new challenges; that preserving our individual freedoms ultimately requires collective action. For the American people can no more meet the demands of today's world by acting alone than American soldiers could have met the forces of fascism or communism with muskets and militias. No single person can train all the math and science teachers we'll need to equip our children for the future, or build the roads and networks and research labs that will bring new jobs and businesses to our shores. Now, more than ever, we must do these things together, as one nation and one people.

This generation of Americans has been tested by crises that steeled our resolve and proved our resilience. A decade of war is now ending. An economic recovery has begun. America's possibilities are limitless, for we possess all the qualities that this world without boundaries demands: youth and drive; diversity and openness; an endless capacity for risk and a gift for reinvention. My fellow Americans, we are made for this moment, and we will seize it—so long as we seize it together.

For we, the people, understand that our country cannot succeed when a shrinking few do very well and a growing many barely make it. We believe that America's prosperity must rest upon the broad shoulders of a rising middle class. We know that America thrives when every person can find independence and pride in their work; when the wages of honest labor liberate families from the brink of hardship. We are true to our creed when a little girl born into the bleakest poverty knows that she has the same chance to succeed as anybody else, because she is an American; she is free, and she is equal, not just in the eyes of God but also in our own.

We understand that outworn programs are inadequate to the needs of our time. So we must harness new ideas and technology to remake our government, revamp our tax code, reform our schools, and empower our citizens with the skills they need to work harder, learn more, reach higher. But while the means will change, our purpose endures: a nation that rewards the effort and determination of every single American. That is what this moment requires. That is what will give real meaning to our creed.

We, the people, still believe that every citizen deserves a basic measure of security and dignity. We must make the hard choices to reduce the cost of health care and the size of our deficit. But we reject the belief that America must choose between caring for the generation that built this country and investing in the generation that will build its future. For we remember the lessons of our past, when twilight years were spent in poverty and parents of a child with a disability had nowhere to turn.

We do not believe that in this country freedom is reserved for the lucky, or happiness for the few. We recognize that no matter how responsibly we live our lives, any one of us at any time may face a job loss, or a sudden illness, or a home swept away in a terrible storm. The commitments we make to each other through Medicare and Medicaid and Social Security, these things do not sap our initiative, they strengthen us. They do not make us a nation of takers; they free us to take the risks that make this country great.

We, the people, still believe that our obligations as Americans are not just to ourselves, but to all posterity. We will respond to the threat of climate change, knowing that the failure to do so would betray our children and future generations. Some may still deny the overwhelming judgment of science, but none can avoid the devastating impact of raging fires and crippling drought and more powerful storms.

The path towards sustainable energy sources will be long and sometimes difficult. But America cannot resist this transition, we must lead it. We cannot cede to other nations the technology that will power new jobs and new industries, we must claim its promise. That's how we will maintain our economic vitality and our national treasure—our forests and waterways, our crop lands and snow-capped peaks. That is how we will preserve our planet, commanded to our care by God. That's what will lend meaning to the creed our fathers once declared.

We, the people, still believe that enduring security and lasting peace do not require perpetual war. Our brave men and women in uniform, tempered by the flames of battle, are unmatched in skill and courage. Our citizens, seared by the memory of those we have lost, know too well the price that is paid for liberty. The knowledge of their sacrifice will keep us forever vigilant against those who would do us harm. But we are also heirs to those who won the peace and not just the war; who turned sworn enemies into the surest of friends—and we must carry those lessons into this time as well.

We will defend our people and uphold our values through strength of arms and rule of law. We will show the courage to try and resolve our differences with other nations peacefully—not because we are naïve about the dangers we face, but because engagement can more durably lift suspicion and fear.

America will remain the anchor of strong alliances in every corner of the globe. And we will renew those institutions that extend our capacity to manage crisis abroad, for no one has a greater stake in a peaceful world than its most powerful nation. We will support democracy from Asia to Africa, from the Americas to the Middle East, because our interests and our conscience compel us to act on behalf of those who long for freedom. And we must be a source of hope to the poor, the sick, the marginalized, the victims of prejudice—not out of mere charity, but because peace in our time requires the constant advance of those principles that our common creed describes: tolerance and opportunity, human dignity and justice.

We, the people, declare today that the most evident of truths—that all of us are created equal—is the star that guides us still; just as it guided our forebears through Seneca Falls, and Selma, and Stonewall; just as it guided all those men and women, sung and unsung, who left footprints along this great Mall, to hear a preacher say that we cannot walk alone; to hear a King proclaim that our individual freedom is inextricably bound to the freedom of every soul on Earth.

It is now our generation's task to carry on what those pioneers began. For our journey is not complete until our wives, our mothers and daughters can earn a living equal to their efforts. Our journey is not complete until our gay brothers and sisters are treated like anyone else under the law—for if we are truly created equal, then surely the love we commit to one another must be equal as well. Our journey is not complete until no citizen is forced to wait for hours to exercise the right to vote. Our journey is not complete until we find a better way to welcome the striving, hopeful immigrants who still see America as a land of opportunity—until bright young students and engineers are enlisted in our workforce rather than expelled from our country. Our journey is not complete until all our children, from the streets of Detroit to the hills of Appalachia, to the quiet lanes of Newtown, know that they are cared for and cherished and always safe from harm.

That is our generation's task—to make these words, these rights, these values of life and liberty and the pursuit of happiness real for every American. Being true to our founding documents does not require us to agree on every contour of life. It does not mean we all define liberty in exactly the same way or follow the same precise path to happiness. Progress does not compel us to settle centuries-long debates about the role of government for all time, but it does require us to act in our time.

For now decisions are upon us and we cannot afford delay. We cannot mistake absolutism for principle, or substitute spectacle for politics, or treat name-calling as reasoned debate. We must act, knowing that our work will be imperfect. We must act, knowing that today's victories will be only partial and that it will be up to those who stand here in four years and 40 years and 400 years hence to advance the timeless spirit once conferred to us in a spare Philadelphia hall.

My fellow Americans, the oath I have sworn before you today, like the one recited by others who serve in this Capitol, was an oath to God and country, not party or faction. And we must faithfully execute that pledge during the duration of our service. But the words I spoke today are not so different from the oath that is taken each time a soldier signs up for duty or an immigrant realizes her dream. My oath is not so different from the pledge we all make to the flag that waves above and that fills our hearts with pride.

They are the words of citizens and they represent our greatest hope. You and I, as citizens, have the power to set this country's course. You and I, as citizens, have the obligation to shape the debates of our time—not only with the votes we cast, but with the voices we lift in defense of our most ancient values and enduring ideals.

Let us, each of us, now embrace with solemn duty and awesome joy what is our lasting birthright. With common effort and common purpose, with passion and dedication, let us answer the call of history and carry into an uncertain future that precious light of freedom.

Thank you. God bless you, and may He forever bless these United States of America.

Critical Thinking

1. How is our nation's diversity a strength?
2. What are the most vital concerns facing our nation today?

Create Central

www.mhhe.com/createcentral

Internet References

Obama Inaugural Address: The Unapologetic President
www.huffingtonpost.com/2013/01/21/obama-inaugural-address_n_2521206.html

The White House
www.whitehouse.gov

Office of the Press Secretary, January 21, 2013.

Unit 12: The Bureaucracy

Political Executives:
A Government of Strangers

Hugh Heclo

Learning Outcomes

After reading this selection, you should be able to:

1. Identify the statistically elite characteristics of political executives.
2. Recognize transience as the single-most obvious characteristic of political appointees.
3. Explain why the observation of political executives' "going native" is an apt image.

Hugh Heclo has been recognized by students and scholars of public administration and public policy as an expert on the federal bureaucracy. The following selection is excerpted from Heclo's *A Government of Strangers: Executive Politics in Washington* (Brookings Institution, 1977), what many political scientists consider to be one of the most significant contributions to the study of the Washington bureaucracy and the recruitment and appointment of political executives. In the book, Heclo focuses on how high-ranking professional bureaucrats attempt to maintain administrative stability and how political appointees attempt to dominate and manipulate the administrative bureaucracy. In addition, he analyzes how government careerists, or professional administrators, attempt to resist the efforts of political appointees to consolidate power within their respective departments or agencies. This book has shifted the theoretical focus of administrative behavior to emphasize the relations of political appointees with bureaucrats and the president.

Heclo depicts the political executives or political appointees as members of the social economic elite of American society. He claims that, in contrast to many private organizations, high-ranking public officials and administrators in the executive branch of the national government are less familiar and less informed about their working environment than administrative subordinates.

Heclo is the Clarence J. Robinson Professor of Public Affairs at George Mason University. He has also taught at Yale University (where he received his Ph.D.), Essex, and the Massachusetts Institute of Technology, and he has been a research associate with the Brookings Institution in Washington, D.C. Heclo has been a staff assistant on domestic policy in the Office of the Vice President of the United States and a consultant to the Department of Health and Social Security for the British government. His research has focused on American government and politics, public policy, social welfare, the presidency, and comparative politics.

Key Concept: political characteristics of executive branch appointees

To speak of political appointees in Washington is obviously to embrace a wide variety of people and situations. Political appointments cover everything from the temporary file clerk recouping a campaign obligation to the cabinet secretary heading a department organization larger than many state governments or the national administrations of some foreign countries. . . .

The Political Executive System

From the outset political executives share one broad feature: all hold an ambivalent leadership position in what might loosely be termed the American "system" of public executives. To appreciate the peculiarity of their political situation, one must return to the basic rationale for having a number of non-elected political appointees in the executive branch in the first place. According to the Founding Fathers' design, power for the legislative functions of government was spread among the various representatives from states and congressional districts; for the executive function, power was deliberately unified in one elected chief executive. A single president to nominate and supervise the principal officers of the executive branch would promote the unity and vigor of executive operations, while requiring the Senate's consent to make appointments final would safeguard against any presidential abuse of the appointment power and would stabilize administration.[1] Theorists of party government later elaborated on what some of the Founders only hinted at—that competition in the electoral marketplace would result in choices between alternative political teams and policies.

The idea of a single chief executive entering office to promote his measures through a band of loyal political supporters in the executive branch is an easily understood model. It fits well with the media's desire to focus on the central presidential personality, and the notion of undertaking public service at the call of the President attracts many new political appointees to Washington. Astute scholars have pointed out that in reality the President's formal power as the single chief executive is often illusory, that even within his own executive branch he must persuade others and calculate his power stakes rather than cudgel his minions. This revisionist view, however, has not altered the customary concentration on the President and, like the standard constitutional or party government models, it relegates the bulk of political executives to a secondary, derivative role in the executive branch. . . .

Characteristics of Political Executives

Although reliable information about political executives' behavior is lacking, a surfeit of data exists concerning their biographical characteristics. These data add up to a description of a statistical elite—statistical because there is little evidence of a self-conscious group seeking agreed upon goals and screening out other entrants; elite because political appointees in the federal government are consistently drawn from the most socially and economically advantaged portions of the population. With a degree of certainty rare in social science, political executives can be predicted to be disproportionately white, male, urban, affluent, middle-aged, well educated at prestige schools, and pursuers of high-status white-collar careers. They are unlikely to be female, nonwhite, wage-earning, from a small town, or possessors of average educational and social credentials.[2]

Work Experience

These socioeconomic data, however, reveal little about the kind of experience political executives gain on the job. For this type of information, researchers have examined job tenure and mobility in hopes of describing the government executives' opportunities to learn about their working environments. Such information does not entirely support several commonly held assumptions about the characteristics of political appointees. One is that the top political layers are filled with newcomers to government—politically imported outsiders credited by defenders with introducing a fresh view of government

operations and labeled by detractors as ignorant intruders. Another common view (and one of the chief justifications for the extensive use of political appointments in government) is that those in the top strata resemble the Founding Fathers, in that they are "in-and-outers," that is, people who periodically interrupt their private careers to move in and out of the public service. Qualifying, if not entirely dispelling, each of these assumptions leaves behind a more realistic picture of the public careers of political executives. . . .

It is worth emphasizing the general point evident in such data: unlike the situation in most private organizations, in the U.S. executive branch those in the top positions of formal authority are likely to be substantially less familiar with their working environment than both their civil service and political subordinates. . . .

These statistics . . . should not summon up images of a top government layer peopled with men of public affairs who, like modern counterparts of Cincinnatus or George Washington, repeatedly exchange private lives for public offices. While prominent examples of such men do exist (Nelson Rockefeller, Clark Clifford, Averell Harriman, etc.), true in-and-out careers are much less common than usually thought. Such careers would presumably show a periodic interchange of public service and private employment, possibly with several appointments in different administrations. In fact, these characteristics are uncommon. . . .

In sum, political appointees are generally people who will move in and sometimes up. They will cope as best they can and move out without returning. The few top executives with continual government experience may be extraordinarily valuable, but as a former civil servant said, "What most people don't realize is that an in-and-outer usually ends up staying an outer." The conventional image of Washington in-and-outers erroneously suggests a political team of utility players, when what actually exists is a one-time sequence of pinch hitters.

Birds of Passage

The single most obvious characteristic of Washington's political appointees is their transience. While most take up their appointments with somewhat more government experience and have a more terminal government career than is usually assumed, political executives are not likely to be in any one position for very long. The standard figure quoted is that the average undersecretary or assistant secretary remains in his job for about twenty-two months. More detailed breakdowns show this average to contain a large number of very short tenures; about half the top political executives can expect to stay in their jobs less than two years. . . .

Much more important than the experience or inexperience of political appointees as individuals is their transience as a group. Cabinet secretaries may bring with them a cadre of personal acquaintants to fill some of their subordinate political positions, but in general public executives will be strangers with only a fleeting chance to learn how to work together. This characteristic is worth examining in a little more detail.

One of the most persistent themes in comments from political executives of all recent administrations is the absence of teamwork characterizing the layers of appointees. This absence of unifying ties is foreordained, given the fractionalized, changing, and job-specific sets of forces that make up the selection process. But it is not only methods of selection that put mutually reinforcing loyalties at a premium. Rapid turnover intensifies all the other problems of political teamwork.

In many ways what matters most is not so much an individual's job tenure as the duration of his executive relationships. Those in superior positions need to assess the capacities of their subordinates; subordinates need to learn what is expected of them. Political appointees at the same hierarchical level need to learn each other's strengths, weaknesses, priorities, and ways of communicating. Normally the opportunity to develop these working relationships is even shorter than the time span for learning a particular job. . . .

The Larger Picture

The unstable teams within departments are positively collegial when compared with the attenuated relations of political appointees across departments. At least within departments there may be the shared need to protect and promote a common set of agency programs. Weighed against this territorial imperative, political appointees elsewhere can seem like alien tribes.

Few political appointees are likely to be united by bonds of party loyalty, the academics' favorite prescription for overcoming political incoherence in Washington. Though they may be in broad agreement with the President's general approach, political executives usually will not have been active members of his party and only a small minority will have struggled together against common opponents in electoral campaigns. Civil servants are identifying a fundamental characteristic of executive leadership in Washington when they report that they have worked for many political appointees but rarely for a politician.[3] Most would probably agree with the assistant secretary who said, "As far as I can tell, in this town a political appointee is simply someone whose career isn't in this department."

None of this inexperience necessarily means a lack of partisanship in "nonpolitical" political appointees. Quite the opposite. Many of those eventually known as the most partisan of Nixon's appointees came from backgrounds with a minimum of party-political experience. "I came to Washington with absolutely no party or political background," one of them said. "I had a naive idea of managing as in private enterprise but quickly learned political factors are all pervasive."

The record of the Nixon White House demonstrated in a number of cases how those least politically experienced can be susceptible to developing more extreme personal partisanship than those accustomed to regular political interaction and its inevitable compromises. Often the zealousness of the new convert to Washington politics can make effective political teamwork that much more difficult. One official summed up his experience in four administrations by observing: "Inexperienced people tend to lack the political instinct. . . . Sometimes the political instinct means the best politics is no politics. And it knows where that's true, it's not pure partisanship."

Lacking any larger political forces to help unify political executives, the lines of mutual interdependence normally run vertically down the departments and their loosely related programs—not horizontally across the layers of political leadership in various departments. Insofar as top political executives need each other (as opposed to needing the President's support or endorsement) the needs are temporary and issue-specific, not enduring. Even at the height of public criticism concerning the placement of Nixon loyalists in the departments, many of those placed recognized the lack of any workable horizontal contacts. As one appointee said: "For all the talk about teams, I have no contact that amounts to anything with other appointees outside the department. The few lunches we have aren't of much use for getting business done. There is no strong mechanism for getting political appointees together. As a group there's no trust."

It would be a mistake, however, to conclude that political executives are averse to creating alliances. At any given moment, informal communications and networks do exist throughout the political levels and across the departments in Washington. But as participants and issues change frequently, so do the nature and location of these relationships. Some political appointees will have enough common objectives and mutual knowledge to create fairly close informal groups. "There are me and six other assistant secretaries from other departments," said one such man. "We've got some management techniques we want to move on." A year later two of these executives were left in government. Another appointee was trying to draw his counterparts into monthly meetings but recognized "the problem is how to get continuity and institutionalize this sort of thing to keep it going." A year later, he too was gone and his group largely dismantled.

Equally revealing of the flux confronting any outsider is the fact that the last man quoted was like many resigning political appointees. He did not depart for reasons bearing any relation to the substance of what he was doing in government but because his own political patrons were leaving. While resignation for reasons of conscience or policy are relatively rare,[4] the chancy circumstances that create political executives in the first place can just as easily lead to their departure. Political executives and their particular sets of relationships with each other not only fade, but fade fortuitously. Even a close observer of these political comings and goings is likely to pick up confusing signals about whether an executive personnel change is a case of tactics, accident, or grand political strategy. . . .

Yet if there were to be such a serious effort at decision-making by enduring teams of political leaders across the top of departments, the U.S. presidency would look far different than it does today or ever has. In such a system cabinet secretaries would need each other as a group more than they would need their departmental identifications and more than they would need any individual member, including the President. Presidents may be advised that they need more collegial help and reactivated cabinets, and they may with good reason even take such advice, at least for a while. But barring any profound institutional and structural changes, no modern president can be expected to be like a foreign prime minister, merely the first among equals. He needs the particular colleagues in his cabinet too little; his colleagues need him too much and each other too little for that to happen. No public executive short of the President has a vested interest in coordinating political leadership in the executive branch as a whole. Political appointees out in the departments and agencies can expect to remain in their twilight zone.

Because the executive branch has a single head, its political leadership is inherently noncollegial—except for a sharing of some executive powers with Congress. That is the way the Founders designed it. That is the way it functions. But "single" does not mean unitary. The political executives' very lack of coequality—no one is the President's peer—means that their successes are likely to be expropriated by the President, their failures left behind in the departments with little effect on the appointees' real vocations outside government. Since there is only one chief executive but many sources of political support and inspiration, top political appointees do not necessarily hang separately if they fail to hang together. *E unibus plurum.*

A Summary and Look Forward

Any commitment to democratic values necessarily means accepting a measure of instability in the top governing levels. Democratic elections are, after all, "a political invention to assure uncertainty of leadership, in what are deemed to be optimum amounts and periods of time."[5] But to the inherent electoral changes, the American executive political system adds a considerably greater range of nonelectoral uncertainty to political leadership. This system produces top executives who are both expendable over time and in a relatively weak, uncertain position at any one time.

The number of political executives is small vis-à-vis the bureaucracy but large and fragmented in relation to any notion of a trim top-management structure. To the

normal confusions of pluralistic institutions and powers in Washington, the selection process contributes its own complexities. White House personnel efforts have rarely been effectively organized. Political forces intervene from many quarters, and their interests in political appointments often bear little relation to presidential needs or to qualifications required for effective performance by public executives. White House efforts at political recruitment can be effective, but the organizational requirements are difficult to master. A White House operation that veers too far in the direction of centralized control can easily become self-defeating by overlooking the need for political executives to balance their responsiveness to the President with their usefulness to the departments. . . .

Weaknesses among political executives lead inevitably to White House complaints about their "going native" in the bureaucracy. The image is apt. To a large extent the particular agencies and bureaus *are* the native villages of executive politics. Even the most presidentially minded political executive will discover that his own agency provides the one relatively secure reference point amid all the other uncertainties of Washington. In their own agencies, appointees usually have at least some knowledge of each other and a common identity with particular programs. Outside the agency it is more like life in the big city among large numbers of anonymous people who have unknown lineages. Any common kinship in the political party or a shared political vocation is improbable, and in the background are always the suspicions of the President's "true" family of supporters in the White House. Political appointees in the larger Washington environment may deal frequently with each other, but these are likely to be the kind of ad hoc, instrumental relations of the city, where people interact without truly knowing each other.

Yet the political appointee's situation is not so simple that he can act as if he is surrounded by a random collection of strangers outside the confines of his agency village. Everywhere extensive networks of village folk in the bureaucracy, Congress, and lobby organizations share experiences, problems, and readings on people and events. An appointee may or may not be in touch with people in these networks, but they are certain to be in touch with each other independently of him. In sociological terms his networks are thin, transient, and single-stranded; theirs are dense, multiple, and enduring. Among public executives themselves there is little need to worry about any joint action to enforce community norms, because there is no community. In dealing with outside villagers who know each other, however, appointees can find that reprisals for any misdeeds are extraordinarily oblique and powerful. The political executive system may be a government of strangers, but its members cannot act as if everyone else is.

Now one can begin to see the real challenge to the political executives' statecraft in Washington. They must be able to move in two worlds—the tight, ingrown village life of the bureaucratic community and the open, disjointed world of political strangers. A public executive in Washington needs the social sensitivity of a villager and the political toughness of a city streetfighter. It is an increasingly unlikely combination. Despite all the resources devoted to more topside staff, new management initiatives, more elaborate analytic techniques, and so on, there remain few—probably fewer than ever—places where political executives can look for reliable political support in any efforts at leadership in the bureaucracy. Political appointees in Washington are substantially on their own and vulnerable to bureaucratic power.

Notes

1. For the political appointment process and the decision against a plural executive, see Arthur Taylor Prescott, *Drafting the Federal Constitution* (Louisiana State University Press, 1941), pp. 544–646; and Alexander Hamilton, James Madison, and John Jay, *The Federalist*, Max Beloff, ed. (Oxford: Basil Blackwell, 1948), nos. 70, 72, and 76. There is some question about how far the Founders actually intended the President to function alone or with the cabinet and Senate as a semicollegial group.
2. See David T. Stanley, Dean E. Mann, and Jameson W. Doig, *Men Who Govern* (Brookings Institution, 1967), pp. 9–36; and Thomas R. Dye and John W. Pickering, "Governmental and Corporate Elites," *Journal of Politics*, vol. 37 (1974), pp. 913–15.
3. Although data are not entirely comparable, certainly less than half the political executives in all recent administrations had any record of political party activity, if by that is meant experience as campaign or party officials, convention delegates, elected officials, or political candidates or their staff members. See Stanley, Mann, and Doig, *Men Who*

Govern, table E-1, p. 132; and Dean E. Mann, *The Assistant Secretaries* (Brookings Institution, 1965), table A-9, p. 295.
4. See Edward Weisband and Thomas Franck, *Resignation and Protest* (Penguin, 1976), especially pp. 121–63 and fig. 1, app. B, p. 201.
5. Dwight Waldo, *Perspectives on Administration* (University of Alabama Press, 1956), p. 14.

Critical Thinking

1. Does it impair the effectiveness of the U.S. executive branch for those appointees in the top positions of authority to be substantially less familiar with their working environment than both their civil service and political subordinates?
2. In the context of the executive branch having, by design, a single head, why does "single" not mean "unitary"?
3. What could an American political executive do to strategically strengthen his or her position in what is generally regarded as the weak, uncertain standing of the Washington "in-and-outer"?

Create Central

www.mhhe.com/createcentral

Internet References

C-SPAN
www.c-span.org

United States House of Representatives
www.house.gov

United States Senate
www.senate.gov

The White House
www.whitehouse.gov

From *A Government of Strangers: Executive Politics in Washington* by Hugh Heclo (Brookings Institution, 1977). Copyright © 1977 by Brookings Institution. Reprinted by permission.

Bureaucracy and the Public Interest

James Q. Wilson

Learning Outcomes

After reading this selection, you should be able to:

1. Compare the standards of efficiency in the private sector to those in the public sector.
2. Discuss the effects of "mission madness."
3. Consider the distinctions between essential and marginal constraints.

James Q. Wilson (b. 1931), a scholar of public administration, regulatory politics, and the federal bureaucracy, published an article entitled "The Rise of the Bureaucratic State" in the Fall 1975 issue of *The Public Interest*. This essay became a landmark in the contemporary scholarly study of administrative behavior. In it, Wilson linked the historical development and expansion of the national government and the executive branch in particular with the evolutionary enlargement of the federal bureaucracy. He emphasized the fundamental risks posed to democratic government in the United States by the concentration of power among unelected bureaucratic appointees in relatively unaccountable executive departments in the modern bureaucratic state.

This essay served as an intellectual precedent to Wilson's contemporary study of the federal bureaucracy and public administration entitled *Bureaucracy: What Government Agencies Do and Why They Do It* (Basic Books, 1989), from which the following selection is taken. The book investigates the inevitable weaknesses and problems of American bureaucracy and offers a theoretical explanation of the restrictions placed upon public agencies. In particular, Wilson analyzes differences in standards of efficiency and performance between the public sector and the private sector. Wilson sees governmental agencies as less productive than private corporations primarily because of the excess restrictions placed on public institutions. The sources of many of the problems confronted by the federal bureaucracy are the American constitutional principles of separation of powers, federalism, governmental accountability, and accessibility to diverse popular interests and preferences. Many public administration and policy scholars have adopted Wilson's constructive criteria to evaluate the effectiveness of governmental agencies.

Wilson received his M.A. and Ph.D. from the University of Chicago, and he taught at Harvard University as the Henry Lee Shattuck Professor of Government. Wilson is currently the Ronald Reagan Professor of Public Policy at the Pepperdine University School of Public Policy. He has also served on numerous national commissions concerned with public policy. Wilson's research and publications have focused on such diverse fields as criminal justice, public administration, organization behavior, and public policy.

Key Concept: suggested reforms of the federal bureaucracy

A Few Modest Suggestions That May Make a Small Difference

To do better we have to deregulate the government.[1] If deregulation of a market makes sense because it liberates the entrepreneurial energies of its members, then it is possible that deregulating the public sector also may help energize it. The difference, of course, is that both the price system and the profit motive provide a discipline in markets that is absent in non-markets. Whether any useful substitutes for this discipline can be found for public-sector workers is not clear, though I will offer some suggestions. But even if we cannot expect the same results from deregulation in the two sectors we can agree at a minimum that detailed regulation, even of public employees, rarely is compatible with energy, pride in workmanship, and the exercise of initiative. The best evidence for this proposition, if any is needed, is that most people do not like working in an environment in which every action is second-guessed, every initiative viewed with suspicion, and every controversial decision denounced as malfeasance.

James Colvard, for many years a senior civilian manager in the navy, suggests that the government needs to emulate methods that work in the better parts of the private sector: "a bias toward action, small staffs, and a high level of delegation which is based on trust."[2] A panel of the National Academy of Public Administration (NAPA), consisting of sixteen senior government executives holding the rank of assistant secretary, issued a report making the same point:

> Over many years, government has become entwined in elaborate management control systems and the accretion of progressively more detailed administrative procedures. This development has not produced superior management. Instead, it has produced managerial overburden. . . . Procedures overwhelm substance. Organizations become discredited, along with their employees. . . . The critical elements of leadership in management appear to wither in the face of a preoccupation with process. The tools are endlessly "perfected"; the manager who is expected to use these tools believes himself to be ignored. . . . Management systems are not management. . . . The attitude of those who design and administer the rules . . . must be reoriented from a "control mentality" to one of "how can I help get the mission of this agency accomplished."[3]

But how can government "delegate" and "trust" and still maintain accountability? If it is a mistake to foster an ethos that encourages every bureaucrat to "go by the book," is it not an equally serious problem to allow zealots to engage in "mission madness," charging off to implement their private versions of some ambiguous public goal? (Steven Emerson has written a useful account of mission madness in some highly secret military intelligence and covert-action agencies.[4]) Given everything we know about the bureaucratic desire for autonomy and the political rewards of rule making, is there any reason to suppose that anybody will find it in his or her interest to abandon the "control mentality" and adopt the "mission accomplishment" mentality?

Possibly not. But it may be worth thinking about what a modestly deregulated government might look like. It might look as it once did, when some of the better federal agencies were created. At the time the Corps of Engineers, the Forest Service, and the FBI were founded much of the federal government was awash in political patronage, petty cabals, and episodic corruption. Organizing an elite service in those days may have been easier than doing so today, when the problems are less patronage and corruption than they are officiousness and complexity. But the keys to organizational success have not changed. The agencies were started by strong leaders who were able to command personal loyalty, define and instill a clear and powerful sense of mission, attract talented workers who believed they were joining something special, and make exacting demands on subordinates.

Today there is not much chance to create a new agency; almost every agency one can imagine already has been created. Even so, the lessons one learns from changing agencies confirm what can be inferred from studying their founding.

First: Executives should understand the culture of their organizations—that is, what their subordinates believe constitute the core tasks of the agency—and the strengths and limitations of that culture. If members widely share and warmly endorse that culture the agency has a sense of mission. This permits the executive to economize on scarce incentives (people want to do certain tasks even when there are no special rewards for doing it); to state general objectives confident that subordinates will understand the appropriate ways of achieving them; and to delegate responsibility knowing that lower-level decisions probably will conform to higher-level expectations.

A good executive realizes that workers can make subtle, precise, and realistic judgments, but only if those judgments refer to a related, coherent set of behaviors. People cannot easily keep in mind many quite different things or strike reasonable balances among competing tasks. People want to know what is expected of them; they do not want to be told, in answer to this question, that "on the one hand this, but on the other hand that.". . .

These advantages of infusing an agency with a sense of mission are purchased at a price. An agency with a strong mission will give perfunctory attention, if any at all, to tasks that are not central to that mission. Diplomats in the State Department will have little interest in embassy security; intelligence officers in the CIA will not worry as much as they should about counterintelligence; narcotics agents in the DEA will minimize the importance of improper prescriptions written by physicians; power engineers in the TVA will not think as hard about environmental protection or conservation as about maximizing the efficiency of generating units; fighter pilots in the USAF will look at air transport as a homely stepchild; and navy admirals who earned their flag serving on aircraft carriers will not press zealously to expand the role of minesweepers. . . .

Second: Negotiate with one's political superiors to get some agreement as to which are the *essential* constraints that must be observed by your agency and which the marginal constraints. This, frankly, may be impossible. The decentralization of authority in Congress (and in some state legislatures) and the unreliability of most expressions of presidential or gubernatorial backing are such that in most cases you will discover, by experience if not by precept, that all constraints are essential all of the time. But perhaps with effort some maneuvering room may be won. A few agencies obtained the right to use more flexible, less cumbersome personnel systems modeled on the China Lake experiment, and Congress has the power to broaden those opportunities. Perhaps some enlightened member of Congress will be able to get statutory authority for the equivalent of China Lake with respect to procurement regulations. An executive is well advised to spend time showing that member how to do it.

Third: Match the distribution of authority and the control over resources to the tasks your organization is performing. In general, authority should be placed at the lowest level at which all essential elements of information are available. Bureaucracies will differ greatly in what level that may be. At one extreme are agencies such as the Internal Revenue Service or maximum-security prisons, in which uniformity of treatment and precision of control are so important as to make it necessary for there to be exacting, centrally determined rules for most tasks. At the other extreme are public schools, police departments, and armies, organizations in which operational uncertainties are so great that discretion must be given to (or if not given will be taken by) lower-level workers.

A good place in which to think through these matters is the area of weapons procurement. The overcentralization of design control is one of the many criticisms of such procurement on which all commentators seem agreed. Buying a new aircraft may be likened to remodeling one's home: You never know how much it will cost until you are done; you quickly find out that changing your mind midway through the work costs a lot of money; and you soon realize that decisions have to be made by people on the spot who can look at the pipes, wires, and joists. The Pentagon procures aircraft as if none of its members had ever built or remodeled a house. It does so because both it and its legislative superiors refuse to allow authority to flow down to the point where decisions rationally can be made. . . .

Fourth: Judge organizations by results. This book has made it clear that what constitutes a valued result in government usually is a matter of dispute. But even when fairly clear performance standards exist, legislatures and executives often ignore them with unhappy results. William E. Turcotte compared how two state governments oversaw their state liquor monopolies. The state that applied clear standards to its liquor bureaucrats produced significantly more profit and lower administrative costs than did the state with unclear or conflicting standards.[5]

Even when results are hard to assess more can be done than is often the case. If someone set out to evaluate the output of a private school, hospital, or security service, he or she would have at least as much trouble as would someone trying to measure the output of a public school, hospital, or police department. Governments are not the only institutions with ambiguous products. . . .

The fifth and final bit of advice flows directly from the limits on judging agencies by their results. All organizations seek the stability and comfort that comes from relying on standard operating procedures—"SOPs." When results are unknown or equivocal, bureaus will have no incentive to alter those SOPs so as better to achieve their goals, only an incentive to modify them to conform to externally imposed constraints. The SOPs will represent an internally defined equilibrium that reconciles the situational imperatives, professional norms, bureaucratic ideologies, peer-group expectations, and (if present) leadership demands unique to that agency. The only way to minimize the adverse effect of allowing human affairs to be managed by organizations driven by their autonomous SOPs is to keep the number, size, and authority of such organizations as small as possible. If

none of the four preceding bits of advice work, the reader must confront the realization that there are no solutions for the bureaucracy problem that are not also "solutions" to the government problem. More precisely: All complex organizations display bureaucratic problems of confusion, red tape, and the avoidance of responsibility. Those problems are much greater in government bureaucracies because government itself is the institutionalization of confusion (arising out of the need to moderate competing demands); of red tape (arising out of the need to satisfy demands that cannot be moderated); and of avoided responsibility (arising out of the desire to retain power by minimizing criticism).

In short, you can have less bureaucracy only if you have less government. Many, if not most, of the difficulties we experience in dealing with government agencies arise from the agencies being part of a fragmented and open political system. If an agency is to have a sense of mission, if constraints are to be minimized, if authority is to be decentralized, if officials are to be judged on the basis of the outputs they produce rather than the inputs they consume, then legislators, judges, and lobbyists will have to act against their own interests. They will have to say "no" to influential constituents, forgo the opportunity to expand their own influence, and take seriously the task of judging the organizational feasibility as well as the political popularity of a proposed new program. It is hard to imagine this happening, partly because politicians and judges have no incentive to make it happen and partly because there are certain tasks a democratic government must undertake even if they cannot be performed efficiently. The greatest mistake citizens can make when they complain of "the bureaucracy" is to suppose that their frustrations arise simply out of management problems; they do not—they arise out of governance problems.

Bureaucracy and the American Regime

The central feature of the American constitutional system—the separation of powers—exacerbates many of these problems. The governments of the United States were not designed to be efficient or powerful, but to be tolerable and malleable. Those who devised these arrangements always assumed that the federal government would exercise few and limited powers. As long as that assumption was correct (which it was for a century and a half) the quality of public administration was not a serious problem except in the minds of those reformers (Woodrow Wilson was probably the first) who desired to rationalize government in order to rationalize society. The founders knew that the separation of powers would make it so difficult to start a new program or to create a new agency that it was hardly necessary to think about how those agencies would be administered. As a result, the Constitution is virtually silent on what kind of administration we should have. At least until the Civil War thrust the problem on us, scarcely anyone in the country would have known what you were talking about if you spoke of the "problem of administration.". . .

Today, the United States at every level has big and active governments. Some people worry that a constitutional system well-designed to preserve liberty when governments were small is poorly designed to implement policy now that governments are large. The contrast between how the United States and the nations of Western Europe manage environmental and industrial regulation . . . is illuminating: Here the separation of powers insures, if not causes, clumsy and adversarial regulation; there the unification of powers permits, if not causes, smooth and consensual regulation.

I am not convinced that the choice is that simple, however. It would take another book to judge the advantages and disadvantages of the separation of powers. The balance sheet on both sides of the ledger would contain many more entries than those that derive from a discussion of public administration. But even confining our attention to administration, there is more to be said for the American system than many of its critics admit.

America has a paradoxical bureaucracy unlike that found in almost any other advanced nation. The paradox is the existence in one set of institutions of two qualities ordinarily quite separate: the multiplication of rules and the opportunity for access. We have a system laden with rules; elsewhere that is a sure sign that the bureaucracy is aloof from the people, distant from their concerns, and preoccupied with the power and privileges of the bureaucrats—an elaborate, grinding machine that can crush the spirit of any who dare oppose it. We also have a system suffused with participation: advisory boards, citizen groups, neighborhood councils, congressional investigators, crusading journalists, and lawyers serving writs; elsewhere this popular involvement would be taken as evidence that the administrative system is no system at all, but a bungling, jerry-built contraption wallowing in inefficiency and shot through with corruption and favoritism.

That these two traits, rules and openness, could coexist would have astonished Max Weber and continues to astonish (or elude) many contemporary students of the subject. Public bureaucracy in this country is neither as rational and predictable as Weber hoped nor as crushing and mechanistic as he feared. It is rule-bound without being overpowering, participatory without being corrupt. This paradox exists partly because of the character and mores of the American people: They are too informal, spontaneous, and other-directed to be either neutral arbiters or passionless Gradgrinds. And partly it exists because of the nature of the regime: Our constitutional system, and above all the exceptional power enjoyed

by the legislative branch, makes it impossible for us to have anything like a government by appointed experts but easy for individual citizens to obtain redress from the abuses of power. Anyone who wishes it otherwise would have to produce a wholly different regime, and curing the mischiefs of bureaucracy seems an inadequate reason for that. Parliamentary regimes that supply more consistent direction to their bureaucracies also supply more bureaucracy to their citizens. The fragmented American regime may produce chaotic government, but the coherent European regimes produce bigger governments.

Notes

1. I first saw this phrase in an essay by Constance Horner, then director of the federal Office of Personnel Management: "Beyond Mr. Gradgrind: The Case for Deregulating the Public Sector," *Policy Review* 44 (Spring 1988): 34–38. It also appears in Gary C. Bryner, *Bureaucratic Discretion* (New York: Pergamon Press, 1987), 215.
2. James Colvard, "Procurement: What Price Mistrust?" *Government Executive* (March 1985): 21.
3. NAPA, *Revitalizing Federal Management: Managers and Their Overburdened Systems* (Washington, D.C.: National Academy of Public Administration, November 1983), vii, viii, 8.
4. Steven Emerson, *Secret Warriors* (New York: G. P. Putnam's Sons, 1988).
5. William E. Turcotte, "Control Systems, Performance, and Satisfaction in Two State Agencies," *Administrative Science Quarterly* 19 (1974): 60–73.

Critical Thinking

1. If there were one federal agency that could benefit most from Wilson's "modest suggestions," what agency would that be?
2. How does the separation of powers exacerbate the problems of bureaucracy?
3. Will the coexistence of "rules and openness" in American government always trump the temptation to create a more efficient, more coherent regime?

Create Central

www.mhhe.com/createcentral

Internet References

C-SPAN
www.c-span.org

United States House of Representatives
www.house.gov

United States Senate
www.senate.gov

The White House
www.whitehouse.gov

From *Bureaucracy: What Government Agencies Do and Why They Do It* by James Q. Wilson (Basic Books, 1989). Copyright © 1989 by James Q. Wilson. Reprinted by permission of Basic Books, a division of HarperCollins Publishers.

Unit 13: The Judiciary

Marbury v. Madison

John Marshall

Learning Outcomes

After reading this selection, you should be able to:

1. Describe the principle of judicial review.
2. Discuss the relevance of mandamus to *Marbury v. Madison*.

In the 1803 landmark decision *Marbury v. Madison* (1 Cranch 137), from which the following selection is taken, the U.S. Supreme Court articulated an opinion that is considered by American political scientists and constitutional legal scholars to be one of the most significant decisions of the Court. The judgment of the Court established judicial review, which refers to the power of the Court to declare congressional and presidential acts invalid because they are unconstitutional. This was the first case in which the U.S. Supreme Court explicitly found unconstitutional a particular act of Congress. This decision enabled the Court to become a very powerful judiciary body.

The election of 1800 was a disastrous defeat for President John Adams and the Federalists. In 1801, at the very end of his administration, Adams and his Federalist colleagues attempted to immediately implement Federalist political objectives and judicial principles. The Judiciary Act of 1801 limited the size of the Supreme Court to five justices, established several new circuit courts consisting of 16 new judgeships, and released the Supreme Court justices from circuit court duties. Subsequently, the Federalist Congress passed legislation authorizing Adams to appoint an unlimited number of justices of the peace on five-year terms for the District of Columbia. In the final days of his administration, Adams attempted to appoint all of these new judicial vacancies with supportive Federalists. Although these "midnight appointments" were signed and sealed prior to Thomas Jefferson's occupation of the office, in the confusion of the transition of administrations several commissions were not delivered.

William Marbury's appointment as justice of the peace for the District of Columbia was among four commissions that had not been delivered when Jefferson took office. Marbury petitioned the U.S. Supreme Court to issue a *writ of mandamus* (an order issued by a court to require the performance of an act) compelling Madison to deliver him his commission.

Chief Justice John Marshall delivered the unanimous opinion of the Court. He contended that the provision of the Judiciary Act of 1789 granting the Court authority to issue the *writ of mandamus* was unconstitutional. Furthermore, Marshall declared that the Court had lacked jurisdiction to decide the case, although Marbury deserved his commission.

Key Concept: the Supreme Court's power of judicial review

Mr. Chief Justice Marshall delivered the opinion of the Court, saying in part:

In the order in which the court has viewed this subject, the following questions have been considered and decided.

1st. Has the applicant a right to the commission he demands? [The Court finds that he has.]

2d. If he has a right, and that right has been violated, do the laws of his country afford him a remedy? [The Court finds that they do.]

3d. If they do afford him a remedy, is it a mandamus issuing from this court? . . .

This, then, is a plain case for a mandamus, either to deliver the commission, or a copy of it from the record; and it only remains to be inquired,

Whether it can issue from this court.

The act to establish the judicial courts of the United States authorizes the Supreme Court "to issue writs of mandamus in cases warranted by the principles and usages of law, to any courts appointed, or persons holding office, under the authority of the United States."

The Secretary of State, being a person holding an office under the authority of the United States, is precisely within the letter of description, and if this court is not authorized to issue a writ of mandamus to such an officer, it must be because the law is unconstitutional, and therefore absolutely incapable of conferring the authority, and assigning the duties which its words purport to confer and assign.

The constitution vests the whole judicial power of the United States in one Supreme Court, and such inferior courts as congress shall, from time to time, ordain and establish. . . .

In the distribution of this power it is declared that "the Supreme Court shall have original jurisdiction in all cases affecting ambassadors, other public ministers and consuls, and those in which a state shall be a party. In all other cases, the Supreme Court shall have appellate jurisdiction.". . .

If it had been intended to leave it in the discretion of the legislature to apportion the judicial power between the supreme and inferior courts according to the will of that body, it would certainly have been useless to have proceeded further than to have defined the judicial power, and the tribunals in which it should be vested. . . .

The question, whether an act, repugnant to the constitution, can become the law of the land, is a question deeply interesting to the United States; but, happily, not of an intricacy proportioned to its interest. It seems only necessary to recognize certain principles, supposed to have been long and well established, to decide it.

That the people have an original right to establish, for their future government, such principles, as, in their opinion, shall most conduce to their own happiness is the basis on which the whole American fabric has been erected. The exercise of this original right is a very great exertion; nor can it, nor ought it, to be frequently repeated. The principles, therefore, so established, are deemed fundamental. And as the authority from which they proceed is supreme, and can seldom act, they are designed to be permanent.

This original and supreme will organizes the government, and assigns to different departments their respective powers. It may either stop here, or establish certain limits not to be transcended by those departments.

The government of the United States is of the latter description. The powers of the legislature are defined and limited; and that those limits may not be mistaken, or forgotten, the constitution is written. To what purpose are powers limited, and to what purpose is that limitation committed to writing, if these limits may, at any time, be passed by those intended to be restrained? The distinction between a government with limited and unlimited powers is abolished, if those limits do not confine the persons on whom they are imposed, and if acts prohibited and acts allowed, are of equal obligation. It is a proposition too plain to be contested, that the constitution controls any legislative act repugnant to it; or, that the legislature may alter the constitution by an ordinary act.

Between these alternatives there is no middle ground. The constitution is either a superior paramount law, unchangeable by ordinary means, or it is on a level with ordinary legislative acts, and, like other acts, is alterable when the legislature shall please to alter it.

If the former part of the alternative be true, then a legislative act contrary to the constitution is not law: if the latter part be true, then written constitutions are absurd attempts, on the part of the people, to limit a power in its own nature illimitable.

Certainly all those who have framed written constitutions contemplate them as forming the fundamental and paramount law of the nation, and, consequently, the theory of every such government must be, that an act of the Legislature, repugnant to the constitution, is void.

This theory is essentially attached to a written constitution, and, is consequently, to be considered, by this court, as one of the fundamental principles of our society. It is not therefore to be lost sight of in the further consideration of this subject.

If an act of the Legislature, repugnant to the constitution, is void, does it, notwithstanding its invalidity, bind the courts, and oblige them to give it effect? Or, in other words, though it be not law, does it constitute a rule as operative as if it was a law? This would be to overthrow in fact what was established in theory; and would seem, at first view, an absurdity too gross to be insisted on. It shall, however, receive a more attentive consideration.

It is emphatically the province and duty of the judicial department to say what the law is. Those who apply the rule to particular cases, must of necessity expound and interpret that rule. If two laws conflict with each other, the courts must decide on the operation of each.

So if a law be in opposition to the constitution; if both the law and the constitution apply to a particular case, so that the court must either decide that case conformably to the law, disregarding the constitution; or conformably to the constitution, disregarding the law; the court must determine which of these conflicting rules governs the case. This is of the very essence of judicial duty.

If, then, the courts are to regard the constitution, and the constitution is superior to any ordinary act of the Legislature, the constitution, and not such ordinary act, must govern the case to which they both apply.

Those then who controvert the principle that the constitution is to be considered, in court, as a paramount law, are reduced to the necessity of maintaining that courts must close their eyes on the constitution, and see only the law.

This doctrine would subvert the very foundation of all written constitutions. It would declare that an act which, according to the principles and theory of our government, is entirely void, is yet, in practice, completely obligatory. It would declare that if the legislature shall do what is expressly forbidden, such act, notwithstanding the express prohibition, is in reality effectual. It would be giving to the legislature a practical and real omnipotence, with the same breath which professes to restrict their powers within narrow limits. It is prescribing limits, and declaring that those limits may be passed at pleasure.

That it thus reduces to nothing what we have deemed the greatest improvement on political institutions, a written constitution, would of itself be sufficient, in America, where written constitutions have been viewed with so much reverence, for rejecting the construction. But the peculiar expressions of the constitution of the United States furnish additional arguments in favor of its rejection.

The judicial power of the United States is extended to all cases arising under the constitution.

Could it be the intention of those who gave this power, to say that in using it the constitution should not be looked into? That a case arising under the constitution should be decided without examining the instrument under which it arises?

This is too extravagant to be maintained.

In some cases, then, the constitution must be looked into by the judges. And if they can open it at all, what part of it are they forbidden to read or to obey?

There are many other parts of the constitution which serve to illustrate this subject.

It is declared that "no tax or duty shall be laid on articles exported from any State." Suppose a duty on the export of cotton, of tobacco, or of flour; and a suit instituted to recover it. Ought judgment to be rendered in such a case? Ought the judges to close their eyes on the constitution, and only see the law?

The constitution declares "that no bill of attainder or ex post facto law shall be passed."

If, however, such a bill should be passed, and a person should be prosecuted under it; must the court condemn to death those victims whom the constitution endeavors to preserve?

"No person," says the constitution, "shall be convicted of treason unless on the testimony of two witnesses to the same overt act, or on confession in open court."

Here the language of the constitution is addressed especially to the courts. It prescribes, directly for them, a rule of evidence not to be departed from. If the legislature should change that rule, and declare one witness, or a confession out of court, sufficient for conviction, must the constitutional principle yield to the legislative act?

From these, and many other selections which might be made, it is apparent, that the framers of the constitution contemplated that instrument as a rule for the government of courts, as well as of the legislature. . . .

Why does a judge swear to discharge his duties agreeably to the constitution of the United States, if that constitution forms no rule for his government? if it is closed upon him, and cannot be inspected by him?

If such be the real state of things, this is worse than solemn mockery. To prescribe, or to take this oath, becomes equally a crime.

It is also not entirely unworthy of observation, that in declaring what shall be the supreme law of the land, the constitution itself is first mentioned; and not the laws of the United States generally, but those only which shall be made in pursuance of the constitution, have that rank.

Thus, the particular phraseology of the constitution of the United States confirms and strengthens the principle, supposed to be essential to all written constitutions, that a law repugnant to the constitution is void; and that courts, as well as other departments, are bound by that instrument.

The rule must be discharged.

Critical Thinking

1. How did the establishment of judicial review help define the judiciary power of the U.S. Supreme Court?
2. If an objective of Chief Justice Marshall in *Marbury* was to assure that the Court would not be in the business of serving partisan political agendas, how well has his intention stood up in American supreme law?
3. Despite being the subject of more than 200 years of critical analysis and debate, why has the *Marbury* judgment remained a cornerstone of our constitutionally driven government?

Create Central

www.mhhe.com/createcentral

Internet References

C-SPAN
www.c-span.org

United States House of Representatives
www.house.gov

United States Senate
www.senate.gov

The White House
www.whitehouse.gov

Supreme Court of the United States, 1803.

Prepared by: James Newman, *University of Maryland University College*

Judicial Independence and the Federal Courts

Bruce Ragsdale

Learning Outcomes

After reading this selection, you should be able to:

1. Discuss some attempts to ensure judicial independence

Bruce Ragsdale is the director of the Federal Judicial Center's Federal Judicial History Office since 1995. He has served as associate historian of the United States Hour of Representatives. He co-edited the "Biographical Directory of the United States Congress (1989)." He is the editor-in-chief of the "History of the Federal Judiciary," an on-line encyclopedia of federal court history at www.fjc.gov/history/home.nsf.

In this article, Ragsdale makes the case that judicial independence is critical to the integrity of checks and balances. How to ensure judicial independence can be problematic. Currently, our judges and justices have lifetime appointments. Ragsdale weighs the impact of lifetime tenure in the judiciary.

Key concept: independent judiciary

Constitutional Protections and Political Debates

A central principle of the United States system of government holds that judges should be able to reach decisions free from political pressure. The framers of the Constitution shared a commitment to judicial independence, and they organized the new government to ensure that federal judges would have a proper measure of independence from the executive and legislative branches. The Constitution guaranteed that judges would serve "during good behavior" and would be protected from any reduction in their salaries, thus preventing removal by a President who opposed their judicial philosophy and congressional retaliation against unpopular decisions. These twin foundations of judicial independence were well established in the British judicial system of the eighteenth century and had been enacted by many of the new state constitutions following independence from Great Britain. But the constitutional outline for the judiciary also ensured that the court system

would always be subject to the political process and thus to popular expectations. The Constitution's provision for "such inferior courts as the Congress may from time to time ordain and establish," granted the legislative branch the most powerful voice in deciding the structure and jurisdiction of the nation's court system. The appointment of judges by the President, with the advice and consent of the Senate, further ensured that important aspects of the judiciary would be part of the political process. The inherent tension between provisions for judicial independence and the elected branches' authority to define the court system has led to recurring debates on judicial tenure and the federal courts' jurisdiction.

Throughout United States history, unpopular court decisions and the general authority of the federal judiciary have prompted calls to limit judges' terms of office, to define more narrowly the jurisdiction of the federal courts, or to limit judicial review—the courts' authority to determine the constitutionality of laws. Underlying the debates on judicial independence have been basic questions about the proper balance of Congress's authority to define the court system and the need to protect a judge's ability to reach decisions independent of political pressure. The debates have also addressed the extent to which the judiciary should be independent of popular opinion in a system of government where all power is based on the consent of the governed. Other debates have raised the need for safeguards for judicial independence in addition to those provided by the Constitution.

Debates on the Constitution

The delegates to the Constitutional Convention accepted with little debate the provisions for service during good behavior and for protected salaries. Only during the ratification debates in the states did political writers more fully explore the Constitution's definition of judicial independence. The most famous commentary came in *The Federalist* essays of Alexander Hamilton, who argued that "the complete independence of the courts of justice is peculiarly essential in a limited Constitution," by which he meant a Constitution that placed limits on the authority of all government office-holders. The judiciary's responsibility, according to Hamilton, was to enforce the people's will as expressed in the Constitution and thus to prevent the abuse of power by the executive and especially the legislature. "Permanent tenure" was the most important foundation of the courts' role as "bulwarks . . . against legislative encroachments."

A prominent Anti-Federalist critic of the Constitution acknowledged the importance of judicial independence as secured by service during good behavior, but "Brutus" also recognized that the judicial independence envisioned by the Constitution was unprecedented. Judges would be removable only by impeachment and conviction of "high crimes and misdemeanors" rather than by a vote of the legislature, as was the case in most other governments with judicial tenure during good behavior. "Brutus" warned that regardless of errors of judgment or inability to carry out their duties, federal judges would be "independent of the people, of the legislature, and of every power under heaven." He also worried that these largely unaccountable judges would have the final say on the meaning of the Constitution, but Hamilton and other framers of the proposed government thought that the courts' responsibility to determine the constitutionality of laws, and thus to protect individual rights, was precisely the reason for the extraordinary protections of judicial independence. Hamilton dismissed concerns about unchecked judicial power, since the courts had "no influence over either the sword or the purse."

Political Parties and the Federal Courts

The framers' hopes for judicial independence were quickly challenged by the unexpected emergence of political parties in the 1790s. By the end of the decade, nominations of judges and any legislation relating to the courts became intertwined with the intense political struggle between Federalists and Republicans. After passage of the Sedition Act of 1798, Federalists used prosecutions in the federal courts to silence political opposition, and in 1801 the Federalist majority in Congress expanded federal jurisdiction at the expense of state courts and created new courts with additional judgeships that were filled by the lame-duck President, John Adams. Republicans came into power soon thereafter determined to curb what they saw as the partisan bias of federal judges. The Republican Congress abolished the new courts and judgeships and impeached two highly partisan judges. Republicans argued that the Constitution granted Congress full authority to establish the judicial system and that the constitutional protections of tenure during good behavior and undiminished salary did not prevent Congress from abolishing courts that were no longer needed. Republicans also argued that the partisan actions of Federalist judges, particularly in the Sedition Act prosecutions, had undermined all pretense of impartiality and judicial independence. Federalists meanwhile decried what they saw as an assault on the constitutional guarantee of tenure during good behavior. The Constitution, they declared, made the judges independent so as "to control the fiery zeal, and to quell the fierce passions" of a newly elected party. Repeal of the Judiciary Act of 1801 and the precedent of depriving judges of their office, Federalists warned, would render all judges the tools of political parties and bring about the collapse of constitutional government.

Despite the private doubts of Chief Justice John Marshall and other justices, the Supreme Court in 1803 issued a decision that let stand the law abolishing the courts and judgeships established in 1801. Republican fears about the judiciary were heightened, however, by the Supreme Court's decision one week earlier, in which Chief Justice Marshall, in *Marbury v. Madison*, asserted the judiciary's right to declare an act of Congress unconstitutional and, more alarming to Republicans, the Court's authority to compel executive compliance with an act of Congress. After the Senate failed to convict Supreme Court Justice Samuel Chase in his impeachment trial of 1805, a truce of sorts fell into place as Republicans abandoned their impeachment plans and the most overtly partisan Federalist judges, like Chase, curtailed their political activity. The temporary lull in public debates, however, did not signify a consensus on the proper measure of judicial independence.

Throughout the early decades of the nineteenth century, unpopular decisions in the Supreme Court and, more often, in the federal trial courts, sparked recurring demands for restricting judicial tenure or limiting federal jurisdiction. Thomas Jefferson, as President and during his long retirement, advocated fixed, renewable terms of office for federal judges. Jefferson asserted that with impeachment the only means of removal, the judges "consider themselves secure for life; they skulk from responsibility to public opinion." Members of Congress and the majorities of several state legislatures repeatedly called for restrictions on the authority of federal courts to review the decisions of state courts or an end to federal jurisdiction over suits between residents of different states. Others submitted amendments to allow for the removal of judges on the vote of super-majorities in Congress or to place age limits on judicial service. None of these proposals succeeded, but their introduction into nearly every Congress before the Civil War indicated that judicial independence remained a subject of political debate.

An Independent Judiciary in a Reconstructed Union

The crisis of union surrounding the Civil War brought new challenges to judicial independence. Unionists and supporters of the anti-slavery movement were highly suspicious of the federal courts because of decisions in support of slavery and particularly because of the Supreme Court's 1857 *Dred Scott* decision, which, among other things, denied all African Americans any rights under the Constitution. Following the close of the Civil War, Republicans in Congress feared that the federal courts would disallow much of their ambitious legislation designed to ensure full citizenship rights for freed slaves and all other African Americans. Congress debated numerous proposals to strip the federal courts of specific jurisdiction and to reorganize the courts. Congress redrew circuit boundaries to ensure that Southern states would no longer hold a majority of seats on the Supreme Court. In 1868, the Congress repealed the Supreme Court's jurisdiction over appeals of habeas corpus petitions, thus preventing former Confederates from challenging the custody of military courts. The House of Representatives in 1868 approved legislation that would have required a majority of seven justices for the Supreme Court to disallow any congressional statute, although the Senate Committee on the Judiciary failed to report the bill.

The willingness of Congress to reorganize the judiciary and to restrict jurisdiction in pursuit of the goals of Reconstruction was counter-balanced by the congressional Republicans' reliance on the federal courts to enforce federal law in the former Confederate states. In 1869, Congress established nine circuit judgeships in the hope, as expressed by Senator Lyman Trumbull, that "nothing would do more to give quiet and peace to the southern country than an efficient enforcement of the laws of the United States in the United States courts." In 1875, Congress extended federal jurisdiction to encompass all cases arising under the Constitution and federal law, so that by the close of Reconstruction in 1877 the federal courts had unprecedented authority and independence.

The Federal Courts and the Politics of an Industrial United States

The most sustained effort to make federal judges more directly accountable to public opinion and to the elected branches of government arose between the 1890s and the 1920s when the federal courts became involved in labor struggles and in debates over government regulation of the economy. The federal courts' approval of injunctions to halt labor strikes and the Supreme Court's disallowance of regulatory legislation contributed to support for various restrictions on judicial authority. Populists seeking to regulate railroad shipping rates, labor unions trying to establish the right to strike, and Progressives defending their extensive program of social welfare and regulation of corporations all in turn advocated legislation to restrict the jurisdiction of the federal courts or to make judges more responsive to shifts in public opinion. The most common proposals included the election of federal judges, fixed judicial terms, narrow limits on federal jurisdiction, and the abolition of judicial review or requirements for a super-majority of the Supreme Court to invalidate federal or state laws. For nearly thirty years, Justice Walter Clark of the North Carolina Supreme Court cultivated national support for the election of federal judges and limits on judicial review. Senator George Norris of Nebraska personally favored the abolition of the lower federal courts and introduced more widely supported bills to restrict judicial review, impose fixed terms on judges, and strip the courts of authority to issue labor injunctions. In 1924, Senator Robert LaFollette, the Progressive Party candidate for President, proposed a constitutional amendment that would have prohibited the lower federal courts from invalidating any congressional statute and would also have authorized Congress to reenact any legislation overturned by the Supreme Court.

Although the House of Representatives Committee on the Judiciary in 1894 reported a bill to limit judges to 10-year terms, few of the proposals to limit judicial independence gained much ground in Congress over the next 40 years, and the diverse critics of the courts never unified behind a common program. The critique of the federal courts, however, was steady and became an important part of the broader public debates on the effectiveness of government in a time of rapid social and economic change. The proposals to limit the authority of the federal judiciary paralleled the movement in the states to subject local judges to recall by popular vote.

Throughout the early decades of the twentieth century, the defense of the existing judicial system was led by the organized bar, especially the American Bar Association. Defenders of tenure during good behavior and judicial review warned that a judiciary beholden to public opinion would never be able to protect civil liberties and economic rights. William Howard Taft, as President, then as dean of Yale Law School, and after 1921 as Chief Justice of the United States, was an important advocate for the established protections of judicial independence. Taft conceded that the federal courts would always be subject to popular criticism because their role was to protect "the guaranties of personal liberty . . . against the partisan zeal of the then majority."

"Court Packing" and the Defense of Judicial Independence

After several years of Supreme Court decisions that challenged key New Deal programs, President Franklin Roosevelt in 1937 proposed a sweeping change in the appointment of all federal judges. Never in United States history had a proposal about the judiciary excited such political debate. The Judicial Reorganization bill would have authorized the President to appoint an additional judge whenever a sitting judge on any federal court did not retire within six months of reaching the age of 70. If approved, the bill would have allowed Roosevelt to appoint immediately as many as 50 new federal judges, including six Supreme Court justices. Roosevelt alleged that the declining abilities of aging judges contributed to a backlog of cases, but he also argued that a regular appointment of new judges was necessary "to bring to the decision of social and economic problems younger men who have had personal experience and contact with modern facts and circumstances under which average men have to live and work."

For months, the judiciary proposal dominated public debate throughout the nation. While many New Dealers supported the bill, defections from Roosevelt's own party doomed the legislation and led the Senate Committee on the Judiciary to recommend that the bill not pass. The Senate committee report described the bill as "an invasion of judicial power such as has never been attempted in this country" and warned that the bill would set a dangerous precedent allowing a Congress or a President to impose constitutional beliefs on the courts. While some attributed the lack of support to the Supreme Court's recent willingness to uphold New Deal legislation (the so-called "switch in time that saved nine"), the opposition to Roosevelt's bill rested on fundamental beliefs about the independence of the judiciary. Roosevelt had clearly challenged a widely shared, popular commitment to the balance of power between the branches of government. Even older Progressives who had supported limited tenure for judges and restrictions on federal jurisdiction shied away from what they saw as Roosevelt's attempted power grab for the executive branch. The administration drafted a revised bill, but that too met with opposition, and the Senate never voted on it. The retirement of Supreme Court justices soon gave Roosevelt the opportunity to appoint a majority of that court, but the court-packing crisis in many ways strengthened support for an independent judiciary and

discouraged further proposals for any comprehensive reorganization of the judiciary.

The Persistence of Court Critics

Despite greater public acknowledgment of the principle of judicial independence in the years following the New Deal, critics of federal court decisions continued to call for limits on federal jurisdiction or for changes in judicial tenure. In the 1950s, in response to *Brown v. Board of Education* and subsequent court enforcement of school desegregation, segregationists advocated various measures to deprive federal courts of jurisdiction over issues related to local schools. In the 1960s, a series of Supreme Court decisions on the rights of criminal defendants, school prayer, and reapportionment of congressional seats fueled a campaign to impeach Chief Justice Earl Warren. To this day, controversial court decisions are often followed by proposals to "strip" the federal courts of specific jurisdiction or even challenges to judicial tenure during good behavior. Like similar proposals dating back 200 years, few have gained serious congressional consideration.

Institutionalization of Judicial Independence

Over the course of the twentieth century, judicial independence was greatly strengthened by the development of institutions for the federal courts' self governance. In an address to the American Bar Association in 1914, William Howard Taft recognized that widespread public criticism of the courts imposed on judges and lawyers the responsibility to ensure a court system worthy of public respect. Taft became a leader in the development of institutions that have allowed the judiciary to govern itself and to guarantee the public a fair and efficient system of justice. Through much of the country's history, the courts received administrative support from various departments of the executive branch. Taft's support for the establishment in 1922 of a conference of chief judges from each circuit was the first step toward independent judicial administration. In 1939, Congress established the Administrative Office of the U.S. Courts, which reported to the conference of judges and provided courts with the support formerly given by the Department of Justice. The congressional act of 1939 also established in each circuit judicial councils with responsibility for improving the administration of all courts within the circuit. The establishment of the Federal Judicial Center in 1967 gave the federal courts their own agency for education of judges and court staff and for research on improving judicial administration.

Public Trust

As Taft recognized in the early decades of the twentieth century, the independence of the judiciary depends not only on the constitutional protections of judges, but also on public faith in a fair and responsive court system. The debates on Roosevelt's court-packing plan revealed that public trust in the judiciary was also based on confidence that the federal courts would not be dominated by another branch of government or by one political party. Critics of judicial independence have always been part of political life in the United States, but in the 200 years following the debates between Federalists and Republicans, the changing majorities in Congress have been reluctant to endorse sweeping changes in the federal judiciary, especially in response to specific court decisions or to further partisan policy.

Create Central

www.mhhe.com/createcentral

From *Federal Judicial Center Publication*, pp. 1–18.

Critical Thinking

1. Should federal judges have a life appointment?
2. Why is a judiciary, free from partisanship, vital in a democratic society?
3. Is a mandatory retirement age appropriate for federal judges?

Internet References

Supreme Court of the United States Blog
www.scotusblog.com

Exploring Constitutional Law
http://law2.umkc.edu/faculty/projects/ftrials/conlaw/home.html

Prepared by: James Newman, *University of Maryland University College*

Resolved: United States Supreme Court Justices Should Be Subject to Term Limits

A Brief in Topic Analysis and Debate Strategy

Duncan Stewart

Learning Outcomes

After reading this selection, you should be able to:

1. Discuss advantages and disadvantages of justices holding lifetime appointments.
2. Understand why the framers of the Constitution allowed justices to hold lifetime appointments.

Duncan Stewart is a student at the University of Utah. His article suggests lifetime appointments no longer have a place in the judiciary.

Key concept: term limits for judges

"In June 2005, at the end of its October 2004 Term, the U.S. Supreme Court's nine members had served together for almost eleven years, longer than any other group of nine Justices in the nation's history. Although the average tenure of a Supreme Court Justice from 1789 through 1970 was 14.9 years, for those Justices who have retired since 1970, the average tenure has jumped to 26.1 years. Because of the long tenure of recent members of the Court, there were no vacancies on the high Court from 1994 to the middle of 2005." —Steven Calabresi

The Resolution in Simple Terms

In recent years discourse in federal courts has been rife with "term limit" talks. Currently all Supreme Court Justices enjoy lifetime appointments contingent on "good behavior," justices may be impeached on the grounds of "high crimes and/or misdemeanors." In application, justices effectively tenure lifetime appointments or retire by stepping down. The advantage of which is that they're insulated from the political process. The removal of justices from the political landscape is the basis of American check and balance on the webs of government power. From this place of tradition is where most of the debate will be framed. The overarching claim being that, it is necessary to remove justice(s) from the political process if it is to be fair and true justice. The disadvantages: it inspires presidents to appoint younger, less experienced judges than they might otherwise appoint, and it motivates justices to stay on the bench long after fair reason would have them retiring. In 1991 Virginia state law ruled in what was characterized as "the dangers of age 70" that "the threat of deterioration at age 70 is sufficiently great, and the alternatives for removal sufficiently inadequate, that they will require all judges to step aside" after the age of 70. (William 2008) Thus, there is a pull of age, too young or too old, and you are no longer qualified. The debate however, extends far past age. It is a foundational political question; should the judiciary be involved in the political process? Those agreeing, or seeing judicial involvement inevitable, argue a term limit for justices of the highest federal court is an extension of democracy. In reformation, control of the courts will have a new semblance of power to the people, if there are term limits it will, in probability, give way to a new election/appointing process of justices.

The most popular idea, pursuant article five of the constitution, is an amendment to article three. This is proposed by Steven Calabresi and James Lindgren to provide term limits—the most commonly discussed limit is 18 years. (Calabresi, Lindgren 2006) Another proposal is a structural change. It would entail adding a new justice every two years. That is two new federal judicial appointments a presidential term. Linda Greenhouse summarized it best in an article appearing in *Slate*: "There are a number of rationales for ending life tenure. For me, the main one has little to do with the court itself—I don't think age or decrepitude is a major problem, and I would sign John Paul Stevens at 92 up for any task I could think of—but rather with court-related politics. Since Supreme Court vacancies occur so randomly (Carter with none, Nixon with four), each vacancy is a cataclysmic event for which the president's and Senate's business basically comes to a standstill. With the twice-per-term vacancies that the 18-year term limit would deliver, everyone would know that their party would have its share (assuming they could elect the right president) and it might lower the temperature surrounding each vacancy. People would vote for president knowing for sure, rather than in the abstract, that they were also voting in effect for two Supreme Court justices." (Greenhouse 2012)

The value that will often be heard on both sides of this debate is that of justice, as it is the courts purpose. The value in the context of this debate round will most likely be defined on the fringes of 'the justness of the Supreme Court,' and/or 'creating the court which will yield the most justice.' Be sure to ask your opponent what *justice* means in the frame of their case. The debate will come down to the means of achieving or measuring said justice, your criterion. A few that you may hear are:

1. Representative Democracy

This criterion is to be run on the affirmative side of the debate. People can effectively elect the justices they wish to see in the court. In the broadest sense representative democracy is the ideal that an elected person should represent a group of people, and that the elected person is accountable to the electorate. Currently the appointment of justices is random because vacancies are random. Which the affirmative can argue is destroying the representative democratic process, thus term limits build representative democracy.

The criticism for the negative: Involving the judicial branch in the political process of identification is a dangerous line as it would subsequently involve short term appointments. Meaning political goals would also be

sought short term, this combined with evidence of political corruption would prove an ineffective court. Well carded argumentation such as this will make it difficult for the affirmative to achieve their value.

2. Checks and Balances

This criterion is to be run on the negative. Your argument is the only way in which the court acts as an effective check is when it is aside the political spectrum. It will prove relatively easy to find a plethora of evidence articulating that the court's involvement in frequent vacancies will: first politicize it, but second corrupt it. If a justice is sure of their seat, they are free to vote based on their judgment rather than party lines. Fear can sway a decision a certain way. "The judicial branch checks the executive and legislative because it is not up for re-election." (Calabresi and Presser 2006) It is insulated from both public opinion and politics. At the point where this is no longer true your opponent is in trouble two fold.

1. The court is now ineffective, or less effective due to an ominous fear of re-election or retirement security; they loose the debate as this mitigates justice.
2. The court is less of a check on the executive and legislative branches, poor laws are made. This mitigates justice. Game over.

(These considering justice is the value, and is impacted well.)

The criticism for the affirmative: The representative democracy which a continual vacancy would foster will act as a greater check against the other two branches. The Judiciary would still have the same powers plus representation.

3. Governmental Legitimacy

This may even be used as a value pretty commonly; indeed the resolution is a fundamental question of what is and what makes a legitimate government. This can be approached from several different places. The first being the social contract, Hobbes, Locke, or most any other author whom wrote a treatise on government and and societal contracts, it depends on how you wish to approach the debate. The second being democracy, that a legitimate government involves representative democracy. This is where governmental legitimacy and representative democracy can be interchanged as a value or criterion; contingent on what you see to be the most strategic option.

Key Terms and Definitions

1. The United States Supreme Court—is the judicial branch of the United States' government. It is composed of nine justices, one of which is the chief justice. Justices are elected by presidential nomination and senate confirmation, serving a

term of life. The constitution of the United States doesn't explicitly give the court the power of judicial review; however it is a concrete precedent. (*Marbury v. Madison* 1803)

2. Tenure—literally means to occupy permanently or to possess a permanent post. In this debate it refers to the seats which the justices hold.

3. Term Limit—this is what the resolution proposes; the term limit will be the allotted amount of time a justice is allowed to occupy a seat.

4. Vacancy—occurs when a justice retires or dies leaving a seat open for presidential nomination.

5. Article 5—of the constitution allows it to be altered.

6. Article 3—is the portion of the constitution which establishes the judicial branch of the federal government. It allows judges to hold their offices "during good behavior," this interpreted to mean life.

7. Justice and "Justice"—a "judge" on the Supreme Court bench is referred to as a "Justice"; please don't confuse this with a value debaters commonly employ.

8. Representative Democracy—the elector and electorate have a direct relationship. The latter is accountable to the first. (See the criterion)

9. Checks and Balances—gives unique powers to each of three branches of government to equalize power. (See the criterion)

10. Governmental legitimacy—the question of whether a government in its current state is justified in having its power exercised. (See the criterion)

Case Ideas/Strategies

1. The Affirmative
   A. Age

Detailed in a recent article by Professor David Garrow, "the advanced age of some Supreme Court Justices has at times led to a problem of 'mental decrepitude' on the Court, whereby some Justices have become physically or mentally unable to fulfill their duties during the final stages of their careers." (Garrow 2006) It is a legitimate argument for the affirmative to say that lifetime tenure is: First harsh on judges of old age, but worst it leaves them incapable of performing their tasks, or they perform under impaired judgment. A commentary in *The Boston Globe* presents a discussion on the subject which highlights that there has been some troubling examples throughout the recent history of justices who simply are no longer up to the task. "What's troubling is some of this information only came out after the justice in question died or retired. I can't help but wonder how many important decisions were made by law clerks or, worse yet, by justices who no longer had complete control of their mental faculties." (Jacoby 2010)

   B. Democratic Ideals

Following the retirement of Justice Sandra Day O'Connor in 2005, five of the nine members of the court had served together for seventeen years, three of them sitting on the bench together for the past 22 years. This position will argue that the constitutions granting of lifetime tenure is fundamentally flawed because

it reduces the efficacy of the check that the nomination process enforces on the court's membership. This happens because there *are fewer and fewer* vacancies appearing in the court. Further, "The increase in the longevity of Justices' tenure means that life tenure now guarantees a much longer tenure on the Court than was the case in 1789 or over most of our constitutional history. Moreover, the combination of less frequent vacancies and longer tenures of office means that when vacancies do arise, there is so much at stake that confirmation battles have become much more intense." (Lindgren 2006) With the amount of power that Supreme Court justices now hold, it is unwise, in a framework of democracy, to let it go unchecked for decades. In some cases five or more decades. It may have been sensible when life expectancy was below the age of forty. The Federalist Papers which addressed the court intended the judicial branch to be the weakest branch of the government. Today I think it is the most powerful; nine people are the final arbiters of legislation and governmental action. Your argument will be currently these people are unchecked by the other two branches of government.

Further, the Supreme Court has become highly politicized over recent years, thus tanking democratic values. By no means does lifetime tenure help this. " . . . Political motives [have become] a more important factor in Justices' retirement decisions, which could have resulted in their deciding to stay on the Court longer for strategic reasons. While it has always been recognized that the Court has had some influence on politics, in the last fifty to eighty years the Court has come to be seen as a more important player than ever before i.e., effectuating political and social change. As a result, the political views of individual Justices have become correspondingly more important. To sitting Justices contemplating retirement, the political views of a likely replacement (and hence those of the presiding President) may lead to their timing their resignations strategically. Such strategic resignations may have led more politically minded Justices to stay on the Court longer and later in age, which has expanded the real-world, practical meaning of life tenure."(Calabresi 2006) Such a politic disallows the equal distribution of party representation, and therefore the Supreme Court is yet again unchecked. A justice will resign when his or her party controls the White House. Thus it works in a cyclical manner. First, judges live longer; second, they are more powerful than ever before; third, they retire strategically, and thus remain unchecked. Term limits would break the cycle and that is the affirmative argument.

2. The Negative
   A. Insulation from the Political Process

Currently Justices enjoy lifetime tenure; this ensures insulation from the political process. Term limits will enter the Supreme Court into the political arena as products for legislative goals. This can be argued to destroy the justice of the Justice system; this would open the court to lobbyists and party lines to become further rooted in its process. In addition most career politicians don't discontinue their involvement in the political process until actual retirement. Thus a justice would have to have future careers or jobs in mind while making decisions between state dispute and legislation. Here is where the speaker argues that the given Justice's decision will be influenced by future employers and/or constituents.

B. Court Backlogs

Integral to democratic ideals is having a voice in the political process, and Supreme Court term limits hamper that. This is because; Supreme Court appointments are highly political. Federal, but not Supreme Court, Justice Robert Bork, an attempted supreme court appointee, was debated for over a year, and prevented anything else from getting done in the Senate. Since 2011, there have been judicial emergencies all over the country, meaning that there were a large number of cases that had not been heard. There are currently not even enough judges to handle cases, and every time the federal government attempts to move someone into the Supreme Court, all other appointments are delayed. (The crux of your argument.) With evidence to support this you can argue voices aren't heard, democratic ideals are decreased, hindered, and haltered, i.e., values aren't achieved and opponents loose. Further, appointments often come from current judges, meaning that once they are appointed to a higher court, their old seat must be filled.

The senate will often use the filibuster in order to prevent a candidate that doesn't meet their ideals from being appointed. This can go on forever in a highly split congress like ours today. This means every time we attempt to promote a new justice, they are debated for an extended period of time. This greatly differs from the first appointments by George Washington which took around a day. In a world such as this values on the negative could be argued in terms of a legitimate government. If a legitimate government supports democratic ideals, that are a multiplicity of voices in the political process, and term limits decrease this, you win a negative ballot.

C. Political Consequence and Spillover

This argument overlaps quite a bit with the others. It functions on the basis that continual appointments to the Supreme Court are a regular part of the partisan political culture. Public perception is negatively impacted when there is opportunity to make a political problem out of court appointments. That being when a term of a senator ends, there must be another appointment immediately and, depending on term length, there are many more chances for a partisan legislature to delay and negate a president's wish for justices. This creates further backlog as well as introducing politics to the sphere of nonpartisan justice. Arguments exist to describe how people will reinforce themselves with their party more than logical

rationale; therefore having debates over the Supreme Court much more often will require people to be inundated in the process, limiting the critical thinking that goes into making decisions which are important to the well-being of the US citizenry. In the current process, Senators must account for the experience, ability, nonpartisanship and longevity of a justice while in a system where the mentality becomes, "This will only last for two (or some) years," every time there is an appointment, the debate is the same and we continually are appropriated partisan justices because of the devolving nature of debates into arguments over personal ideologies. A past "what if" could be seen in the decision on the Affordable Care Act. Justice John Roberts surprised the country with his vote because he is traditionally seen as conservative, but voted based on his interpretation of the constitution, wider than the politics that surrounded the issue. A more politicized and partisan branch of the government is not what we need, nor would it have been beneficial for the Supreme Court debates, regardless of the current or possible decision. This argument combined with a value of checks and balance or the legitimacy of the political/constituent process would make an effective case. The weaknesses of this, however, is it's a confusing argument, may not have a strong link, but does give a basis which I predict what most cases will have a semblance of.

Critical Thinking

1. Should justices have a mandatory retirement at age 70? At any age?
2. Should justices have term limits?
3. Should the judiciary act as an agent of social change?
4. If you were to create occupational requirements for a justice, what would you require?

Create Central

www.mhhe.com/createcentral

Internet References

Term Limits for the Supreme Court: Life Tenure Reconsidered
http://papers.ssrn.com/sol3/papers.cfm?abstract_id=701121

Life Tenure, Term Limits, and Supreme Court Justices
www.scotusblog.com/2007/09/life-tenure-term-limits-and-supreme-court-justices

Works Cited
Calabresi, Steven, and Lindgren, James. "Term Limits for the Supreme Court: Life Tenure Reconsidered." 2006. Web.

Calabresi, Steven. *The Future of the Supreme Court: Institutional Reform and Beyond.* Minneapolis, MN: University of Minnesota Law School, 2006. Print.

Calabresi, Steven. "Reintroducing Circuit Riding: A Timely Proposal." Minnesota Law Review, 2006. Web.

"How Can We Fix the Constitution?" *Slate Hive.* 2012. Web <http://hive.slate.com/hive/how-can-we-fix-constitution/article/the-18-year-bench>

Jacoby, Jeff. "MinnLawyer Blog." *MinnLawyer Blog RSS.* Boston Globe, <http://minnlawyer.com/minnlawyerblog/2010/07/14/what-happens-when-your-supreme-court-justice-loses-it>

"Kevin Drum." *Mother Jones.* <www.motherjones.com/kevin-drum/2011/09/term-limits-supreme-court>

Leiter Professor, William. "Laissez Faire Redux: The Supreme Court and Age/Disability Discrimination" Paper Presented at the Annual Meeting of the Midwest Political Science Association, Palmer House Hotel, Chicago, IL, Apr 12, 2007. 2013-05-08. Print.

"Term Limits for Supreme Court Justices." *PostPartisan.* Web. <http://voices.washingtonpost.com/postpartisan/2010/04/term_limits_for_supreme_court.html>

"Term Limits for the Supreme Court: Life Tenure Reconsidered." By Steven G. Calabresi, James Lindgren. USC Law, Web. <http://papers.ssrn.com/sol3/papers.cfm?abstract_id=701121>

United States Congress. *The Federalist Papers.* By Alexander Hamilton, James Madison, and John Jay. Cong. Bill. [Washington, D.C.]: Library of Congress, 1996. Print.

Copyright © 2013 by Duncan Stewart. Reprinted by permission of the author.

Unit 14: Domestic Public Policy Making

Lessons: Lost Opportunities

Haynes Johnson and David S. Broder

Learning Outcomes

After reading this selection, you should be able to:

1. Assess the historic significance of health care reform in the United States.
2. Identify the meaning of the phrase "credibility gap" and when it entered our language.
3. Discuss the consequences of President Clinton's reliance on his party's congressional leadership.

Haynes Johnson (b. 1931) and David S. Broder (b. 1929) have collaborated as news journalists and correspondents for over 30 years. The following selection is an excerpt from their book *The System: The American Way of Politics at the Breaking Point* (Little, Brown, 1996), a contemporary classic on President William Jefferson Clinton's initiative to provide universal health insurance for Americans and the subsequent political struggle between supporters and adversaries of this plan. Filling a gap in the contemporary literature on this subject, the authors analyze the most significant problems of current American health care in the context of the critical behavior and roles performed by the president, the Congress, the political parties, the lobbyists, the press, and other key decision makers of the U.S. political system. These two distinguished journalists use their insider's position to conduct interviews of key political players (e.g., President Clinton, Hillary Rodham Clinton, the congressional leadership, and powerful lobbyists) who were directly involved in the design, advocacy, and rejection of a very controversial comprehensive public policy and social reform.

In the following selection, Johnson and Broder depict the failure of health care reform in the Clinton administration—which occurred without any roll call vote in the Democratic Congress and which was immediately followed by the Republicans' regaining control of Congress in 1994, after a 40-year absence—as one of the most significant lost political opportunities of the twentieth century. The authors contend that there were multiple contributing factors that caused the collapse of President Clinton's health care reform legislation, including the sustained and intense efforts by the Republican congressional leadership to regain control of Congress and promote a revolutionary conservative political agenda (i.e., the "Contract With America") in conjunction with the strongly mobilized, greatly financed, and sophisticated lobbying effort of many special interest groups. Johnson and Broder acknowledge that one of the most egregious failures of the Clinton administration in its attempt to promote comprehensive reform legislation was its inability to understand the limitations on the president's power due to electoral results (i.e., Clinton did not gain majority support, as he won 43 percent of the popular vote). Beyond focusing on the specific stages of the failed health care legislation, the authors analyze the fundamental problem of private interests' increasing power to influence and manipulate the political process and public policy and the political system's inability to promote the public interest.

Johnson received his M.S. in American history from the University of Wisconsin. He has been a reporter, columnist, and national correspondent for the *Washington Star* and the *Washington Post*, and he was the Ferris Professor of Journalism at Princeton University. He is a frequent news commentator on such national television programs as *Today, Washington Week in Review,* and *The NewsHour With Jim Lehrer.* Among his numerous honors and awards is the Pulitzer Prize in national reporting in 1966 for outstanding national coverage of the civil rights demonstrations in Selma, Alabama.

Broder received his M.A. in political science from the University of Chicago. He has been a reporter and national political correspondent for the *Congressional Quarterly, Washington Star, New York Times,* and *Washington Post,* and he was a fellow of the Institute of Politics at Harvard University, a Poynter fellow at Yale University and Indiana University, and a fellow of the Institute of Policy Science and Public Affairs at Duke University. He is a frequent news commentator for CNN, NBC's *Meet the Press, The NewsHour With Jim Lehrer,* and PBS's *Washington Week in Review.* Broder received the Pulitzer Prize in journalism in 1973 and the National Society of Newspaper Columnists Lifetime Achievement Award in 1997.

Key Concept: the American political system's failure to achieve comprehensive health care reform

*I*n one of our early interviews, Secretary of Health and Human Services Donna Shalala described the battle launched by President Bill Clinton and his wife, Hillary Rodham Clinton, as one for "the last great social policy of this century." Enumerating the programs passed during the previous decades, she said, "This is the last piece, the country focusing on improving the quality of life for its people at the turn of the century."

She was correct in those judgments, but the battle represented much more than an attempt to forge a major policy. It became a fundamental test of the clashing elements in The System. As Shalala pointed out in that interview, for the first time in a dozen years one party had been entrusted by the voters with control of the executive and legislative branches of government. "If this Democratic Party doesn't move to cover people who get up in the morning and go to work in minimum-wage jobs," she said, "then it's not only lost its soul, it's lost its political coalition for the future."

When she spoke, she and others in the Clinton administration were optimistic. But in the end, the Democratic Congress adjourned without even a roll call on reform, and the Clinton White House barely addressed its demise—an outcome that no one, including its most determined opponents, thought possible when the fight began. As Shalala feared, the Democratic coalition collapsed in the historic midterm election of 1994: a widely recognized public need went unfulfilled; Republicans ended forty years of Democratic control of Congress and initiated the great struggle over the role and purpose of the federal government that will continue through the 1996 presidential election and beyond. Thus the story of the life and death of health reform shines a harsh light on the way The System—and the men and women in it—succeeds or fails. As Paul Starr, the Princeton scholar and author who played a major part in designing the Clinton health care reform, ruefully said later, "The collapse of health care reform in the first two years of the Clinton administration will go down as one of the great lost political opportunities in American history. It is a story of compromises that never happened, of deals that were never closed, of Republicans, moderate Democrats, and key interest groups that backpedaled from proposals they themselves had earlier co-sponsored or endorsed. It is also a story of strategic miscalculations on the part of the President and those of us who advised him."

He also accurately said, "The Republicans enjoyed a double triumph, killing reform and then watching jurors find the President guilty. It was the political equivalent of the perfect crime."

It is easy in retrospect to say that this kind of fundamental change was too much for The System to resolve. But another ambitious proposal, the tax reform bill of 1986, was enacted in a divided government, and there were many moments when different decisions could have produced a different result. As we have seen, the lessons of that earlier tax reform battle and the 1989 fiasco

with Medicare catastrophic health insurance were either ignored or forgotten. They are instructive not only for our story, but also for future attempts to achieve major reform on controversial issues. . . .

It is our view, as well, that in this great test The System failed the people it was designed to serve. The goal of providing affordable quality health care for all—more substantially addressed, if not fully achieved, by every other advanced industrial country in the world—is farther from realization in the United States in 1996 than it was at the beginning of the decade. When the debate began, a broad public bipartisan consensus had developed on the need for fundamental reform, although not on the best policy to pursue or on the solutions people were ready to support. The battle was fought amid the most favorable conditions in this century. Paul Starr's epitaph is correct: The loss of this battle will be recorded as one of the great lost opportunities in American history.

How great a failure this turned out to be became clear over the next year. Many of the problems that prompted the Clinton initiative remain, and one of them, the number of uninsured Americans, grows steadily larger. Medical inflation continues. Public health services for the poorest Americans rapidly erode, and older Americans in need of health care find themselves threatened with higher costs for reduced services. States, counties, and cities, which face sharply reduced federal support, search in vain for local tax dollars to maintain basic services. Major public hospitals close. The already great chasm separating America's haves from its have-nots continues to widen. At the end of 1995, a year after the Clinton effort crashed, the triumphant Republican majorities in Congress struggled with the same runaway costs of the largest federal health programs, Medicare and Medicaid, that led Clinton to try to reform them. The increasingly fractious battle between the Democratic President and the Republican Congress over the federal budget that resulted in the longest shutdown of the federal government in history exposes the greater struggle that health care symbolizes: over two conflicting visions of the role of American government and the values of the society at century's end.

The failure of The System on health care reform might not loom so large if other great challenges facing the society were being met. They are not. Personal safety, economic opportunity, international peace, and health care are the four great security questions by which the American people judge the quality of their lives. On all but one of these, international peace, the last quarter of the twentieth century has witnessed the failure of The System to meet the legitimate expectations of the people it is supposed to be serving.

. . . Increasingly embittered debates over such intensely divisive issues as Vietnam and Watergate have added to the feeling that confrontation, not consensus, drives The System. More and more Americans now view both Democrats and Republicans as intent on tearing down opponents rather than building up the country. Energy policy fails to ensure conservation of natural resources or sufficient protection of the environment. Tax policy produces bewildering complexities. Crime policy involves more posturing than policing. In the most glaring failure, government has been unable to put its fiscal house in order. Annual deficits on a previously unimaginable scale accumulate; future generations are burdened with a geometrically rising national debt that threatens their personal prospects and the American future.

It was in this context that the battle between the President and the Congress over health reform was waged. Difficult and complex as that battle proved to be, restoring a sense of personal safety and fostering economic security are far more daunting. The twin scourges of crime and drugs are fed by powerful sociological forces that include the breakdown of the family structure and the disappearance, in many neighborhoods, of adult males capable of imposing discipline and establishing role models for a generation of alienated and increasingly violent teenagers. The Information Age transforms the entire marketplace from one with primary dependence on the creation and distribution of tangible goods to one relying mainly on the generation and transmission of data. In a time when billions of dollars of currency and investment whiz around the world in fractions of a second of microchip activity, debates about tariffs and trade seem antique. Clearly, education and training are even more important keys to individual prosperity than in the past. Yet Americans entering the workplace face a formidable new problem: No one knows how many and what kind of jobs there will be and where they will be located. There are no easy solutions; most of the problems are structural, having developed over decades. They present long-term challenges to a System, and a society, fixated on the immediate moment.

In contrast to these immensely complex challenges, the goal of providing access to quality health care for everyone was not an impossible dream. No doubt the credibility of the Clintons would have been enhanced had they admitted from the beginning that hard choices were involved—and acknowledged, too, that some people would have to pay a price in dollars, convenience, or freedom of choice for a new system that enabled everyone, not just the 85 percent with insurance, to receive care. There were reasons to be skeptical of Ira Magaziner's belief that waste in the existing health care system was so great that fine-tuning could produce sufficient savings to finance universal care, but no one seriously challenged his assertion about its enormous inefficiencies. Shortchanging such preventive measures as immunization has resulted in millions of people seeking expensive, unreimbursed care in hospital emergency rooms for conditions that could—and should—be treated far more cheaply and humanely at earlier stages of the illness. The administrative costs of competing insurance companies could—and should—be cut significantly by some mechanism, whether termed a purchasing

cooperative or an alliance, that draws small groups or individuals into larger blocks of health care consumers. Real competition could—and should—limit medical inflation even more than private business was beginning to experience when the Clintons began their effort. Even if one rejects the government-financed single-payer plan, which the Congressional Budget Office says would provide health insurance for everyone at lower overall total cost, room clearly existed for reforms that made practical economic and social sense.

Failure to achieve any of those possible changes was a failure of The System and every one of its parts: the presidency, the Congress, the political parties, the interest groups, and the press.

We cannot render a tougher judgment on Bill Clinton and his administration than the one he pronounced on himself: "I set the Congress up for failure." The errors of judgment, of omission and execution, that he and First Lady Hillary Clinton and their associates made were critical. While they deserve great credit for tackling a problem that Presidents had found reasons to postpone for six decades or more, and for placing it at the center of national debate and consciousness, they cannot avoid blame for the ultimate failure. Though many factors contributed to that end, we agree with Paul Starr's retrospective judgment: The lesson for the next time in health care reform is faster, smaller. "We made the error of trying to do too much, took too long, and ended up achieving nothing." Even worse, Starr said, is the ultimate irony that appears to be coming true a year after the end of the Clinton attempt; a movement that began with liberal proposals to control costs and expand coverage has produced conservative legislation that raises costs and reduces coverage.

Of all the mistakes, the greatest was the failure to recognize the limits on the President's authority imposed by the election returns. Conventional wisdom holds that you do not build bold agendas on small majorities, and Bill Clinton had no majority at all. He won with 43 percent of the popular vote, while his party lost ten seats in the House and just held its own in the Senate. Clinton limped into Washington, trailing the popular vote district by district of almost every member of Congress and with few longtime political alliances on which to draw. Moreover, health care reform was not the only item on his agenda or, to a majority of his advisers, the most important. During his presidential transition discussions in Little Rock, the highest priority, understandably and inevitably, was placed on dealing with the soaring budget deficit he had inherited. By reducing the deficit, he hoped to stimulate the economic growth he had promised in the campaign. . . .

Despite all the warning signals, the Clintons marched ahead, fortified by a belief that the rightness of their cause and the hard work they were prepared to expend on it would overcome all obstacles. They did not. Indeed, the Clintons compounded their problems by the structure they themselves designed.

The decision to create the special White House task force headed by Hillary Rodham Clinton and Ira Magaziner was a major mistake. Magaziner did a thorough job of devising a plan that was internally consistent and that addressed as many of the complex problems as any public policy could. The First Lady was an eloquent, tireless, and, for the most part, effective advocate for the cause. But the consequences of the President's decision to entrust the task to them were overwhelmingly negative. Having Hillary at the head of the task force inhibited the political debate within the administration. The secrecy under which it operated alienated not only important congressional leaders but others in the administration whose support was critical for its success. These people, in significant instances, resorted to the classic Washington tactic of making their objections public by leaking damaging (and often inaccurate) information to a press corps thoroughly frustrated by the curtain of silence erected by Hillary Clinton and Ira Magaziner. Leaks that plagued the project reflected an extraordinary lack of discipline and cohesion in the heart of the government. These repeated and destructive leaks exposed a larger problem: Despite the obvious importance both the President and the First Lady attached to health care reform, it remained something of an orphan within their administration. The White House staff for domestic policy, budget, politics, and lobbying, to say nothing of aides at Treasury, Health and Human Services, and other departments, were never fully committed to a project from which they felt excluded. The task force joke about living on "Planet Ira" contained a hard truth: Many in the White House said of the reform group, "They're so smart. Let them figure out how to pass it." That attitude was echoed, and amplified, on Capitol Hill.

All these were political mistakes, and the ultimate responsibility for them goes to the man in charge, who, as we have seen, was more than ready to take the blame. We've already explored two of these errors: first, the mismatch between the scale of reform and the political capital available to achieve it; second, the decision to place responsibility for devising the plan on a small group within the White House in a way that made their officials with expertise feel circumvented and that cast doubt on the President's claim to policy flexibility. A third set of errors involves the Congress.

The White House never resolved the contradiction between a House strategy based on the Democratic Left and a Senate strategy aimed at achieving consensus on a bill by winning moderates of both parties. Even within the Senate, the chairmen of the two committees, each believing he had White House backing, operated under very different assumptions about what served the President's interests. And there was another problem: Few on Capitol Hill could claim any expertise on the subject; fewer were even vaguely familiar with the program

he chose to support, and many of them disagreed with Clinton's version as they examined it. . . .

Americans have learned, from bitter experience, not to take their Presidents at their word. The phrase "credibility gap" entered the language with Lyndon Johnson and Vietnam: the phenomenon it described grew with every successive President. From Watergate to "read my lips," Americans have been disillusioned again and again and again. Whitewater, and a host of lesser stories, shattered Clinton's credibility—and Hillary's as well—during the time health care was on the national agenda. Trust was destroyed. In the end, Hillary was literally driven offstage by near-fanatical opponents, and the President was forced to participate in a political charade when he supposedly removed his name from the health care bill. . . .

Another fateful decision Clinton made early in his presidency was to rely heavily on the advice and judgment of the Democratic congressional leaders to pass his program. As we have noted, Clinton ran against Washington and constantly pressed Magaziner and others to get beyond "conventional Washington thinking" on the substance of his health care program.

But at a dinner in Little Rock, during his transition period, Clinton listened attentively as Vice President Gore, Speaker Foley, House Majority Leader Gephardt, and Senate Majority Leader Mitchell begged him not to repeat the "*error*" Jimmy Carter had made by holding himself aloof from the congressional Democrats. Let us be your foot soldiers, they said. Gephardt and Mitchell were particularly forceful in warning that Carter's legislative program had been crippled by the early divorce between him and the congressional Democrats. This miscalculation left him vulnerable to a serious renomination challenge from an esteemed legislator, Senator Edward M. Kennedy, and ultimately led to his defeat by Reagan.

No matter how narrow Clinton's victory, no matter how slim the congressional majorities, the leaders assured the new President that the congressional Democrats would deliver for him—if he gave them a chance. Gephardt said many Democrats like himself, who were newcomers when Carter became President, had learned their lesson: Failure to back your President opens the White House door to the Republicans. They would not make that mistake again, Gephardt said. But, please, Mr. President, he added, once you've given us our marching orders, let us carry them out *our* way.

Clinton cannot be seriously faulted for listening to them, even though none of them had been a close ally in helping him win the nomination or the election. They were the veterans. They knew The System. It hardly made sense to begin his term by refusing to agree to cooperate with his own party leaders, especially given the hostile signals from the Republicans. . . .

In the 1980s, facing Republican Presidents, Democrats in Congress realized that they might have gone too far in democratizing their institution and began to strengthen their leadership. They gave the Speaker and the two majority leaders more say in committee assignments; they beefed up their policy and communications staffs; occasionally they even disciplined a notable defector, like Phil Gramm, by removing him from an influential committee. But these steps did not alter the basic fact that when the health care battle began, the centrifugal forces of personal ambition and predilection were far more powerful in both houses of Congress than the cohesive forces of party loyalty.

Forming a unified, disciplined political front was nearly impossible in that Congress. Because the Clintons' health care reform would touch the jurisdictions of at least five major committees of the House and Senate in major ways, and an additional eight or nine in peripheral ways, some thought was given to creation of an ad hoc supercommittee in each chamber that could move the bill promptly to the floor. As we have seen, the First Lady ardently sought this approach. Gephardt, Foley, and Mitchell immediately rejected the idea; the members of the committees with jurisdiction would never yield that much power to a select group appointed by the leaders.

And, as we have also seen, the obstacles in the multicommittee approach proved to be so formidable that the leaders were unable to get a measure to the point of being voted up or down in either the House or the Senate. Responsibility was hopelessly, destructively, fragmented. . . .

The health care battle exposed as clearly as any recent legislative effort the infirmities that had developed in Congress under the long period of Democratic control. Clinton was not to blame for them; he was their victim. And when he had to sit and watch, in August of 1994, as the very leaders he had trusted to deliver for him squabbled for weeks over petty, parochial jurisdictional questions while health care reform went down the tubes, he must have wondered whether he had made a mistake in trying to move this broken system.

The fight also exposed the weakness of the Democratic Party—and led directly to its further dismemberment in the election of 1994. What Donna Shalala told us was the simple truth: Bringing health insurance within reach of every American family was the final piece of the Social Security system the Democrats had begun assembling under Franklin Roosevelt. It represented the single most important unfulfilled commitment of that party to its working-class and middle-class base. The very rich and the very poor had health care coverage. So did the elderly. The millions of ordinary working Americans without coverage were the people for whom the Democrats supposedly stood.

The most stunning fact about this entire effort is that when the Democrats controlled both houses of Congress and had in the White House in Bill and Hillary Clinton the two most knowledgeable and committed advocates

of universal health care coverage in history, they failed over two years even to bring the measure to a vote.

This failure spoke to weaknesses in both the presidency and in Congress. But it screamed to the world that the Democratic Party, the oldest and arguably most successful political institution in the free world, had lost its core, lost its heart, lost its soul. . . .

The political strategy the Republicans employed to demolish the Clinton plan was brilliant in its boldness. If Ira Magaziner thought the administration could "make complexity our ally," the Republican pollsters quickly discovered that the specter of a Big Government health care bureaucracy was their most powerful weapon. They took only a few weeks to recover from the initial favorable wave of stories about the President's speech and Hillary Clinton's round of appearances at congressional committees before they launched a series of ever-stronger attacks on "government health care." . . .

Republicans were far from alone in playing narrow politics. Dozens of interest groups that the Democrats had counted on also demonstrated how parochial they could be; how fixated on their own agendas, how heedless of the necessity to compromise to achieve a larger goal. At every stage of the story, many of them—from the giant American Association of Retired Persons to the tiny Foundation for Hospice and Home Care—declined to say flat out, "Help pass the Clinton plan."

Not that the White House was always skillful in negotiating with these interest groups. But administration ineptitude did not justify their holding back their vital support. Talking with their lobbyists and directors after the battle, we heard repeatedly, "We always assumed we would get something through Congress. We just wanted to get the best deal we could." But this was a classic case where the perfect became the enemy of the good—and of the attainable. Thus, these groups must ultimately share the blame for the fact that the country got nothing.

In the end, this battle revealed something even more significant about the interest groups that were so determined to defeat the Clinton reform. On the evidence of this struggle, they have so far outgrown the conceptions and definitions of past interest-group operations that it is necessary to rethink the way The System works.

For many decades, we have known that the schoolbook model of representative democracy obscures the reality. We remember the disillusioned reaction of the dedicated young White House Delivery Room volunteer who, when invited to speak to his hometown high school students about the lessons he had learned about our democracy, would not tell them how The System *really* works for fear it would make them even more cynical. One of those lessons is that the majority does not always—or automatically—prevail. Our system of government is littered with constitutional and political roadblocks that make it hard for huge policy changes like health care reform to be enacted quickly. We agree, up to a point, with those who point this out and who conclude that The System operated exactly as it is supposed to in the health care battle: Where no strong consensus exists, major change should wait.

But that argument ignores a deeper truth about the critical role that public opinion plays in The System. In many respects, the story of the life and death of health care reform is the story of how to manufacture and manipulate public opinion. A fundamental question that emerges from this story is, Why did the anticipated, and needed, great public debate about what kind of health care Americans want never occur? And why did the initially favorable American public become so frightened by the President's reform?

The answer is that "public opinion" was largely an artifact of the groups that mobilized to defeat reform. They created opinion with their grassroots and media efforts. Then they invoked that public opinion to convince, or provide a rationale for, the members of Congress who for reasons of self-interest wanted to vote no.

One of the most striking aspects of this battle is that, from beginning to end, 70 percent or more of those polled said they agreed with two fundamental propositions underlying the Clinton plan; that all American families should have health insurance and that all employers should contribute to paying for their workers' premiums.

Seventy percent-plus agreement on anything is most rare in American politics. It suggests a strong climate for change. Yet when we asked pollsters and lobbyists working to defeat the Clinton plan why these public attitudes did not represent a clear public mandate for reform, the answer we got went like this: "Of course, people want employers to pay for their health insurance. Why wouldn't they? But if you ask a follow-up question, 'Do you want the government to require business to pay for health insurance if it means lower wages and fewer jobs?' the number of those supporting reform turns around."

The interest groups opposing Clinton successfully persuaded much of the public that his plan would mean not only lower wages and fewer jobs but less freedom to choose a doctor, a hospital, or an insurer. It would mean more bureaucracy and lower-quality care. They spread this largely false message relentlessly in a campaign that cost literally hundreds of millions of dollars and involved the use of every technique developed for the modern high-tech election campaign.

Critical Thinking

1. How is it that presidential election returns can impose appreciable limits on the president's authority, even though obviously the president was the victorious candidate?
2. If the Republicans had not regained control of Congress in 1994, would the comprehensive health care reforms launched by Clinton have been achieved?
3. So far in the twenty-first century, how applicable has the expression "credibility gap" been to the American presidencies?

Create Central

www.mhhe.com/createcentral

Internet References

Office of Management and Budget
www.whitehouse.gov/omb

From *The System: The American Way of Politics at the Breaking Point* (Little, Brown & Co., 1996). Copyright © 1996 by Haynes Johnson and David S. Broder. Reprinted by permission of Hachette Book Group USA.

Unit 15: American Foreign Policy

The Erosion of American National Interests

Samuel P. Huntington

Learning Outcomes

After reading this selection, you should be able to:

1. Draw a connection between the Cold War and American national interests.
2. Identify the "commercial diplomacy" of the Clinton Administration.
3. Recognize culture and creed as, historically, the two primary components of American identity.

Samuel P. Huntington (b. 1927) is considered one of the most productive and influential contemporary scholars of American foreign policy and international relations. As a prolific author of major, innovative, scholarly publications on American foreign policy and global politics, his works are often cited and referred to by political scientists and foreign policy decision makers. Huntington's article "The Erosion of American National Interests," *Foreign Affairs* (September/October 1997), from which the following selection is taken, is a landmark interpretative analysis of American foreign policy because it has promoted the contemporary scholarly study of American national interests.

Huntington is currently the Albert J. Weatherhead III University Professor at Harvard University, where he has taught for many years. He is also director of the John M. Olin Institute for Strategic Studies at Harvard University and chairman of the Harvard Academy for International and Area Studies. His expertise on foreign policy has enabled him to influence foreign policy decisions through his membership in various important advisory organizations, including the National Security Council, in which he was director of security planning for the Carter administration; the Social Science Research Council; the Institute of Strategic Studies; and the Council on Foreign Relations. He has been awarded numerous fellowships, including a Guggenheim Fellowship. He was the founder and coeditor of the journal *Foreign Policy* and president of the American Political Science Association. Huntington's many publications include *Political Order in Changing Societies* (Yale University Press, 1969), *The Soldier and the State: The Theory and Politics of Civil-Military Relations* (Belknap Press, 1981), *American Politics: The Promise of Disharmony* (Harvard University Press, 1983), *American Military Strategy* (University of California, 1986), *The Third Wave: Democratization in the Late Twentieth Century* (University of Oklahoma Press, 1993), and *The Clash of Civilizations and the Remaking of World Order* (Simon & Schuster, 1996).

The following selection is a critical analysis of the current confusion in precisely identifying American national interests in the post-Cold War period. This article has filled a critical intellectual gap in the contemporary literature on American foreign policy and strategic defense planning because it has promoted serious reexamination of the specific sources responsible for the formulation of American national interests. Huntington argues that erosion of a coherent understanding of American national identity has been accelerated by the demise of the Cold War and by complex social, cultural, and demographic transformations in American society. This has resulted in a confused awareness of American national interests. Huntington's classic essay is a unique contribution to the study of American foreign policy in that he attempts to demonstrate that such policy and American national interests have shifted from legitimate broad global concerns to highly parochial commercial and ethnic objectives. In addition to promoting the commercial or economic interests of particular American businesses, contemporary American foreign policy has also been shaped by dominant transnational or nonnational ethnic interests.

In lieu of an American foreign policy of particularism oriented toward the fulfillment of specific commercial and ethnic interests, Huntington advocates a renewal of commitment by Americans to central, identifiable national interests. Instead of an abstract foreign policy based upon idealistic goals, a comprehensive strategy, or moralistic visions, Huntington prescribes a reconceptualization of American foreign policy guided by the pragmatic principle and realistic objective of a national interest of national restraint, which would have the broad support of the American people. According to Huntington, this would reduce American commitments in the global arena in conjunction with a planned reduction of American resources promoting narrow commercial and ethnic objectives.

Key Concept: the replacement of American national interests by narrow commercial and ethnic interests

The Disintegration of Identity

The years since the end of the Cold War have seen intense, wide-ranging, and confused debates about American national interests. Much of this confusion stems from the complexity of the post-Cold War world. The new environment has been variously interpreted as involving the end of history, bipolar conflict between rich and poor countries, movement back to a future of traditional power politics, the proliferation of ethnic conflict verging on anarchy, the clash of civilizations, and conflicting trends toward integration and fragmentation. The new world is all these things, and hence there is good reason for uncertainty about American interests in it. Yet that is not the only source of confusion. Efforts to define national interest presuppose agreement on the nature of the country whose interests are to be defined. National interest derives from national identity. We have to know who we are before we can know what our interests are.

Historically, American identity has had two primary components: culture and creed. The first has been the values and institutions of the original settlers, who were Northern European, primarily British, and Christian, primarily Protestant. This culture included most importantly the English language and traditions concerning relations between church and state and the place of the individual in society. Over the course of three centuries, black people were slowly and only partially assimilated into this culture. Immigrants from western, southern, and eastern Europe were more fully assimilated, and the original culture evolved and was modified but not fundamentally altered as a result. In *The Next American Nation*, Michael Lind captures the broad outlines of this evolution when he argues that American culture developed through three phases: Anglo–America (1789–1861), Euro–America (1857–1957), and Multicultural America (1972–present). The cultural definition of national identity assumes that while the culture may change, it has a basic continuity.

The second component of American identity has been a set of universal ideas and principles articulated in the founding documents by American leaders: liberty, equality, democracy, constitutionalism, liberalism, limited government, private enterprise. These constitute what Gunnar Myrdal termed the American Creed, and the popular consensus on them has been commented on by foreign observers from Crevecoeur and Tocqueville down to the present. This identity was neatly summed up by Richard Hofstadter: "It has been our fate as a nation not to have ideologies but to be one."

These dual sources of identity are, of course, closely related. The creed was a product of the culture. Now, however, the end of the Cold War and social, intellectual, and demographic changes in American society have brought into question the validity and relevance of both traditional components of American identity. Without a sure sense of national identity, Americans have become unable to define their national interests, and as a result subnational commercial interests and transnational and nonnational ethnic interests have come to dominate foreign policy.

Loss of the Other

The most profound question concerning the American role in the post-Cold War world was improbably posed by Rabbit Angstrom, the harried central character of John Updike's novels: "Without the cold war, what's the point of being an American?" If being an American means being committed to the principles of liberty, democracy, individualism, and private property, and if there is no evil empire out there threatening those principles, what indeed does it mean to be an American, and what becomes of American national interests?

From the start, Americans have constructed their creedal identity in contrast to an undesirable "other." America's opponents are always defined as liberty's opponents. At the time of independence, Americans could not distinguish themselves culturally from Britain; hence they had to do so politically. Britain embodied tyranny, aristocracy, oppression; America, democracy, equality, republicanism. Until the end of the nineteenth century, the United States defined itself in opposition to Europe. Europe was the past: backward, unfree, unequal, characterized by feudalism, monarchy, and imperialism. The United States, in contrast, was the future: progressive, free, equal, republican. In the twentieth century, the United States emerged on the world scene and increasingly saw itself not as the antithesis of Europe but rather as the leader of European-American civilization against upstart challengers to that civilization, imperial and then Nazi Germany.

After World War II the United States defined itself as the leader of the democratic free world against the Soviet Union and world communism. During the Cold War the United States pursued many foreign policy goals, but its one overriding national purpose was to contain and defeat communism. When other goals and interests clashed with this purpose, they were usually subordinated to it. For 40 years virtually all the great American initiatives in foreign policy, as well as many in domestic policy, were justified by this overriding priority: the Greek-Turkish aid program, the Marshall Plan, NATO, the Korean War, nuclear weapons and strategic missiles, foreign aid, intelligence operations, reduction of trade barriers, the space program, the Alliance for Progress, military alliances with Japan and Korea, support for Israel, overseas military deployments, an unprecedentedly large military establishment, the Vietnam War, the openings to China, support for the Afghan mujahideen and other anticommunist insurgencies. If there is no Cold War, the rationale for major programs and initiatives like these disappears.

As the Cold War wound down in the late 1980s, Gorbachev's adviser Georgiy Arbatov commented: "We are doing something really terrible to you—we are depriving you of an enemy." Psychologists generally agree that individuals and groups define their identity by differentiating themselves from and placing themselves in opposition to others.[1] While wars at times may have a divisive effect on society, a common enemy can often help to promote identity and cohesion among people. The weakening or absence of a common enemy can do just the reverse. Abraham Lincoln commented on this effect in his Lyceum speech in 1837 when he argued that the American Revolution and its aftermath had directed enmity outward: "The jealousy, envy, avarice incident to our nature, and so common to a state of peace, prosperity, and conscious strength, were for a time in a great measure smothered and rendered inactive, while the deep-rooted principles of hate, and the powerful motive of revenge, instead of being turned against each other, were directed exclusively against the British nation." Hence, he said, "the basest principles of our nature" were either dormant or "the active agents in the advancement of the noblest of causes—that of establishing and maintaining civil and religious liberty." But he warned, "this state of feeling must fade, is fading, has faded, with the circumstances that produced it." He spoke, of course, as the nation was starting to disintegrate. As the heritage of World War II and the Cold War fades, America may be faced with a comparable dynamic.

The Cold War fostered a common identity between American people and government. Its end is likely to weaken or at least alter that identity. One possible consequence is the rising opposition to the federal government, which is, after all, the principal institutional manifestation of American national identity and unity. Would nationalist fanatics bomb federal buildings and attack federal agents if the federal government was still defending the country against a serious foreign threat? Would the militia movement be as strong as it is today? In the past, comparable bombing attacks were usually the work of foreigners who saw the United States as their enemy, and the first response of many people to the Oklahoma City bombing was to assume that it was the work of a "new enemy," Muslim terrorists. That response could reflect a psychological need to believe that such an act must have been carried out by an external enemy. Ironically, the bombing may have been in part the result of the absence of such an enemy. . . .

In Search of National Interests

A national interest is a public good of concern to all or most Americans; a vital national interest is one which they are willing to expend blood and treasure to defend. National interests usually combine security and material concerns, on the one hand, and moral and ethical concerns, on the other. Military action against Saddam Hussein was seen as a vital national interest because he threatened reliable and inexpensive access to Persian Gulf oil and because he was a rapacious dictator who

had blatantly invaded and annexed another country. During the Cold War the Soviet Union and communism were perceived as threats to both American security and American values; a happy coincidence existed between the demands of power politics and the demands of morality. Hence broad public support buttressed government efforts to defeat communism and thus, in Walter Lippmann's terms, to maintain a balance between capabilities and commitments. That balance was often tenuous and arguably got skewed in the 1970s. With the end of the Cold War, however, the danger of a "Lippmann gap" vanished, and instead the United States appears to have a Lippmann surplus. Now the need is not to find the power to serve American purposes but rather to find purposes for the use of American power.

This need has led the American foreign policy establishment to search frantically for new purposes that would justify a continuing U.S. role in world affairs comparable to that in the Cold War. The Commission on America's National Interests put the problem this way in 1996: "After four decades of unusual single-mindedness in containing Soviet Communist expansion, we have seen five years of ad hoc fits and starts. If it continues, this drift will threaten our values, our fortunes, and indeed our lives."[2]

The commission identified five vital national interests: prevent attacks on the United States with weapons of mass destruction, prevent the emergence of hostile hegemons in Europe or Asia and of hostile powers on U.S. borders or in control of the seas, prevent the collapse of the global systems for trade, financial markets, energy supplies, and the environment, and ensure the survival of U.S. allies.

What, however, are the threats to these interests? Nuclear terrorism against the United States could be a near-term threat, and the emergence of China as an East Asian hegemon could be a longer-term one. Apart from these, however, it is hard to see any major looming challenges to the commission's vital interests. New threats will undoubtedly arise, but given the scarcity of current ones, campaigns to arouse interest in foreign affairs and support for major foreign policy initiatives now fall on deaf ears. The administration's call for the "enlargement" of democracy does not resonate with the public and is belied by the administration's own actions. Arguments from neoconservatives for big increases in defense spending have the same air of unreality that arguments for the abolition of nuclear weapons had during the Cold War.

The argument is frequently made that American "leadership" is needed to deal with world problems. Often it is. The call for leadership, however, begs the question of leadership to do what, and rests on the assumption that the world's problems are America's problems. Often they are not. The fact that things are going wrong in many places in the world is unfortunate, but it does not mean that the United States has either an interest in or the responsibility for correcting them. The National Interests Commission said that presidential leadership is necessary to create a consensus on national interests. In some measure, however, a consensus already exists that American national interests do not warrant extensive American involvement in most problems in most of the world. The foreign policy establishment is asking the president to make a case for a cause that simply will not sell. The most striking feature of the search for national interests has been its failure to generate purposes that command anything remotely resembling broad support and to which people are willing to commit significant resources.

Commercialism and Ethnicity

The lack of national interests that command widespread support does not imply a return to isolationism. America remains involved in the world, but its involvement is now directed at commercial and ethnic interests rather than national interests. Economic and ethnic particularism define the current American role in the world. The institutions and capabilities—political, military, economic, intelligence—created to serve a grand national purpose in the Cold War are now being suborned and redirected to serve narrow subnational, transnational, and even nonnational purposes. Increasingly people are arguing that these are precisely the interests foreign policy should serve.

The Clinton administration has given priority to "commercial diplomacy," making the promotion of American exports a primary foreign policy objective. It has been successful in wringing access to some foreign markets for American products. Commercial achievements have become a primary criterion for judging the performance of American ambassadors. President Clinton may well be spending more time promoting American sales abroad than doing anything else in foreign affairs. If so, that would be a dramatic sign of the redirection of American foreign policy. In case after case, country after country, the dictates of commercialism have prevailed over other purposes including human rights, democracy, alliance relationships, maintaining the balance of power, technology export controls, and other strategic and political considerations described by one administration official as "stratocrap and globaloney."[3] "Many in the administration, Congress, and the broader foreign policy community," a former senior official in the Clinton Commerce Department argued in these pages, "still believe that commercial policy is a tool of foreign policy, when it should more often be the other way around—the United States should use all its foreign policy levers to achieve commercial goals." The funds devoted to promoting commercial goals should be greatly increased; the personnel working on these goals should be upgraded and professionalized; the agencies concerned with export promotion need to be strengthened and recognized. Landing the contract is the name of the game in foreign policy.

Or at least it is the name of one game. The other game is the promotion of ethnic interests. While economic interests are usually subnational, ethnic interests are generally transnational or nonnational. The promotion of particular businesses and industries may not involve a broad public good, as does a general reduction in trade barriers, but it does promote the interests of some Americans. Ethnic groups promote the interests of people and entities outside the United States. Boeing has an interest in aircraft sales and the Polish-American Congress in help for Poland, but the former benefits residents of Seattle, the latter residents of Eastern Europe.

The growing role of ethnic groups in shaping American foreign policy is reinforced by the waves of recent immigration and by the arguments for diversity and multiculturalism. In addition, the greater wealth of ethnic communities and the dramatic improvements in communications and transportation now make it much easier for ethnic groups to remain in touch with their home countries. As a result, these groups are being transformed from cultural communities within the boundaries of a state into diasporas that transcend these boundaries. State-based diasporas, that is, trans-state cultural communities that control at least one state, are increasingly important and increasingly identify with the interests of their homeland. "Full assimilation into their host societies," a leading expert, Gabriel Sheffer, has observed in *Survival*, "has become unfashionable among both established and incipient state-based diasporas . . . many diasporal communities neither confront overwhelming pressure to assimilate nor feel any marked advantage in assimilating into their host societies or even obtaining citizenship there." Since the United States is the premier immigrant country in the world, it is most affected by the shifts from assimilation to diversity and from ethnic group to diaspora.

During the Cold War, immigrants and refugees from communist countries usually vigorously opposed, for political and ideological reasons, the governments of their home countries and actively supported American anticommunist policies against them. Now, diasporas in the United States support their home governments. Products of the Cold War, Cuban-Americans ardently support U.S. anti-Castro policies. Chinese-Americans, in contrast, overwhelmingly pressure the United States to adopt favorable policies toward China. Culture has supplanted ideology in shaping attitudes in diaspora populations.

Diasporas provide many benefits to their home countries. Economically prosperous diasporas furnish major financial support to the homeland, Jewish-Americans, for instance, contributing up to $1 billion a year to Israel. Armenian-Americans send enough to earn Armenia the sobriquet of "the Israel of the Caucasus." Diasporas supply expertise, military recruits, and on occasion political leadership to the homeland. They often pressure their home governments to adopt more nationalist and assertive policies towards neighboring countries. Recent cases in the United States show that they can be a source of spies used to gather information for their homeland governments.

Most important, diasporas can influence the actions and policies of their host country and co-opt its resources and influence to serve the interests of their homeland. Ethnic groups have played active roles in politics throughout American history. Now, ethnic diaspora groups proliferate, are more active, and have greater self-consciousness, legitimacy, and political clout. In recent years, diasporas have had a major impact on American policy towards Greece and Turkey, the Caucasus, the recognition of Macedonia, support for Croatia, sanctions against South Africa, aid for black Africa, intervention in Haiti, NATO expansion, sanctions against Cuba, the controversy in Northern Ireland, and the relations between Israel and its neighbors. Diaspora-based policies may at times coincide with broader national interests, as could arguably be the case with NATO expansion, but they are also often pursued at the expense of broader interests and American relations with long-standing allies. Overall, as James R. Schlesinger observed in a 1997 lecture at the Center for Strategic and International Studies, the United States has "less of a foreign policy in a traditional sense of a great power than we have the stapling together of a series of goals put forth by domestic constituency groups. . . . The result is that American foreign policy is incoherent. It is scarcely what one would expect from the leading world power."

Schlesinger had to recognize, however, that multiculturalism and heightened ethnic consciousness have caused many political leaders to believe this is "the *appropriate* way to make foreign policy." In the scholarly community some argue that diasporas can help promote American values in their home countries and hence "the participation of ethnic diasporas in shaping U.S. foreign policy is a truly positive phenomenon."[4] The validity of diaspora interests was a central theme at a May 1996 conference on "Defining the National Interest: Minorities and U.S. Foreign Policy in the 21st Century." Conference participants attacked the Cold War definition of national interest and what was described as "the traditional policy community's apparent animosity toward the very idea of minority involvement in international affairs." Conferees explored "the experiences of Jewish-Americans and Cuban-Americans and sought to extract lessons from the way these two groups succeeded in influencing foreign policy while others failed." The sponsorship of this conference by the New York Council on Foreign Relations, once the capstone institution of the foreign policy establishment, was the ultimate symbol of the triumph of diaspora interests over national interests in American foreign policy.

The displacement of national interests by commercial and ethnic interests reflects the domesticization of foreign policy. Domestic politics and interests have always inevitably and appropriately influenced foreign policy. Now, however, previous assumptions that the foreign and domestic policymaking processes differ from each other for important reasons no longer hold. For an understanding of American foreign policy it is necessary to study not the interests of the American state in a world of competing states but rather the play of economic and ethnic interests in American domestic politics. At least in recent years, the latter has been a superb predictor of foreign policy stands. Foreign policy, in the sense of actions consciously designed to promote the interests of the United States as a collective entity in relation to similar collective entities, is slowly but steadily disappearing.

The Push and Pull of American Power

A decade after the end of the Cold War, a paradox exists with respect to American power. On the one hand, the United States is the only superpower in the world. It has the largest economy and the highest levels of prosperity. Its political and economic principles are increasingly endorsed throughout the world. It spends more on defense than all the other major powers combined and has the only military force capable of acting effectively in almost every part of the world. It is far ahead of any other country in technology and appears certain to retain that lead in the foreseeable future. American popular culture and consumer products have swept the world, permeating the most distant and resistant societies. American economic, ideological, military, technological, and cultural primacy, in short, is overwhelming.

American influence, on the other hand, falls far short of that. Countries large and small, rich and poor, friendly and antagonistic, democratic and authoritarian, all seem able to resist the blandishments and threats of American policymakers. On issues of protectionism, sanctions, intervention, human rights, proliferation of weapons of mass destruction, peacekeeping, and others, officials of foreign governments listen politely to American demands and entreaties, perhaps express general agreement with the ideas advanced, and then quietly go their own way. This tendency "to follow their own counsels," Jonathan Clarke observed in *Foreign Policy* in 1996, "includes both great and small nations. . . . "

Particularism vs. Restraint

American foreign policy is becoming a foreign policy of particularism increasingly devoted to the promotion abroad of highly specific commercial and ethnic interests. The institutions, resources, and influence generated to serve national interests in the Cold War are being redirected to serve these interests. These developments may have been furthered by the almost exclusive concern of the Clinton administration with domestic politics, but their roots lie in broader changes in the external and internal context of the United States and changing conceptions of American national identity.

The likelihood that these contextual factors will shift in the near future seems remote. Conceivably China could become a new enemy. Certainly, important groups in China think of the United States as *their* new enemy. A China threat sufficient to generate a new sense of national identity and purpose in the United States, however, is not imminent, and how serious that threat is judged to be will depend on the extent to which the Americans view Chinese hegemony in East Asia as damaging to American interests. Reviving a stronger sense of national identity would also require countering the cults of diversity and multiculturalism within the United States. It would probably involve limiting immigration along the lines proposed by the Jordan Commission and developing new public and private Americanization programs to counter the factors enhancing diaspora loyalties and to promote the assimilation of immigrants. These developments may well occur, but given the extent to which, in Nathan Glazer's phrase, "we are all multiculturalists now," it will be a while before the recent denationalizing trends are reversed.

The replacement of particularism would require the American public to become committed to new national interests that would take priority over and lead to the subordination of commercial and ethnic concerns. At present, as polls show, majorities of the American public are unwilling to support the commitment of significant resources to the defense of American allies, the protection of small nations against aggression, the promotion of human rights and democracy, or economic and social development in the Third World.[5] As a result the articulation of these and other broad goals by administration officials produces little follow-through, and with rare exceptions the calls of establishment figures for American leadership generate no effective action. Unable to deliver on its broad promises, American foreign policy becomes one of rhetoric and retreat, with the active energies of the administration concentrated on the advancement of particularistic concerns. Foreign governments have learned not to take seriously administration statements of its general policy goals and to take very seriously administration actions devoted to commercial and ethnic interests.

The alternative to particularism is thus not promulgation of a "grand design," "coherent strategy," or "foreign policy vision." It is a policy of restraint and reconstitution aimed at limiting the diversion of American resources to the service of particularistic subnational, transnational, and nonnational interests. The national interest is national restraint, and that appears to be the only national interest the American people are willing to support at this time in their history. Hence, instead of formulating unrealistic schemes for grand endeavors abroad, foreign policy elites might well devote their energies to designing plans for lowering American involvement in the world in ways that will safeguard possible future national interests.

At some point in the future, the combination of security threat and moral challenge will require Americans once again to commit major resources to the defense of national interests. The *de novo* mobilization of those resources from a low base, experience suggests, is likely to be easier than the redirection of resources that have been committed to entrenched particularistic interests. A more restrained role now could facilitate America's assumption of a more positive role in the future when the time comes for it to renew its national identity and to pursue national purposes for which Americans are willing to pledge their lives, their fortunes, and their national honor.

Notes

1. See Vamik D. Volkan, *The Need to Have Enemies and Allies: From Clinical Practice to International Relationships,* Northvale, NJ: Aronson, 1994, and Jonathan Mercer, "Anarchy and Identity," *International Organizations,* Spring 1996, pp. 237–68.
2. *America's National Interests, A Report from the Commission on America's National Interests,* Cambridge: Center for Science and International Affairs, John F. Kennedy School of Government, Harvard University, 1996, p. 1.
3. Lawrence F. Kaplan, "The Selling of American Foreign Policy," *The Weekly Standard,* April 23, 1997, pp. 19–22.
4. Yossi Shain, "Multicultural Foreign Policy," *Foreign Policy,* Fall 1995, p. 87.
5. See John E. Reilly, ed., *American Public Opinion and U.S. Foreign Policy 1994,* Chicago: Chicago Council on Foreign Relations, 1995, and Arthur M. Schlesinger, Jr., "Back to the Womb? Isolationism's Renewed Threat," *Foreign Affairs,* July/August 1995, pp. 2–8.

Critical Thinking

1. Is it always necessarily true that national interest derives from national identity?
2. In what specific ways have commercial and ethnic interests replaced America's national interests?
3. How would the core message of this article have been affected had Huntington written it not in 1997, but after 2001?

Create Central

www.mhhe.com/createcentral

Internet References

The Council on Foreign Relations
www.cfr.org

American Foreign Policy Council
www.afpc.org

Reprinted by permission of *Foreign Affairs*, September/October 1997. Copyright © 1997 by the Council on Foreign Relations, Inc.

The Crisis of Liberal Internationalism

Stanley Hoffmann

Learning Outcomes

After reading this selection, you should be able to:

1. Provide a general description of liberal democratic internationalism.
2. Identify the two differing perspectives of human nature from which liberalism is founded.
3. Point out the critical norms responsible for much of the confusion over the liberal agenda.

Stanley Hoffmann (b. 1928) is a contemporary scholar of global politics, particularly European politics, French culture and politics, international law, international organizations, and American foreign policy. He received his M.A. from Harvard University and his LL.D. from the University of Paris. He is the Paul and Catherine Buttenwieser University Professor at Harvard University, and served as chairman of the Center for European Studies at Harvard University, where he has taught for over 40 years. Hoffmann has received numerous prestigious honors and awards, including the Carnegie Prize in International Organization and the Prix Alphonse Bentinck. The scholarly insights articulated in his numerous writings, particularly in international relations, European politics, and American foreign policy, have made him one of the most frequently cited authors in these areas of study. His numerous publications include *France Seventeen Eighty-Nine to Nineteen Hundred* (Viking Penguin, 1986); *Janus and Minerva: Essays in the Theory and Practice of International Politics* (Westview, 1987); *The New European Community: Decisionmaking and Institutional Change* (Westview, 1991), coedited with Robert O. Keohane; *International Relations: The Long Road to Theory* (Irvington, 1993); and *The European Sisyphus: Essays on Europe, 1964–1994* (Westview, 1995). Hoffmann is a frequent contributor to international and comparative scholarly journals, including *Foreign Policy, Foreign Affairs, Daedalus,* and the *New York Review of Books.*

The following selection is an excerpt from "The Crisis of Liberal Internationalism," *Foreign Policy* (Spring 1995), Hoffmann's classic study of the declining influence of the ideology of liberal democratic internationalism in the contemporary global context. Liberal democratic internationalism, or Wilsonianism, is the twentieth-century foreign policy approach that prescribes that the United States should design its foreign policy decisions according to idealistic moral criteria, universal ethical principles, and abstract philosophical ideals, such as the promotion of democracy, global human rights, and free trade. Hoffmann contends that American hegemony was responsible for promoting this perspective, particularly in its containment of totalitarianism and Soviet communism and its opposition to colonialism and imperialism. He also argues that there has been a recent erosion of consensus by the American people and political leadership for a U.S. policy of liberal internationalism due to perceived extensive human and financial costs. Instead, many Americans have argued for a return to the traditional realistic approach to global relations, which recommends that the United States design its foreign policy objectives to conform to its perception of its concrete, nonideological national interests. Hoffmann also contends that liberal democratic internationalism is itself responsible to some degree for its failures in the contemporary global arena.

Hoffmann says that the contemporary threat to the implementation of the liberal internationalist vision of global stability and cooperation consists of global social and political anomie and chaos. This is a world characterized by disintegrating states due to such complex factors as the collapse of the Soviet Union, pervasive conflicts, and civil wars among rival ethnic, religious, and political factions. It is in this context of disintegrating states that Hoffmann examines the four critical norms that are responsible for much of the confusion over the liberal agenda: sovereignty, self-government or democracy, national self-determination, and human rights. In this classic essay, which should have a profound impact upon contemporary foreign policy scholars and leaders, Hoffmann calls for a serious reformulation of liberal internationalism. A concept of human rights that would entail limitations on the principles of sovereignty and self-determination would be the cornerstone of his prescription for a reinvigorated liberal vision of the world.

Key Concept: the decline and reformulation of liberal internationalism

*C*ommunism is dead, but is the other great postwar ideology, liberal internationalism, also dying? A recent book by political scientist Tony Smith as well as several speeches by National Security Adviser Anthony Lake have reminded Americans that "liberal democratic internationalism, or Wilsonianism, has been the most important and distinctive contribution of the United States to the international history of the twentieth century," as

Smith states it. Lake, presenting the Clinton administration's foreign policy as a pragmatic Wilsonianism, has explained that it aims at expanding democracy and free trade, at defending democracy from its foes, at quarantining repressive and pariah states, and at protecting and promoting human rights.

After two years, however, pragmatism is more visible than Wilsonianism. In a speech at Harvard, Lake stated that the promotion of democracy and the defense of human rights would entail the use of force only if, among other qualifications, there were clearly defined American interests. He also suggested that the spread of liberalism was not *ipso facto* an American interest: an inadvertent but remarkable concession to traditional realism. As in the Carter years, the different elements of the liberal agenda are again in competition with one another—human rights versus the expansion of free trade, as one example. Whether the liberal agenda should be carried out by multilateral means or, in case of need, by the United States alone, has again become a source of confusion and grief, as in Bosnia. Meanwhile, the nation's enthusiasm for bearing the human and financial costs of carrying out a policy of liberal internationalism has waned. Whereas containment had provided a reasonably clear rationale for policy and a lever for mobilizing public support, neo-Wilsonianism seems a guideline made of rubber and has left the American public deeply ambivalent.

This is not new. As Tony Smith establishes in *America's Mission*, the golden ages of liberal democratic internationalism were the periods that followed the two world wars, and, to some extent, the 1980s, when the Cold War was being "won" by the West and the "third wave" of democratization occurred. This is not a coincidence; it suggests that in order to understand the current difficulties of liberalism on the world stage there is a need to go far beyond the all too familiar and depressing litany of what is wrong with Bill Clinton's foreign policy. An examination of the plight of liberal internationalism must shift to the flaws and limitations of liberalism itself. . . .

But liberalism's embrace of national self-determination raised more questions than it answered. There was, once more, the dilemma of intervention for the emancipation of oppressed nationalities. In addition, there were formidable new question marks. Nationalities do not come in neat packages. One could conceive abstractly of a world of distinct liberal states, but a world of separate nation-states would leave vast areas of confusion: minorities in existing nation-states, plus the vexing problem of what is the "self" that is entitled to self-determination (what, in other words, distinguishes a group that deserves to become a nation-state from one that does not). There were also questions of whether self-determination was necessarily synonymous with sovereignty, and whether a world of independent sovereign nation-states would find harmony as easily as the world of states envisaged by seventeenth- and eighteenth-century liberals—precisely because of the conflicts that were likely to result from the problems of minorities and of who can claim to form a nation.

Second, the national cause might be separate from the liberal one: There could be authoritarian versions of nationalism, definitions of the nation in terms of "blood and earth," not consent—conceptions that make of the individual a pure product of his national community, and not the master of his civic fate. Non-liberal nationalisms thus could give new strength and relevance to authoritarian doctrines and might derail the philosophy of historical progress that predicted the gradual triumph of liberal government over tyranny. The replacement, on the illiberal Right, of divine right (or the power of tradition) with the needs and demands of the nation was to give a formidable new lease on life to ideas previously associated with obsolescent aristocracies, a reactionary Church, or frivolous courts.

Third, liberalism's embrace of nationalism introduced into liberalism a philosophical incongruity. The appeal of liberalism had been an appeal to reason—the reason embodied in John Locke's Natural Law, Kant's idea of a Good Will rooted in human reason, and the rationalism of utilitarian calculations of pleasure and pain. Nationalism has much more to do with will than with reason; its connections are with Rousseau's General Will, which is exclusively that of the separate community, and with Jacobinism. If the legitimacy of power is derived not merely from rational consent to a system of checks and balances and to a careful separation between a public sphere and a domain of individual liberty, but also from the existence of a common national will, are there not serious risks that such a will, however democratic, could overrun the restraints on power and remove the barrier that protects individuals? Nationalism, in other words, reopened the inherent tension between liberalism and democracy that had broken out in the French Revolution, and thus threatened both the liberal program at home and the cosmopolitan vision abroad—by creating new sources of intense conflict between states with different conceptions of the nation and overlapping nationalities, and by weakening the two transnational pillars of the liberal international order: a transnational economy and world public opinion.

Liberal Internationalism and Realpolitik

With such blind spots and contradictions, how could liberal internationalism nevertheless have been as successful as it has been at times, particularly in the period that followed the Second World War? A part of the answer is undoubtedly provided by American hegemony in the vast areas in which the United States was able and willing to exert its influence after the calamitous insulation of the interwar period. It is already paradoxical enough that the progress of liberal vision, in the creation of a transnational economy as well as in the development of cooperation among liberal states, should depend so much on the preponderance of power in one state, and on its willingness to provide others with a variety of public goods. After all, the kind of liberal internationalism achieved through hegemony raises questions both about what happens "after hegemony," and about the fairness of the order thus established. But one has to go deeper and examine both why the "hegemon" acted as decisively as it did and why others were willing to accept some of the costs.

The reason is another paradox. Liberal internationalism, a vision of harmony that remained rather vague about how to reach nirvana, has been best at performing what might be called negative tasks. In the economic realm, this was, of course, exactly what the doctrines of laissez-faire demanded. Liberalism has—under the impulse of a hegemon for which self-interest and liberal conviction converged—succeeded in removing a vast number of barriers to trade and communication, and thus in establishing that transnational economic society that liberalism itself called for. The same result was achieved within the European Community, where many of the powers given up by the states have gone not to the new central institutions, but to the market. And there, progress resulted not from the hegemony of one power, but from a consensus among liberal regimes. In the political realm, however, liberalism, in order to reach its conception of peace, had to give priority to battle. Liberal internationalism has both fueled and supported the revolt against colonialism and imperialism, thus carrying forward Wilson's call that "no nation should seek to extend its polity over any other nation or people." Liberal internationalism has spoken up against violations of human rights, especially in the last 20 years. Above all, it waged a protracted cold war against Soviet totalitarianism in order to "contain" it, in the expectation, formulated in 1946–47 by George Kennan, that the Soviet system would eventually succumb to its internal flaws.

Thus the prelude to liberal harmony had to be a skillful exercise in limited war—limited both because of the liberal aversion to war and because of nuclear weapons. But it was the force of the totalitarian challenge that resolved the ambivalence of liberalism toward international activism and neutralized, for a long while, its noninterventionist potential. Even many of the "positive" missions accomplished by liberal internationalism after 1945—the democratization of Germany and Japan, the establishment of the European Community, the integration of the world capitalist economy—were undertaken or advanced as essential parts of the battle against the Soviet totalitarian threat. It was a remarkable fusion of realpolitik and liberal internationalism. But that fusion was not without strains. Some were over priorities: Was the containment of Soviet influence or of communism's expansion so overriding a goal that it

left little space for the nurturing of liberal democracy in, say, Greece in 1967–74, in the Shah's Iran, or in Central American and Caribbean countries? Was the Soviet version of communism so dangerous that it became necessary to court and accommodate Moscow's communist rivals—especially in China—and to close one's eyes to the crimes committed by them against human rights? What should one do when anti-imperialism struck at interests America's main allies deemed essential (Suez), or when there was a dramatic confluence of communism and anti-imperialism (Vietnam)?

There was also a problem of means: Did not the battle against communism entail a risk of using distinctly "illiberal" methods, particularly in the realm of subversion or in so-called revolutionary wars like Vietnam? And there was one issue whose importance was barely realized in the momentous sweep of decolonization: The support the United States and liberals in Europe provided to the revolts against colonialism put the demand for self-determination (that is, against alien rule) ahead of any concern for self-government (that is, liberal democracy). These revolts resulted in the establishment of states within the borders arbitrarily drawn by the imperial powers, and amounted to a grant of self-determination not to nations, but often to heterogeneous collections of peoples living within these borders. . . .

Liberalism's Modern Predicament

Basically, the plight of the liberal vision results from the fallacy of believing that all good things can come together. They rarely do, and many that were expected to be good have turned out rotten. More specifically, the liberal vision was focused on one particular enemy: the Moloch of power, wherever found, either arbitrary and excessive at home or imperial and militaristic abroad. Insofar as abuse of power is a hardy perennial, liberalism remains an indispensable source of inspiration and value. But there is another enemy in today's world: not the violence that results from the clash of mighty powers or from the imposition of the power of the strong on the weak, but the violence that results from chaos from below. The world today is threatened by the disintegration of power—by anomie, which denotes the absence of norms but can also refer to the collision of norms.

The Wilsonian edifice, its Rooseveltian version of 1945, the Bush coat of fresh paint of 1990, all were undertaken to deal with a world of interstate conflicts. All three assumed that the nature of the regime is a key determinant of state behavior: that liberal nation-states do not fight each other. It is difficult to provide decisive evidence for such a hypothesis, however, and neo-realists believe that the anarchic "structure" of international relations imposes the same kind of behavior on all states. But even if that hypothesis is true, wars among states are only one of the perils of the post-Cold War international system. What is now at stake is the very nature of the state. The "Westphalian" system that has inspired all theories of international relations presupposed well-determined states, clashing or cooperating. Both realism and liberalism shared that assumption; Marxism rejected it, but only because of its belief that the "logic" of state behavior was merely an expression of the logic, and contradictions, of capitalism—that states were, so to speak, puppets manipulated by the global economic system. Liberalism—or the U.N. Charter—finds it difficult to cope with a variety of phenomena: the disintegration of the Soviet Union and Yugoslavia; ethnic conflicts in the successor states; civil wars among rival ethnic, religious, or political factions in countries long ravaged by the Cold War (such as Cambodia or Afghanistan) or in much of Africa; the failure of many post-colonial states, especially in Africa but also in parts of Asia, to become nation-states; and the attempts by Islamic or Hindu fundamentalists to replace a secular with a religious and thus highly exclusionary definition of the state. To arrive at a world of liberal polities, there must be a clear idea of the state. If the world consists of disintegrating states, then the cooperative processes and institutions that are supposed to fuel harmony under the banner of liberal internationalism are easily overwhelmed by millions of refugees who flee massacres and disasters and seek asylum in liberal states, or call for protection whenever they cannot escape.

Liberal internationalism thus faces a predicament. First, it needs a set of clear principles to set goals. Yet, in two crucial respects all it finds is a cacophony of principles governing two issues that are anything but new: what to do about violations of human rights by tyrannical regimes—in places such as Haiti, Burma, or China—and how to react to the imposition of alien rule on reluctant peoples—such as the Kurds of Iraq (or Turkey), the Tibetans of China, the East Timorese of Indonesia. On both issues the old split about whether or not to intervene is a deep as ever. On balance, however, the noninterventionist impulse is strengthened by the disappearance of the Soviet threat and rationalized with the argument that the propagation of political liberalism will ultimately result from the spread of global economic liberalism. Thus, paradoxically, the principle of state sovereignty (which is not particularly liberal, since many states are not based on consent) is often given precedence over the liberal norms of self-government and of national self-determination. The old argument for nonintervention was that intervention even for liberal causes would multiply violent conflicts, whereas liberalism's aim was to dampen them. A new argument is that in a world where chaos is now a major peril, intervention even for good liberal causes may only create more chaos.

It is precisely in the realm of chaos I described above—the realm of disintegrating states—that the clash of norms is the most evident and paralyzing: Sovereignty (as a principle of order and, still, a barrier against aggressive or imperial designs), self-government or democracy, national self-determination (with all its ambiguities and flaws), and human rights (which are not devoid of ambiguities of their own, as debates over the priority of political over economic and social rights, and over the rights of individuals vs. the rights of peoples and groups indicate) are four norms in conflict and a source of complete liberal disarray. Human rights—the major strand of non-utilitarian liberalism—often cannot be protected without infringing upon another state's sovereignty, or without circumscribing the potential for a "tyranny of the majority" entailed by national self-determination and by Jacobin versions of democracy. The trouble-making potential of self-determination, both for interstate order and for human rights, is not so obvious that many liberals want to curb it or even get rid of it, yet the demand for it simply cannot be ignored, and denying its legitimacy would rarely be a recipe for order of democracy. Inconsistency is the result of this confusion: the international "community" has recognized Croatia, Bosnia, and Eritrea, but not Biafra, Chechnya, or the right of the Kurds and Tibetans to states of their own.

In a search for a thread that would allow them to set priorities and a strategy, liberal statesman receive little help from liberal philosophers. In his recent lectures, titled "The Law of Peoples," John Rawls fails to discuss the meaning of "peoples." Cosmopolitan liberals such as Martha Nussbaum, who stress the moral arbitrariness of borders (between states or between nations), step outside the limits of traditional liberalism (which saw the universal values of its creed realized in and through a world of states, not a world state). They also go far beyond what the moral traffic will bear. Communitarian liberals such as Michael Walzer are torn between the cosmopolitan and interventionist implications of their liberalism—when "domestic brutality, civil war, political tyranny, ethnic or religious persecution" become intolerable—and the noninterventionist and relativist implications of their communitarianism. What is needed, and still missing, is a complex and sophisticated rethinking of liberal internationalism; its Ariadne's thread would be human rights (including the right to participate in one's government, and the right to be part of, but not a slave to, national community). It would curtail sovereignty—so that the powers entailed by it could be shared at home and pooled abroad—and it would limit self-determination so that minorities everywhere could have a genuine choice between assimilation and protection of their distinctiveness, and so that the desire for self-rule need not take the form of full state sovereignty in every instance.

Intervention and the Use of Force

Liberal internationalism is also in disarray over methods for defending or promoting its vision. Among liberals today, two sets of alternatives intersect. On the one hand, there is an argument over intervention. Some remain sufficiently suspicious of outside interventions (whether unilateral or collective) to prefer not stepping beyond humanitarian operations whose aim is to protect the victims of natural or manmade disasters. Others fear that the politics of band-aids will only allow the do-gooders to feel good, and leave unaltered the deeper causes of the disasters: murderous gangs and armies, as in Liberia, Somalia, and Rwanda; ethnic absolutists, like Serbs or Bosnian Serbs; tyrants such as Saddam Hussein, and so on. The logic of that viewpoint leads, of course, to far deeper foreign involvements, indeed to protectorates or trusteeships (Cambodia being one current example).

The other great division is over the use of force. Traditionally, liberalism has tried to limit legitimate force to self-defense and collective defense against aggression. But the scope of state chaos, as well as the murderousness of some contemporary tyrannies, has led many liberals to endorse in principle the idea of an outside resort to force whenever domestic chaos threatens the peace and security of other states (for instance through the mass flight of refugees) or whenever domestic chaos or tyrannical government results in massive violations of human rights, such as ethnic cleansing and genocide. Other liberals are doubly dubious about the resort to force because of a traditional tendency to look at it as an instrument of last resort only, and because of a conviction that many of these uses of force could only lead to quagmires and entrapments. Both sides often agree on the dispatching of U.N. peacekeepers, but when it comes to having these troops actually *use force* (except in self-defense), or to having "peace-builders" with missions far more extensive than peacekeepers, disagreement reappears. The Bosnia fiasco has been the result of all these cleavages. Bosnia has been the victim of the imbalanced compromise between those who gave priority to the restoration of peace, however unfair the solution may be, and those who gave priority to the suppression of what they saw as a double assault on liberal values: Serb aggression and ethnic cleansing.

A final predicament concerns not norms or methods, but agents. Who should be the secular arm of liberal action? Great powers (global or regional) claiming to act as enforcers of community norms inspire suspicion, even if, as in the case of India's intervention in Bangladesh, the ratio of self-interest to common good was clearly tilted toward the latter. There is a second problem with hegemonic enforcers: What happens when they choose not to act, failing to realize that the spread of chaos or the triumph of tyranny are antithetical to their interests as great powers? What has happened in the Clinton years, and may happen even more in the second, "Republican" half of the Clinton era, is ominous. Deprived of the relatively clear and widely shared goals that had pushed America to the fore of what was propagandistically called the free world, Washington has been left with Anthony Lake's laundry list of worthy goals, but appears incapable of turning them into a coherent strategy. The administration, sensing the reluctance of its public and Congress

to have America play the role of world policeman, and marked by memories of Vietnam, suggested that if vital interests were not at stake, force would be used only multilaterally. But the story has been one of a double retreat: from military intervention (except in Haiti, where force was coupled with a very limited or ambivalent mandate) and from multilateralism—except when the latter made inaction or minimal action "legitimate," as in Bosnia. Unilateralism has become a way to appease anti-internationalists (a loose collection of realists and of American nationalists) and to justify doing very little.

The alternative to great powers as enforcers would be international organizations, but the lesson of recent years is that the United Nations tends to act effectively only when great powers provide the necessary leadership. When the powers are divided or predominantly reluctant, operations become fiascoes, as has been the case in Somalia and Bosnia, or too little and too late, as in Rwanda (largely because of American pressure to keep the intervention small in size and scope). The United Nations—like traditional liberalism—was designed for a world of interstate conflicts: Many of the tasks it has had thrust on it since 1991 therefore exceed its capacities. As an institution it suffers from the contradiction between a liberal vision that makes harmony depend on the right kind of state (liberal-national) on the one hand, and an international system that requires a heavy dose of international regimes and organizations aimed at overcoming the drawbacks of state sovereignty on the other. The fact that the U.N. has been provided neither with the enforcement institutions Chapter VII of the U.N. Charter had foreseen for collective security nor with a permanent force capable of preventive action or of peace-building in domestic crises has resulted both in calamitous conflicts of loyalty for the contingents that states placed at the U.N.'s disposal and in massive inefficiencies. It would be unfair to accuse liberals of having neglected international agencies, but the literature on regimes has focused much more on norms and institutions at the crossroads of interstate economic cooperation and the transnational world economy than on norms and institutions that deal with what I have called the domain of chaos. Liberals have also paid a lot of attention to agencies for the international protection of human rights. But the gap between liberal theory and practice on human rights is wide indeed. It is explained by the existence of so many states with skeletons in their closets and no desire to do more than pass resolutions on subjects as thorny as minority rights, political freedoms, the rights of migrants and refugees, and international criminal justice.

The Rise of Transnational Society

So far, we have analyzed the plight of liberalism in the world of states. What about the other side of its vision for the planet: transnational society, constraining the capacity of states for evil? Insofar as world public opinion is concerned, Wilson's hopes have not been realized for many reasons. First, when one looks only at the public opinion of open and liberal societies, as expressed in their media, one finds a reflection of the diversity of ideological and religious positions, as over population issues. One also finds the diversity of national perspectives, such as the frequent American reluctance to look at economic and social rights as genuine claims. Second, this is still a world half free and half not. A large number of authoritarian regimes still control the formation and expression of public opinion. They succeed, especially in discussions of human rights issues, in hiding their abuses behind arguments for relativism and the defense of local customs and norms. A variety of economic issues has also put up road blocks on the way to Wilson's vision. In dealing with the problems of distributive justice associated with the allocation of wealth and resources among and within states, and with the intra- and intergenerational choices in environmental policies, liberalism has traditionally been rather silent. When it has raised its voice, it has been torn between its pure laissez-faire types who favor efficiency over equity, defend the status quo, and maintain their faith in the "trickle down" effects of growth on the one hand, and on the other more socially troubled or New Dealish types who are eager to find safety nets for the poor, to orient free enterprise toward "sustainable human development," and to entrust international agencies with some redistributive functions and resources. As a result, on issues of singular importance for the vast majority of humankind, "world public opinion" has not been a cohesive force orienting governments. It has been divided—often along the lines of the rich vs. the poor, with significant elements in each camp crossing over and adopting the arguments of the other. And it has fluctuated over time. This is not to deny the importance of nongovernmental organizations in many areas and their capacity to graduate from "world public opinion" to "transnational actors." But one must face the limits as well.

The formation of global transnational economy constitutes a triumph of the liberal vision that first appeared in the eighteenth century (when philosophers saw private interests cutting across borders as potential tamers of clashing state passions), but it also provides evidence of the fact that fulfillment of the vision has mounting costs and unexpected consequences. Liberalism has always been a somewhat delicate coalition of two different perspectives on human nature. One of them emphasizes selfishness, defines interests in material terms, and celebrates the (general) benefits from individual greed. The other touts the moral aptitudes of human beings, focuses on rights and duties, and emphasizes both moral self-fulfillment and civic virtues. Many liberal philosophers—particularly the utilitarians—have tried to make the two strands converge. Much of the admiration Alexis de Tocqueville had for America came from his belief that here they had indeed been merged. Many of his doubts about liberal democracy's future came from his fears

about the possible victory of greed and individual self-interest. It should not be surprising that in the drive to create a global economy through the dismantling of state barriers, concerns for human rights, democracy, or self-determination have often been submerged or twisted according to the highly debatable assumption that free economies must "ultimately" lead to free polities as well. The assumption may turn out to be correct, but it is fair to say that the jury is still out.

The new transnational economy has not merely, and beneficially, constrained the power of states. It has not only deprived them of much of their capacity to build command economies that ignore the signals given by markets and produce colossal inefficiencies. It has, alas, also deprived them of some of their ability to perform necessary tasks, to carry out basic functions liberalism never intended to remove from them. The free flow of drugs and the free circulation of crime have accompanied the formation of a global world economy. Governments find it difficult to restore against such "bad goods" the controls they have removed to facilitate the flow of the good ones. Moreover, the ability of governments to define their own monetary policies and to orient investments, employment, and growth has been seriously curtailed by the very size and weight of the transnational economy. The case of the European Monetary System and of its two huge crises in the summers of 1992 and 1993, when private capital movements played havoc with the exchange rates set up by the European Community and overwhelmed the efforts of central banks, is an extreme but important example of what is happening. The liberals of past centuries had thought primarily in terms of trade. We are now moving toward an integrated world market of trade, production, and distribution. The new world economy is made of national and multinational corporations operating across borders, and of millions of individual bond holders, shareholders, and holders of savings accounts in search of maximal and quick profits across borders. That has two effects, also unforeseen by liberal internationalism, and both contribute to the prevalence of chaos. One is the creation of a huge zone of irresponsibility: The global economy is literally out of control, not subject to the rules of accountability and principles of legitimacy that apply to relations between individuals and the state. States hesitate to impose their own rules unilaterally, out of fear of inefficiency and self-damage. Thus liberalism, successful in reducing the state's power, has created a formidable anonymous new power. It affects both states and individuals, but is treated as if it were merely an extension of the individual's sphere of protected freedoms. What is desperately needed is a theory that acknowledges the public aspects and effects of such private activities across borders and establishes a kind of common government for those activities—just as within civil societies liberalism aimed at setting up legitimate central institutions in order to rule out the flaws of a "state of nature.". . .

Liberal internationalism has never been very good at specifying what liberal state interests were, beyond physical security and survival, and whether setting up an international system of liberal states was a vital interest, and not merely a legitimate aspiration, of liberal states. It has not been good at confronting the illiberal aspects of nationalism and the destructive potential of national self-determination. It has not paid enough attention to the contradiction between a cosmopolitan but uncontrolled world economy and a world of sovereign albeit cooperating states. Nor has it heeded the need for strong common institutions capable both of coping with whatever states cannot accomplish by themselves and of regulating what may soon be seen as a transnational Frankenstein monster.

Marxism is discredited. Realism promises only the perpetuation of the same old game and is no better equipped to face the politics of chaos than is liberalism. Liberalism remains the only comprehensive and hopeful vision of world affairs, but it needs to be thoroughly reconstructed—and that task has not proceeded very far, either in its domestic or its international dimensions.

Critical Thinking

1. Could any issue other than human rights provide the cornerstone for reinvigorating a liberal vision of the world?
2. Is the argument wise that says that the modern world is imperiled by such chaos that intervention for even the best of liberal causes may only worsen the chaos?
3. How justified was Alexis de Tocqueville in his belief that America had succeeded in merging the self-centered material side of liberalism with the virtuous duty-driven side of liberalism, and would he contend as much today?

Create Central

www.mhhe.com/createcentral

Internet References

The Council on Foreign Relations
www.cfr.org

American Foreign Policy Council
www.afpc.org

From *Foreign Policy*, Spring 1995. Copyright © 1995 by the Carnegie Endowment for International Peace. Reprinted with permission. www.foreignpolicy.com.